Liberalism without Illusions

Liberalism

without

Illusions

*Essays on Liberal Theory and
the Political Vision of Judith N. Shklar*

Edited by
BERNARD YACK

THE UNIVERSITY OF CHICAGO PRESS
Chicago & London

Bernard Yack is professor of political science at the University of
Wisconsin—Madison. He is the author of *The Longing for Total
Revolution* (1986) and *Problems of a Political Animal* (1993).

The University of Chicago Press, Chicago 60637
The University of Chicago Press, Ltd., London
© 1996 by The University of Chicago
All rights reserved. Published 1996
Printed in the United States of America
05 04 03 02 01 00 99 98 97 96   1 2 3 4 5

ISBN: 0–226–94469–7 (cloth)
0–226–94470–0 (paper)

Library of Congress Cataloging-in-Publication Data

Liberalism without illusions : essays on liberal theory and the
   political vision of Judith N. Shklar / edited by Bernard Yack.
      p.   cm.
   Includes bibliographical references and index.
   ISBN 0-226-94469-7 (alk. paper). — ISBN 0-226-94470-0 (paper :
alk. paper)
      1. Liberalism.   2. Shklar, Judith N.   I. Shklar, Judith N.
   II. Yack, Bernard, 1952–   .
   JC574.L525   1996
   320.1'3—dc20   95-18561
                                                          CIP

♾ The paper used in this publication meets the minimum requirements of the
American National Standard for Information Sciences—Permanence of Paper for
Printed Library Materials, ANSI Z39.48–1984.

For Dita

Contents

Preface

THE LAST TWENTY YEARS have seen a considerable reinvigoration of the liberal political imagination. During much of the cold war, liberalism stood for all that is safe, familiar, and reliable in political theory, a comfortable haven from past terrors and dangerous modern innovations. Original insight, creativity, and theoretical daring were not virtues that one generally associated with liberal theory during this period. But that has changed. New political circumstances have challenged liberal theorists to think creatively about a host of problems associated with identity, pluralism, and the national community that their predecessors ignored or regarded as settled. Liberalism, it has become clear, is far from complete, either as a theory or as a set of political practices. As a result, debates about its characteristic goals, means, and limitations are now far more imaginative than in past decades.

Judith Shklar played a major role in this reinvigoration of liberal political thought, perhaps as great a role as her Harvard colleague John Rawls. Hers was an intensely political and skeptical form of liberalism. While most American liberals argue about rights and virtues, Shklar focused on wrongs and vices. Rights were important for her as well, but as a means of defusing dangers, not as the end of liberal politics. Instead of proposing a new conception of individual rights, she sought to deepen our understanding of the unpleasant facts of life that make liberal institutions desirable.

Foremost among these unpleasant facts of life for Shklar was the depth and persistence of the human disposition toward cruelty. "Putting cruelty first" among the vices was Shklar's way of reformulating liberalism's categorical imperative. By redefining liberalism in this way, Shklar sought to highlight the psychological origins and burdens that accompany a commitment to liberal politics. Putting cruelty first, she argued, obliges us to seek ways of limiting the opportunities for the exercise of physical cruelty. It reflects a judgment that cruelty is the most fearful and dangerous of human vices, the vice to which we should commit the greatest resources to control. But in order to limit the opportunities for the exercise of cruelty, we must impose constraints on ourselves as well as on the power of public officials. For as Shklar made clear throughout her work, putting cruelty first means learning to live with injustice, cowardice, disloyalty, and the other vices of everyday life; above all, it means learning to constrain our inclinations to strike out harshly against these vices and the people who bear them.

Shklar complained that because American academics are the beneficiaries of an unusually long and uninterrupted experience of political freedom and stability, they tend to underestimate the strength and variety of humanity's illiberal dispositions. As a result, the repeated emergence of new or forgotten strains of antiliberalism, as after the collapse of communism in Eastern Europe, is always catching them by surprise. Shklar emphasized the vices in order to correct this kind of naïveté. She feared that contemporary liberal academics' preoccupation with rights and rationality conceals from us the concerns about human character that inspired liberalism in the first place.

Indeed, Shklar's greatest contribution to contemporary political thought was to restore some lost psychological depth and realism to the liberal political imagination. Like a fine novelist, Shklar sensed that the way to truth leads through the details of character and context. In place of arid generalizations about rationality and self-interest, she brought to life a complex world in which every vice has distinctive political consequences and every virtue unavoidable costs.

Shklar's contribution to the revival of liberal political thought is not as widely known as many other thinkers' because, until recently, that contribution came more through personal influence than through her publications. For thirty-five years Judith Shklar was an extraordinary presence in the Harvard government department. Her boundless curiosity and unflinching honesty—not to mention her legendary critical faculties—moved generations of students and colleagues to reconsider their settled and familiar understandings of liberalism. Encounters with Shklar have thus left their mark on a very large group of contemporary political theorists, including, of course, those who have contributed to this volume.

Shklar's first books were, for the most part, studies of classical political theorists such as Rousseau and Hegel who shared her fascination with the moral psychology of modern individuals. Some elements of her vision of liberal politics appear already in her second book, *Legalism* (1964). But it was only in her later books, such as *Ordinary Vices* (1984) and *The Faces of Injustice* (1990), that Shklar began to speak about liberalism clearly and distinctly in her own voice.

Sadly, Shklar's sudden and premature death in September 1992, at the age of sixty-three, has silenced that voice at the height of its creativity. In this volume we friends and students of Judith Shklar try to keep alive the conversation about liberal politics that she began. The essays collected here explore Shklar's distinctive understanding of liberalism as well as some of the figures in the history of liberal political thought and issues in contemporary liberal politics that most concerned her. While all these essays reflect Shklar's influence, they display a wide range of intellectual concerns and political commitments. Nothing was more antithetic to Shklar's taste or intellectual ambition than the idea of collecting a school of like-minded disciples. The lively play of different points of view in these essays thus carries on the analysis of liberal politics in the open-ended spirit that she celebrated.

The volume opens with my introduction to Shklar's political thought. It then proceeds with a number of essays that consider different aspects of Shklar's understanding of liberalism. The first chapter, by Michael Walzer, assesses the strengths and limitations of Shklar's negative understanding of liberal politics, a chapter that is nicely balanced by Stanley Hoffmann's reflections, at the close of part 1, on Shklar's broader aims as a political thinker. Nancy Rosenblum brings out the important but little noticed egalitarianism of Shklar's understanding of liberalism in "The Democracy of Everyday Life." Seyla Benhabib and John Dunn explore the viability of Shklar's fierce anti-utopianism. Amy Gutmann then offers an argument for an evolution in Shklar's understanding of liberal politics away from the primarily negative view emphasized by Walzer, Benhabib, and Dunn.

The chapters in part 2, on the history of liberal political thought, reflect the emphasis on the relationship between individual freedom and moral psychology that was so central to Shklar's understanding of liberalism. This emphasis is especially evident in Stephen Holmes's chapter, "Ordinary Passions in Descartes and Racine." It can also be seen in Tracy Strong's and Patrick Riley's treatments of Rousseau, a thinker whose psychological acuity made him Shklar's favorite political theorist. Isaac Kramnick explores the tension between the skeptical attitudes—so heavily emphasized by Shklar—and visionary goals of Enlightenment liberalism through a discussion of Harold Laski's political thought. Finally, Quentin Skinner explores Thomas Hobbes's "antiliberal" theory of liberty and the challenge it poses to Shklar's understanding of liberal politics.

Part 3 addresses problems in contemporary liberal theory and practice. Dennis Thompson's chapter on hypocrisy and democracy and my own on active and passive justice each begin with one of Shklar's original insights and attempt to develop it in new directions. Bruce Ackerman and George Kateb, focusing on the role of constitutional courts and of free speech in a liberal polity, explore fundamental issues of liberal constitutionalism. Finally, Rogers Smith's "The Unfinished Tasks of Liberalism," an attempt to summarize the unfinished business of liberal politics in American society, provides an appropriate conclusion to a volume that approaches "liberalism without illusions."

I have said little about Judith Shklar's life in this introduction because that story is much better told in her marvelous autobiographical lecture, which we include as an appendix to this volume. This lecture, one of a series presented by various scholars to the American Council of Learned Societies, provides such an uncannily accurate sense of Shklar's voice and personality that any biographer's efforts would seem lifeless beside it. Dita began her autobiography by confessing, "I am a bookworm." We are all the richer for that fact and honor her memory here by trying to keep alive the intellectual adventure that she crafted out of her reading.

Liberalism without Illusions:
An Introduction to Judith Shklar's Political Thought

Bernard Yack

JUDITH SHKLAR DEVOTED relatively little time to explaining her most original ideas or relating them to more familiar approaches to moral and political problems. For her restlessly inventive mind, each new insight was a spur to further thinking rather than an occasion for public celebration. As a result, she found the packaging of old insights a rather tedious chore. She expressed her ideas—on the printed page, as in conversation—in great torrents rather than in clear and steady streams of argument. We are tremendously indebted to her for this cascade of insights, although, like travelers on white water, we sometimes find ourselves exhausted and a little confused about exactly where we have ended up after reading her work. This essay offers some bearings for those who take up the journey through Judith Shklar's moral and political thought.

Shklar's commitment to liberal politics anchored all of the various projects she undertook. An introduction to her political thought is thus an introduction to her vision of liberalism. Accordingly, I focus here on three of Shklar's most distinctive and original contributions to contemporary liberal political thought: her deepening of liberal moral psychology, her critique of abstract and formalistic understandings of liberal politics, and her emphasis on cultural erudition as a source of moral and political insight.

Moral Psychology and Liberal Theory

Of the many charges leveled at liberals and liberalism, naïveté is probably the most frequent. Liberals have been repeatedly ridiculed

1

for their naïveté about rationality, progress, and our capacity to reform social practice; for their naïveté about the universality of liberal sentiments and ideals; and, above all, for their naïveté about human psychology, about the rationality, predictability, and basic decency of human behavior.

No one could accuse Judith Shklar of such naïveté. Her commitment to liberal politics grew from her apprehensions about the inexhaustible and ever-changing constellation of human vices. Liberalism was for her a way of ranking vices rather than a celebration of progress and rationality. Liberals, in her account, put physical cruelty at the top of their list of vices and are willing to take strong measures to minimize the opportunities for human beings to exercise cruelty toward each other. Moreover, they must bear the strain of tolerating a whole range of unpleasant vices such as cowardice, hypocrisy, and disloyalty that their emphasis on cruelty allows to flourish in their communities. Liberal theorists, she insists, need to face up to liberalism's "deep and enduring debt to misanthropy"[1] and to devote greater attention to the vices and the darker side of human psychology.

Shklar's interest in moral psychology pervades all of her books, from her interpretative studies of Rousseau, Hegel, and Montesquieu to her reinterpretations of key concepts in liberal political thought such as legalism, injustice, citizenship, and obligation. Shklar shared with Montaigne and Montesquieu, her favorite liberal theorists, a fascination with the everyday vices and prejudices that defeat our attempts to rationalize our social lives. Like them, she believed that any opinion, no matter how foolish or irrational, can inspire human beings to harm themselves and others. This deep skepticism about our capacities for public and private rationality, a skepticism reinforced by the extraordinary violence and irrationality of politics in twentieth-century Europe, inspired her distinctive view of liberal politics, which she describes as the "liberalism of fear."[2]

Shklar contrasts this "liberalism of fear" with the "liberalism of rights" popular in contemporary academic circles. The liberalism of rights owes its origins to Locke and Kant rather than to Montaigne and Montesquieu, and dominates most contemporary discussion of liberalism through the influence of Rawls, Nozick, Dworkin, and other liberal academics. It treats liberal politics as a means of securing and enhancing some set of individual rights. In order to justify the primacy of these rights, however, its advocates are often forced to defend the implausible assumptions that make liberalism so vulnerable to charges of naïveté. Examples of such assumptions include the benign consequences of enlightened self-interest, the invariably beneficial effects of ideological competition in the free marketplace of ideas, exclusive definitions of rationality (as risk avoiding or risk taking, depending on the rights one prefers), and the coherence and consistency of public culture in a liberal democratic community.

Shklar, in contrast, sees the pursuit of rights as secondary. For her, individual rights represent a means of diminishing public cruelty and the fear it inspires rather than the primary end of liberal politics. There are some things, she argues, that human beings cannot regulate—for example, the practice of religion or sexual behavior—without indulging their propensity to cruelty. And there are some necessary state functions, such as punishing criminals, that inevitably promote fear by presenting opportunities for public cruelty and therefore must be hemmed in with procedures that depersonalize the exercise of power.[3] For Shklar, the goal of liberal theory is the development of defenses against the ever-changing threat of public cruelty rather than the discovery and application of the definitive understanding of human rights. Protection against the fear of cruelty is "both the beginning and an end of political institutions such as rights." Those who, like many contemporary American academics, make demands for rights primary do so only, in Shklar's words, because they "have relatively little experience of protracted and uninterrupted fear."[4]

Shklar's focus on the dangers posed by the cruel and irrational passions of other human beings might suggest parallels with Hobbes's understanding of politics. After all, Hobbes too constructs a political system based on fear of our neighbors' cruel and irrational passions. But there is a crucial difference between these two examples of a politics of fear. For Hobbes, fear of the sovereign must be used to minimize our fear of each other. He argues that the only rational way of maximizing our individual security and freedom is to create an unlimited power that can overawe all of the individuals, from proud aristocrats to querulous priests, who seek to use us cruelly. For Shklar, in contrast, such concentration of power and fear tends only to increase the kind of cruelty it is designed to minimize. Following Montesquieu's critique of despotism, she argues that continuous fear of the sort inspired by Hobbesian sovereigns is an uncontrollable "physiological reaction" that paralyzes judgment and makes room for all of the basest and most irrational human passions.[5] Cringing subjects are likely to be cruel subjects. We have reason, therefore, to "fear a society of fearful people."[6]

Nor should we identify Shklar's liberal politics with the minimal or "night watchman" state preferred by libertarians and laissez-faire capitalists. Libertarian politics is also a liberal politics of fear. It recoils from state power as *the* threat to individual freedom and creativity. Like many other liberals, Shklar rejects this version of liberalism because it rests on a completely unjustified faith that governmental power is always more threatening to our freedom and security than the power of private actors such as large corporations.[7] More originally, she also argues that advocates of the minimal state tend to exaggerate the extent to which nongovernmental sources of harm are beyond human control, thereby portraying them as unfortunate facts of life rather than injustices. In *The Faces of Injustice* (1990) Shklar shows that the distinction that we draw between natural misfortune and human injustice inevitably reflects subjective aims and viewpoints rather than a simple search for objective causes of harm. While public officials and spectators, not to mention advocates of enlightened selfishness, have a great interest in insisting that most suffering "couldn't be helped," victims have an opposing interest in identifying the actions and omissions that might have prevented their suffering. Victims may often exaggerate blameworthiness as they seek to characterize their suffering as injustice rather than misfortune. But Shklar insists that, given the limits of our cognitive capacities, there are insights into injustice that only the experience of victimization can provide.[8] Accordingly, she vehemently rejects the hard and fast distinction between government control and impersonal social forces that support most arguments for the minimal state.

The most original part of Shklar's vision of liberal politics is her account of the moral and psychological burdens of a liberal way of life. Liberalism is usually described as an easy doctrine to live with. As long as you pay your taxes and avoid interfering with the freedom of other individuals, you can live as you please. A relaxed and ignoble lassitude is the quintessentially liberal attitude, according to this widespread view. Laissez-faire and laissez-aller, rather than strenuous self-discipline, characterize the liberal soul.

"Nothing," Shklar counters,

> could be more remote from the truth. . . . The very refusal to use public coercion to impose creedal unanimity and uniform standards of behavior demands an enormous degree of self-control. Tolerance consistently applied is more difficult and morally demanding than repression. . . . Far from being an amoral free-for-all, liberalism is, in fact, extremely difficult and constraining, far too much so for those who cannot endure contradiction, complexity, diversity and the risks of freedom.[9]

Liberal self-discipline may lack the drama and intensity associated with celebrated acts of Christian or Plutarchian virtue. But the liberal's struggles with ordinary, everyday vices are no less real than saintly and heroic struggles with extraordinary vices and circumstances. It is painful to live amidst a variety of popular and influential opinions that offend one's moral and aesthetic sensibilities. And it is immensely gratifying to strike out at the objects of one's disgust. Clearly, a liberal's life is filled with denied as well as delayed gratification.

Liberals have to struggle, in particular, with the costs of putting cruelty first among the human vices, according to Shklar. This means that they have to be willing to tolerate a range of painful vices that cannot be attacked without opening the door to human cruelty. Many liberal theorists try to conceal the pain of tolerating these vices by arguing that private vices like greed will in the aggregate promote public goods like prosperity. Shklar accepts no such comforting formulas. Toleration of everyday vices such as hypocrisy, cowardice, and betrayal is painful. If we tolerate them it is because we should be worried about worse vices, not because we believe in invisible hands that turn vices into virtues.

Shklar's understanding of the goals of liberal politics, with its emphasis on minimizing the occasions for public cruelty, is clearly negative in character. But it departs from more familiar negative understandings of liberalism in its psychological depth. The barriers that Shklar asks us to build against public cruelty are internal as well as external. They include painful forms of self-restraint as well as legal and institutional constraints. In order to put cruelty first she asks us to find ways of constraining our recurring desire to attack many of the vices that make social life so unpleasant. These psychological restraints are, for Shklar, just as important—and perhaps more difficult to maintain—as the external barriers that we must build against tyrants, torturers, and other known abusers of power. For we bear the source of public cruelty within us even when we live in relative security within the protections provided by the liberal state.

Abstraction and Legalism in Liberal Theory

Shklar welcomed the recent revival of normative theorizing among liberal academics. But she was deeply concerned about their increasingly abstract and apolitical characterization of liberalism. Shklar believed that the best way to analyze political concepts was to think through the experiences that make them necessary and to test their limits. For example, her major study of the rule of law points us toward political trials, such as those at Nuremberg, rather than conceptual debates about the definition of law.[10] And when in her last years she undertook a study of obligation and loyalty, she turned first to the experience of political exiles, for whom issues of loyalty and obligation are most acute.[11]

This abstraction from actual political experience and conflict alarmed Shklar for two reasons. First of all, she believed that it leads to the misrepresentation and trivialization of liberal practices such as the rule of law, individual rights, and political pluralism. It inspires blood-less and overly formal characterizations of liberal politics that serve only to resolve academic puzzles. Second, she believed that such abstraction tends to promote conclusions that unintentionally threaten liberal commitments to diversity and the legitimacy of political disagreement.

One reason for this trend toward abstract and apolitical arguments is the increasing influence of moral philosophers and legal theorists in debates about the meaning of liberalism. Shklar notes that these two groups of scholars are trained in a way that emphasizes conceptual and doctrinal analysis rather than reflection on the contingencies of historical and political experience.[12]

But Shklar shows that this trend toward abstraction in liberal theory has far deeper and more enduring sources than the changing distribution of labor within American universities. Its deepest roots lie in basic liberal commitments to legalism and pluralism. Both commitments lead liberal theorists to search for a few uncontroversial principles that all individuals do or should—were they to render consistent their basic aims and desires—accept. This pressure to come up with actual or hypothetical consensus on basic liberal principles is what pushes liberal theory in ever more abstract and apolitical directions. In her work on legalism and injustice, Shklar gives us the tools with which to explain and resist this trend.

A strong dose of lawfulness is a crucial component of liberal political culture, according to Shklar. For we can only minimize fear of public cruelty by following intricate constitutional and procedural rules that constrain government's power to punish. The problem with reliance on legal rules to constrain power is that it allies liberalism with a powerful and much broader ideology, which Shklar describes as legalism. Legalism, in its broadest form, is an ethic of rule following. It encompasses a broad set of attitudes that inclines us to measure behavior against a set of general rules and principles.[13] Legalism models moral and political reasoning on adjudication. It makes the discovery of the relevant general rule and its impartial application to particular cases the key steps in any practical judgment.

Legalism in contemporary society reigns most powerfully, according to Shklar, among lawyers and law professors, for whom legalism is a "professional ideology."[14] Their penchant for legalist approaches to moral and political judgments tends to obscure the controversial political purposes behind a variety of liberal practices such as the rule of law.[15] In the heated debate about the legitimacy of the Nuremberg trials, for example, the major issues raised by most liberal legal theorists concern whether the trials violated the rule of law norms that support due process and condemn retroactive criminal legislation. For Shklar, the violation of some of these norms in the Nuremberg trials was unquestionable and unavoidable. But that hardly settles questions about how we should judge the political value of the trials. Shklar argues that we must also consider the specific political purposes and potential consequences of extraordinary cases such as the Nuremburg trials and that, to do so, we can no longer follow legalism's adjudicatory model of political judgment. She concludes that the Nuremburg trials were justified because the legalized punishment of Nazi war criminals served to revive and reinforce the older and more decent traditions of politics and criminal law that had been swept away by the violent passions unleashed by Nazi rule. In Japan, where no such traditions existed, it made no sense to hold war crime trials since they would be seen as nothing but expressions of the conquerors' military superiority. In Germany, in contrast, the drama of such trials could serve, despite their unavoidable departures from ordinary rule of law norms, to revive respect for legal constraints on the exercise of power.[16]

The more general conclusion that Shklar draws from her analysis of the Nuremburg trials is that we must exercise political judgment, judgment about the purposes and consequences of our choices, in order to determine the value of limits of legal rules and ideals. Shklar was attacking the fabled law/politics distinction long before it became fashionable to do so. But unlike most contemporary critics of liberal legal theory, she recognized that skepticism about the distinction between law and politics is the beginning, not the end, of an evaluation of the rule of law in liberal societies. Proving that legal judgment cannot be separated entirely from controversial political purposes does not necessarily defeat arguments for the rule of law. Everything depends on the nature of those purposes and the extent to which rule of law norms can serve them.

Commitments to the rule of law make liberal theorists especially susceptible to legalist perspectives when they deal with questions of social conflict and controversy. Many of the most influential liberal theorists have followed legalism's adjudicatory model of political judgment by searching for, as the foundation of their theories, the general rules and principles that we all implicitly or explicitly accept. Natural rights and self-evident principles of reason were the most popular candidates for this role among eighteenth-century philosophers. These concepts have lost much of their appeal for contemporary philosophers and liberal theorists. But the search for uncontroversial and generally accepted foundational principles proceeds apace.

One new method of identifying such principles, far more respectable to contemporary philosophers, is to recover them from the common usage of language, in the way that, for example, H. L. A. Hart defends the distinction between legal and moral rules. Analysis of our everyday conceptual vocabularies requires no unrealistic leap into the realms of metaphysics or philosophical anthropology. But, apart from a tendency to impose an unrealistic uniformity on our use of language, it ignores the political commitments that often shape the use of language. So Hart's distinction between legal and moral rules, far from reflecting neutral and uncontroversial "facts" about the way in which we use language, reflects a central but controversial liberal commitment: to try to protect a certain realm of behavior, which Hart calls morals, from the state's powers of punishment.[17] It is far more practical and intellectually honest, according to Shklar, to accept the burden of directly defending such controversial principles rather than to insist lamely that something so malleable as linguistic usage implicitly commits your opponents to your beliefs.

More recently, a number of political theorists and moral philosophers have turned to shared cultural experience as a way of identifying social consensus about fundamental liberal principles of political organization. What were once described as self-evident truths or facts of reason are being rediscovered as the shared meanings and principles embedded in "our" cultures. Richard Rorty presents the bluntest version of such arguments when he insists that an "ethnocentric" view of our culture yields us precisely the liberal principles that previous philosophers sought in the mirror of nature.[18] John Rawls makes a similar, though softer, move in this direction when he argues that Kantian principles of moral personality are "embedded" in our "liberal democratic culture."[19] And Michael Walzer stakes his pluralist theory of justice on the existence of "shared social meanings," meanings that allow us to determine what "we" in any particular culture believe about the principles that should guide the distribution of different goods.[20]

Shklar directly challenges this approach to liberal theory and its claims to have discovered an implicit consensus for perpetually controversial principles. These convenient "intimations of shared meaning, as divined by prophetic or traditionalist avatars of the people, are never checked against actual opinions, least of all those of the most disadvantaged and frightened people."[21] Were they investigated in this way, it would become clear that the facts of cultural life are no less complex and controversial than the facts of nature or reason. Moreover, Shklar warns that even were we to discover apparent shared meanings in our society, we should be suspicious of our findings since what we view as the predominant opinions in any society will inevitably reflect the views of the social and intellectual elites who have the greatest access to public modes of expression. "In the absence of a clear and free account of their feelings we should assume that the least advantaged members of a society resent their situation [and their society's "shared" principles], even though—like many a black slave—they smile and sing in a show of contentment."[22] Accordingly, Shklar urges liberal political theorists to give up their vain quest for a consensus on basic political principles and listen more carefully to the discordant voices that exist within their communities. "Conflict among 'us,'" she declares, is "both ineluctable and tolerable, and entirely necessary for any degree of freedom." Indeed, far from searching for consensus, she strained "to make 'us' even more aware of our incompatibilities and their consequences."[23]

As the previous paragraphs should make clear, Shklar's analysis of the influence of legalism on liberal theory takes her well beyond questions about legal rules and institutions. In particular, *The Faces of Injustice* extends her critique of legalist abstractions to the way in which we think about justice and injustice. Most conceptions of justice are legalist in character, since they portray justice as a body of rules and basic principles governing the distribution of benefits and burdens within a community. Injustice, according to this "normal model" of justice, occurs whenever we depart from any of these general norms.[24]

Most contemporary liberal theories of justice are, as we have seen, drawn to a particular version of the normal model of justice, one in which a society's most basic rules and principles reflect an actual or implicit consensus. The problem with all normal models of justice, according to Shklar, is that they exaggerate a community's ability to identify potential forms of injustice.[25] Normal models of justice treat injustice as nothing but a departure from standards of justice; if no departure from such a standard has occurred, one cannot complain about being treated unjustly. Our ability to recognize an injustice thus depends, according to these models, on the prior existence of a society's established or consensual understanding of justice.

Such an account of injustice, Shklar complains, tends to blind us to the myriad sources of injustice—sources that victims are often the only ones to recognize[26]—that go beyond departures from recognized standards of justice. Liberal versions of the normal model add to the indignity of the victims of such injustices by insisting that the victims themselves at some level do—or should, after sufficient reflection— recognize that they have not really suffered an injustice. Reliance on the normal model of justice thus leads some liberal theorists to close their ears to the diverse experiences of fear and public cruelty that liberal institutions, in Shklar's view, should be designed to diminish.

The Importance of Historical and Cultural Erudition

It might seem rather commonplace to praise a prominent scholar for her erudition, even when her learning is as broad and deep as Judith Shklar's. Nevertheless, Shklar's intellectual breadth, her insistence that we treat the whole of our literary, scientific, historical, and philosophic inheritance as a source of insight, is one of her most important contributions to contemporary moral and political theory. For it is not at all self-evident that moral and political theory, especially liberal theory, should be grounded in the kind of intellectual erudition that Shklar emphasized—as even a casual glance at many contemporary works in the field demonstrates. Shklar gives us reasons to view such erudition as a source of moral and political insight rather than as mere decoration for the hard work of conceptualization and justification.

"Historical memory," Shklar suggests, "is the faculty of mind [on which] the liberalism of fear draws most heavily."[27] Recollections of the startling variety and violence of public cruelty, of its unexpected attractions to individuals and peoples, of the way in which past illusions about the progress of liberal civilization have been repeatedly shattered, these historical memories inspire Shklar's liberalism of fear. Without such historical knowledge we tend to grow complacent about liberal politics, forgetting just how a fragile an achievement they represent.

Other traditions of liberal thought—not to mention the circumstances of modern social life and education—tend to diminish the importance of historical awareness. The liberalism of progress, which still survives even after World War I and Auschwitz, encourages us to look at history through the distorting haze of teleology and self-glorification. That one can still be taken seriously today when talking about the "end of history" in the triumph of liberal democratic institutions,[28] even after the nightmare of violence and cruelty that shattered similar dreams earlier this century, shows just how far the liberalism of progress can weaken our historical sense. The liberalisms that focus on natural rights and personal development also discourage historical awareness by abstracting from specific historical experiences in their justifications of liberal politics. As Shklar notes, neither of the "patron saints" of these two forms of liberalism, Locke and Mill, "had a strongly developed historical memory."[29]

Shklar also urged moral and political theorists to follow the example of Hegel, "who took whatever he could find in the treasure trove of our literature."[30] Great works of art and literature were for her an inexhaustible source of stories about moral conflict and judgment, a source that she increasingly drew upon in her later writings. Most importantly, these works of imagination offer political theorists the finest insights into the human vices. For while philosophers have been loath to discuss cruelty and the other vices at any length, art and literature have focused on little else.[31] Reflection on artistic and literary representations of moral psychology represent, for Shklar, an indispensable corrective to the ever-increasing abstractness of contemporary moral and political philosophy.

Shklar was one of the last of the generation of Central European intellectuals that the Nazis drove to the United States, a generation whose cultural education dazzled and enormously enriched American intellectual life.[32] Like most of the other European emigrés who have influenced academic political theory in America, such as Arendt, Adorno, Marcuse, and Strauss, Shklar thought that there was much for Americans to learn from the European catastrophe of the first half of the twentieth century. Like this group of emigré theorists, she feared that disinterest in history and long experience of political stability make Americans rather naïve about the dangers that threaten a decent political order. But unlike most of them, Shklar never expressed a sense of cultural superiority and disdain for American mass society and everyday politics. To her it seemed very strange that survivors of the shipwreck of European culture and politics looked down upon the stable and relatively decent society that gave them such a safe and comfortable refuge. Americans had achieved things in political life that Europeans had manifestly failed to achieve. Whatever its problems—and Shklar was always searing in her criticism of distinctly American injustices such as the treatment of African Americans—Shklar believed that American society and institutions had as much to teach the emigrés as they had to teach Americans. Shklar's liberalism of fear reflects her idiosyncratic synthesis of American and European experience.

Shklar's appreciation of American politics and society helped her purge Central European *Bildung* of the vices that frequently accompanied the emigrés' most influential arguments: anti-intellectual disdain for the achievements of modern science and technology, nostalgic illusions about premodern societies, and an inflated sense of the importance of theoretical knowledge for the fate of human civilization. In her hands, European appreciation for historical and literary culture serves to enhance—rather than disenchant us with—our lives in modern societies.

Moreover, although her skepticism was legendary, Shklar had little patience for the epistemological nihilism so popular in contemporary literary and cultural studies. There were for her simply too many important and fascinating things to think about to worry too long about the final adequacy of the claims we make to understand them. Of course we can never fully get beyond the social and linguistic influences that constrain our pursuit and expression of knowledge. Of course all we can offer are our interpretations of social and cultural experience. But there is so much that we need to interpret and argue about, so many surprising contingencies to discover and comment upon, that epistemological despair was for Shklar a self-indulgent waste of time.

Shklar once described her work as "a ramble through a moral minefield."[33] Her writing, like such a ramble, offers much excitement but little comfort. Shklar's insights make us intensely aware of both the unseen dangers that surround us and the unexpected richness of our everyday moral experience. Her vision of liberal politics thus not only helps us to navigate the "moral minefields" within which we conduct our lives but makes the journey a far more interesting and rewarding one.

Notes

1. *Ordinary Vices* (1984), 3. All citations to Judith Shklar's works in this volume will appear in the text and notes with abbreviated titles and implied attribution. Full titles and complete bibliographical information may be found in the bibliography near the end of the book.

2. "The Liberalism of Fear" (1989). See also *Ordinary Vices*, 5, 237–49.

3. See "The Liberalism of Fear" and "Political Theory and the Rule of Law," (1987).

4. *Ordinary Vices*, 237.

5. *Montesquieu* (1987), 84–85.

6. "The Liberalism of Fear," 29. See also *Ordinary Vices*, 23–24.

7. "The Liberalism of Fear," 31.

8. *The Faces of Injustice* (1990), 3–8, 51–82.

9. *Ordinary Vices*, 4–5.

10. *Legalism*, 151–90.

11. See "Obligation, Loyalty, Exile" (1993). This article is a preliminary study for a set of five lectures on this subject that Shklar was to have presented at Cambridge University in 1993.

12. *Legalism*, preface to 2d edition (1986), x–xi.

13. Ibid., 1–2.

14. Ibid., 8–10.

15. See in general "Political Theory and the Rule of Law."

16. *Legalism*, 151–90.

17. Ibid., 41–42.

18. See Richard Rorty, "Postmodernist Bourgeois Liberalism," *Journal of Philosophy* 80 (1983): 583–89; "Solidarity and Objectivity," *Nanzen Review of American Studies* 6 (1984): 1–19; and "The Priority of Democracy to Philosophy," in *The Virginia Statute for Religious Freedom*, ed. M. D. Peterson and R. C. Vaughan. (Cambridge, 1988), 257–81.

19. John Rawls, "Justice as Fairness: Political, not Metaphysical," *Philosophy*

and Public Affairs 15 (1985): 223–51. See also *Political Liberalism* (New York; 1993), 13–14.

20. Michael Walzer, *Spheres of Justice* (New York, 1983).

21. *The Faces of Injustice,* 115.

22. Ibid.

23. *Ordinary Vices,* 227.

24. *The Faces of Injustice,* 17.

25. Ibid.

26. Ibid., 36–37. For further discussion of Shklar's arguments about injustice see Bernard Yack, "Injustice and the Victim's Voice," *Michigan Law Review* 89 (May 1991): 1334–49.

27. "The Liberalism of Fear," 27.

28. As in Francis Fukuyama's popular book, *The End of History and the Last Man* (New York, 1992).

29. "The Liberalism of Fear," 27.

30. *Ordinary Vices,* 229.

31. Ibid., 7.

32. Shklar tells the story of her family's escape from Riga in the autobiographical lecture included at the end of this volume. Characteristically, she emphasizes the black-comedic elements of her story.

33. *Ordinary Vices,* 6.

Part One

Liberal Troubles

1

On Negative Politics

Michael Walzer

JUDITH SHKLAR OFTEN TALKED as if her politics was largely negative in character, and I think that is the way the "liberalism of fear" is most often understood. Fear is a negative emotion, manifest in a movement away, a backing off from danger, a defensive reaction to the threatening object or person. A similarly motivated politics would be similarly manifest—the state conceived, say, as shield and shelter, protecting individuals even from its own agents. "Putting cruelty first" means starting with what we most want to escape. This is a politics founded equally on the history of war and revolution in the twentieth century and on Shklar's own experience: as she escaped from the Gestapo, so should we all. The liberalism of fear is a bulwark against Nazism in particular and the secret police in general.

It is a necessary bulwark, and I shall assume that readers of this essay are as ready as Shklar was, as I am, to build and defend it. The question that I want to pose is whether this readiness can possibly form the substance of a political position, either intellectually or practically. Is there such a thing as a purely or simply or even largely negative politics? After all, a bulwark and its defenders stand in front of something. What is it that they are defending? On behalf of what are we fearful? The answer most consistent with a negative politics is life itself, physical security. But this is a curious answer since it is at least sometimes true that the best way to save our lives, if that is all we mean to save, is to surrender to whatever it is that threatens us—or to give up politics entirely and hide from the threatening forces, in accordance with the classical wisdom of Proverbs: "When the wicked rise to power, the wise run for cover." A purely negative politics might well require radically nonpolitical behavior.

When we defend the bulwarks, we are usually defending something more than our lives; we are defending our way of life. The cruelty that we are putting first includes but is certainly not limited to death and torture; it extends also to betrayal, dispossession, exile, the breakup of families, the defeat of everyday expectation and hope. These negatives correspond to a highly diverse set of positives: different cultures, different property and kinship systems, different understandings of the normal life course. There is a certain sameness on the other side of the bulwarks, but a great diversity on this side. On the other side are invaders and usurpers, ruthless tyrants and their gangs of violent men who rule or plan to rule in their own interest and not in the common interest (the first of the ancient definitions of tyranny) or who seize the women and property of their subjects (the second ancient definition) or who seek to impose an absolutist and all-encompassing ideology (the most important of the modern definitions). On this side of the bulwarks are men and women, complexly related, with their personal status and sense of themselves; families and their varied holdings; customary rights and privileges; established communities of many sorts; different institutional arrangements; different moralities and religions. We oppose the tyrants in the name of all these; negative politics always has a substantive subject—a certain necessary positivity.

We probably should support a politics of this sort even when we have qualms about or are opposed to what it protects—so long as the forces on the other side of the bulwarks are violent and tyrannical. I don't mean to rule out revolutionary politics, but vanguard revolutions, pressed forward against the wishes not only of the rulers but also of the ruled, are clearly excluded. Imagine a group of people defending a hierarchical society—where priests rule lay people, or landlords rule peasants, or capitalists rule workers—against a band of revolutionary terrorists: we have learned to fear terrorism more than hierarchy. Or, better, we have learned that the hierarchy of terrorist and terrorized is the very worst kind. That is the real meaning of our negativism. It requires that we defend, or support the defense of, a wide range of regimes and societies whenever they face a common threat. What is defended, however, is always *something*, different in each case, even if the threat is similar in kind

I

A "liberalism of fear" might describe just this defense of something, with *liberal* defining the means of defense, the architecture, so to speak, of the bulwarks: constitutional government, civil liberties, a free press, and so on. Or it might describe the things we most value and most readily defend: a particular regime and culture, individual autonomy, and the social space within which free men and women enact their life plans. These individuals with plans constitute liberal positivity, and it is hard to imagine any liberalism, however fearful, without them. Compare the liberalism of fear to the doctrine of "negative freedom," which is probably its philosophical analogue. Negative freedom has the same positive subject. Its purpose is to give the individual, conceived as an agent, room for agency; its negativity is a bulwark against intrusive and high-handed officials, armed with laws, seconded by the police.

What makes this negativity seem sufficient unto itself is the givenness of the individuals behind the bulwarks. They are just there, like natural beings, autonomous unless constrained. But this givenness is in fact a problem. One can't build the bulwarks just anywhere and expect to find autonomous men and women behind them. Here are the physical individuals; why aren't they busily shaping projects, developing and enacting life plans? So we are led to think about education, culture, politics, and everything else that is necessary to the formation of the positive subjects of negative freedom. The case is the same with the liberalism of fear: before we can be fearful in a liberal way, we must learn what it means to be liberal.

Consider a more particular example: the free market as an instance of negative freedom. Many economists believed that what was required, and all that was required, to transform the state-run economies of Eastern Europe into market economies was the destruction of the existing constraints on entrepreneurial activity. So the constraints were destroyed, and freedom proclaimed. Where are the entrepreneurs? It turns out that disciplined energy, methodical work, deferred satisfaction, and a readiness to take risks are more rare than the economists thought. Entrepreneurs are not natural beings but cultural formations.

In much the same way, liberalism is a particular social-historical construction, and it isn't made by throwing up bulwarks around a piece of social space. It requires work within that space. Insofar as this work is intentional, it will be driven by some positive vision of its purpose. So the liberalism of fear depends upon what we might call the liberalism of hope. I don't mean this in any sentimental way but quite literally: what we are afraid of is that the things we have come to value, our accomplishments until now, and our plans for the future will be destroyed by violent men. When we defend the bulwarks, then, we are committing ourselves to an ongoing engagement and a pattern of activity. For what the bulwarks are meant to defend doesn't exist naturally, has to be made, and isn't finished.

I must stress again that this engagement and activity represent not only the positive side of the liberalism of fear but also the particularist side. They are doubly particularist, first and most obviously because they are liberal and not conservative or communitarian or fundamentalist, and second because they are liberal in a specific way. I shall illustrate this latter point by considering in some detail the positive content of Judith Shklar's liberalism. But first I suggest a brief look at how one puts cruelty first in an American context. In a purely negative sense, and from the standpoint of the person at risk, the opposite of cruelty is physical safety: injury and torture are what I am safe from. But when Shklar writes about America, she is more focused on social or psychological degradation than on bodily injury, and the opposed state is equality, independence, dignity. When I am independent, I can't be degraded. Slavery is the key to her account of American history—slavery imagined (with Orlando Patterson) as a form of social death rather than physical vulnerability. Since this is a kind of dying or, better, killing that is still remembered and still, in various mitigated forms, endured, putting cruelty first means attending to it. And this attention makes for a highly specific American liberalism.

II

Consider now Shklar's positive account of this liberalism in her book *American Citizenship* (1991). In her view, liberalism requires first a certain sort of political community, constituted as a democracy of citizens, political equals with suffrage and civil rights and, second, a certain sort of political economy in which everyone is guaranteed the chance to work for a living wage. These two requirements are elaborated against the background of slavery (understood, again, as the denial of citizenship and free labor) but also with reference to the women's movement and the trade union movement. The standard left analogies—"domestic slavery" and "wage slavery," though Shklar is always careful to distinguish them from the real thing—make sense to her. Hence she defends the "struggles" of workers against the threat of unemployment and dependency and of women for voting rights and jobs—the crucial political and economic status markers. She doesn't assert the intrinsic value of participation or work; hers is in no sense a moralizing account of liberal politics. Nor does she dwell much on the instrumental value of participation (to defend interests) or of work (to make money). She is interested above all in their cultural or symbolic value: this is how individuals achieve equal standing and dignity in American society.

We don't give the members of the American political community a special name like *citizen* and *comrade* in the French and Russian revolutions. Nonetheless, membership is very important in establishing individual autonomy, and the vote is its crucial symbol—probably more important in the context of a multiracial immigrant society than in any of the countries of Europe. At the same time, America has never been, despite its revolutionary origin and republican tradition, a radical republic where individual standing is wholly determined by citizenship and participation. It is also a capitalist society, where standing is determined by work and wealth. Hence the parallel importance that Shklar attributes to suffrage on the one hand and employment on the other. Hence, too, her most radical proposal: that liberalism in America requires for its completion what seems least likely—an American version of social democracy.

An *American* version, for this is a social democracy focused on the working individual, not the working class. Shklar argues that the liberal state, representing the political community as a whole, has a "comprehensive commitment . . . to provide opportunities for work to earn a living wage for all who need and demand it."[1] Work is a right, she says, but not a right of the sort that philosophers usually describe. It is "a right derived from the requirements of local citizenship, not a primary human right."[2] People around the world cannot claim this right, though they no doubt have others, both primary and secondary. Nor can its American claimants look to the courts for its enforcement. Primary rights are presumably enforceable by the courts; rights like this one are closer to "presumptions guiding our policies." It would be better to say "presumptions that ought to guide our policies"—insofar as we understand our history and society.

I take that first person plural pronoun to be very important. Of course, the aggressors and usurpers and would-be tyrants against whom we defend the bulwarks are *our* enemies, but they are also, or ought to be, everyone's enemies. We have rights against them that we share with all humanity. The locally derived right to work is ours in a stronger sense. It reflects the particularism of positivity. When we imagine a society of voting and working members where the vote and the work guarantee individual membership but don't provide the necessary content of individuality, where men and women are free to plan a life beyond voting and working, then we are imagining an American liberalism. We give expression, with Shklar, to an American imagination.

III

So the point of the liberalism of fear is to open up social space for many liberalisms, including our own. I don't mean to suggest that fear doesn't constrain what goes on within this open space. I have been using the bulwarks metaphor in too literal a way, as if there really was a wall around the city. Sometimes there is, of course, and sometimes the defense of the bulwarks is an actual endeavor. But the walls are also within the city, and the more liberal the city is, the more pervasive are the walls. Liberalism is a culture of barriers, animated by a deep suspicion of power, protecting every individual member against the rampages of the powerful. Though it cannot form the content of a way of life, negativity penetrates more deeply into substantive liberalism than into any other political formation. Here lies liberalism's claim to universality: that its doctrinal arguments and institutional arrangements reflect a common fearfulness whereas every other politics is naïve about or complicitous in the power of aristocrats or kings or bureaucrats or vanguards. Obviously, this claim is only plausible if made on behalf of a liberalism that is not itself naive about or complicitous in the power of plutocrats and corporate managers. Nonetheless, it makes sense to see liberal suspicion as a universally useful force and the culture of barriers as a common good.

Should we, then, all be liberals? If we regard liberalism now as a purely negative politics, this is not something that we can *be*. We can only be something else *in a liberal way*, subject to liberal constraints. *Liberal*, in this sense, is properly used as an adjective: liberal monarchist, liberal democrat, liberal socialist, and insofar as the major religions are political in character, liberal Jew, Christian, Muslim, Hindu, and so on. In these formulations, the adjective expresses our fears, the noun, our hopes. This isn't a universally necessary usage, for liberalism is also, as I have been arguing, a substantive politics. Focused on individualism and autonomy, it may require modifiers of its own—as in *social* or *communitarian* liberalism—which address the local pathologies of autonomy. But *liberal* as an adjective, expressing fearfulness and negativity, is likely to be useful everywhere. I cannot imagine a political regime that I would not want constrained in at least some of the ways that it suggests. And the constraint that comes first to mind is one focused on the cruelties of power.

How does liberal negativity work? I don't think that it does anything more than intensify and institutionalize the negative features of other political doctrines and regimes. Defenders of monarchy, for example, will always claim that the monarchy they defend is not tyranny. Their kings rule or are supposed to rule in a not arbitrary, not capricious, not irresponsible, not lawless, not oppressive way. Liberal monarchy is a regime where these negatives are realized politically, where the king, at least in the ordinary course of events, *cannot* rule arbitrarily, capriciously, and so on. But it won't necessarily be autonomous individuals who are protected against the royal will; it may well be ancient guilds or chartered towns or an established church or even hereditary aristocracy. Similarly, the king may choose a mercantilist economic policy and still be a "liberal" king in this negative sense—if his choice is made with the consent of parliament, say, or through some legal process, and without overriding the customary rights and privileges of his subjects.

When these subjects join together to defend their ancient "liberties" against a usurping king, are they liberals? They probably think of themselves as true monarchists; their hopes lie in a good king. But their politics is very much like (a local version of) the liberalism of fear: it misses the substance of liberalism but captures the essential negatives. Think how many revolutions start in this way, driven by fear, aiming at the constraint of power, and then are taken over from within by the advocates of an illiberal positivity. Substantive liberalism certainly can be a revolutionary ideology—in fact it has been that, briefly in the French and more lastingly in the American case—but the negative version seems more powerful. It is also characteristically episodic and recurrent; every abuse of power brings a "liberal" response.

Liberal socialism has a form similar to liberal monarchy, though the doctrinal connections are very different. Central socialist doctrines make individual liberation the long-term goal of the movement; they claim, in effect, to incorporate liberal positivity. But the idea of class struggle, the dream of "seizing" power and using the state to bring about rapid social and economic transformation, the acceptance of "vanguard" leadership—all these, for many socialists, undermined the commitment to negative constraints. If the proletariat was in theory a "universal" class and in practice a majority class, and if it acted in the interests of all humanity, and if everything it did was historically determined, why were constraints needed? The proletariat was the world-historical good king. But the actual rule of the bad advisors of this good king quickly produced not only a straightforwardly liberal but also a liberal socialist opposition. The latter was led by men and women still committed to the substantive means and ends of socialism, who advocated at the same time a variety of limits on the exercise of political power: an independent judiciary, a free press, a strong civil society.

I call these features of a political system negative, though they obviously have positive content (and value) because their content is not given by liberal doctrine. "The liberal method of taking part in the political contest," wrote Carlo Rosselli, author of a book called *Liberal Socialism* (1937), "cannot be qualified; it is not and cannot be either bourgeois or socialist, conservative or revolutionary."[3] This seems to me wrong, since liberalism in fact can both qualify and be qualified. Even within liberal limits, a political contest can take very different forms involving different protagonists, different kinds of mobilization, different degrees of participation, different styles of debate. Socialism should press these differences in one direction (class-based or ideological parties, mass mobilization, intense participation), substantive liberalism is another. We defend the "liberal method," however it is positively expressed, for the sake of the protection it provides against tyranny.

A last question: Does liberal negativity set limits on substantive liberalism, too? If there is a liberal (and illiberal) socialism, is there also a liberal (and illiberal) liberalism? I think that *libertarianism* is the name we use for a liberalism set loose from its own negativity. In this version of liberal politics and society, individual autonomy, unlimited in its scope, gives rise to a pattern of domination: the strong over the weak, the rich over the poor. Since such a pattern, once established, opens the way for cruelty and oppression, it is certain to produce, as a characteristic recoil, the liberalism of fear. What fear will dictate in this case is a defensive reaction aimed at setting limits on liberty itself in order to secure the basic interests of the weakest members of society. If these fearful liberals move beyond defensiveness and try to make this or that version of autonomy universally available, they will become liberals of a positive sort, driven by hope as well as fear, "social" liberals, say; or they will reach toward some further positivity and become liberal socialists.

We always have to be afraid of political power; that is the central liberal insight. But this is an insight into a universal experience that wasn't discovered, only theorized, by liberal writers. Nor does this fear by itself make for an adequate theory of political power. We must address the uses of power as well as its dangers. And since it has many uses, we have to choose among them, designing policies, like Shklar's guaranteed employment, that enhance and strengthen what we most value in our way of life. Then we try to enforce those policies; carefully, if we are wise, remembering the last time we were fearful and acting within the limits of liberal negativity.

Notes

1. *American Citizenship: The Quest for Inclusion*, 99.
2. *American Citizenship*, 100.
3. Carlo Rosselli, *Liberal Socialism,* ed. Nadia Urbinati, trans. William McCuaig (Princeton, 1994), 94.

2

The Democracy of Everyday Life

Nancy L. Rosenblum

American citizenship finds its glory not simply in the right to political participation but in the democracy of everyday life.
The Faces of Injustice [1990], 43

JUDITH SHKLAR DESCRIBED THE TASK of intellectual history as an attempt to discover the spiritual antecedents of contemporary thought, and her most influential work focused on the precursors of the "liberalism of fear" (1989). A number of recent commentators claim to see a shift in Shklar's later writings, away from this grim preoccupation with warding off the worst official cruelties and toward a positive theory of social democracy. It is true that Shklar was increasingly interested in democratic citizenship, American citizenship in particular, but attempts to recruit her as a social democrat or philosopher of equality go too far.[1] It is not surprising, after all, that the author of a study of Rousseau would see the sense of injustice as "the core of the modern democratic political sensibility" (*The Faces of Injustice*, 92, 86). But Shklar consistently declined to engage in the business of systematic normative theory, where notions of social justice and responsibility are given solid ground. On the contrary, she always insisted that the experience of injustice has "an exuberant life of its own," which no system of justice can grasp. Nor did she subscribe to the collection of political preferences that define social democracy, and where we find some overlap of sympathy or policy her reasons diverged from the conventional ones. For example, she recommended a "right to work" for Americans because, for reasons specific to our shameful history of slavery, earning has become a prerequisite for first-class citizenship. She continued to see "ac-

I would like to thank Peter Berkowitz, Rogers Smith, and Catherine Zuckert for comments on an earlier version of this essay.

tive citizenship" as a self-protective response to injustice and declined to celebrate political participation and collective action.

It is truer to what is distinctive in Shklar's work to say that from the start her interest went beyond the history of political philosophy and the texts of Rousseau, Hegel, and Montesquieu and extended to the way ideas move out into political culture. From her early writing on the decline of utopianism and on legalism, her attention was drawn to political ideology. Why we resort to particular ideas, what cycle of mutual accusations is initiated, what they blind us to, what actions are likely to follow, and what actions are inconceivable, these were her standard questions. Her later writings focused on the capacity of political ideology to address the injustices of everyday life, and the ambiguities of American citizenship in particular. The job of political theory, as she saw it, was to confront us with the paradoxes and incoherences of our working political ideas.

Shklar's first business was to deliver the grim reminder that even in American political thought, liberal democratic ideas compete, often unsuccessfully, with a variety of full-blown, virulently antidemocratic ideologies. The "liberalism of fear" was not in eclipse. Our fund of historical and literary memories comprises not just constitutional democracy, as we like to imagine, but slavery, racism, nativism, sexism, and religious bigotry (*American Citizenship*, 13). The psychological logic of the play of political ideologies is as complex in American political culture as elsewhere—something standard accounts of a historical progression toward civic equality and inclusion miss.[2]

Liberal democracy also generates its own internal incoherences and contradictions. Shklar insisted that pluralism, with its dispersion of power, is a description of liberal society and a condition of freedom, but many of her most provocative insights had to do with the way pluralism invites social inequalities and cultivates what we know to be vices. An unstable dynamic of trust and distrust is built into representative government. Social mobility creates a sensation of betrayal in personal as well as public life. Pluralism insures that our commitment to public institutions will be partial and that the loyalties of families, ethnic groups, and religious sects will often overwhelm public justice. And at the heart of her analysis is the observation that pluralism generates intended and unintended exclusions so that outsiders are inevitably rebuffed. Snobbery—"the habit of making inequality hurt"—is a by-product of multiplicity (*Ordinary Vices*, 87). These tensions of American pluralist democracy are inescapable because citizens belong to "two interlocking public orders, one egalitarian, the other entirely unequal" (*American Citizenship*, 63).

Inequality mattered to Montesquieu and Montaigne, Shklar's own spiritual antecedents, because it created opportunities for cruelty, but they did not treat social equality as a positive good (*Ordinary Vices,* 28). Liberal democrats must, and Shklar looked back to the Jacksonian era as the point of reference for thinking about American citizenship and equality today. First-class citizenship is a sham without civil rights and public standing, of course, but there is more to democratic culture. Beyond right principles, well-designed political institutions, and allegiance to constitutional order are regular habits of equality, among them the inclination to behave toward others "identically and with easy spontaneity" (*Ordinary Vices,* 136). This democratic disposition is developed in public and in private: "Active citizenship shades over into bordering private spheres . . . the phrase *good citizen* is now very commonly used to refer to people who behave well on the job and in their immediate neighborhood" (*American Citizenship,* 5). At the heart of American liberal democracy, then, is the collection of attitudes and ways of relating to others Shklar called the democracy of everyday life. It is an unusual subject for political theory. But we have some familiarity with democratic types from experience, and we encounter them writ large in characters in American literature.

How can we recognize the democracy of everyday life; what conditions support it; for whom is it psychologically tenable? I explore these questions later in this chapter with the help of characters from novels by Nathaniel Hawthorne and Saul Bellow, who bring the democratic disposition home to us. In the following section I underscore in greater detail Shklar's interest in the way political ideology frames what we see as possible. It is a prelude to understanding why she saw the democracy of everyday life as a possibility for us. It also invites us to consider the elements of contemporary democratic ideology that inhibit others from sharing her optimism.

Political Ideology and Psychological Possibility

It is a mistake to imagine that we can consider political theory without psychology, which helps us to comprehend the holding power political ideas have for us. Shklar used historical cases and literary set pieces to evoke the psychological reality behind political thought, and to jar recognition. Literary examples do not illustrate anything, she explained, but reveal something directly: "They are there for their own sake, for their ability to force us to acknowledge what we already know imperfectly. They make us recognize something as if it were obvious" (*Ordinary Vices,* 229). Vivid historical examples, too, "force us to acknowledge what we know about ourselves and each other" (ibid., 138, 195). Politically important opinions are rarely locked in groups whose perspectives are unintelligible to outsiders, Shklar insisted, signaling her distance from postmodernist insistence on the inaccessible extremes of power and powerlessness, "self" and "other." Since Shklar could not abide the arrogance of prophets of "shared meaning" who talked confidently about what "we" know and believe, and since she found most imputations of feeling and opinion to herself and others both untrue and condescending, how did she confirm that she got "us" right? Literary portraits served as a check. She could be confident that she got the political dimension of snobbery right, for example, if it is confirmed in the Pyncheon family of Hawthorne's *House of the Seven Gables.*

There are limits to political psychology, of course. We cannot know the irreducibly subjective component of victimhood. The effects of exclusion from full citizenship on self-respect, say, are purely personal, and not-so-rare displays of fortitude and pride should give political theorists pause before they attribute a deficit of self-respect to others. If civil rights and public standing contribute indispensably to public respect, still, they are neither the sole source nor guarantee of individual self-respect at all. In short, the case for democratic equality cannot rest on repairing the loss of self-respect. Nothing was further from Shklar's mind than a political theory based on individual psychology and personal responses. She had no desire to see political theorists become a self-appointed "branch of the counselling industry" (*Ordinary Vices,* 226).

On the other hand, Shklar did not subscribe to any theory of human nature. Her rare psychological generalizations were meant as correctives: she invoked the universalism of pain because she was appalled by the parochial tendency to ignore this *summum malum* and the areas of the world where torture and arrant arbitrariness rage, for example, and she pointed to the physiological gratification revenge provides in the course of considering what the calm enforcement of rules of justice cannot (*The Faces of Injustice,* 101). For the most part, however, what we need to know are the historically specific political ideologies that frame what we see as possible, and the political psychology that gives these ideas their holding power.

Consider Shklar's extended analysis of the "second great age of romanticism" in *After Utopia.* Writing in 1957, she described how extravagant claims by Enlightenment intellectuals and political events in our horrible century contributed to the disappearance of political philosophy. By itself the state of the world could not account for why so many thinkers saw the entire social universe as totalitarian, however, or why they lost faith in Promethean creativity and resigned themselves to the "romanticism of defeat." Shklar offered a psychological not historical logic. Political theory is dependent on mustering a modicum of hope, a "grain of baseless optimism," and the decline of political faith explains its disappearance. Psychological logic also underlies her criticism of romantic substitutes for political thought. Radical optimism is admittedly "insane," but romantic rejection of purposeful social thought and action is itself an irrational fear. Despair and fatalism are self-indulgent. And antipolitical postures are emotionally untenable—since few people can endure romantic isolation it is not surprising that "the last of the many self-inflicted defeats" of romanticism was its ignominious end in ideologies such as blood-and-soil political nationalism, or communism (*After Utopia*, 107). Is anything else possible? Shklar asks at the end of *After Utopia*. This too was a psychological question: whether an adequate theoretical alternative to antipolitical culture consciousness *can be offered*. Shklar's answer could only have appealed to intellectuals: "at present we know too little to feel justified in cultural despair. . . . A reasoned skepticism is consequently the sanest attitude for the present" (ibid., 269).[3]

Shklar demonstrated what it means to temper despair and translate reasoned skepticism into political theory in *American Citizenship: The Quest for Inclusion*, which traced the political ideology that celebrates earning from Franklin to its fruition in the Jacksonians. She judged this ideology incoherent, particularly so today when the disjuncture between social values and the real constraints of industrial society are apparent. Still, her task as a political theorist was to explain how we got to this point: "The American work ethic . . . becomes perfectly comprehensible when it is understood not as a reflection of the class values of preindustrial artisans, but as the ideology of citizens caught between racist slavery and aristocratic pretensions" (*American Citizenship*, 64). She could also see that "the memory of slavery, made potent by racism, still arouses predictable fears among white workers and haunts blacks," and that Jacksonian ideology is echoed in our mutual accusations about welfare dependency today: "The defender of the helpless poor wants to protect them against an army of predatory aristocrats denying them their rights and sustenance; the opposing party of individual effort . . . see the idle poor as no longer citizens" (ibid., 85, 96). Both sides want to make good citizens of the underclass by turning them into earners. These are not the best possible public values, on Shklar's view, and they are not endowed with moral worth by being shared (ibid., 98). Nonetheless, she channeled her skepticism into a decent proposal to create paying jobs geographically close to the unemployed. She had no illusion that this created work had much to do with generating self-respect, or that a paying job cultivates good citizens. But guaranteed paid work provides men and women with what is, for us, an elementary component of public standing, and illustrates her thought that the job of political theory is to review critically the judgments we ordinarily make and the possibilities we usually see (*Ordinary Vices*, 226).

What did Shklar think was possible—psychologically possible, emotionally tenable—for us? She warned that far from being an amoral free-for-all, liberalism is extremely difficult and constraining, "far too much so for those who cannot endure contradiction, complexity, diversity, and the risks of freedom" (*Ordinary Vices*, 5). I have already remarked on the specific form she believed contradiction and complexity to take in pluralist society: "The individual American citizen is in fact a member of two interlocking public orders, one egalitarian, the other entirely unequal." No wonder that boundaries between acceptable and intolerable inequalities are so hard for us, or that as some forms of inequality diminish Americans seem to reinvent others. Things are made harder by the fact that standard resources for overcoming the vicissitudes of pluralism are closed to us. Liberal democracy is incompatible with massive education in civic virtue or efforts to create perfectly socialized citizens for whom public goals take precedence (*The Faces of Injustice*, 45). Nonetheless, Shklar thought that many of us are able to endure "contradiction, complexity, diversity" because some resources for negotiating them are available. The Madisonian solution—multiplying groups so that all can have some occasion for inclusion and exclusion—should make social inequality easier for everyone to bear (*Ordinary Vices*, 136). Another resource for negotiating the complexities and stresses of pluralism is "the democracy of everyday life." Shklar defined it as a matter of treating everyone identically and with easy spontaneity. It entails acting as if social standing and cultural differences were a matter of indifference in our views of one another.

The democracy of everyday life does not attack the myriad distinctions based on styles of consumption, leisure activities, neighborhood, religion, race, or standard of living. It is not a promise of social equality. It would be wrong to see this democratic disposition as an adequate morality or account of character. The democracy of everyday life cannot even be taken as a sure sign of mutual respect. Shklar acknowledged that the democracy of everyday life may be hypocritical. Not all of us are convinced that all men and women are entitled to social respect, only some of us think so. But most of us are able to act as if we really did believe it, and that is what counts for her (*Ordinary Vices*, 77). Every minuscule amount of political decency counts. Each small exhibition of indifference to social inequality contributes to the democracy of everyday life.

It also counts for Shklar that the democracy of everyday life is not absurdly optimistic and so is unlikely to end in a self-inflicted defeat. She had taken our measure: simplicity was a possibility within our psychological powers. The democracy of everyday life is simple because it involves ordinary interactions among individuals and because it does not require us to assess the social place and sensibilities of everyone we meet and adjust our conduct accordingly. Carefully calculating social status, making fine cultural distinctions, and taking exquisite pains to avoid slights are wholly out of keeping with a democratic disposition. The demand to give and receive recognition for one's particular social and cultural attributes, earned or inherited, has always been associated with an antidemocratic ethos, as we see in Hawthorne's description of the haughty Judge Pyncheon in *The House of the Seven Gables:* "As is customary with the rich, when they aim at the honors of a republic, he apologized, as it were, to the people, for his wealth, prosperity, and elevated station . . . putting off the more of his dignity in due proportion with the humbleness of the man whom he saluted, and thereby proving a haughty consciousness of his advantages as irrefragably as if he had marched forth preceded by a troop of lackeys to clear the way."[4]

What does the democracy of everyday life look like? What support does it receive from political ideology? And is Shklar's "grain of baseless optimism" justified?

Holgrave's Choices

The embodiment of the democracy of everyday life is the Jacksonian hero of Hawthorne's *House of the Seven Gables.* Holgrave is the perfect democratic disposition. In scene after scene we see this young artist, poor but independent, engaging directly and with identical forthrightness with everyone. Holgrave's ancestors were the victims of a fraudulent property claim by the prominent Pyncheon family of Salem, but he is not consumed by anger or desire for revenge and deals with the Pyncheon's in his usual manner. These would-be aristocrats are alternately affronted and amazed by his steady, uncalculating demeanor, his lack of ceremony and deference. Except for the most incorrigible of them, the Pyncheons are eventually won over. Old Hepzibah is encouraged by his example to discover that gentility and aristocratic pretensions are terribly restricting; that opening a shop is not a social taint; that treating customers with identical pleasantness is good for trade and improves her own disposition. Holgrave does not take advantage of vulnerability any more than he curries favor with social superiors. He never exploits his "animal magnetism" and mesmeric powers, which make Hawthorne's villains (Westervelt, the self-promoting charlatan, and Hollingsworth, the visionary reformer, in *The Blithedale Romance*) so dangerous. The temptation to exercise empire over another spirit is not strong in him.

For Hawthorne, the deep moral truth in this democratic outlook was that goodness and evil are evenly distributed among high and low, but he does not ascribe this sort of moral reflection to his hero. The source of Holgrave's democratic disposition is simpler—he is boundless, unencumbered, and self-made. Holgrave is an artist—a practitioner of the new art of daguerreotype, but at the age of twenty-two he has already worked as a schoolmaster, a salesman in a country store, the political editor of a country newspaper, a peddler of cologne, a practitioner of dentistry, a traveler, a short-term member of a community of Fourierists, and a public lecturer on mesmerism. Amid all these personal vicissitudes he is responsible neither to public opinion nor to individuals. Lack of fixed expectations insulates him from the terror of change or loss of favor (*Seven Gables*, 112). Open to new possibilities, everyone is interesting to him and has a claim on his attention. Hepzibah and Phoebe, the Pyncheon cousins, struggle to understand his disregard for social position and convention: he is not lawless exactly, but lives by a law of his own, they decide. He follows his conscience. Holgrave's defining trait is that despite putting off and on many exteriors, "he had never lost his identity . . . he had never violated the innermost man" (*Seven Gables*, 157).

As long as democratic mixing does not give way to isolation, Hawthorne was not troubled by living in the present or lack of permanent social affiliations and defining commitments. It did not imply radical contingency or isolation, atomism, or a "thin self." By far the greater danger is the "oyster-like tenacity" with which people cling to family, social affiliation, and settled expectations. Would-be aristocrats are not the only culprits. Hawthorne could see that the weight of antiquity and snobbish longing for European high culture had not been lifted—*The Marble Faun* (1860) tells that story; Puritans and descendents of leading families of the revolution enjoyed inherited status and political influence; the upset of Southern dynasties was a prospect Hawthorne relished if the North were victorious in the Civil War. And there were the recipients of political spoils, who live in fear of party change. A transitory life is what democracy is all about, Hawthorne insisted, so much so that *resisting* change is the deliberate election. To be identified too deeply with some social attribute or role whether it is a perfectionist vision (Hollingsworth), aesthetic sensibility (Clifford), attachment to property or public office (Judge Pyncheon), or connection with one place and one affection (Hepzibah)—is madness or imbecility. It is also a good predictor of cruelty, intended or unintended. Those with fixed ambitions and places to defend are bold, imperious, relentless, and crafty; Judge Pyncheon followed out his purposes "with an inveteracy of pursuit that knew neither rest nor conscience," (112) trampling on the weak and doing his best to beat down the strong.

All this echoes the standard political ideology of Jacksonian democracy, which described the American revolution as unfinished. Disavowal of hereditary conditions was its great promise, but a "regal fungus" survived. "Entails, nobility, hierarchy, and monopolies" are corrupting and a plain affront to democratic equality.[5] Holgrave doubts whether "even our public edifices—our capitols, state houses, court houses, city hall, and churches—ought to be built of such permanent materials as stone or brick." (163) They should crumble to ruin once in twenty years. Here is Paine's ideal of "revolution in every generation" made concrete and brought into daily social life. For those who took these democratic promises to heart, America had devolved into a "Custom House." Hawthorne was its surveyor, recording the strong grip of kinship, estate, and hereditary conditions in a political society that hypocritically pretends they have been erased.

Not everyone agreed with this picture. Henry James thought that the past had time to produce so little that America was a "thinly composed society" without ancient classes, castes, manners, or institutions (his famous litany of what is lacking continues on). To Santayana it seemed as if Hawthorne wrote in an utter social vacuum; his genius was employed in "digestion of vacancy."[6] But Hawthorne insisted that America had enough in the way of inheritance and unearned privilege to foster the pretense of nobility, to undermine the social ethos of voluntary association, and to make the ideal of self-made identity seem like a chimera. He was acutely aware that women especially were constrained by inherited conditions; this was a constant theme. Moreover, Hawthorne sensed that in some form the forces of inherited attachment are ineradicable, for personal past operates whether or not one's ancestors are ancient or illustrious. The family is a closed society and names are our universal inheritance (in keeping with the democratic wish for self-made identity, Hawthorne, born on the fourth of July 1804, changed his, and we learn that Holgrave is an alias). *The House of the Seven Gables* is an extended narrative on the theme, "how much of old material goes to make up the freshest novelty of human life" (12). That is why the democracy of everyday life is only a possibility, and Holgrave is a hero, not a commonplace type. Still, if American society is not fully open and continuously elective, the conditions of "fresh atmosphere" do exist. Even old Hepzibah, the mustiest Pyncheon of them all, left the house of the seven gables for a new life. Hawthorne's striking decision to uncouple self-made identity from its usual tie to youth and illustrate the social malleability of old age is the mark of his hope for cultivating democratic dispositions.

Hawthorne suggests that certain public institutions correspond to the democracy of everyday life, however imperfectly. The most dramatic expression of the idea of self-made identity, fresh beginnings, and self-government was the propensity in the first half of the nineteenth century to form "elective communities" out of a company of strangers. The predictable failures of utopianism are the subject of *The Blithedale Romance*.[7] A more promising institutional expression is elections—rotation in office. Raw ambition, ignorance, and absence of public spirit characterize most politicians, and Hawthorne thought that on the whole the electorate chooses blindly and amiss. Even so, elections, mass political parties, and spoils unsettle authority and institutionalize impermanence, which is all to the good. And the ability to earn a living by political appointments opens office holding to every social class. Hawthorne, an unabashed locofoco surveyor, observed that his post in the Salem custom house and partisan political activities forced him to mix it up. "I look upon it as evidence . . . of a system naturally well balanced, and lacking no essential part of a thorough organization, that . . . I could mingle at once with men of altogether different qualities and never murmur at the change."[8]

The institution that comes closest to mirroring the democracy of everyday life is romantic marriage. Holgrave and Phoebe fall in love and end a generations-long feud between their families. The family is the ever-present frontier. Hawthorne calls it a "neutral territory." Of course, marriage is also the start of another little closed society and round of inheritance: "To plant a family! The idea is at the bottom of most of the wrong and mischief which men do." But this, too, was temporary: "The truth is, that, once in every half century, at longest, a family should be merged into the great, obscure mass of humanity, and forget all about its ancestors" (*Seven Gables*, 164).

The democracy of everyday life has its origin in the Jacksonian era, then, but Hawthorne did not associate it with that political ideology wholesale. The Jacksonian portrayal of society as a conflict between rich and poor, and the image of a single democratic people enjoying a consensus of opinion were simplistic. Hawthorne did not subscribe to the simple solution of transferring social status and political influence from a "paper aristocracy" to laboring classes. Holgrave was not a reverse snob. Nor did Hawthorne share the Democrats' absolute confidence in meritocratic striving. Nothing was more foolish "than the eagerness with which gaunt and gosling-like youths strive to break through the barriers."[9] He did not expect too much from opening up democratic institutions to "public sector Horatio Algers."[10] There is more to democratic character than productive work, earning one's living, and getting ahead.[11]

For Holgrave is not just an independent earner, he is a moral type, which is what the democratic disposition is, however limited. It is a truncated political morality—less than civic virtue and certainly not the whole of character. Phoebe, the incarnation of *caritas* and true goodness, sternly observes that Holgrave is not a Christian. It is true that he lacks humility. But his sense of superior capacity is not tied to social standing and he has no interest in influencing others. Though he is a reformer in principle he is not especially active in righting injustice. But he is neither silent nor passive, and his disposition to forthrightly acknowledge injustice where it exists and to treat people fairly and with easy spontaneity is a democratic tonic.

Hawthorne's novel captures the ideology that rejects inheritance and promises self-made identity, making democratic characters like Holgrave possible, and it points to complementary institutions. Hawthorne makes the social obstacles plain as well: class, privilege, and the newer tendency to reverse snobbism. The limitations of this picture are obvious: there is nothing about slavery or race, or nativism, or ethnic antagonism, which are also ways of making inequality hurt and inhibiting the democracy of everyday life.[12]

The Adventures of Augie March

A later incarnation of the democratic disposition comes in the person of a second generation Jewish boy on Chicago's West Side in the period from the 1920s to World War II. Saul Bellow's Augie March announces himself on the opening paragraph: "I am an American, Chicago born . . . and go at things as I have taught myself, free-style, and will make the record in my own way: first to knock, first admitted; some times an innocent knock, sometimes a not so innocent."[13] Like Holgrave, Augie navigates urban society trying on social relations and roles. For him too, a self-made life begins with living in the present and moving out beyond the small circle of attachments, family and ethnic enclave, that shares the same "history of love" (*Augie*, 285). Sloughing off the past is easier for Augie. Holgrave's roots went back to Puritan Salem; Augie has no memory of his father, who abandoned the family, and his immigrant roots are shadowy, made actual to him through the March's boarder, Grandma Lausch. She is less representative of the family traditions of Jewish Odessa than amorphously "old world," with her aristocratic airs, Machiavellian advice, and czarist domestic tyranny. Her mission is to try to instill in Augie her sense of what is necessary for success in America, pressing on him the thought that to be trusting is to be a chump among the tough and cunning-hearted (*Augie*, 10).

Like Holgrave, Augie insisted that "one is only ostensibly born to remain in specified limits" (*Augie*, 240). The Jacksonian era remains a point of reference here, for work continues to signify independence, not just a way of earning a living, self-made identity remains an aspiration, and the link between shifting involvements and the democracy of everyday life is as strong as it was a century earlier. Holgrave was always self-employed while Augie must work for others, but he manages to avoid becoming a cog in an industrial or bureaucratic machine. Still young at the book's end, Augie has worked for the neighborhood real estate mogul, in an exclusive men's shop, for a luxury dog service; he has been a bum, a book thief, a union organizer, a partner in his brother's coal business, a college student, a WPA housing surveyor; he has been a research assistant for an eccentric millionaire writing a book on the state of the world, a merchant marine, kept by an eccentric lover in Mexico, and at the close is working in Paris as a black marketeer after the war.

To be faithful to the idea that "one is only ostensibly born to remain in specified limits," Holgrave had to resist the contradictions of inheritance, privilege, and aristocratic pretension in a society whose promise was openness. For Augie the forces pushing him to a particular social role and identity are so pervasive in everyday life they do not bear naming: "All the influences were lined up waiting for me. I was born, and here they were to form me" (*Augie*, 43). Augie's brother Simon insists that Augie must not dissolve in bewilderment of choices but must make himself hard. His scrambling friend explains that children of immigrants flock to the factorylike corridors of city colleges to get a card or diploma because "if people don't know what you qualify in they'll never know where to place you, and that can be dangerous. . . . You have to specialize" (189). His employer Mrs. Renling proposed to adopt him and make him her heir. Augie runs from every offer and opportunity. Allowing himself to be adopted would have been a betrayal of his submissively "scrubbing and lugging" mother, for one thing (238). For another, Augie was reluctant to create expectations of loyalty; he resisted being rescued from the rat race or saved by affection because people inevitably felt betrayed when he could not go along with their plans for building enterprises and families. Work is the Rosetta stone to Augie's life, then, and it is clear why he refuses to settle on one position. Different careers signify not just variations of wealth but varieties of subordination and privilege, expectations of friendship and marriage, styles of living and social cliques, and Augie wants to avoid getting stuck. Bellow reminds us that even if they are a matter of adoption, election, or serendipity rather than inheritance, fixed social place and settled affiliation are the enemy of a democratic disposition.

Augie is a romantic sensibility: alive to plenitude, unable to abide constraint, paralyzed by the thought that no external choice faithfully expresses his true inner self. But the democratic character of his resistance is plainly predominant. The lives held up to him as exemplary not only threaten his independence, they are built on small dominations. Simon, set on wealth and keyed to making every situation pay off, is not just an inveterate social climber (there is nothing terribly wrong in that) but a rich "prince": capricious, haughty, critical, arbitrary in his dealings with his wife and daughter, outright mean in his public affairs, taking pleasure in humiliating people. He wants to rule in his petty sphere, and he demands recognition. Einhorn, the neighborhood real estate wheeler-dealer, "had his experts who tinkered with the gas meters; he got around the electric company by splicing into the main cable; he fixed tickets and taxes." He was steeped in lawsuits, legal miscarriages, sour partnerships, welshings and contested wills, and he was obscene (*Augie*, 73). None of this put Augie off as much as the fact that Einhorn was a "selfish autocrat." The strong willed and powerful want to consolidate their sense of who they are and feed their "hungry principles" with fresh recruits. Those who come within their circle of influence are weak and the result is bullying, demands for obedience, and daily injustices that often fall outside the practicable reach of rights and laws. Like high-handed officials who make you empty your pockets, these men and women insisted on demonstrations that Augie was not his own person. Opposition, saying no, was a physiological imperative, as definite a feeling in him as hunger: "I never had accepted determination and wouldn't become what other people wanted to make of me" (28).

Augie knew too much about "more or less permanent pain" to think that happiness is what he is looking for. He is simply trying to refuse to lead a disappointed life. He does not require that others understand him, or recognize him for who he truly is. But he does refuse to let their misunderstandings govern his life. He has his fair share of moral courage. He holds out for a "good enough fate" (*Augie*, 28). The democratic disposition is not all negative resistance, though; it inclines to a positive way of relating to others, which is the heart of the democracy of everyday life. Augie never retreats or craves isolation. Because he is open to possibilities, other people appear endlessly interesting to him, personally and individually. He is the embodiment of political theory's arid, disembodied notion that "identities are formed in open dialogue, unshaped by a predefined social script."[14] Characteristically, Augie finds some good in almost everyone. He respects Einhorn's generosity with money, his energy and courage in overcoming his physical handicap, his thoughtfulness about the world: "he had the intelligence to be sublime" (100). Bellow's Augie March believes in our universal eligibility to rise above our generally detestable characters: "What did Danton lose his head for, or why was there a Napoleon, if it wasn't to make a nobility of us all?" He never found this paragon, but at least "I've never seen any reason why not" (29).

This is a good profession of Shklar's "grain of baseless optimism." For Augie was well acquainted with people who saw human failing as the reality principle, the basic data of experience. One of Augie's lovers warns against bettering people in your mind to make them loveable; she puts every human weakness into the picture—"the bad, the criminal, sick, envious, scavenging, wolfish, the living-on-the-dying" (*Augie*, 437). Another lover (the misanthropists here are women) turns on Augie: he was not mad enough about abominations and wasn't "hard enough against horrors or wrathful about swindles" (209). He made allowances, and wasn't enough of an enemy. Perpetual indignation is egalitarian, too, of course. The inability to abide faulty humanity springs from a vision of a different kind of humanity altogether, and Bellow, like Hawthorne, saw the root of misanthropy in perfectionism. Augie observes that for his friend Thea, "what I'd call average hypocrisy, just the incidental little whiffs of the social machine, was terribly hard on her" (379). The democracy of everyday life is impossible for her because mixing it up with fellows who are "good enough" is unabidable and making allowances is a moral lapse. Hawthorne was the master psychologist of perfectionism and its cruelties in the form of Puritanism and nineteenth-century utopianism. Bellow recaptures its mundane expressions.[15]

When Hawthorne looked for a rough correspondence between the democracy of everyday life and certain institutions he found it in rotation in office, elective community, and romantic marriage. In Bellow's prewar Chicago, labor unions are the principle candidate. Augie's adventures involve him in other institutions: public charities, which he is taught to deceive, and the Works Progress Administration, which provides purposeless work, but his stint at organizing hotel workers excites his democratic idealism. Grammick, the chief organizer, displayed an admirable "consciousness in advance of rights and wrongs that hadn't risen to view yet" (*Augie*, 287). And Augie was thrilled by the Whitmanesque spectacle of the rush to join; organizing was a matter of scrambling to channel the flood of demand for membership that followed the Wagner Act and sit-down strikes in 1935–36.[16] This mass organization brought out the skilled crafts workers of traditionally ethnic unions but also Greek and African-American chambermaids, porters, maintenance men, "short-order grovelers, . . . the humanity of the under-galleries, . . . all varieties of assaulted kissers, infirmity, drunkenness, dazedness, innocence, limping, crawling, insanity, prejudice" (*Augie*, 288–89). Einhorn cynically observes that a closed shop will not "make men out of slobs." Augie makes allowances and finds people good enough. People get up every morning to go to work, he points out to Einhorn; "it isn't right . . . that they should be so grateful for being allowed to continue in their habit that they shouldn't ask for anything more" (293). Night workers "wanted the chance to say those self-rehearsed things that sometimes had been on their hearts too long." Augie had no illusion that workers had a monopoly on right thinking; "true and false light was distributed just about as usual, in my opinion" (290). Like the dishwasher, "leakily thinking," Augie simply wanted to make his "dim contribution to the righting of wrongs" (292).

He was kept from zealousness, however. For one thing, there is some truth in Einhorn's observation that unions are just another big organization "that makes dough" (*Augie*, 293). The workers may have longed for "some fire-fed secret personality that would prepare the moment when they could stand up yelling rebellion" (290), but Augie's role as an organizer consisted of warning workers against direct action, stalling in hearing grievances, trying to get them to comply with the cumbersome mechanics of union elections required by law. Corruption and goon violence may have characterized the Chicago police, but in Augie's experience they arose between members loyal to the recognized union and the masses of those even more underpaid, mostly women, demanding representation by the Congress of Industrial Organizations. Finally, Augie did not want to represent others or to be represented. But that is what organizing is about—rising above individuals, forming associations, asserting group interests and identity, and commanding public recognition. Heady speculations about the meaning of labor and social justice take a back seat to preoccupation with the business of representation. This is a familiar and defensible face of pluralist politics. But it is far from the easy and spontaneous interactions among individuals that make up the democracy of everyday life, which is the face of democracy Augie is fit for.

The democratic disposition looks much the same in these characters created almost a century apart. In neither case does it have much to do with rights or formal civic conduct. It is associated with shifting involvements and a steady moral core. Augie may lack a social identity but *uncommitted* does not adequately describe him any more than Holgrave.[17] He is a positive moral type. He cannot abide cruelty and humiliation of others, in public or private. He is immune to bigotry; he tolerates many vices and crimes, but not these. Augie is incapable of taking advantage of others, or making a strength of disadvantage. He is unfit to be an oppressor, and knows that he is likely to be thought a chump and to be despised. He had no power to hold a grudge, which is one positive moral consequence of living in the present. He makes allowances for ordinary vices. Most important, Augie lacks "an inflamed place of self-distinction." That is always imperial because it tries to command how others should look on you. It demands recognition. Others must affirm by their demeanor or conduct your understanding of who you are, and misrecognition is not just a slight but an unpardonable offense. In contrast, Augie treats everyone with the same easy spontaneity. He is always acutely aware of his own individuality but this has nothing to do with claiming to be better than others or insisting that they comprehend him: "Being Phoebus' boy? I couldn't even dream of it. I never tried to exceed my constitution. In any case, when someone . . . urged me and praised me, I didn't listen closely. I had my own counseling system. It wasn't infallible, but it made mistakes such as I could bear" (*Augie*, 204).

The Democracy of Everyday Life and the Politics of Recognition

These portraits give a sense of what the democracy of everyday life is like and the political ideology of self-made identity that makes democratic dispositions psychologically possible. The democratic disposition involves openness to the vicissitudes of pluralist society and an interest in others personally and individually, which stem in part from a sense of one's own possibilities. This need not entail blind affirmation of social justice or equal opportunity, only confidence that a "good enough fate" is conceivable, and that inheritances and the forces recruiting us to join, however powerful, are not irresistible or inevitably decisive.

If the ideology of self-made identity and the democracy of everyday life seem less likely today, it is not hard to see why. One factor is the contemporary ironic attitude that sees Holgrave's and Augie's ruminations on the possibility of greatness among us as anxious self-aggrandizing not to be taken seriously.[18] Confidence in the democratic disposition will be fragile if it depends on an Emersonian faith in individuals. As Shklar points out, we are not all self-made types who move from social role to social role, land on our feet, never *are* our job or social definition, and who "no aggregate can contain." We are just as likely to be vulnerable, fearful, bullied, or cowed as hopefully adventurous individualists navigating pluralism. The chief ideological inhibition on democratic dispositions, however, is the current political imperative to link individual possibility to group identity—whether belonging is by ascription, inheritance, or joining up. The democracy of everyday life is inhibited if families or groups are closed and exclusive, and if we insist that affiliations and differences are the most important things about us. The comfort some people find in group identity, loyalty, and pride in difference is undeniable. So is the fact that the current "politics of recognition" (or "politics of identity," "politics of difference," or "multiculturalism"), which encourages us to see ourselves as members, amplifies the inevitable vices of pluralism. It heightens sensitivity to presumably defining distinctions and does nothing to moderate mutual mistrust, which has plenty of real causes. It breeds reverse snobbery, a hypocritical pretense that individual variations of experience and disposition among "us" do not matter, and endless accusations of betrayal when they do.

Nothing could be more foreign to Augie March than self-definition in terms of group identity or the thought that being misunderstood is a form of oppression. He encounters prejudice early on; the handful of Jews in his Polish neighborhood were regularly chased, stoned, bitten, and beaten up as Christ killers, "but I never had any special grief from it, or brooded . . . and looked at it as needing no more special explanation than the stone-and-bat wars of the street gangs or the . . . swarming parish punks to rip up fences, screech and bawl at girls, and beat up strangers" (*Augie,* 12). Ethnic hostility and intimidation are so universal that Augie does not feel like a minority. He does not experience people attributing hostile and demeaning characteristics to him as destructive. As he sees it, taking one's turn at being a despised outsider and taking one's lumps at the hands of some angry group is to be expected. Clearly, Augie is assisted in this attitude by the fact that he sees prejudice as spontaneous irrationality; he does not conceive of it as a fully developed antidemocratic ideology. Nor does he discern a systematic impact on his own opportunities or public standing. Not all encounters with prejudice and ethnic antagonism are the same, though, and Augie March is not Everyman.[19] Bellow does not advise us that Augie's adventures could be duplicated by just any young man of any race and background, much less by every young woman.

The politics of recognition is a perfectly understandable response to systematic political exclusion and social inequalities that are made to hurt. If the tension of belonging to "two interlocking public orders, one egalitarian, the other entirely unequal" is brought home to us daily, the impulse to reduce the stress is bound to arise. Everyday offenses will be assigned public significance; regular slights and grievances and ordinary vices will assume a pattern of oppression. Variations of the politics of recognition have in common a determination to hear the voices of the aggrieved, and accept felt injustice as mandates for change (*The Faces of Injustice,* 85). Today, democratic theory accepts the politics of recognition as a prelude to justice, and democratic theorists are thinking through the standards of public reasonableness, procedures for deliberation, and arrangements for representation that make it possible to provide public recognition to groups, overcome mutual distrust, and allow for fair political outcomes, at least in public forums.

But there is no confusing the politics of recognition with the democracy of everyday life, which is a habitual way of going about our ordinary business, not a political or moral theory or prescription for reform. It has to do with day-to-day behavior in realms that will never be congruent with official public culture, and it concerns face-to-face relations among individuals.[20] It is a disposition, not a doctrine. Precisely because it is a way to negotiate the contradictions of pluralism and not a demand on others, the democracy of everyday life cannot suffice for those who insist on "recognition." For the politics of recognition seeks to alter the behavior of others. And outside of civil associations and public forums where group representation and deliberation may be practicable, applied to everyday relations, the politics of recognition is liable to be very demanding. It requires a considerable degree of sociological and cultural sensitivity to discriminate among social and cultural groups in a wildly pluralist society, and to assess the appropriate differential treatment to individuals in ordinary situations. It requires self-discipline to avoid what group members say is a slight, and to adjust our demeanor and conduct to what counts for them as an adequate demonstration of respect. This is especially so if the desired exhibition of respect is experienced as a demand for deference, not equality at all. The politics of recognition requires even more if what is wanted is acknowledgment of the group's merits and accomplishments, the worth of its culture. That this is an invitation to hypocrisy—to currying favor or patronizing compliance rather than political decency—is clear. At the extreme the politics of recognition may signal a retreat from equal respect to a complicated particularist system of status, honor, and offense.

The whole point of the democracy of everyday life, by contrast, is simplicity—*not* having to take the exact social or moral or cultural measure of others in everyday affairs. It is the habit of treating people "identically and with easy spontaneity," a normal disregard for most differences, and a disposition to make allowances rather than take offense or magnify slights. "Whoever feels that he belongs to a group that would arouse the snobbish ire of some potential father-in-law or his equivalent, ought to muster all the personal honor of which he is capable," Shklar advised. "Neither his rights nor his 'true merits,' whatever these may be, will serve him well. What one needs is the courage to be loyal to one's own, which is a way to live, not a way to alter the conduct of other people" (*Ordinary Vices*, 135). When Holgrave declines to revenge the injury to his family, and when he refuses to modulate his form of address or worry about the appropriateness of his intimacy with the Pyncheon cousins, he resists complicity in Judge Pyncheon's assumption of ascriptive hierarchy and in his aristocratic pretensions. Of course, for those intent on public acknowledgment of injustice and collective distinctiveness, there is all the difference in the world between their demand for recognition and Pyncheon's arrogant insistence that others affirm his superiority. Still, it would require more than Shklar's "grain of baseless optimism" to see the democracy of everyday life and the politics of recognition as compatible, much less mutually reinforcing. That only proves what Judith Shklar insisted we could recognize if only we spoke about what we know: the internal complexity and incoherence of American liberal democracy, the difficulty we have negotiating the treacherous terrain of pluralism, and the psychological tension between the political equality of democratic citizenship and the social inequalities of everyday life.

Notes

1. For example, see in this volume Amy Gutmann's essay, "How Limited Is Liberal Government?"

2. For a recent discussion of "ascriptive Americanist traditions", see Rogers M. Smith, "Beyond Tocqueville, Myrdal, and Hartz: The Multiple Traditions in America," *American Political Science Review* 87 (Sept. 1993): 549–66.

3. The same sentiment appears in Saul Bellow's writing: there haven't been civilizations without cities, his hero Augie March reflects, but what about cities without civilization? He concludes that would be impossible, inconceivable: "An inhuman thing . . . to have so many people together who beget nothing on one another" (*The Adventures of Augie March* [New York, 1949], 159). Shklar told the author in a private communication that Bellow had read *After Utopia* and used it in later novels.

4. Nathaniel Hawthorne, *The House of the Seven Gables* (1851; New York, 1990), 118.

5. Stephen Simpson, "Political Economy and the Workers," in *Social Theories of Jacksonian Democracy*, ed. Joseph Blau (New York, 1954), 145, 156. A single rhetoric of unearned privilege captured the opposition of common workers to aristocratic social pretension and of entrepreneurs to monopolists.

6. Henry James had compassion for Hawthorne (and for himself) struggling to draw romance from such meager elements. Henry James, *Hawthorne* (1879), in *The Shock of Recognition*, ed. Edmund Wilson, 460, 436. George Santayana, *The Genteel Tradition* (Cambridge, Mass., 1967), 44. In the same spirit, Irving Howe argued that like all American novelists, Hawthorne was reduced to treating politics as a form of personal experience because there was not enough real political material in the environment (*Politics and the Novel*, [New York, 1943], 163). Lionel Trilling described the lack of solidity of American society, the ab-

sence of palpable weight and force (*Sincerity and Authenticity*, [Cambridge, Mass., 1971], 113).

7. See Nancy L. Rosenblum, "Romantic Communitarianism: *Blithedale Romance* v. *The Custom House*," in *The Liberal-Communitarian Debate* ed. C. F. Delaney (New York, 1994).

8. Quoted in James, *Hawthorne*, 482.

9. Hawthorne, "Hints to Young Ambition," in vol. 17 of *The Writings of Nathaniel Hawthorne* (Boston, 1900), 241. Hawthorne worried that after the Civil War military merit ("or rather, since that is not so readily estimated, military notoriety") would become the sole measure civil distinction ("Chiefly About War Matters," *Complete Writings*, 17:366–67).

10. The phrase is James Morone's in *The Democratic Wish* (New York, 1990), 91.

11. Hawthorne knew from his experience at Brook Farm that labor is not necessarily ennobled by being equitable and cooperative: "the clods of earth, which we so constantly belabored and turned over and over, were never etherealized into thought. Our thoughts, on the contrary, were fast becoming cloddish" (The Blithedale Romance [1852; New York, 1958], 88).

12. Remarkably, Hawthorne had nothing to say in this connection about slavery. He was no ordinary abolitionist; the end of slavery should not be deliberately pursued; if slavery were left alone, "it would by some means impossible to be anticipated . . . vanish like a dream." That was part of his skepticism that "no human effort, on a grand scale, has yet resulted according to the purpose of its projectors" ("Chiefly About War Matters," 419, 402).

13. Saul Bellow, *The Adventures of Augie March* (New York, 1949), 3.

14. Charles Taylor, Multiculturalism and "The Politics of Recognition" (Princeton, N.J., 1993), 36.

15. For an extended discussion of Bellow's use of Breughel's painting "The Misanthrope," see Jeffrey Meyers, "Breughel and Augie March," in *Critical Essays on Saul Bellow*, ed. Stanley Trachtenberg (Boston, 1979), 83–88.

16. Morone, *The Democratic Wish*, 162–67.

17. Robert Penn Warren called his review of *Augie March* "The Man with No Commitments" (*The New Republic*, 2 Nov. 1953, 22).

18. Richard Poirier criticizes Bellow in this vein: despite his "little ironies," he seems to be unaware of "the essential irrelevance, the essential pretension and shabbiness of the self-aggrandizing mind at work in, and for, the hero" ("Bellow to Herzog," *Partisan Review* 32 (1965): 266, 270).

19. Saul Bellow describes "what it was like to set oneself up to be a writer in the Midwest during the thirties. For I thought of myself as a midwesterner and not a Jew" (*American Scholar* 44 (Winter 1974/75): 72).

20. That is why Saul Bellow links the fate of liberal society to the fate of the novel: "a liberal society so intensely political can't remain liberal for very long. I take it for granted that an attack on the novel is also an attack on liberal principles" because the novel's subject is always individuals not corporate destinies, the rise of new classes, cultural intelligentsias ("A World Too Much with Us" *Critical Inquiry* 2 (1975): 9).

3

Hope over Fear: Judith Shklar as Political Educator

John Dunn

"THE LIBERALISM OF FEAR" was one of Judith Shklar's most resonant phrases. First prominently invoked at the beginning of *Ordinary Vices,* and articulated as programmatically as she would ever have cared to set out her own views in an essay in Nancy Rosenblum's 1989 collection *Liberalism and the Moral Life,* it served too, in 1990 and 1991, as axis for each of her two final and most passionately political books, *The Faces of Injustice* and *American Citizenship.* [1] When a voice of such power abruptly falls silent, questions hang in the air. Above all, what, in the end, was she trying to tell us? What, indeed, was she trying to tell herself?

Some skeptics leave behind them quite accessible and aggressive political doctrines: Hobbes, Bayle, Hume, and in his own way Michael Oakeshott. Judith Shklar was very different. She had an instinctive distaste for doctrine of any kind, seeing it as intrinsically absurd and often quite puerile. But she had ample beliefs of her own, and she was far from feeble in the force with which she held them. Moreover, she genuinely valued in others the capacity to believe with energy and imagination, and persisted in doing so even where the beliefs in question struck her as moderately ludicrous, or where she thought their political implications actively pernicious.[2] She was a liberal who loved in others (and especially in the young women and men whom she taught with such verve, insight, and energy) their capacity to probe the human world for themselves, in hope, with feeling, with courage, and with imagination. But she was no sentimentalist. She hated cruelty and injustice—the grim and often pointless harm with which human beings endlessly visit upon one another. But she hated with at least equal passion the harms which they do to themselves, to their own souls: their grotesque capacity for self-deception, their stunning self-righteousness. This last response struck an almost aristocratic note, a trifle at odds with her strenuous distaste for aristocracy as such, and for its casual snobberies.[3] Her exhilarating personal warmth and generosity were balanced by an extraordinary (and plainly often painful) fastidiousness: an intense desire that humans should be other than they are, kinder, truer, finer, wiser, or at the very least less formidably and gratuitously inane.

The liberalism of fear, as we have it, is the hastiest of sketches, as far as it well could be from an intellectual testament. (It is hard to imagine her electing to leave behind her, in any possible world, something as inherently pompous as an intellectual testament.) But for all its cursoriness of outline and briskness of expression, it does show something of the balance of political judgment which she formed at such cost to herself, and which she sought so hard to convey to her charges, colleagues, and friends.

That balance of judgment stands in sharp contrast, plainly enough, to two other styles of liberalism, each of them, even now, more prominent in North America: a liberalism of natural rights, or one of personal self-development.[4] But it stands in just as clear a contrast to many other political viewpoints grounded in taking fear seriously: not just to the full panoply of reactionary repression, but also to the cool instrumental defense of security and physical comfort, not merely to Joseph de Maistre, but also to Thomas Hobbes or even Jeremy Bentham. At its core it was a politics of justice, not one of gratification—a sustained attempt to think (and feel) from the victim's point of view.[5]

The recognition that fear must be taken seriously, even the will to take it seriously, in themselves offer little guidance over just how to do so: how to learn from it with any deftness, reliability, or acumen. The goal of a liberalism of fear is not to eliminate fear—an outcome neither practicable nor unequivocally desirable. "To be alive is to be afraid, and much to our advantage in many cases, since alarm often preserves us from danger." Its goal, rather, is to cut fear down to size: to tame it and thrust it back, and by doing so to open up to the widest possible degree a space in which individual women and men can "make as many effective decisions without fear or favour," about as many aspects of their own lives as will leave their fellow adults equally free to do the same for themselves. So expressed, to be sure, there is little distance between it and a liberalism of natural rights, or even one of personal development. All interpretations of liberalism must in some sense share a single goal. Where they differ most is over the grounds which lend force to that goal, and the means which can be trusted for reaching it. What makes the liberalism of fear so different from most modern liberal political philosophy is its numb sense of the scale of the obstacles to realizing any interpretation of liberalism at all: the power, subtlety, obstinacy, or sheer ferocity of its multifarious adversaries. Hence the focus on a *summum malum*, cruelty, and the fear which it inspires, and the very fear of fear itself,[6] above all the fear of "a society of fearful people."[7] Its political core, therefore, lay in a sense of the scale, intensity, and intricacy of the struggle against the human evil which suffuses all of collective human life, just at it suffuses every individual life also. Because it saw menace in so many quarters (because it was alert to such a variety of dangers), the liberalism of fear was to be notably sparing in its allocation of trust. It doubted the wisdom of every form of categorical trust— trust in the mildly sanitized practices or traditions of particular communities, in the educative state (or church) in the hands of just the right educators, in the sensitively and tremulously interpreted self, or the combat groupings of gender or class or ethnos or ideological bloc. Most discerningly of all, perhaps, it doubted the purifying potentiality of struggle itself (the fight, the wounds, the solidarities, the knowledge of shared sufferings, the keen stimulus of shared contempts). (Here, I should acknowledge a slow, reluctant, and acutely discomfiting personal educational debt.)

Seen against the liberalism of fear, accordingly, most academic political theory comes out as bewilderingly callow: politically naïve and very sparsely informed, psychologically shallow and obtuse, sociologically parochial or imperceptive, self-regarding and self-deceptive, mythagogic at worst, and even at best historically more than a little myopic. This is not a generous estimate. But it remains hard to dispute its validity. What does it really imply?

What it implies for politics itself is understandably opaque: certainly that the latter activity is very difficult to comprehend, still more certainly that it will always remain perturbing to those who do understand it best, but most crucially that we can be confident that it will always be immensely important, without in general being in the faintest degree elevating. Beyond this, generality is apt to be uninstructive. Insight lies in the dense and the particular, in the cumulative outcome of professional social scientific or historical inquiry (for which she retained a vivid collegial respect and appreciation), or in the regular services of a great newspaper.[8] The liberalism of fear, then, is a political science-friendly (or social science-friendly) theory of politics. But the political and social science which it befriends is often more potential than actual: the contribution which still might be made by disciplined inquiry of a kind which many have now been trained to undertake, rather than the modal performance of an existing stratum of academic practitioners. Actually existing political theorists mostly do largely what they ought not to do, and there is little health in them. But even actually existing political scientists are unlikely on inspection to prove *sans reproche*, especially if judged by the ferocious standards which Judith Shklar set for herself. If this is right, the impact is bracing enough, but it is also disconcertingly dispersive. To be told all this simply, didactically, and *ex cathedra* could easily be irritating; but it might well hold the attention. To be told it with the passion, eloquence, learning, and insight of Judith Shklar was for some simply dismaying, indeed even a trifle disabling. To be told it in person, face to face, could be crushing.

For her, there could hardly have been a worse outcome, one which would have pleased her less. What she truly wanted of people was what the Chinese Communist Party used to affect to want of its peasant clients: that they should *stand up*.[9] What made such an outcome possible, though, was something which did please her, and pleased her deeply: her awesome confidence in her capacity to teach, and the source of that confidence in its very palpable justification. None of her books is really a didactic exercise. But they are all intended to teach. They echo the way she taught, and even at times the assurance with which she taught. But they do not in the end *teach* as she taught. They could not, and they never will. There are plenty of academic writers whose books and essays are in many ways more than ample substitutes for their authors, clearer, sharper, more potent, more economical, pruned of personal occasions for irritation or resentment. But Judith Shklar was a teacher first and a writer very much second. Even her political theory was an exercise in teaching - a true political education, not a series of detachable and standardizable conclusions. She taught individual persons to think for themselves. She did not purvey, with vigor and rhetorical accomplishment, propositions she happened to believe true. What she trained was judgment and sensibility, a personal balance of self-confidence and self-doubt, nerve, patience, endurance, clarity of thought, openness of mind. She was superlatively indifferent to fashion. The books remain; and each of them carries a charge and freshness of its own (even those she herself came somewhat to dislike). But they cannot by themselves do what she could do, term after term, and with the greatest of ease.

That is why it is worth looking again at what she sought to teach, as Stanley Hoffman, Bernard Yack, and others have already begun to do,[10] and trying to capture more effectively just what it really implies. It is worth doing so, now that the medium and the message are sundered forever, not because such a quest can hope to dull the personal loss but because what she strove so hard to convey is something which can only hope to travel effectively (only hope indeed now to *survive* as a continuing educational presence) if it enters consciously into the efforts of a great many people. All education is a form of cultural and political struggle. No doubt, in itself, the liberalism of fear was simply a convenient mnemonic—a formula which captured something she was trying to focus for herself—and reappeared thereafter just because it served to remind her of how this could be conveyed with ease, accessibility, and emphasis. But her penchant for it was perceptive. It was, and remains, an effective battle cry for the political education which she devoted her life to trying to impart.

The practical recipes of this education were few, trenchant, and relatively simple: the indispensability of limited government; the immense importance of dispersing power of politically effective action across a variety of social groupings; the insufficiency of purely negative liberty in a drastically unequal and unjust society; the furtiveness, tenacity, and pervasiveness of human injustice; and the sheer misery which it induces. Many of them, unsurprisingly, are lessons which she found most felicitously expressed in the pages of Montesquieu, and in the psychological insight of *Lettres Persanes* as much as in the patient explorations of *L'Esprit des Lois*.[11] What gave this modest and unpretentious vision its depth and power was the energy and rigor with which she conceived and defended it, and the stress she laid on the single resource that can best sustain it, "a strongly developed historical memory." The liberals of fear were right to concentrate predominantly on the avoidance of foreseeable evils. They were right to restrict themselves to politics and to base their agenda firmly on "the physical suffering and fears of ordinary human beings." They had no occasion to blanch at the charges that these choices reflected ignoble tastes or undue simplicity of mind. But if the liberals of fear were in this measure a party of memory rather than a party of hope, that did not mean that they were committed to denying themselves hope (still less that she was somehow so committed). There is nothing lugubrious or fatalistic about a liberalism of fear. It is an intensely activist doctrine, as committed as Kant himself was to taking full responsibility for its own purchase on the world, and for its future possible purchase every bit as much as for its past actual purchase.[12] It is a politics of active apprehension, not one of passive guilt, let alone panic-stricken and compulsive repression.

In some ways Judith Shklar was certainly a conservative thinker. What is conservatism at best if not a party of "strongly developed historical memory" and one which refuses obdurately to ground its politics on unsupported hope of any variety whatsoever? But no conservative could set at the core of their political purposes the endless (and perhaps peculiarly hopeless) struggle against human injustice; and few, even today, would be likely to offer as key criterion for the success of their political efforts the maximization of the scope of free choice over their own lives for every human adult. The categorical and impartial distrust of all governments is not a conservative proclivity. The frank suspicion of the

ethical soundness of every actual tradition is not a conservative sentiment. Judith Shklar could be a punishing critic of *gauchiste* political fantasy. But she was no cold war liberal; and she could remember far too
much history, with far too much discomfort, to take seriously the possibility that history might come to an end.

The educational implications of such a viewpoint do not leap to the
eye. But there is no reason to doubt that it does possess educational implications. There may be an element of absurdity to praising the dead,
however much it helps to relieve the distress of the living. But there is
nothing absurd in trying to learn from the dead. To commend the liberalism of fear need not be an act of misplaced personal mourning. It
might also be (and surely should be) a quite impersonal witness to the
impact of a deeply educative viewpoint and to the experience which
that viewpoint made possible.

Judith Shklar did at one point have occasion to tell the American political science profession at large how she saw its tasks and the place of
political theory within it.[13] She had ample opportunity over the decades
to make clear to her political theory colleagues how she saw the tasks of a
political theorist. She testified, on another occasion, to the strain and
rewards of her own personal career.[14] and on many occasions to the special disabilities and challenges which face women in every walk of life in
every society of the modern world (as they have done in so many ways,
and for so long, virtually throughout human history). A prudent inter-
preter of her legacy would go no further than these and other published
texts. But all of these texts are muted by a quite unaffected personal
modesty about her own achievements as a writer and thinker, and about
the claims of these achievements on the attention of others. She certainly
did not lack confidence in her own intellectual judgment (or even in its
clear superiority to that of many other scholars, often of great weight and
reputation, in particular). But she was incapable of touting the merit of
her own wares. Any serious interpretation of the educational implications of her legacy would have to go beyond the plain evidence of the
texts—would have to infer rather than simply to report.

If we have the gall to try to do so, then, what should we infer? If politics is so important, so obscure, and so treacherous, how should we set
about trying to understand it? (Or, less ingenuously, how should we set
about the business of trying to show others, in detail and at length, how
to try to understand it?) In part this is a question about the academic
division of labor, about the felicity or otherwise of professionally organized instruction and inquiry amongst those who are now employed to
teach others how to understand politics, and to teach themselves how to
do so to the highest accessible standard precisely in order to equip them
best to teach others in this way. At one level this was a matter about

which Judith Shklar was quite decisive (perhaps even excessively so). An utterly (and proudly) professional and deeply modern woman, she needed no convincing either of the value or of the ineluctability of the division of labor. She admired and relished the professionalism of her colleagues right across the discipline of political science, and in a wide variety of other disciplines as well. She learned from them with the utmost assiduity, and a wholly unforced and often touching gratitude. As many have testified eloquently, this made her an extraordinarily rewarding intellectual friend to those of all ages.

But the personal virtues and liberal intellectual convictions expressed in this ubiquity of intellectual curiosity and generosity of intellectual response do not readily transpose into institutional structure or curricular content. Seen in these terms, it might appear that a Shklar university should be simply one which maximized the protected space for free inquiry for all its denizens, taught as much as teachers, and a Shklar curriculum might appear almost limitlessly centrifugal. But this certainly misses a great deal in her approach to either: notably her intense seriousness of mind and spirit, and her capacity for a quite devastating level of severity. She did not approve of dilettantism or frivolity; and she seldom concealed her disapproval, least of all toward those (still almost invariably male) who were in any sense grander in current social perception or more powerful in current political fact. What she approved of was disciplined effort and the active exercise of imagination, not established routine or consolidated and well-defended personal success. A political science profession judged by Shklar standards and not found wanting would have to be very different from the profession which now exists, and not merely in learning, dedication, and integrity of purpose. It would differ, above all, in political awareness and political insight, in the nature of its address to its own subject matter.

How, more concretely, would it have to differ? In political theory itself there was in some measure a Shklar canon. It was a very broad church: by no means a community of fanatical skeptics, contemptuous refusers of belief as such. Plato and Aristotle, Cicero and Augustine, Hobbes and Locke, Montesquieu and Rousseau, Madison and Jefferson, Kant and Hegel, Tocqueville, Emerson, her friend John Rawls: little eccentricity there. More out of the ordinary, and at least as important for her, were the great French anatomists of the passions, above all Montaigne and Pascal, and the leading dramatists of the world (Euripides, Shakespeare, Molière). All of these were read actively and interrogatively, not simply for what they had meant to convey, but also for what could (and should) be learned from them: what they had to teach. What they had to teach, for her, depended ultimately not just on their own transitory and contingent preoccupations but on the enduring

truths about the human political condition, which those preoccupations had just happened to illuminate with special power and precision
—the truths picked out and epitomized in the liberalism of fear. If this
was a community of any discrete sets of persons at all it was above all a
community of those who have heard the terrible news. No current ren-
dition of political theory, however intellectually fluent or graceful in expression, could quite pass muster if it too had not entered this
saddened, chastened, but still purposeful community.

Political theorists paradigmatically read texts, although, as Shklar
was at pains to insist, they could not learn how to read these texts, let
alone what to read them for, without taking the trouble to read a vast
amount else. But most political scientists quite rightly believe the objects of their inquiry to be far more diverse and widely dispersed
around the social world. They, too, in her eyes, if they were to pursue
their profession as they should, must enter the community of those who
have heard the terrible news. Otherwise they could hardly hope to
avoid the inadvertent parochialism or complacency which she viewed
with such withering contempt. But to meet the Shklar standards political scientists did not need to specialize in the nastier aspects of human
collective life or the grimmer bits of the map. They did not need to become experts on genocide, on modern warfare with its abominable
weaponry, on famine, the predicament of refugees, or torture, on Cam-
bodia, Bosnia, or Rwanda. What they needed simply was to be aware of
the prominence and pervasiveness of these horrors: to bear them constantly in mind, not brood obsessively about them. This was what set the
limit (moral, spiritual, but also professional) to an acceptable division of
labor within political science. To teach about politics, for her, was above
all a responsibility, not a job for which one could get paid handsomely,
or an especially interesting and agreeable way of passing the time. It
was a hard responsibility to discharge, perhaps an impossible one to discharge fully. But anyone who grasped it could at least try to meet it.
There was nothing surprising about the special quality of her admiration for Immanuel Kant.

Much about Shklar's personal intellectual approach is missed in a
cursory presentation of this character: notably her stress on the central-
ity of psychology to any serious conception either of politics itself, or of
the peculiar spiritual hazards and cognitive difficulties of studying it adequately. There were few matters on which she was more trenchant
than on the flippancy of any attempt to study politics without taking full
account of earlier amateur exploration and more recent professional
study of the human psyche. But this awareness, which runs prominently through all her writings, never (as far as I am aware) took a pro-
grammatic form or issued organized proposals for the professional

intellectual formation of students of politics. A liberalism of fear must be inured to the need to take the human psyche just as seriously as a source of hazard as it does as a locus of capability, a site of suffering, or an object of respect. But it offers no distinctive insight into how to implement this preoccupation effectively in intellectual practice, a task at which the profession at large has made singularly little headway, and for which the full panoply of rational choice theory or the theory of games offers the most exiguous of aid.

The balance of Judith Shklar's attitudes toward politics was subtle and idiosyncratic. Radical in her sharp focus on the penetralia of oppression, and in her unhesitating and passionate identification with the position of the victims of power, she was also conservative in her conviction of the priority of informed memory over emotionally eager and cognitively gratuitous hope, in her alertness to the snares of self-deception, and in her conviction of the imperative to judge practically with the greatest of care; and she was liberal, above all, in her utter certainty of the value of individual freedom and her determination to defend it against all comers.

For this balance the liberalism of fear is an excellent formula. Driven by an awareness of the overwhelming grimness of much of human political life, its saturation with suffering and evil, the liberalism of fear is in no way an excuse for passivity, still less a counsel of despair. The priority of memory (or fear) over hope which she commended was epistemic, not practical. For her, hope as it should be, appropriate hope, was a category of the will, not a refuge for (or from) the intelligence. Fear, too, reciprocally, was a guide to the intelligence, not a recommended posture for human agents. As a teacher the last thing she wanted was to make cowards of her pupils, to deplete their capacity for courage or to cow their eagerness to resist oppression wherever they found it. But she emphatically did mean to teach them how to distinguish hope from expectation, how to judge for themselves what was likely to occur and what might really be achieved, and to distinguish these as starkly as possible from what they would like to see occur. A political science profession which had learned how to teach its pupils these skills, and which taught them with any consistency and predictability, would indeed offer a political education. We should all have reason to be proud to belong to it. Meanwhile, perhaps less so.

Notes

1. See *Ordinary Vices* (1984), 5; "The Liberalism of Fear," in *Liberalism and the Moral Life*, ed. Nancy Rosenblum (1989); and *The Faces of Injustice* (1990) and *American Citizenship: The Quest for Inclusion* (1991).

54   John Dunn

2. See *Faces of Injustice*, 115; *American Citizenship*, acknowledgments, 99, 114; cf. Michael Walzer, *Spheres of Justice* (Oxford, 1983).

3. See *Ordinary Vices;* "The Liberalism of Fear," 27, 32.

4. "Liberalism of Fear," 26–28.

5. See especially *Faces of Injustice*.

6. "Liberalism of Fear," 29, 21, 29.

7. Cf. Samir al-Khalil, *Republic of Fear*, (London, 1990).

8. See "Liberalism of Fear," 37–38.

9. Cf. William Hinton, *Fanshen: A Documentary of Revolution in a Chinese Village* (New York 1966).

10. See Stanley Hoffmann, "Judith Shklar as a Political Thinker," *Political Theory* 21 (1993):172–80; and Bernard Yack, "Injustice and the Victim's Voice," *Michigan Law Review* 89 (1991):1334–49.

11. *Montesquieu* (1987).

12. "Liberalism of Fear," 27, 31, 30, 33–34.

13. "Redeeming American Political Theory" (1991).

14. "A Life of Learning" (1989).

4

Judith Shklar's Dystopic Liberalism

Seyla Benhabib

RUNNING LIKE A RED THREAD through Judith Shklar's lifework is a "dystopic" vision of liberalism; a liberalism which is not only anti-utopian but self-consciously dystopian. One of the earliest statements of this vision is contained in *Legalism: An Essay on Law, Morals, and Politics*. Published in 1964, with the memories of the Nuremberg trials and the cold war still very much alive, Shklar positioned herself against too much self-congratulation on the part of Western liberal democracies. Drawing a rather sharp line between the ideologies of free-market capitalism and the political essence of liberalism, she wrote of her contribution,

> it is, at its simplest, a defense of social diversity, inspired by that barebones liberalism which, having abandoned the theory of progress and every specific scheme of economics, is committed only to the belief that tolerance is a primary virtue and that a diversity of opinions and habits is not only to be endured but to be cherished and encouraged. The assumption throughout is that social diversity *is* the prevailing condition of modern nation-states and that it *ought* to be promoted.[1]

Shklar gave other names to her "barebones" vision of liberalism. She also called it the "liberalism of permanent minorities,"[2] and in one of her most memorable essays she coined the phrase "*the liberalism of fear.*" "No form of liberalism," she writes,

> has any business telling the citizenry to pursue happiness or even to define that wholly elusive condition. It is for each of us to seek it or reject it in

A version of this chapter appeared under the same title in *Journal of Social Research* 61, no. 2 (Summer 1994): 477–88. Reprinted by permission.

favor of duty or salvation or passivity, for example. Liberalism must restrict itself to politics and to proposals to restrain potential abusers of power in order to lift the burden of fear and favor from the shoulders of adult women and men, who can then conduct their lives in accordance with their own beliefs and preferences, as long as they do not prevent others from doing so as well.[3]

Such statements would clearly place Judith Shklar with those contemporary political philosophers who see liberalism as "political, not metaphysical."[4] In fact, her early book on legalism may be seen as one of the first articulations of an antimetaphysical philosophy of liberalism. Why, however, does she reject a liberalism based upon a more comprehensive doctrine of human nature, history, and society? Unlike for John Rawls, the guiding concern for Judith Shklar is not to establish the conceptual conditions for an "overlapping consensus." She remained too much of a skeptic throughout her life to believe that such consensus was either possible or even desirable. The sources of her antimetaphysical liberalism do not lie in her desire to base liberal constitutional government upon noncontroversial public doctrines which can be also publicly endorsed. Shklar's antimetaphysical view of liberalism derives from her own very distinctive version of antifoundationalism in philosophy and politics.

Shklar distinguished the Lockean liberalism of natural rights theories from the Rousseauian and Kantian tradition of a liberalism of "autonomy," and from the liberalism of self-perfection, as represented by John Stuart Mill. She rejected the first kind of justification of liberalism because she questioned the natural law tradition. Like Hannah Arendt and unlike Leo Strauss, she maintained that the development of modern science and technology had rendered any appeals to nature, understood as a reality untouched by human intervention and manipulation, mythical and fictitious.[5] Nature, including human nature, had become an object of human manipulation. Furthermore, the social sciences lent no support to the belief that there was an unchanging substratum called human nature which existed untouched by time, culture, and social structure. If, in the face of these objections, one still insisted on grounding human rights upon a concept of nature, one fell into philosophical dogmatism. Shklar also agreed with the Kantian tradition that we always had to ask the question, even if this be human nature, is it right or legitimate that we respect its dictates and follow its inclinations? Must we act upon the promptings of human nature, whatever these may be? Are we not also creatures who can choose to act otherwise? Philosophical appeals to nature inevitably end up as disguised appeals to some form of human freedom, reason, dignity, or worth. Thus

Shklar departed from natural law liberalism in order to ally herself with the liberalism of consent and freedom as articulated by Kant and Rousseau.

Nonetheless, although she would defend a liberalism of autonomy against a liberalism of natural rights, she was equally skeptical about the rationalistic view of human nature and the teleological view of history which Kantian liberalism in particular seemed to presuppose. Why? The entire flavor of her œuvre provides the answer. While not a believer in vague philosophical generalizations about natural law and human nature, Shklar was an extremely close, nuanced, and sharp observer of human psychology. Stanley Hoffman has remarked in a recent article that moral psychology was one of her lasting interests.[6] Indeed, the variety and richness of what she herself at one point named her "phenomenological" approach is remarkable.[7] She reflected upon the diversity, ambiguity, opacity, and tenacity of human emotions and motivations throughout her work. She was more concerned to delineate the physiology of injustice than erecting rationalist theorems about justice; she was more concerned to bring into focus the indignities of exclusion from citizenship than to paint a picture of a perfect republican citizenry.[8] Shklar was a shrewd psychologist, and this made her a nonrationalist without being an antirationalist. Her never quite explicit quarrel with Kantian liberalism, including the philosophy of Rawls, has its sources in her radically different view of human psychology.

Philosophical rationalism focuses on what can be shared by all, on what is publicly defensible, on what can be articulated and defended in a public court of appeal. Shklar, by contrast, remained much more interested in the view from the margins. She reasoned about political and psychological phenomena not from the angle of what was visible at the center of public life but from the standpoint of the margins, from the standpoint of those who did not have a voice easily representable at the center. She had a skeptical temperament; one which she shared with Montaigne, Montesquieu, and in some ways Alexis de Tocqueville. And it is this political skepticism, coupled with psychological agnosticism, that makes Judith Shklar seem so "postmodern" to some commentators.[9] Her disbelief in the "metanarratives" of history was fueled though by a different historical sensibility than contemporary postmodern skepticism.

Judith Shklar belonged to the generation of European Jewish emigrés whose world was shattered, and as she expressed it in one of her most poignant, and, to my knowledge, her only piece of autobiographical writing, whose "childhood had been brought to an end" by Hitler. Born to a German-speaking Lithuanian Jewish family of professionals,

Shklar's "barebones liberalism" carried the indelible marks of disbelief in the face of a world gone insane. What is distinctive about her voice as an emigré political theorist, and what sets her so far apart from thinkers like Strauss and Arendt, both approximately twenty years her elders, is the lack of pathos with which she registered the destruction of her familial world and the end of her childhood. This absence of pathos marks her distance from the core tradition of German philosophy. Although brought up in a German-speaking household, Judith Shklar was not a German Jewish philosopher. Her skeptical and restrained temperament would put her rather in the company of Eastern European ironists like Franz Kafka, Milan Kundera, or György Konrad.

For her the rise of European fascism and the Holocaust were not to be interpreted as the "end of western rationality," as the "end of tradition, as we have known it."[10] She was unsure that there had ever been a single tradition of Western reason. Nor did she think that to ward off these phenomena one had to recover the lost treasures of Western political thought. Where Strauss and Arendt remained Grecophiles, Shklar was a decided modernist, more at home in the skeptical temperament of the French Encyclopedists than within the orbit of the German love affair with Hellas. Though tremendously respectful of Hannah Arendt as the towering political philosopher of her generation, Shklar was deeply critical of her as well.[11] She found Hannah Arendt often capricious in her interpretations, and strongly disagreed with Arendt's reading of Kant's political theory. She charged her with incurable romanticism concerning good politics. Arendt's reading of revolutions and particularly her interpretation of the American political experience continued to baffle Shklar. In some ways her last book, *American Citizenship: The Quest for Inclusion,* is a belated answer to Arendt's *On Revolution* (1963). Instead of marginalizing and rendering invisible the plight of African-American slaves in the new republic, Shklar places the injustice of slavery and the wounds it has inflicted on the meaning of American citizenship at the very center of her analysis. By arguing that the status of being a wage earner and a jobholder is just as fundamental to the public identity of Americans as their participation in public life, she shows that, as the first modern civil society in the bourgeois period, the American republic from its inception combined the socioeconomic question with the political one. Against Arendt, Shklar appears to be arguing that categories of economic justice and equality and political independence and participation cannot be and should not be separated.

Her modernist rootedness in the thought of the French Enlightenment, her insistence that the socioeconomic and political questions could not be treated separately gave Judith Shklar's "barebones liberalism" a strongly social-democratic flavor. She was not sure that the "liberalism of fear" could be a sufficient basis for her vision of political liberalism;[12] and ultimately this minimalist vision fails to capture the complexity of her reflections on morality and the rule of law and the interdependence of socioeconomic justice and good government. In Shklar's work there is also a much more activist view of government, a ruthless critique of the culture of officialdom and bureaucracy, an almost aristocratic ethos of public service, and appeals to vigilant citizenship—all of which have more in common with the civic-republican and social-democratic understandings of citizenship than with the liberalism of negative freedom.

• • •

Surely Shklar's discussion of Giotto's sculptures of justice and injustice are among the most memorable pieces of prose produced by one who was consistently a brilliant stylist. "The reason we may feel no joy in contemplating Giotto's Justice," writes Shklar,

> is that she calms our fears but thwarts our highest aspirations, whether they be heroic or civic. . . . She lacks the emotional punch that Injustice delivers and that revenge would also offer us. Giotto's Justice is also not a perfect response to the nightmare of his Injustice in the eyes of a democratic admirer of his art. For any politically organized society, the quality of justice depends crucially on the character of government, both in its structure and in its actions. . . . Certainly, justice cannot by tyrannical, but there is no sign of Ciceronian republican or modern democratic values here. The citizens only play. They do not deliberate, vote, or administer. The queen does it all, handing out whatever is to be distributed, while the citizens are politically completely passive.[13]

Shklar leaves little doubt that she finds Giotto's iconography of injustice more persuasive than his bucolic and frozen portrayal of justice precisely because the former is less impassive, and above all because it shows individuals' moral involvement in the misfortunes as well as injustices which affect them and others. The vision of "citizens only playing" is not to Shklar's liking. While skeptical toward the republican conception of citizenship—a citizenship of vigilance.

In *The Faces of Injustice* she introduces the concept "passive injustice" to describe her concerns. Passive injustice results from the failure of republican citizens to see to it that the rules of justice are maintained and furthermore from their failure to support actively those informal relations of "democracy of everyday life, in the habits of equality, and the mutuality of ordinary obligations between citizens."[14] This concept of passive injustice and the accompanying vision of citizenship are intriguing, for such a view of politics and of public life can hardly be maintained, it seems to me, without making the democratic project of participation absolutely central to liberalism. Resorting to conjugal metaphors, at one point Shklar writes that "liberalism is monogamously, faithfully, and permanently married to democracy—but it is a marriage of convenience."[15]

Much in her work implies, however, that this is more than a marriage of convenience. If a sense of public justice, of the rule of law, and the protection of equal citizenship rights are fundamental to the project of liberalism, then these can only be assured through citizens who do not practice passive injustice in their everyday lives. Passive injustice undermines the rule of law as a living ethos, and as a public political culture. Liberalism, as Shklar understands it, requires a citizenship of vigilance; liberalism then requires democracy as a continuing mate.

Despite this activist conception of citizenship, Shklar hardly considered participatory democracy a viable project, for she had an acute appreciation of the institutional complexity of the modern state. She took the administrative-bureaucratic nature of the modern state very seriously, and insisted that an honorable body of public servants and a group of fair and reliable bureaucrats were just as essential for the realization of social justice as vigilant citizens. The theme of an active citizenship of vigilance is constant in Shklar's work, but is less dominant than her unwavering and ruthless critique of bureaucratic abuse, incompetence, and corruption. I am inclined to suggest that this vision of public officialdom may have been one of the few traces of Prussianism in Judith Shklar's political theory.

In her early book, *Legalism,* Shklar dissected the mind-set of believing that moral conduct is a matter of rule following and that moral relationships consist of rights and duties determinable by set rules.[16] Shklar was not only thinking of well-known twentieth-century phenomena of moral turpitude and political criminality which were widespread among the followers, soldiers, party hacks, and bureaucrats of dictators and totalitarian leaders, but she was also concerned with how the lack of civic courage and independent judgment in democracies could undermine the very rule of law officials were purporting to uphold. Written in 1964—before Watergate, before the Pentagon papers, before the Iran-Contra scandal, and numerous other instances of public and constitutional criminality—Shklar's concept of legalism was uncanny in its anticipation of the moral turpitude that could befall public officialdom.

A citizenship of vigilance, a public officialdom with a deep sense of justice, and the capacity for moral autonomy are the cornerstones of Shklar's vision of liberalism. These principles of political life move her toward the democratic partner in the monogamous marriage between liberalism and democracy while her activist sense of government puts her in the company of political and economic reformers and the social-democratic Left.

One of the most remarkable theses of *The Faces of Injustice* is the claim that the line separating misfortune from injustice is a political choice and not a natural given.[17] Misfortunes of the past, like certain forms of disease and infant mortality, are the injustices of today. If the means for preventing such diseases and conditions are known and can reasonably be carried out by officials and administrators, but if such measures are not undertaken, then misfortune becomes injustice. An earthquake is a striking example here: both technological lack of know-how, official incompetence, lack of adequate social organization, and social corruption can transform this quintessential natural misfortune into a paradigm example of the failure of social justice. Shklar thus introduces a criterion of social justice for demarcating misfortunes from injustice. Commenting on the doctrine of the invisible hand, she writes:

> It seems to me that this is a poor argument because it is evident that when we can alleviate suffering, whatever its cause, it is passively unjust to stand by and do nothing. It is not the origin of injury, but the possibility of preventing and reducing its costs, that allows us to judge whether there was or was not unjustifiable passivity in the face of such disaster. Nor is the sense of injustice irrelevant. The voices of the victims must also be heard first, not only to find out whether officially recognized social expectations have been denied, but also to attend to their interpretations of the situation. Are changes in the order of publicly accepted claims called for? Are the rules such that the victim could have consented to them had she been asked? If the victim's suffering is due to accident or misfortune but could be remedied by public agents, then it is unjust if nothing is done to help. A valid expectation has been ignored and her sense of injustice should assert itself and we should all protest. It is at the very least what one should expect of the citizens of a democracy.[18]

We live in a society where much social injustice and inequity is still presented as a case of personal or natural misfortune. It is an aspect of the proverbial American dream that it paints social conditions and structural constraints as if they were natural barriers to be overcome by extraordinary personal efforts. The persistence of this myth, which served this country deceptively well as long as it was in a period of economic growth and capitalist expansion, coupled with distrust of government and public life in general, have produced a political amnesia which seeks to portray social injustice as natural misfortune. Reading Shklar's reflections on this matter, one can sense how radical her vision of government was and how exacting she was in expecting the most of public officials and of public policy. In her view, it is not the origins of suffering and injustice that are important but the possibility of alleviating them; what is unforgivable is doing nothing when something can be done. Of course, this claim which radically disassociates between merit, desert, and justice would need to be more carefully analyzed.[19] I doubt that it could hold as a principle of distributive justice with respect to all forms of social goods, but its implications for contemporary debates about the culture of poverty, the meaning of welfare, health care, education reform, and rebuilding the inner cities are obvious. If we, as a society, can do something to alleviate the causes of such suffering and injustice, then we are all passively unjust in not hearing the voices of the victims and recognizing their denied expectations.

This vision of an activist and redistributionist government, the call for a citizenship of vigilance, and the insistence upon the moral integrity of public officialdom go far beyond the dystopic liberalism of fear in terms of which Judith Shklar at times characterized her own project. Her vision of liberalism is one of active politics, public rectitude, and social compassion. In this respect her thought reminds me of a political thinker from another tradition, namely, Antonio Gramsci, who wrote of "pessimism of the intellect, and optimism of the will." Her dystopic but social-democratic liberalism is an original, irreverent, and thoughtful voice which we would do well to learn from in contemporary discussions about political liberalism. Judith Shklar's contribution expands the concept of the moral person, which a liberal view of government necessarily presupposes, by enriching the moral psychology of personhood; and her views of the history and institutions of the modern state introduce a dose of "sociological imagination" to contemporary debates around liberalism which has been sorely missing in recent years.

Notes

1. *Legalism* (1964), 5.

2. Ibid., 224.

3. "The Liberalism of Fear" (1989), 31.

4. See John Rawls, "Justice as Fairness: Political, Not Metaphysical," *Philosophy and Public Affairs* 14 (Summer 1985): 223ff., and *Political Liberalism* (New York, 1993).

5. See *Legalism*, 66–67. In these pages Shklar also criticizes natural law theories "for their mildly schizophrenic tone. Natural law is 'there,' and yet it is not 'there'" (67). Cf. Hannah Arendt, *The Origins of Totalitarianism*(1951; New York, 1979), 290ff.; Leo Strauss, *Natural Right and History* (Chicago, 1953).

6. Stanley Hoffmann, "Judith Shklar as Political Thinker," *Political Theory* 21 (May 1993): 172–81.

7. *The Faces of Injustice* (1990), 28, 20ff.

8. See *American Citizenship. The Quest for Inclusion* (1991).

9. See Stephen White, *Political Theory and Postmodernism* (Cambridge: Cambridge University Press, 1991).

10. Hannah Arendt, *On Revolution* (New York: Viking Press, 1963).

11. "Hannah Arendt as Pariah" strikes me as being quite acrimonious and at times ungenerous in spirit. Shklar reads Arendt against the grain on so many issues in this essay that a more detailed examination of her views than can be undertaken here is necessary. I deal with the relation between the two thinkers in *The Reluctant Modernism of Hannah Arendt* (forthcoming). For a different assessment of Arendt, see Shklar, "Rethinking the Past" (1977).

12. "The Liberalism of Fear," 29.

13. *The Faces of Injustice*, 105.

14. Ibid., 42–43.

15. "The Liberalism of Fear," 37.

16. *Legalism*, 1.

17. *The Faces of Injustice*, 5.

18. *The Faces of Injustice*, 82.

19. For a thoughtful discussion of some of the critical questions raised by Judith Shklar's critique of the "normal model of justice," see Bernard Yack, "Injustice and the Victim's Voice," *Michigan Law Review* 89 (May 1991): 1334–49. The normal model presents a picture of justice as a body of rules and principles governing the distribution of burdens and benefits within a community; justice means the impartial enforcement of these rules. Injustice occurs, institutionally and individually, whenever one departs from these norms. Shklar challenges this model's understanding of "injustice" while granting validity to its conceptualization of justice. Yack correctly argues that her critique of the normal model cuts deeper, and that it is difficult to maintain the distinction between a defective view of justice and a defective view of injustice (1347).

5

How Limited Is Liberal Government?

Amy Gutmann

LIBERALISM IS A POLITICAL DOCTRINE of limited government, but how limited is the government that liberalism defends?[1] In "The Liberalism of Fear" ("Fear"), *The Faces of Injustice* (*Injustice*), and *American Citizenship* (*Citizenship*), Judith Shklar offers three different answers, which reflect three increasingly complex and comprehensive understandings of liberalism. I call these understandings negative liberalism, positive liberalism, and democratic liberalism. Negative liberalism and positive liberalism bear a strong resemblance to Isaiah Berlin's negative and positive liberty. Democratic liberalism—an intimate marriage of democracy and liberalism (not one merely of convenience[2])—is the version of positive liberalism whose understanding of limited government I defend in this essay by examining pivotal arguments in "Fear," *Injustice*, and *Citizenship*.

I begin, as Shklar begins "Fear," with concerns about securing personal liberty and limiting governmental power for the sake of combating cruelty. I show how the concern for combating cruelty that inspires the defense of negative liberalism in "Fear" supports the more positive understanding of liberalism evident in *Injustice*, with its less limited understanding of government. The concern for securing the social standing of all individuals as citizens, in turn, supports the democratic version of positive liberalism that appears in *Citizenship*. I end by suggesting that a liberal government should be no more nor less limited than is needed, first, to secure basic liberties and opportunities for all individuals, and, second, to respect the outcomes of fair democratic procedures as long as they are consistent with the constitutional constraints of securing basic liberties and opportunities for all. This is the limited government of democratic liberalism. Its scope is not limited by negative liberty per se, as negative liberalism would require. Its legitimate power is limited instead by the constitutional constraints of securing basic (civil and political) liberties and opportunities for all individuals.

The Limits of Negative Liberalism

"Liberalism has only one overriding aim: to secure the political conditions that are necessary for the exercise of personal freedom. . . . Apart from prohibiting interference with the freedom of others, liberalism does not have any particular positive doctrines about how people are to conduct their lives or what personal choices they are to make."[3] This view of liberalism, which Shklar says is "the original and only defensible understanding," parallels Berlin's concept of negative liberty, meaning freedom from interference. Just as negative liberty entails freedom from interference and nothing else, so negative liberalism protects the political conditions necessary for the exercise of personal freedom, and nothing else.[4]

Shklar's telling term for a liberalism whose overriding goal is to protect negative liberty from state power is *the liberalism of fear,* the fear above all of cruelty, and cruelty above all at the hands of oppressive political powers, "because the fear and favor that have always inhibited freedom are overwhelmingly generated by governments."[5] Negative liberalism finds its most obvious origins in post-Reformation Europe, in reaction to the cruelty inflicted by the religious wars of Christianity. We have since seen more than enough cruelty at the hands of political powers, both secular and religious, to keep the call for limited and tolerant government alive as an inspiring, and inspired, political doctrine. But fear of political atrocities is not the only, perhaps not even the most steady and reliable, source of inspiration for negative liberalism. Without negative freedom, we would no longer be human beings with our own lives to live. Pursuing our own good in our own way is part of what it means to live a fully human life.[6] Whether or not this is universally true, it is true enough for human beings as we now know them.

Valuing the externally unimpeded pursuit of our own good does not presuppose moral skepticism, the view that there is no morally better or worse way to live one's life (from which it is said to follow that all individuals should be free to pursue their own good in their own way). The freedom to live as we choose is more often tied to moral skepticism by its critics than its defenders, and for good reason. Moral skepticism is not a logical source of the defense of negative liberty, although there may be psychological affinities between moral skepticism and an attitude of toleration. The moral skeptic doubts that one way of life is any better than another, and therefore criticizes political persecutions conducted in the name of the true religion or any other allegedly superior moral doctrine. But the critic of liberal toleration then asks: if all ways of life are equally good, what recommends toleration as a way of life above all the others? If the skeptic's answer is that toleration is no better or worse than intolerance as a way of life, then liberalism fails to defend toleration and limited government. Moral skepticism seems to require this answer, which is all the more reason to recall the classical liberal defense of toleration, one rooted not in moral skepticism but rather in a belief that is fiercely at odds with it. The belief, which John Locke enlists in *A Letter Concerning Toleration,* is that true faith cannot be commanded.[7] Forced faith is false faith. The government should stay out of the business of *making* people virtuous because the virtue business, managed by the state, is bound to bankruptcy.

Although negative liberalism is neither born of moral skepticism nor logically connected to it, its overriding aim—to free individuals from political oppression so they may live their own lives, provided they respect the like freedom of others—may have strong psychological affinities to moral skepticism. Moral skeptics are not even *tempted* to intervene in anyone else's life for moralistic or paternalistic reasons because they do not believe that anybody's life can be morally misguided. They therefore need not restrain an impulse—common among nonskeptics —to enlist state power to set things right. Liberals with robust moral commitments, on the other hand, may be tempted to intervene in what they take to be morally misguided lives. The psychological tension between belief in both toleration and moral misdirection accounts for the practical fragility of liberalism. Suppose I am a liberal who believes that there are morally better and worse ways of life. I restrain myself from interfering with other people's pursuit of immoral ways of life by a moral conviction that no one should be forced to act morally except when force is necessary to prevent intrusion on someone else's liberty. I expect other people similarly to restrain themselves, or be restrained by the liberal state. If my immorality is intrusive, then I can be forced to respect other people's liberty even if I am made to do so for fear of punishment rather than out of my own moral conviction. The liberal state must force me to let *other* people be free, without forcing me to be free in the sense of leading a thoroughly moral life. This understanding of liberal toleration is unavailable to the moral skeptic.

Moral skeptics can still consistently defend toleration as a modus vivendi. The moral skeptic may claim that it is *prudent* for people to live and let live lest they too perish by the intolerance of others. Sometimes this is the case, but often it is not. The modus vivendi defense of toleration is therefore weaker than the Lockean defense because it is far less generally applicable. There are many political conditions where nothing short of a moral commitment provides sufficient reason for people to tolerate views that they believe to be mistaken, heretical, sinful, or otherwise pernicious. Intolerance may be more prudent for people who are part of a politically dominant group, whose dominance is likely to endure at least as long as their lifetime. If politics is guided only by prudence based on self-interest and not by moral standards, then enlisting the state to spread one's sectarian faith will often be the dominant strategy, preferable to toleration. The Lockean rationale for toleration is more robust.[8] It offers even members of a dominant group good reason to desist from forcing their faith on others: people should be able to live their own lives according to their best lights provided they do not violate anyone else's rights. A government that respects religious and philosophical pluralism builds on this core commitment to what might be called personal integrity or dignity.

Respect for personal integrity (or dignity) requires governments to protect some but not all negative freedoms. Negative liberalism goes too far if it gives absolute priority to negative freedom beyond what the protection of personal integrity can sustain.[9] Shklar's account of liberalism's *summum malum*, the avoidance of cruelty, also challenges her earlier identification of liberalism with protecting *all* negative liberties. A liberalism that is concerned above all with damage control—limiting the infliction of physical and emotional pain on persons—need not prevent government generally from interfering with the negative freedom of individuals. Similarly, as Berlin recognizes, a liberal who values negative freedom need not deny the need to limit negative freedom for the sake of realizing some other "ultimate" values, such as social justice. Not all negative liberties are equally valuable, and not all kinds of cruelty can be prevented by securing negative liberty.[10] Governments may rightfully infringe upon some negative freedoms, such as freedom from government regulation of working conditions and freedom from taxation, in order to protect people from cruelty. Concern for the integrity or dignity of persons rather than the value of negative liberty above all else makes more sense of the liberal commitment to avoid cruelty and to secure religious toleration.

The political task of protecting personal integrity makes sense of Shklar's focus on freedom from fear, and fear of governments above all else. Governments are the institutions that have the greatest capacity for intolerance and cruelty. We must quickly add that governments do not monopolize the means of intolerance and cruelty. We are reminded every day of the prevalence and fear of private cruelty in the form of murder, rape, assault, battery, and child abuse. Still greater is the political capacity for cruelty in the form of "arbitrary, unexpected, unnecessary, and unlicensed acts of force and by habitual and pervasive acts of cruelty and torture performed by military, paramilitary, and police agents."[11] But liberalism need not choose between combating public cruelties and preventing private ones. Both typically constitute assaults on personal integrity. To the extent possible, liberal governments should protect people from cruelty, whatever the source.

The purely negative conception of liberalism is inadequate to this task. We reasonably fear not only interference with our freedom, but starvation, impoverishment, sickness, homelessness, joblessness, and other conditions that would render us incapable of making effective use of our freedom. The night watchman state of negative liberalism adequately addresses only some of these politically relevant fears, and Shklar implicitly acknowledges as much when, in *Injustice*, she distances herself from libertarianism's exclusive concern with protecting negative liberty and criticizes Friedrich Hayek's identification of the unregulated market with individual freedom.[12] Liberalism's commitment to combating cruelty and fear in all its political forms imposes more positive duties upon government than the securing of negative liberty. These duties are required by any conception of liberalism whose purpose is to combat cruelty and other assaults on the integrity of persons. Attributing positive duties to government extends liberalism's scope beyond the protection of negative liberty, and therefore takes us beyond negative liberalism.

From Negative to Positive Liberalism

In contrast to negative liberalism, positive liberalism is committed to securing basic liberties, those liberties necessary for the integrity of persons, rather than liberty per se. But the concerns of positive liberalism do not begin and end with protecting basic liberties. Positive liberalism not only limits the liberties that a liberal state *must* protect, it also holds governments responsible for securing conditions that enable people to make effective use of their liberty. The paradigm of positive liberalism is Rawls's conception of justice in *Political Liberalism*.[13] Positive liberalism gives priority to basic liberty, not liberty per se. It also secures basic opportunity for all members of society, those opportunities that are necessary for living a decent life.

The relationship between negative and positive liberalism parallels that between negative and positive liberty, as Berlin famously describes it. Negative and positive liberty, on one interpretation of Berlin, are inherently at odds with one another, an open war having been waged between proponents of negative and positive liberty. On this interpretation, the pursuit of positive liberty on behalf of other people is necessarily incompatible with a commitment to permit people to live their own lives free from the interference of others, particularly the interference of political authorities. Any government that is committed to helping people realize their "higher selves" is bound to become tyrannical, forcing people to live according to a blueprint not of their own making.

But this is not the only interpretation of the relationship between negative and positive liberty, or the strongest one. On a second interpretation, the relationship is far less hostile. An "open war" between negative and positive liberty is waged only by one-eyed proponents of each value who are blind to the legitimate claims of the other. The two concepts of liberty are importantly distinct, but positive liberty—which includes the freedom to be educated as a child or to be protected from starvation or oppressive working conditions as an adult—often adds to the value of a negative liberty, rather than detracts from it. Berlin repeatedly warns us that while positive liberty may add to the value of negative liberty, it should not be confused with that value: "The fact that given examples of negative freedom . . . —say the freedom of parents or schoolmasters to determine the education of children, of employers to exploit or dismiss their workers, of slave-owners to dispose of their slaves, of the torturer to inflict pain on his victims—may, in many cases, be wholly undesirable, and should in any sane or decent society be curtailed or suppressed, does not render them genuine freedoms any the less." Berlin therefore argues that "useless freedoms should be made usable, but they are not identical with the conditions indispensable for their utility."[14]

On this second interpretation, negative and positive liberty are more compatible, but not completely so. Positive liberty supplements negative liberty because freedom from interference is insufficient for a good life. People also want and need to be free to achieve valuable ends of their own choosing. Some negative liberties (such as the freedom of employers to exploit their workers) are even unnecessary to realize this liberal vision of people being free to live good lives of their own choosing.

The relationship between negative and positive liberalism is analogous to this second (and, I think, superior) understanding of the relationship between negative and positive liberty. If negative liberalism takes cruelty to be the worst of all political evils, then it cannot be identified with freedom from interference, and nothing else. Shklar herself does not hold fast to this identification even in "Fear." She extends the political mandate of liberalism from the protection of personal freedom to the securing of opportunities for all individuals effectively to exercise their freedom. In defending "the elimination of such forms

and degrees of social inequality as expose people to oppressive practices,"[15] she moves beyond negative liberty to a defense of basic opportunity, which is part of positive liberty.

Eliminating oppressive social inequalities is not the same as protecting personal freedom, nor is it the same as creating the conditions for
limited government, unless one tautologically identifies limited government with the ending of oppressive social inequalities. Although
Shklar begins by insisting that liberalism is a single-value political theory, resting exclusively upon personal freedom, her attempt to assimi-
late all the commitments of liberalism to protection of personal
freedom fails.[16] Any government that is committed to securing the liberty of all individuals to make "as many *effective* decisions without fear
or favor as is compatible with a like freedom of every other adult" is
committed to far more than protecting freedom.[17] It is also committed
to providing people with the *opportunity* to make effective use of their
freedom.

Positive liberalism can (and should) still abide by Berlin's adamant
warning to distinguish between the political conditions that support liberty, the effective opportunity to enjoy liberty, and liberty itself.[18] Berlin's case for clearly defining negative liberty is a conceptual as well as a
moral point, about how best to understand the concept of liberty and to
keep alive its distinct value, the value of people living their own lives,
free to choose ("and not to be chosen for").[19] But it simply does not follow that we should identify liberalism as a political doctrine that is dedicated exclusively to the protection of negative liberty. Berlin's
conceptual argument that liberty should be understood as freedom
from interference serves an independently important purpose. If we
cannot even notice when someone's liberty is restricted, we are incapable of defending freedom from interference when it ought to be defended. But the argument that "liberty is liberty, not equality or fairness
or justice . . . or human happiness or a quiet conscience" says nothing
about *how* limited liberal government should be.[20]

According to positive liberalism, government should do both less
and more than defend negative liberty. A liberal government need not
protect all negative freedoms. It must protect those freedoms that are
necessary for combating cruelty and preserving the integrity (and dignity) of persons. A liberal government must also do more than protect
negative freedom. It must provide basic opportunity for all individuals.
Why should defenders of negative liberalism accept the extension of
liberal government beyond the protection of individual liberty? Because a government that protects all negative liberties cannot succeed
in fulfilling what advocates of negative liberalism take to be the most
fundamental aim of liberalism, namely, combating cruelty. To combat

cruelty a government must do what it can to eliminate those forms and degrees of social inequality that expose people to oppressive practices.

Once liberalism extends its concerns beyond the protection of negative liberty, it invites us further to question the extent of limited government. At least in some social contexts, the internal logic of a liberalism committed to combating cruelty calls for even more governmental action than protecting basic liberties and eliminating those "inequalities that expose people to oppressive practices."[21] Consider the problem of health care coverage in the United States. Many of the working poor in the United States are born so poor that from infancy they lack access to adequate health care, while other Americans are fortunate enough to be born to parents able to provide them with good health care and therefore with a normal life expectancy and a decent set of life chances. Whatever people do later in life, surely they did nothing at birth to deserve adequate or inadequate health care. Without adequate health care, people cannot enjoy their freedom. Yet nobody limits the negative liberty or actively oppresses Americans who lack access to adequate health care.

The lack of access to adequate health care counts as an instance of what Shklar calls "passive injustice," the failure on the part of government to save people from unnecessary suffering. Sometimes passive injustice consists of the "civic failure to stop private and public *acts* of injustice."[22] The government's failure to stop unjust private action was the problem in the infamous case of Joshua DeShaney. Doctors and case workers knew that Joshua's father was brutally beating him. The final caseworker, as the Supreme Court noted, "dutifully recorded these incidents in her files . . . but she did nothing more."[23] As a result, Joshua became permanently brain damaged. Shklar criticizes the decision of the Court's majority: "The state, the U.S. Supreme Court held, could not be held responsible for Joshua's end under the Due Process Clause of the Constitution, but Justice William Brennan is hardly alone in thinking that doing nothing under such circumstances amounts to as great an injustice as any that a modern state can commit."[24]

Even as a matter of American constitutional law, which should not be identified with the whole of liberal justice, Justice Brennan presents a powerful argument that governmental agents can be held responsible for their inaction under the Due Process Clause when governmental agencies have *already* acted in such a way as to make citizens dependent upon them for protection. Even though the Due Process Clause "is phrased as a limitation on the State's power to act, not as a guarantee of certain minimal levels of safety and security,"[25] the distinction between governmental action and inaction does not dispose of this case for the Court, for reasons that are relevant to a defense of positive liberalism.

When the government has already acted so as to render citizens reliant on its aid, as it did in the *DeShaney* case, whether or not such action was morally obligatory in the first place, public officials can be held responsible for subsequent inaction. This is essentially what Brennan argued in his dissent in *DeShaney:* "if a State cuts off private sources of aid and then refuses aid itself, it cannot wash its hands of the harm that results from its inaction." The *DeShaney* case illustrates the instability of negative liberalism in cases where governments act beyond their allegedly negative mandate. In virtue of its child welfare laws, the State of Wisconsin had directed "citizens and other governmental entities to depend on local departments of social services . . . to protect children from abuse." Because the law directs all complaints of child abuse to the Department of Social Services, "it simply belies reality, therefore, to contend that the State 'stood by and did nothing' with respect to Joshua."[26]

Suppose we assume that the Due Process Clause has only the negative liberal purpose of prohibiting government from abusing its power or employing it as an instrument of oppression. Even an exclusive focus on this negative liberal purpose does not decide cases like *DeShaney* in the direction the Supreme Court's majority took. The simple distinction between action and inaction cannot settle cases like *DeShaney*, where the government acts to protect people and then fails to fulfill the expectation of protection that its action has reasonably created. If governmental agencies try to protect citizens, displacing alternative sources of protection, then their "inaction can be every bit as abusive of power as action," Brennan concludes. Whether or not inaction is every bit as abusive is beside the point. Inaction can constitute a major abuse of power. The premises of negative liberalism are consistent with Brennan's conclusion that "oppression can result when a State undertakes a vital duty and then ignores it."[27]

This critique of *DeShaney* shows that government inaction is not a decisive defense against the charge of political oppression. But it does not go so far as to defend a main tenet of positive liberalism, the obligation of government to act in the first place to protect citizens from avoidable suffering that results from inaction, rather than from someone's immoral action. Although Brennan contends that the government undertook "a vital duty," his argument, based on due process, does not depend on showing that it was the government's duty to act in the first place. To make a more robust case for positive liberalism, we must move beyond *DeShaney* and the Supreme Court to consider the broad responsibilities that fall upon liberal governments, rather than the considerably narrower responsibilities of the judiciary.

In many situations of injustice, as in the case of the approximately thirty million Americans who now lack adequate health care coverage, there are no *acts* analogous either to the brutal beating of Joshua or to the creation of a Department of Social Services. There are instead only actions that should be, but are not, initiated by government to provide the basic life chances that can be afforded to every American. These basic life chances, such as the opportunities afforded by adequate health care, add to the value of basic liberty, but they can be guaranteed only if government either directly or indirectly secures basic opportunities as well as basic liberties for all members of society, to the extent possible.

If liberal governments should secure basic opportunities as well as basic liberties (as Berlin and other defenders of negative liberty grant), then the failure of governmental action can constitute an injustice by liberal lights even when there are no unjust acts to restrain or prior commitments to complete. Shklar's vivid depiction of the unjust public person, gleaned from Giotto's *L'Inguistizia,* supports this critical perspective of positive liberalism. The unjust public person is "either bold enough to deprive others of their dignity and life *or indifferent to it.*"[28] The claim that public officials can be responsible for failure to aid people, even in the absence of an established institutional expectation, moves us decisively into the territory of positive liberalism. Liberal expectations are no longer that governments will simply desist from harming people, but that they will also do what they can—within principled limits—to protect people from what a liberalism that refused to look beyond negative liberty would consider politically irremediable misfortune. Positive liberalism obligates governments to do far more than desist from oppressing or harming anyone. Governments also should afford everyone an effective opportunity to live a decent life.

We now can characterize the relationship between negative and positive liberalism in a way that more fully captures the spirit of a liberal moral vision. Positive liberalism does not only expand the limits of responsible government set by negative liberalism; it also supplants its single-valued doctrine, first by limiting the responsibility of government in the realm of liberty to securing the *basic* liberties of all persons—liberties that are necessary for the integrity of persons. Liberalism should be understood not as a doctrine that indiscriminately protects *all* negative liberties, but rather one that gives priority to protecting the *basic* liberties of all individuals. So understood, liberalism remains an inspiring but incomplete political doctrine.

The second way in which positive liberalism supplants negative liberalism is by committing governments to providing basic opportunities for all. Some negative freedoms that are not necessary for personal integrity, such as the freedom to exploit workers or retain all of one's

pretax income, come into conflict with the aim of securing basic opportunities for all individuals. That is why we should say that positive liberalism defends the basic liberiy of all individuals, those liberties necessary to the integrity and dignity of the person rather than personal
freedom or negative liberty per se.

Defenders of positive liberalism therefore refuse to give priority "to
liberty as such, as if the exercise of something called 'liberty' has pre-
eminent value and is the main if not sole end of political and social justice." Positive liberalism protects "certain specific liberties," those that
are "essential social conditions" for people to exercise their capacity for
a conception of the good life and a sense of justice. Among these liberties are "freedom of thought and liberty of conscience, the political liberties and freedom of association, as well as the freedoms specified by
the liberty and integrity of the person; and finally, the rights and liberties covered by the rule of law."[29] Even if this list is incomplete, it shows
that positive liberalism goes a long way down the road with negative liberalism but stops short of absolutely protecting all negative liberties.

Freedom from taxation for redistributive purposes, for example, is
conspicuously absent from the list of freedoms that are protected by
positive liberalism, and rightly so. The rationale for omitting this freedom from the list of basic liberties is that redistributive taxation to fund
education and health care, for example, can promote basic opportunity
without interfering with anyone's basic liberty. If governments are capable of securing basic opportunity and fail to do so, their policies promote injustice. When your society is capable of ensuring everyone in
need a decent standard of living and adequate health care, it is not mere
misfortune to die young due to poverty and inadequate health care.
Positive liberalism provides an unequivocal basis for criticizing such
governmental inaction to provide basic opportunity for all individuals
as injustice. This expansive understanding of injustice tracks Shklar's
judgments in *Injustice* far better than the negative definition of liberalism that she offers in "Fear."

Democratic Liberalism

We have said little so far about democracy, yet every credible conception of positive liberalism assumes the context of a constitutional *democracy*. Shklar's argument for expanding governmental action in *Injustice*
explicitly presupposes a constitutional democracy.[30] And among the
basic freedoms included by Rawls in the priority of liberty are political
liberties: the right to vote, run for public office, and other distinctively
democratic freedoms. To what extent does the limited government of
liberalism make room for democratic activity on the part of citizens?

One common answer is that the liberal commitment to political liberties (and therefore to democratic citizenship) is purely instrumental to the protection of civil liberties. The value of political liberty is therefore not on a par with that of civil liberties, which are valuable for their own sake. This is the answer that is often associated with liberalism, and Berlin's distinction between negative and positive liberty. "Perhaps the chief value for liberals of political-'positive'-rights, of participating in the government," Berlin writes, "is a means for protecting what they hold to be an ultimate value, namely individual-'negative'-liberty." Democracy, on this liberal view, is not itself a liberal value; it is valuable only insofar as it serves to realize fundamentally liberal values.[31] In "Fear," Shklar suggests an answer along these lines when she writes that liberalism is "monogamously, faithfully, and permanently married to democracy—but it is a marriage of convenience." Democracy is a valuable political instrument because "without enough equality of power to protect and assert one's rights, freedom is but a hope."[32] Democratic rights, so understood, have value as a means of protecting personal freedom and securing basic opportunity for all. Equal suffrage, for example, is an instrument for realizing liberal values. It is not itself a fundamentally liberal value.

Is the marriage of liberalism and democracy best understood as one merely of convenience? Berlin sometimes suggests otherwise, as when he writes that valuing liberty for its own sake "underlies both the positive demand to have a voice in the laws and practices of the society in which one lives, and to be accorded an area . . . in which one is one's own master, a 'negative' area in which a man is not obliged to account for his activities to any man so far as this is compatible with the existence of organized society."[33] Perhaps Berlin means to say that suffrage rights are instrumental to civil rights, but here he seems to put the two kinds of rights on the same footing, as valuable for the freedom that they accord individuals.

Positive liberalism gives us reason to doubt that democracy is solely instrumental to securing other, more essential values. If we compare the political rights necessary for democratic government with civil rights such as freedom of religion, we find that neither is instrumental in the sense of being a purely *external* condition for realizing other, more fundamentally liberal values. At least in the context of the United States, and probably in many other contemporary contexts, it is a public indignity for an adult American to be denied equal political liberties. In many modern societies, democratic rights are the primary public expression of the equal standing of individuals who share a common state. Rawls recognizes this when he places political freedom among the basic liberties that are protected by the first (and prior) principle of justice.

In *Citizenship*, Shklar also gives us reasons for rejecting the purely instrumental view of democracy's relationship to liberalism. "The ballot has always been a certificate of full membership in society, and its value depends primarily on its capacity to confer a minimum of social dignity." The ballot *certifies* full membership. It *confers* social dignity. It is not only an instrumental means of realizing liberal values that are only contingently related to democratic citizenship. Democratic citizenship, at least in the United States, Shklar writes, "has never been just a matter of agency and empowerment, but also of social standing as well." The right to vote is one of the "*attributes*" of an American citizen." It is regarded as more than a means of promoting a person's particular interests, and as something other than a means of self-realization. It is a sign, a recognition and representation, of social standing: "The struggle for citizenship in America has . . . been overwhelmingly a demand for inclusion in the polity, an effort to break down excluding barriers to recognition, rather than an aspiration to civic participation as a deeply involving activity."[34]

The democratic version of positive liberalism recognizes the relationship of liberalism and democracy as intimate, and not merely a marriage of convenience. Democratic liberalism counts the *political* freedoms of constitutional democracy as among the liberties that are basic to publicly representing, and thereby expressing, the dignity of persons. To the extent that equal voting rights, for example, are necessary to represent publicly the equal dignity of persons, the marriage of liberalism and democracy is intimate, not one of mere convenience. Equal voting rights in the United States, as the discussion in *Citizenship* suggests, serve this representational, noninstrumental role. They publicly affirm the equal civic status of adult members of our society. Unequal voting rights serve the opposite representational purpose; they express the unequal civic status of citizens, and are taken as an affront to the dignity of (and by) those adults who are given less than equal political rights. Suffrage rights also serve important instrumental purposes, but democracy need not be courted by liberals just for convenience. It is not only our *exercise* of suffrage but our publicly affirmed *right* to vote that has signified deeply: "Without the right one was less than a citizen."[35] For women or African Americans to be considered something less than citizens was in itself an injustice, quite apart from whether our other liberties and opportunities were therefore unjustly distributed as a consequence of our unequal political liberties (which they generally were).

The lack of public representation as an equal citizen is only part of the problem that democratic liberalism needs to address. The full representational value of political rights cannot be realized without their effective exercise. Voting rights signify less if they are continually unused, especially if their disuse by a disadvantaged minority reflects the widely perceived fact that their exercise would not gain the minority the basic opportunities, say, of education, health care, and productive work, to which they are entitled. For political rights to realize their full representational value, they must also have potentially good consequences for law and public policy. Otherwise, political rights are likely to be perceived as something of a sham, and may even begin to lose their value of representing the dignity and social standing of citizens.

Equal voting rights, truly competitive elections, public accountability of officials, publicity of laws and public policies, and other procedurally fair democratic practices are necessary but not sufficient to constitute a defensible form of democratic liberalism. A democracy that is restrained only by democratic procedures would be too unlimited to secure other distinctively liberal values. Democratic liberalism therefore depends on constitutional constraints that go beyond the defense of democratic values alone. We have already introduced those constraints as part of positive liberalism. The constitutional principles of basic liberty and basic opportunity rightly constrain democratic decision making. The constraints are ideally self-constraints, informing the political decision making of citizens along with legislators, judges, and other public officials.

But the constitutional constraints on democratic action of positive liberalism do not yield a comprehensive politics. If they did, they would leave no room for democratic discretion, and democracy would be only instrumental to the realization of nondemocratic values. Quite the contrary, the constitutional constraints of the democratic version of positive liberalism *include* authorization of democratic discretion and recognition of the legitimate authority of citizens and their accountable representatives to make laws and public policies that reach beyond the protection of basic liberties and opportunities, while respecting them. The democratic deliberations of citizens and accountable public officials are valuable for at least three reasons: they can help develop the most publicly defensible interpretations of some constitutional constraints; they can contribute to the representation and respect of all adults as equal citizens; and they can lead to the creation of legitimate public policies that reach beyond the constitutional constraints of securing equal liberties and opportunities for all.

The ideal of democratic liberalism is therefore more than simply self-government. It is deliberative and constitutional self-government: popular rule that deliberatively constrains itself or is rightly constrained by respect for the basic liberties and basic opportunities of all individuals. The constitutional limits that democratic liberalism places on self-government should make it clear that democracy does not promise self-realization through political participation. Democratic liberalism takes politics beyond the protection of negative liberty, but it does not succumb to Berlin's critique of those who overestimate and thereby abuse the value of positive liberty, first by identifying positive liberty with self-mastery, and then by justifying tyrannical political authority exercised in the name of our higher or truer selves.

Good citizenship, by the ideal of democratic liberalism, is not "the call for perfect republican virtue." That call is inconsistent with giving priority to basic liberty and respecting our freedom to choose among many good ways of life that are not primarily political. By the lights of democratic liberalism, citizens are free to devote their lives to politics, but no one is required to do so. Democratic liberalism rejects the idea, rightly or wrongly associated with Rousseau, that civic virtue requires a life devoted to politics, which transforms one's identity into that of a true citizen. "There is very little evidence to show that there are many Americans who contemplate such transformative politics with interest, let alone enthusiasm," Shklar writes. "The paradox of an ideal democratic citizenship that has no appeal to the people it is supposed to favor is not without irony."[36]

Good citizenship by the ideal of democratic liberalism also eschews nationalism in its many pernicious forms. The source of the standing of citizens must not be our ethnic, religious, or racial identity, but our integrity and dignity as persons. Although a liberal democracy, were one ever to exist in ideal form, could not secure equal liberties and opportunities for everyone throughout the world, each liberal democracy must at minimum desist from violating the rights of people who live beyond its borders. Nationalistic doctrines encourage governments and ordinary citizens to violate even this minimal moral obligation to strangers.[37] Liberal democracies owe more than negative duties to people who live beyond their borders, but if liberalism respects the basic liberties of all individuals, regardless of their nationality, it can counter the most prevalent and pernicious forms of nationalism.

What, then, are the implications of democratic liberalism for the liberal ideal of limited government? The rights of democratic citizenship expand the limits of liberal government beyond those of negative liberalism and nondemocratic forms of positive liberalism. For the rights of democratic citizenship to be meaningful, citizens must be able to govern themselves, but they must do so within constitutional limits that respect all liberal values, not just democratic ones. A law or policy that fails to safeguard basic liberty or secure basic opportunity is unjustified on liberal grounds, regardless of whether it is democratically authorized. By the same token, any restriction of equal political liberties that is not necessary for safeguarding constitutional rights is also un-justified. Democratic freedoms are among the basic liberties. Liberal governments therefore are unduly limited in scope if they restrict the exercise of democratic freedoms beyond what is necessary to safeguard basic liberties and opportunities.

Limited government has a different meaning for democratic liberalism than it does for negative liberalism. While negative liberalism limits the scope of government by requiring it to desist from doing anything that violates negative liberty, democratic liberalism limits government not by its scope but by virtue of its constitutional constraints. Although democratic liberalism extends the responsibilities of government beyond safeguarding negative liberties to providing basic opportunities, it does not constrain government to a limited scope because democratic citizenship is a fundamental constitutional right. It is more than a necessary means to protecting other constitutional rights even though it is less than a sufficient limit on state power. Democratic rights are instrumentally valuable, to be sure, but they are also a direct expression of our interest in publicly representing ourselves and being publicly represented as equal citizens. Democratic rights enable us to enjoy the equal standing of citizens and they also leave the scope of limited government open to ongoing deliberation.

Democratic liberalism does not therefore require us to spend a major part of our lives participating in politics. It permits us to use our discretionary authority as citizens to shape our society in constitutionally consistent ways. Democratic liberalism, so understood, is still unambiguously "a political doctrine, not a philosophy of life such as has traditionally been provided by various forms of revealed religion and other comprehensive *Weltanschauungen.*"[38] The boundaries of legitimate governmental action are constrained by constitutional principles but not closed by them. Beyond constitutional constraints, democratic deliberation itself limits the legitimate authority of government. Liberalism and democracy are therefore tied together not by convenience, or by love, but ideally by mutual respect of individuals with their own good lives to live and a polity to share and shape on fair terms together.

Notes

1. On some accounts, liberalism is more than a political doctrine. It is also a philosophy of life that is committed to cultivating individuality and/or autonomy. But on all accounts, liberalism is at least a political doctrine of limited government.

2. "The Liberalism of Fear," 37.

3. Ibid., 21.

4. Ibid. See also Isaiah Berlin, "Two Concepts of Liberty," in *Four Essays on Liberty* (Oxford, 1969), 122–31: "I am normally said to be free to the degree to which no man or body of men interferes with my activity. . . . You lack political liberty or freedom only if you are prevented from attaining a goal by human beings. Mere incapacity to attain a goal is not lack of political freedom" (122). Negative liberty, Berlin adds, "is not the only goal of men. . . . But nothing is gained by a confusion of terms. To avoid glaring inequality or widespread misery I am ready to sacrifice some, or all, of my freedom: I may do so willingly and freely: but it is freedom that I am giving up for the sake of justice or equality or the love of my fellow men" (125).

5. "The Liberalism of Fear," 21.

6. See John Stuart Mill, *On Liberty* [1859]. See also Berlin, "Two Concepts of Liberty," 127.

7. See John Locke, *A Letter Concerning Toleration*, ed. James Tully (Indianapolis, 1983), 23, 26–29, 38.

8. For a comparative assessment of the philosophical cases for toleration based on skepticism and on Lockean premises, see Amy Gutmann and Dennis Thompson, "Moral Conflict and Political Consensus," *Ethics* 101 (Oct. 1990): 65–72.

9. Berlin's defense of negative liberty suggests as much: "I should like to say once again to my critics that the issue is not one between negative freedom as an absolute value and other, inferior values." There is, he argues, "the paramount need to satisfy the claims of other, no less ultimate, values: justice, happiness, love, the realization of capacities to create new things and experiences and ideas, the discovery of the truth." But, he hastens to add, "nothing is gained by identifying freedom proper . . . with these values, or with the conditions of freedom, or by confounding types of freedom with one another" (Berlin, introduction to *Four Essays on Liberty*, lvi).

10. "To take a concrete example: it is, I believe, desirable to introduce a uniform system of general primary and secondary education in every country, if only in order to do away with distinctions of social status that are at present created or promoted by the existence of a social hierarchy of schools in some Western countries, notably my own. . . . If I were told that this must severely curtail the liberty of parents who claim the right not to be interfered with in this matter . . . I should not be ready to dismiss this outright. But I should maintain that when (as in this case) values genuinely clash, choices must be made" (ibid., liv).

11. "The Liberalism of Fear," 29.

12. *The Faces of Injustice*, 76–82.

13. See John Rawls, *Political Liberalism* (New York, 1993), 228–30; cf. Rawls, *A Theory of Justice* (Cambridge, Mass., 1971).

14. Berlin, introduction, lvi–lvii, liv.

15. "The Liberalism of Fear," 28.

16. "Every adult should be able to make as many effective decisions without fear or favor about as many aspects of her or his life as is compatible with the like freedom of every other adult. That belief is the original and only defensible meaning of liberalism" ("The Liberalism of Fear," 21). The problem of identify-

ing liberalism solely with liberty is built into this definitional statement. To make as many effective decisions is not a matter of liberty alone, it is a matter of effective liberty, which includes a strong dose of opportunity to make use of one's liberty. Shklar never admits that a commitment to opportunity is built in to this definition of liberty, although her substantive defense of liberalism is fully consistent with a commitment to liberty and opportunity for all.

17. "The Liberalism of Fear," 21 (emphasis added).

18. Shklar acknowledges this in addressing Berlin's insistence that liberty not be confused with the conditions of liberty. But she does not qualify her defense of negative liberty in recognition that the reduction of social inequalities entails a significant restriction of liberty, for the sake not of liberty but its effective exercise or enjoyment. See "The Liberalism of Fear," 28–29.

19. Berlin, introduction, lx.

20. Berlin, "Two Concepts of Liberty," 125.

21. "The Liberalism of Fear," 28.

22. *The Faces of Injustice*, 6 (emphasis added).

23. *DeShaney v. Winnebago County Department of Social Services*, 489 U.S. 189 (1989), 193.

24. *The Faces of Injustice*, 6.

25. *DeShaney*, 195.

26. Ibid., 207, 208, 210.

27. Ibid., 212.

28. *The Faces of Injustice*, 48–49 (emphasis added).

29. Rawls, *Political Liberalism*, 292–93, 291.

30. *The Faces of Injustice*, 6.

31. Berlin, "Two Concepts of Liberty," 165.

32. "The Liberalism of Fear," 37.

33. Berlin, introduction, lx.

34. *American Citizenship*, 2, 3 (emphasis added).

35. Ibid., 37.

36. Ibid., 5, 12.

37. For an important exception, see Yael Tamir's defense of *Liberal Nationalism* (Princeton, N.J., 1993).

38. "The Liberalism of Fear," 21. Cf. John Rawls, *Political Liberalism* (New York, 1993), xvi–xviii.

6

Judith Shklar as a Political Thinker

Stanley Hoffmann

THE SUDDEN DEATH OF JUDITH N. SHKLAR on 17 September 1992 is a tragedy. It is a tragedy first of all for her family, then for her friends, and for her students, on whom she lavished encouragement and affection without ever censoring her formidable capacity for intellectual argument and criticism. The torrent of letters, memories, and testimonies provoked by her death reveals the depth of the mark she left on all those who had approached and learned from her. In one of Edmond Rostand's plays there is an invocation to the sun: "Without you, things would only be what they are." Those who knew Dita Shklar were sometimes warmed, occasionally scorched, and always dazzled by her radiance; the world is a much drabber and grimmer place without her incisive intelligence, her rapier mind, her colossal energy, her incredible all-encompassing erudition, her limitless curiosity, her impatience with false pretenses, the enthusiasm with which she read, wrote, taught, and inspired.

It is a tragedy, also, because she still had so much to give. In ordinary mortals, the level of energy and creativity tends to decrease with age. Hers increased in ways that were a source of wonder for her friends. In the last ten or twelve years of her life, as she gained the international recognition she had always deserved, her intellectual productivity, which had already been high, exploded. She left a profusion of papers and drafts, many of which were written in the last six months of her life. She was planning at least two more major works; one, which she had

A version of this chapter appeared under the same title in *Political Theory* 21 (May 1993): 172–89. Reprinted by permission of Sage Publications, Inc.

begun, on the rights and obligations of exiles throughout history, and another on the history of American political science.

Her friends and her students can talk for hours about the intellectual nourishment, moral support, and emotional comfort she provided (with abundance, firmness, and tact, respectively), about the power of her mind and the strength of her personality (I have never heard so many people say, after remarking on her intellectual toughness, "I loved her"). Nevertheless, nothing is more striking than the absence of serious and extensive work about *her* work. Dita Shklar has written with insight and respect about Hannah Arendt. I would argue that her writings are just as worthy of analysis and reflection as those of that other, better-known refugee. Her friends John Rawls and Michael Walzer, whom she admired and cherished, are widely recognized as profound and influential thinkers. Her work is equally rich. Is it because, unlike them, she preferred to reveal her ideas obliquely, through the study of others or through the examination of ordinary ideologies or "ordinary vices"? Is it because she was not a hedgehog but a fox? Whatever the answer, the time has come, alas, for a systematic exploration of an extremely rich mine. Dita's studies of the Enlightenment, of American political thought and of political obligation, her restatement of liberalism for men and women living after the great catastrophes of the twentieth century, are enormous contributions to political philosophy.

The notes that follow are triply incomplete. I am not a political theorist (teaching a course on modern ideologies with Dita was a humbling, albeit exhilarating, experience). I have had neither the time nor the necessary detachment to read again all her published works, and to try to do for them what she did so well for so many classic authors. Nor have I finished reading the unpublished essays she left. What follows, then, is just a series of suggestions for further research.

I

When one tries to embrace this impressive mass of writings, two features stand out. The first is the decisive impact of her own family origins and early experiences (she deals with them—discreetly because she was close to believing, like Pascal, that *le moi est haïssable*—in her marvelous 1989 lecture for the American Council of Learned Societies, "A Life of Learning"). She came from a family of German-speaking Jews in Riga, and thus belonged to a triply besieged minority; unpopular in Latvia, threatened by the Bolshevik mastodon next door, and by the rise of Hitler nearby. In 1939 her family fled, just in time, to Sweden, and then, fearing a German invasion, all the way through the Soviet Union to Japan, then to the United States (where they were briefly jailed!) and to Canada, where they settled. She went to school and college in Montreal. As she wrote in a recent critique of Walzer, her disagreement with his longing for community is "a dialogue between an exile and a citizen."[1] Her experience as a refugee, as well as her later life as an immigrant in America, explain her outlook on power. She once wrote that there are two kinds of political scientists, those who study power because they would like to exert it, and those who study it because they fear it—those who would like to ride the horse of power, and those who are scared of being trampled by it. She always put herself (and me) in the second category. This was the germ of her most important contribution, the liberalism of fear. It was the same experiences that made her focus on the problems of citizenship, on the conflicts between the individual and the group (not just the state), on the dialectic of inclusion and exclusion. She often said that her interest was the study of evil, and that she therefore didn't risk running out of topics. Where that interest came from, for a transplanted European, is clear enough.

A second feature is the increasing self-assurance which marks the evolution of her work. She began with criticism (in *After Utopia* and in *Legalism*) and with exegeses (in her books on Rousseau and Hegel). One could without much difficulty discover her own point of view, but it remained subordinated to her analysis of the perspectives of others. In her works of the eighties and nineties, while she continues to produce erudite and incisive commentaries on a variety of writers, she deals much more directly with her own thoughts about politics; *Ordinary Vices, The Faces of Injustice, American Citizenship,* and several of her essays of this period, provide us with her own political philosophy.

In a sense, she left three distinct bodies of works. One consists in all the remarkable essays in which she extracted the meaning and described the context of the ideas of such authors as Rousseau, Hegel, Harrington, Bergson, Montesquieu, d'Alembert, Jefferson, Emerson, Henry Adams, Pope, Orwell, Arendt, and Walzer. The second is her own contribution to age-old debates about political obligation and loyalty, the rights and duties of citizens, the conditions for and institutions of democracy, the nature of justice and injustice, the foundations of liberalism. A third group includes all her studies and thoughts about the history of political theory and political science. The former, she argued, revived after a period in which, following the exhaustion of the grand ideologies of the nineteenth century, political philosophy itself seemed exhausted; the latter, in her view, owed much to the practical concerns of American's Founding Fathers.[2]

Among the many themes in her works, I would like to single out three that seem central to me. The first one is the importance and autonomy of the sphere of politics. The thrust of her critique of romanticism, in *After Utopia,* was that "the romantics were anti-political" and their "one concern . . . was to defend non-political man against the encroachments of public life."[3] She was often eager to defend political man against the encroachments of abusive groups and states. But it was the political person who interested her, it was the social being and the citizen (or the person excluded from citizenship), not the private individual cultivating his own garden who was her central concern. Her defense of his rights was always accompanied by an emphasis on his obligations. The tension between the private and the public, between independence and freedom, between "men" and "citizens," is at the heart of her studies of Rousseau and Hegel.

For her, as for all liberals, liberalism meant the maintenance of a (far from immobile) barrier between the personal and the public domain. But the preservation of that barrier did not require only the division and dispersion of public power, the fostering of pluralism, and a reduction of the kind of extreme social inequality which could "expose people to oppressive practices."[4] The public sphere, on which she focused, was seen by her as a realm of collective *decisions.* To be sure, these decisions may be guided and facilitated by existing legal rules, or by the "shared understandings" celebrated by Walzer. But her attack on legalism and her critique of Walzer make it crystal clear that, to her, legalism was a kind of ideological escape from the need to face directly "the social actualities with which (legalism) purports to deal," and what she first called the "liberalism of permanent minorities"[5] made her deeply suspicious of groups, be they voluntary associations or nations—whose "historical record is grim" toward such minorities, for instance, "the poor, the Black and the injured" in this country,[6]—or the Jews in much of Europe. These collective decisions must, of course, be based on certain principles, and it is to the elucidation and discussion of these that what I have called the second body of her works is devoted.

The second theme is, indeed, the protection of the (social and political) individual against all the perils that threaten him or her, especially in contemporary society. What is the nature and what are the limits of his or her obligations to the state? (She was particularly careful in distinguishing obligations from loyalty, that is, duties based on rules from affective commitments.) What are the qualities needed by the citizen of a liberal democracy? This was the question behind the marvelous moral essays and psychological sketches of *Ordinary Vices*—a question raised by her awareness of the fact, already noted by Montesquieu, that the citizen of a modern republic cannot be the virtuous public man of the Greek city-state, and by her conviction that, nevertheless, not *all* vices are equally compatible with the just functioning of a modern liberal regime.

Her concern for minorities, exiles, the excluded, and the victims led her in two highly original directions. One was her profound investigation of political injustice. She was particularly concerned with distinguishing injustice from misfortune, in order to concentrate on the harm done *by people* to other people, rather than on all the cruelties that can unfairly affect our lives. And she pointed out that there are two main faces of injustice: acts and failures to act—the injustice of, say, deliberate cruelty, and the injustice that consists in failing to help "actual and potential victims"; the active injustice of the evil citizen verses the passive injustice of the bad citizen. Focusing on the latter allowed her to show that injustice was not just the opposite of justice, that what she called the normal model of justice was unsatisfactory, and that there was no way of ever eliminating the sense of injustice; every reform, as well as the refusal to reform, feeds it, and therefore the best way of dealing with this fact is—once again—the establishment of a "system of effective and continuous citizen participation in which no one wins or loses all the time."[7]

The other direction was the "liberalism of fear." Here too, by adopting (entirely the wrong word; she didn't adopt it, she embodied it!) the perspective of the victim in a century of collective crimes, she both exposed the fallacies of and rejuvenated something that was as dear to her as justice: liberalism. She agreed with John Rawls that the liberalism that needed to be defined anew was only a political doctrine, not a "comprehensive" "philosophy of life."[8] But she did not follow Rawls in his arduous search for abstract principles acceptable to and for an "overlapping consensus" of all reasonable individuals. She proceeded from a distrust of abstract rules and a conviction that conflict was the stuff of life: *her* liberalism was anti-utopian, which did not mean that it was only valid for Western political cultures, for her attack on communitarian relativism was blistering. It was to be both of universal relevance, and based on the humbling psychological and political conclusions that historical memory, especially that of twentieth-century victims, suggested as the foundations of liberal reconstruction. The liberalism of the eighteenth century, the century in which she often said she felt most at home, was propelled by an aggressive faith in reason and in historical progress. Shklar, who distrusted collective emotions, knew only too well the feebleness of reason pitted against or drafted by them, and what had happened "after utopia." But the fact that the individual had been turned from a self-reliant conquering hero into a member of an endangered species made it even more imperative to circumscribe his obligations and to protect his rights, which she saw not as "natural" or given but as "licenses and empowerments that citizens must have to . . . protect themselves against abuse."[9]

The only possible liberalism now, therefore, is a liberalism that tries above all to defend the individual from cruelty—in a century of holocaust and torture—and from the most blatant forms of injustice. Montaigne was the hero of *Ordinary Vices* because "he put cruelty first"; Montesquieu was another hero of that book, and the subject of a brilliant intellectual biography, because he identified fear as the spring of despotism, and despotism as the scourge of humanity. "The fear of fear does not require any further justification, because it is irreducible. It can be both the beginning and an end of political institutions such as rights."[10] Her distrust of unlimited government, based on a suspicion of power that reminds one, at times, of the French philosopher Alain, was complemented by an equally deep suspicion of the oppressive and stifling power of communities, particularly of nationalism. There was a "positive" side to the liberalism of fear: on the one hand, it meant the rule of law and of procedural fairness—including access of all to "courts, legal services and police protection" (something a pure "law and order" state resigned to extreme inequality would make impossible)—the dispersion of power as well as that of property (because it is an abusable form of power"), and consent as a continuous process under conditions of "personal freedom." (This is a crucial sentence, for it condenses her dislike of the paternalism, however well meaning, she deemed characteristic of many efforts to build a welfare state that assume the "noncompetence" of its charges.)[11] On the other hand, it meant the possibility (not the guarantee!) that the different "selves" protected from fear could do something with their lives. This is why (Walzer notwithstanding) Shklar's liberalism was not merely an adjective (*liberal*) qualifying a more substantive political doctrine—except that of democracy, given the monogamously, faithfully, and permanently "necessary" marriage of convenience between democracy and liberalism.[12]

A third important theme is what could be called American distinctiveness. A fine book could be formed with the essays written by Shklar about American thinkers, institutions, and history, in addition to the masterpiece that turned out to be her last book, *American Citizenship*. Some of these essays were lectures prepared, in French as well as in English, for French-speaking audiences. At a time when the French, having repudiated the Marxist and para-Marxist ideologies that had dominated their "market of ideas" for so long, were rediscovering the conservative liberalism of Constant and Guizot, she explained that in the United States, her friend Isaiah Berlin's distinction between negative and positive liberty made no sense because the essential concept and institution here is rights (which are not merely barriers, fences, defenses, but acts of empowerment) and claims on the government aimed at goading it into positive action. She admired the Founding Fathers' mix of philosophical reflections and practical concerns, their capacity to apply the former to the formidable concrete tasks of founding a new polity (Tocqueville had blamed the French Enlightenment for its lack of practical sense—an excessive charge, I believe—and he rather understated the importance of political philosophy among the practical Americans). *American Citizenship* is a Tocquevillian attempt at circumscribing the originality of American public life. But it is also pure Shklar, for she focuses on citizenship as social standing from the viewpoint of the excluded: slaves and, to a large extent, women, and shows how American citizenship has actually been defined, so to speak, against the background of slavery—the condition of those who neither vote nor are freely remunerated. Voting as the synonym of citizenship and earning as the necessary condition for public respect have been the American way of coping with "the stress of inherited inequalities" and especially with "the remnants of black chattel slavery." While she admired American society for its commitment "to political equality and to the principle of inclusion,"[13] she had no illusions about the flaws of America: the massive failures to vote, the citizens' preference of "peace and quiet to justice,"[14] the recurrent witch-hunts, the inability to include fully African Americans, that is, the continuing legacy of slavery. She knew that even in America, those rats Camus wrote about in *The Plague* could land and ravage ordinary lives.

II

In this brief sketch, something needs to be said not only about Shklar's main themes but also about her approach (the word *method* would have been angrily rejected by a writer who loved Montaigne for his unsystematic discursiveness, and who, like Montaigne, preferred telling stories and moving in and out of topics to writing Cartesian essays built with steel rods).

A characteristic which gives its particular value to her first body of works—her studies of other authors—is her scrupulous search for the meaning they gave to their writings. She never imposed her meanings on them; and while she agreed with the modern "hermeneutists" about the multiplicity of possible interpretations of texts,[15] her own was always based on a triple concern: for the author's intentions as expressed by him, for the general design and construction of his entire work, and for the precedents, antecedents, and references, explicit or not, he may have had in mind. Thus her books and essays in this category are models of objective *explications de textes;* she disliked subjectivism in all of its manifestations, and certainly did not believe that a text can be made

to say anything a reader fantasizes about. This is also why her book re-
views were so carefully crafted and required so much labor: she wanted
to tell her reader about the substance of the author's arguments rather
than about how *she* would have written a book on the subject under review. (When her own work was reviewed in a way that put the reviewer
first and the meaning of the book second, she was, rightly, furious.) As a
result, she produced what is probably the best study of Rousseau's political philosophy and a study of Hegel that scraped away the crust of interpretations that made him mainly "the precursor of Marx and
Nietzsche" and restored the portrait of a "successor of Rousseau and
Kant."[16]

Another characteristic, related to the previous one, but surprising in
a political philosopher, was her concern for the *psychology* of political
action. In our course on ideologies I was the intellectual historian of
ideas, she was the psychologist of ideological appeals and effects. It was
the psychologist of the human heart who fascinated her in Rousseau,
and the "spiritual picture-gallery" of "brilliant psychological and group-
psychological portraits"[17] that interested her in Hegel's *Phenomenology
of the Mind*. She—like Montesquieu—was interested in how "character
and government constantly mold each other." Dealing with liberal regimes, she focused not on elites and central institutions but on the ordinary citizens, the daily victims, and their problems—a view from below
(a *démarche* that reminds one of Simone Weil, whom, as far as I know,
she never mentioned). Like Weil, Shklar believed that justice meant not
doing more harm. Both because of her perspective—that of the people
at the receiving end, so to speak—and because of her disenchantment
with the liberalism of hope and progress, she is above all concerned
with avoiding evil, rather than with fostering good. Thus she sketches
the character a "good liberal" would need, in terms of avoiding cruelty,
snobbery, misanthropy, and betrayal (and also the self-righteousness
that so often comes with fighting the good fight against vice); a dose of
hypocrisy is tolerated, and could even be useful. She notes that "Kant's
character is profoundly negative"; so is hers, because "all our virtues
are, in fact, avoidance of vices." It is her psychological insight which
makes her understand both the power and the danger of utopias—the
risk that visions of the good will lead to murderous human
experiments—and it is that insight makes her focus on avoidance
rather than on fulfillment: on evil rather than on good, on fear rather
than on virtue ("because fear is the ultimately evil moral condition"),[18]
on injustice rather than on justice, because the sense of injustice corre-
sponds to the universal experience of citizens (or exiles) and to the basic
language of politics. Courses on political psychology should turn to

Shklar's work instead of Freudian models, and learn from her application of La Bruyère's method of portraits to the study of political character.

Finally, one cannot fail to be struck by the practical orientation of her political philosophy. She was, according to herself, *not* a philosopher. But her "phenomenological and historical political theory" did more than "sort out" political questions "in terms of the way in which they have been treated in literature, political writings and debates . . . and in political history."[19] She was passionately concerned with the significance of political concepts and theoretical issues for the daily lives of people, and one could derive from her works, especially her later ones, a set of modest proposals about the kinds of institutions and policies that would flesh out the liberalism of fear, carry out the politics of inclusion, and provide good government for people like "us."[20] Just as she wanted to relate ordinary vices to "a whole social and religious scheme," or to our contemporary "nonscheme," liberal democracy (whose "ethos of determined multiplicity" she praised),[21] she taught her students always to relate political theory to the study of politics. She wrote that she had been interested, as a young student, in "high class literary journalism."[22] Her interest in political science, in the political life of the U.S. and Europe, in the evolution of international politics, was insatiable. This woman who seemed to have read all of political philosophy, and all the books written about political theorists, was just as knowledgeable about contemporary debates on the economy, or on crime, or on science. She was, unostentatiously—she hated ostentation and pompousness —a Renaissance mind; never has the MacArthur "genius grant" been more appropriately given than when it was given to her, in 1984. The knowledge accumulated by that "bookworm" could leave her friends (surely not just me!) with a fearful sense of their own inadequacy. But she was not only a bookworm: the exile, or refugee, was a deeply worried citizen, and not merely a witness but a restless, imaginative, and generous consciousness, as well as an unpretentious but demanding conscience.

There was no one else like her, and it is high time that we study and learn from what she has given us—not only so as to measure the depth of our loss, but better to realize how much we owe her.

Notes

1. Paper on the work of Michael Walzer, delivered at American Political Science Association convention, 1991; unpublished.

2. "Redeeming American Political Theory," *American Political Science Review* 85 (1991): 3–15.

3. *After Utopia,* 96.

4. "The Liberalism of Fear," 28. Have there been many essays that pack so much thought in so few (seventeen!) pages?

5. *Legalism,* 223, 224.

6. From her essay on Walzer.

7. *The Faces of Injustice,* 40, 121. See also Bernard Yack, "Injustice and the Victim's Voice," *Michigan Law Review* 89 (May 1991): 1334–49.

8. "The Liberalism of Fear," 21.

9. *Ibid.,* 37.

10. *Ordinary Vices,* 237.

11. *The Faces of Injustice,* 122, 118–20.

12. "The Liberalism of Fear," 37. Actually, it is communitarianism which needs to be qualified by an adjective, since it can be liberal, authoritarian, totalitarian, secular, religious, etc... Shklar's liberalism of fear may not have been "comprehensive", but it was a thoroughly coherent philosophy of political life.

13. *American Citizenship,* 101.

14. Unpublished paper on justice and citizenship, 1992.

15. See "Squaring the Hermeneutic circle."

16. *Freedom and Independence,* xiv.

17. Patrick Riley, "In Memoriam Judith Shklar," unpub.

18. *Ordinary Vices,* 235, 234, 242.

19. Unpublished lecture on loyalty and obligation, at the University of Toronto, October 1991.

20. Cf. her definition of *us* in *Ordinary Vices,* 226–27.

21. *Ordinary Vices,* 248.

22. "A Life of Learning."

Part Two

Liberal Political Thought

7

Ordinary Passions in Descartes and Racine

Stephen Holmes

NOT EVEN THE MOST CIRCUMSPECT political theorist can refrain from making controversial assumptions, however latent or inchoate, about elemental human endowments and proclivities. The choice between pessimistic and optimistic assessments of mankind's capacity for rational behavior reminds us that unspoken psychological premises may also have sweeping political implications. The anti-utopian liberalism of Montesquieu, Constant, and Tocqueville, for instance, is deeply indebted to classical French moral psychology. Liberal political theory, as they developed it, depends less on a fantasy model of rational egoism than on seventeenth-century theories of violent and mindless passions and the extraordinary unlikelihood of self-control. As Bernard Yack has remarked, such apprehensions were also central to Judith Shklar's "liberalism of fear." Her political theory—like that of her liberal heroes—was founded on an unflattering but plausible conception of human character and motivation. In this chapter I will examine, in a modestly Shklaresque vein, the account of destructive and self-destructive behavior contained in two of the most provocative and influential works of classical French moral psychology. Descartes's theory of mental fixation, coupled with Racine's portrait of emotional dissonance and its consequences, helps give strikingly precise contours to the irrationality postulate underlying so much of modern liberal thought.

Descartes's Physiology of the Mind

The Passions of the Soul (1649) is devoted almost entirely to the "unruliness" of human passion in general.[1] Descartes conceives passion as a perturbation of consciousness. It is an inner "agitation" or a disorderly commotion that our body inflicts upon our soul.[2] Passions "gnaw the heart" and cloud the head.[3] They can wholly "take away or pervert the use of reason," making prudence impossible and inducing thoughtless or mindless behavior.[4] They transform even the most cautious people into hopeless *inconsidérés*.[5]

Descartes mentions disinterested goodness, of course—and in an uplifting way, as one would expect. But he thinks that passions typically make human beings disinterested in a less flattering sense. Passion-driven individuals are indifferent to their own advantage, not because of any nobility of spirit but, on the contrary, because their minds are, like Racine's Phèdre's, too tormented, distracted, and bewildered to focus steadily on the difference between a cost and a benefit. They cannot think straight and cannot begin to weigh advantages against disadvantages. Their behavior is impulsive or compulsive, impetuous or rigid. It is neither clear-eyed nor calculating. The passionate individual acts *malgré lui*. He is swept along (*emporté*) by emotions.[6] He lacks self-control and cannot pursue goals in a methodical way. No surprise, then, if he often ends up destroying himself.

The peculiar Cartesian theory of mind-body interaction naturally provides crucial background for this discussion. Much of Descartes's analysis is physiological, a bottom-up or anatomical account of psychic turbulence. Passions are obscure and confused thoughts excited in the soul by a jostling of nerves and a swish of the blood. Psychosomatic compulsions represent the body's tyranny over the soul. As a child, for instance, Descartes fell in love with a girl who squinted in a cross-eyed fashion. The fortuitous conjunction of the feeling of love with the sight of squinty eyes produced a crease (*un pli*) in Descartes's brain. This cerebral pleat, in turn, inclined him thereafter to love anyone who squinted.[7] Infantile imprinting on the basis of fluke association explains some of the most irrational and inappropriate forms of human behavior.[8]

In general, the body is the sole source of human irrationality.[9] This is Descartes's succinct rebuttal of what we can anachronistically call the rational actor theory. *Man could be a truly rational maximizer only if he could live without a body.* Because people have bodies, for good or ill, they can almost never be wholly rational. Our soul is constantly irritated and disturbed because it is so closely united with "the machine of our body."[10] Within this bodily machine, the apertures of the heart flap open and shut mechanically, while microscopic particles of agitated blood career violently through a labyrinth of canals, eventually colliding with the pineal gland and thereby upsetting and flummoxing the soul. Descartes occasionally describes the passions as instruments by which the body deftly manipulates the soul into doing its bidding. In such passages, he stresses the utility of passions such as hunger for the conservation of the body.[11] But most of his examples suggest that the body is relatively stupid or inept at rational self-preservation. Many objects that stir irresistible or addictive cravings are obviously harmful, for instance.[12] Similarly, passions frequently divert us from repulsing physical injuries which could quite easily be avoided if our minds were unclouded and on the alert.[13]

We experience passions as involuntary spasms. We blush, blanch, cringe, tremble, weep, faint, or explode with laughter—without any contribution of our will.[14] We are "seized" by passions and turned into helpless automations. It is not surprising, given this somewhat ridiculous state of affairs, that the soul can both desire and not desire the same object at the same time.[15] To illustrate the lack of self-control characteristic of passion-besotted souls, Descartes emphasizes both unaccountable mood swings and inner inconsistency.[16] Even a husband who feels a "secret joy" at the death of his wife will nevertheless cry involuntarily at her funeral, because that is what his body, aroused by the sight of coffins and crepe, incites his soul to do.[17]

The Dominant Human Passion

So far I have documented Descartes's general doubts about the human capacity for rational behavior. But the most original thesis in the *The Passions of the Soul*, as well as the one most relevant to our discussion of *Phèdre* below, concerns "the first of all the passions."[18] What is the dominant emotion in the human mind, according to Descartes? What is the ultimate source of all irrational behavior? It is, surprisingly enough, the inability to control one's attention. All secondary passions—such as love and hate—are permeated by this primary passion, which has a physiological source and accounts for the inherent irrationality of all passion-driven behavior. Although this claim is somewhat unfamiliar, it is extremely important and deserves to be examined in some detail. Descartes is thinking, first of all, of stupefaction or paralyzed fascination. Fastened to the machine of its body, the mind tends to be awestruck, say, by surprise and, as a result, to lose full control over attention.[19] New and strange situations stun, mesmerize, and paralyze the soul. Our minds are amazed before they can assess the advantages or disadvantages of a captivating object. Like a deer petrified by a headlight, human consciousness becomes rigidly fixated on observed things solely because they are unexpected or rare, not because they are useful or intrinsically worthy of careful consideration. We gape, like fools. This compulsive infatuation of consciousness is imposed by the body which, for its part, freezes up like a statue.[20] The ability to be wonder struck or astonished (*étonné*) may have been planted by nature to make men capable of learning. But, in practice, astonishment inhibits learning, transfixing our gaze on mere surfaces, precluding detached, flexible, and free-ranging inquiry, and thus preventing rationally adaptive behavior. Destructive passions have a tendency to congeal into destructive habits. In this case, people become senselessly addicted to the unexpected, that is, physically hooked on entranced states of mind in which purposiveness, calculation, and appropriateness to the situation lie beyond their powers.

Passion deprives the will of the ability to control or guide mental concentration. That is the main "mechanism" by which it subverts rationality, explaining why Descartes ascribes psychological primacy to stupefaction or mental fixation. Love and hate, for example, would not be such ruinous passions if they did not rigidly dictate the focus of all our thoughts. Passions make rational behavior difficult or impossible because they physiologically compel the mind to dwell hypnotically on useless or harmful thoughts. They turn our attention away from achievable goals, for instance, gluing the mind helplessly to unfulfillable projects and wild dreams.[21] Central to Cartesian psychology, therefore, is the category of irrational desire, inherited from classical and scholastic thought but now explained in physiological terms, as a product of consciously unmasterable fixation.[22]

Emotion-driven assessments of reality are utterly untrustworthy because based on a highly selective view of the relevant facts. Formulated differently, man is an essentially irrational animal because the focus of his attention, what captivates his mind and eye, is seldom controlled by rational estimates of available opportunities or costs and benefits. Descartes sometimes makes this basic point by describing passion as a magnifying glass built into the soul. It produces cognitive distortion by exaggerating the importance of the goods and evils to which it staples our attention.[23] Passion makes bad reasons seem more convincing than they are, while dimming the force of good reasons. It stirs us to respond with more ardor than we should. It leads us to concentrate fussily on paltry matters to the neglect of what, from a prudential standpoint, are much more significant dangers and opportunities. In other words, emotions demolish any sense of perspective or proportion. This should come as no surprise since, as everyone knows, rational comparison becomes impossible in the frenzy of passion.

Jealousy is a good example.[24] On the flimsiest possible evidence, a jealous individual will lurch uncontrollably into a torrent of suspicions. Other emotions, too, make us respond inappropriately to objects and events. Sexual attraction is a case in point. Our body compels our soul to conceive sexual intercourse as the *summum bonum,* "the greatest of all imaginable goods."[25] This is not a rational assessment, according to Descartes. Romantic love (defined clinically as a gurgling of warm particles around the heart) is a form of mesmerization. It is a confused thought that inclines us to focus obsessively and adhere physically to whatever we love. It is irrational, as the case of Phèdre will amply demonstrate, because it induces maniacal fixation and tunnel consciousness. Love is therefore even more dangerous than hate. For the frivolous pleasures of the loved one, it will bring about the ruin of the world. Love will sacrifice everything to "the extravagance of its fury."[26]

Cowardice is a similarly irrational emotion, a "coldness" that spreads through the limbs and that "diverts the will from useful actions" simply by *blinding* the coward to available chances for self-defense.[27] Fright is defined as "a trouble and astonishment in the soul" that prevents a person from fighting back when attacked.[28] It is a physiological convulsion that interferes with a cool survey of the circumstances and therefore prevents the choice of a situationally adequate response. Congealed into a habit, this momentary stupor becomes dejection, moroseness, abjectness, and weakness of the will—character traits described jointly as *la bassesse,* or "self-mistrust."[29] Such dispositional weaknesses are in no one's self-interest and add nothing to the survivability of either the species or the group. To emphasize the physiological origins of this kind of pathological modesty, Descartes notes that it is communicated involuntarily. People can "read" your self-contempt from your twisted posture, skulking gait, and downcast eyes.

A truly rational actor, according to Descartes, will focus on the future, not on the past. He will not mope listlessly over spilled milk, but will concentrate shrewdly on outcomes that can be influenced by planning and effort. Passion-driven behavior is additionally irrational, therefore, whenever it involves a retrospective rather than consequentialist twist of mind. Regret is always an error.[30] Some people are so thoroughly crushed by guilt and remorse that they even turn a blind eye to oncoming problems, making matters worse.[31] Here again, human attention is being emotionally misdirected. Busy licking their wounds, people do not even notice when they are about to be attacked a second time. Remorse sometimes gels into a habit, a feeling that pervades all of life independent of changing circumstances. People afflicted with this malady feel culpable or derelict automatically—no matter what they do or fail to do.[32]

Loyalty, Envy, and Revenge

But what about the irrational sources of violence and physical aggression? Writing in seventeenth-century France, Descartes naturally
associates psychological with social chaos, the inward anarchy of the
passions with the outward anarchy of Europe's religious civil wars. Not
by chance, therefore, he identifies one of the most ruinous of all the
passions as *dévotion,* or selfless loyalty. This emotion again involves a
prerational channeling of human attention, a kind of erotic identification with (and submission to) a leader or a group. We project our identities onto our prince or country and become, thereby, willing to kill and
die for their sake.[33] Loyalty of this sort leads the individual to neglect
his self-interest, narrowly understood, and to sacrifice himself for the
object of his devotion.[34] Needless to say, blind loyalty is a mind-fixating
emotion supremely useful to secular or religious leaders involved in dy-
nastic or sectarian squabbles and annexationist adventures.

From the nation builder's viewpoint, loyalty is a two-edged sword.
The state needs loyal citizens. But if subjects passionately identify with
lesser notables and rival subgroups within the community, civil war may
well result. Factionalism, too, thrives upon the universal human propensity for selfless devotion. Descartes speaks in this regard of "false
devotion," meaning loyalty unregulated by the rational desire for civil
peace. Because zeal is often irrational, in this sense, it can propel fac-
tions into "the greatest crimes that men can commit—such as betraying
cities, assassinating princes, and exterminating entire peoples simply
because they do not share their opinions."[35] Given the amount of blood
shed in the name of groups, Nannerl Keohane probably devotes too
much attention, in her discussion of Descartes's psychology, to his
search for an "antidote to radical individualism."[36] The most powerful
disintegrative force in French history was obviously not individualism,
but its opposite, namely, man's social instinct, his passion-dictated tendency to cluster into homogeneous groups.

That "certain people take offense at the good things they see hap-
pening to other men" appears perfectly obvious to Descartes.[37] He defines envy, in fact, simply as "a kind of hate."[38] A wholly rational man
would be perfectly nonenvious. He would never allow his mind to lin-
ger painfully on an enviable neighbor, but would deftly refocus his attention toward equals or perhaps toward people who are worse off than
himself, and who may even envy him.[39] But the mind almost never se-
lects the objects of its fascination in order to maximize utility. In fact,
the mind does not select the object of its attention at all. There is no
rational choice in this fundamental domain because there is no choice
at all. An unmistakable sign of the irrationality of the envious is their

pitiable tendency to afflict themselves, to exacerbate their own misery by dwelling obsessively—as they have no good reason to do—on their own relative disadvantage.[40] Envious behavior is agitated, confused, and driven by a perverse and insatiable desire to cut others down to one's own size.[41] Descartes writes explicitly about traits and possessions that are esteemed less if widely shared.[42] In his correspondence he invokes the following example: "a man who possessed only a thousand pistols would be very rich, if there was no one else in the world who had so many; but the same man would be very poor if everyone else owned more."[43] Here the value we derive from ownership is strictly derivative from the symbolic superiority this ownership conveys. The universal human scramble for positional goods is an irrational perversion of course. Goods which are truly valuable—such as virtue, science, and health—retain their value even if widely shared. But most people cannot attend exclusively to such absolute values to the neglect of positional goods because they are unable to master their passions, that is, they simply cannot control the focus of their thoughts.

Descartes has a similar view of the "ardent desire for vengeance."[44] Like all acts committed in anger, revenge is irrational. By concentrating fixedly on retaliation, we expose ourselves to fresh injuries coming from new and unexpected enemies. Like remorse, moreover, revenge is backward looking. From a strictly rational standpoint, the original injury for which one craves revenge is water under the bridge. Nothing one does now will undo the original damage. Indeed, revenge breeds revenge, in a notoriously endless cycle. Thus, from a coolly consequentialist standpoint, retaliation is morally insane: it will make everyone worse off. But people throw themselves into cycles of revenge because they are not rational. They brood obsessively over every loss of face, spending sleepless nights plotting to take an eye for an eye. They imagine absurdly that revenge stands to injury as soap to dirt, that vengeance will wipe clean a hideous stain in the world.

Descartes argues that "the desire to repulse harmful things and to avenge oneself" is the "most urgent" of all the secondary passions.[45] His fullest discussion of the irrationality of revenge occurs in a famous letter of 1645. The relevant paragraph is worth citing at length:

> Anger can sometimes excite in us desires for vengeance so violent that it makes us imagine more pleasure in punishing our enemy than in conserving our honor or our life—and they make us imprudently risk both for such a cause. Whereas, if reason examined the good, or the perfection, on which this pleasure of revenge is founded, it would discover no other (at least when revenge does not prevent someone from injuring us again) than this: it makes us imagine that we have some advantage over

those on whom we take revenge. But this is often nothing else than an absurd fancy [*une vaine imagination*], that merits no respect compared to honor or life, or even compared to the satisfaction one derives from seeing oneself master one's anger in abstaining from revenge.[46]

Violent passions subvert common rationality and derail the instinct of self-preservation by fixating the mind on a shadowy mirage. Or rather, the longing for revenge colonizes the instinct for self-preservation itself, making the vengeful man believe that the "higher self" he must preserve involves a socially acknowledged superiority over the person or group who has purportedly done him wrong. If we made a rational comparison we would often see the wastefulness or even idiocy of retaliation. But the passion-besotted mind is maniacal and knows no comparisons. By contrast to backward-looking vengefulness, the forward-looking desire for self-preservation is a cool and rational motivation.

In several important passages, Descartes notes that the will cannot control the passions directly, but must instead resort to indirection by manipulating the focal point of attention. By conjuring up an emotionally charged image, the soul can provoke a psychophysical response. It can thus control one passion by arousing another with contrary effects. His principal example here is the classical one: the passion of fear can be defeated by the passions of glory and shame.[47] When we are about to run away from battle, we can focus our minds on the disgrace of cowardice, the embarrassing thought of how others will view our craven flight, and thus keep ourselves dutifully at our post. For students of the Hirschman thesis, this example is interesting because it shows that glory itself was originally conceived as a countervailing passion.[48] Indeed, one might even say that the Hobbesian appeal to the fear of death against the longing for glory was nothing but a reversal of the traditional appeal to glory against fear.

Descartes explicitly advocates the use of countervailing passions, including glory against fear, because passions cannot be controlled directly. But he is not at all consistent on this point. He also denounces the very idea of countervailing passions on the grounds that conflict between passions will produce not equilibrium but chaos. We may have a situation, for example, in which "fear represents death as an extreme evil that can be avoided only by flight" and, at the same time, "ambition represents the infamy of flight as an evil worse than death." In this case, "these two passions will act differently on the will." Obeying first one and then the other passion, the will will be "constantly opposed to itself," rendering the soul "enslaved and unhappy."[49] This pathetically divided condition is relatively common. Inner emotional conflict, in fact, is an immensely important source of human irrationality. To explore this theme, we can do no better than to turn to Racine's most famous work.

Psychological Conflict in Racine

In his ingratiating preface to *Phèdre* (1677), Racine inexplicably presents this deeply disquieting play as a wholesome moral lesson. Here we see passions leading to disorder, he writes. Here we see vice mercilessly punished. What better evidence can a playwright provide that the theater is indeed a school of virtue?[50] Readers of the play, however, have searched in vain for the "useful instructions" that Racine purportedly planted there. What leaps to the eye, by contrast, is the unprecedented juxtaposition of savagery and propriety. This clash between bestiality and courtesy, between breathtaking cruelty and fastidious etiquette, leaves the audience with a sense of rawness and unease—a discomfort exacerbated, despite prefatory reassurances, by the lack of any edifying moral lesson. Virtue is not rewarded. No cosmic balance is restored. Racine casts an imperturbably icy gaze upon the excruciating conflict within Phèdre between her love and her shame. While Phèdre views her own passion for Hippolyte morally or judgmentally, Racine views it amorally or neutrally—clinically, one might even say, in the manner of Descartes.

Ultimately, *Phèdre* remains an endlessly fascinating work, first of all, because of the affectless way it explores affectual conflict. But readers educated on the motivational assumptions of modern economics will probably be most surprised by Racine's Cartesian disregard for enlightened self-interest. The calculating pursuit of personal advantage plays only a marginal role in the dramatic events of the play. The behavior vivisected is compulsive, not calculating. The characters are swept away by passions or gripped by inherited injunctions laying down what must (and especially what must not) be done. They seldom think strategically about foreseeable consequences or about alternatives they might reasonably choose. The entire play is a drawn-out act of suicide, conveying unmistakably that Racine does not view self-preservation as the decisive human motivation. What he emphasizes instead is the self-destructiveness of Phèdre's sentiments and actions.[51] Her self-hate inundates her self-love.

The treacherous passion that most preoccupies Racine is love—what he calls *fol amour*.[52] Love is a kind of madness, a disorder in the soul, more destructive than hate. Racine describes it as a frenzy, a delirium, a furious fire, an insane longing, and a fatal poison.[53] Being in love is an *égarement*, a having lost one's way. This raging passion blinds the eyes and clouds the mind. It robs you of your wits.[54] The lover is spellbound, dazed, enthralled. Such trancelike rapture puts a comparison of costs and benefits utterly beyond one's powers. Phèdre is agitated, confused, and internally torn. She is literally "beside herself" (*hors d'elle-même*), unable to perceive her interests or act upon her sense of justice.[55] To show that amorousness is impetuous, even convulsive, Racine stresses love's physiological symptoms, very much along the lines laid down in *The Passions of the Soul*. At the sight of the beloved, the lover burns and shivers, trembles involuntarily, falls speechless, draws a mental blank, and gapes like someone bewitched.[56] Phèdre would be much better off if she could simply divert her attention to other matters or look the other way, but, as Descartes would have said, she is an empassioned woman and therefore cannot control the focus of her thoughts.[57]

In the grip of passionate love, Phèdre is utterly helpless. She battles valiantly against her infatuation and manages to appear appropriately *pudique* for a time. But eventually her resolve is shattered by circumstances. Despite her vow of silence, she blurts out to Hippolyte her crazed longing, precipitating the tragic denouement.[58] In another crucial scene, she seems to have resolved to tell Thésée that Hippolyte is innocent of an attempt to seduce her. But the news that Hippolyte loves Aricie hits her like a lightning bolt.[59] Shocked minds cannot act reasonably. Her jealousy is so acute that it ties her tongue, preventing her from acting on her obviously sincere commitment to truth and justice. Even when such a passion-induced state of panic endures only for a moment, it can set irreversible processes in motion and thereby do permanent damage. Jealousy momentarily (but fatally) overwhelms Phèdre's sense of justice. One motive tips the scales against another, producing inner confusion and outward disaster.

Love itself is not presented here as soft and lyrical. It is less companionate than possessive—even vindictive. The sheer violence and brutality of love is conveyed by the striking image of Venus, ravenously gnawing at the person who has fallen in love, her wounded prey.[60] Aricie describes her own love for Hippolyte in martial terms, as a conquest in which she can gain honor by subduing a yet unvanquished foe.[61] What most excites her about Hippolyte is the thought of causing him to pine and struggle futilely against his chains.[62] In his helplessness, she will be able to contemplate triumphantly her own power. To fall in love is to suffer, as Venus's painful arrow also makes brutally clear.[63]

Along with her love, of course, Phèdre feels guilt, or perhaps shame. She is tortured by remorse. Her passion for Hippolyte is always accompanied by inward distress: she is repulsed by her love even while she feels it.[64] Her burning desire is inseparable from a burning sense of self-disgust, a profound belief that hers is the foulest of desires. This specific psychological conflict, central to the play, cannot be accurately described as a clash between passion and reason.[65] Her shame is not particularly reasonable. Indeed, it is just as hysterical and delirious as her love. The source of Phèdre's shame is a half-conscious belief that she has violated some primitive incest taboo.[66] But this belief is not especially reasonable. Neither is her inner attachment to the incest taboo presented as strategic or even a matter of thought. Shame wells up inside her, involuntarily, very much like love. It, too, is a compulsive reflex of the mind, with physiological symptoms, and which has nothing whatever to do with calculations of personal advantage. She has internalized a norm, and it seizes her emotionally. When she violates this norm, she suffers physiological torments: burning, choking, trembling. Phèdre's shame is not powerful enough to suppress her illicit love. But it certainly affects her action, poisoning her existence and driving her to suicide.

Racine, as mentioned, views this ruinous conflict between love and shame with a cold, clinical, and amoral eye. He does not take sides or draw our attention to helpful lessons. His amazing refusal to paint moral norms as morally admirable, in a conventional manner, is conveyed, for instance, by Oenone's brutal statement that Phèdre should sacrifice everything to her honor, even if this means Hippolyte's death.[67] The unspeakable cruelty of the ordinary ideal of honor is also displayed in Thésée's response to the false report that his son has attempted to seduce his wife. He begs Neptune, with palpable sincerity, to drown Hippolyte in his own blood.[68] Here, it seems safe to say, addiction to the social norm of shameless honor, to an unstained reputation, is presented as just as violent and irrational as the ferocious passion of love. This even-handed treatment of norms on the one hand and passions on the other is reinforced by Racine's description of Thésée's reaction to the false report. He responds automatically, reflexively, without thinking. His total lack of self-awareness is emphasized when he confronts Hippolyte. He is unable to hear anything Hippolyte says, of course. But he also accuses his son of viewing adultery as some kind of a game—a risible accusation since that is exactly the way Thésée himself views adultery.[69]

The fundamental love/shame conflict within Phèdre's emotional-mental world leads directly to self-hate.[70] Inner divisions, if sufficiently intense, trigger wildly aggressive behavior toward oneself. Phèdre is nauseated by her own feelings, to the point of despising her very existence.[71] She experiences herself as a defiling presence—as if all living creatures found her physically repulsive. To snuff out her noxious passion, she is willing to extinguish her life. To die is to remove her pollution and foulness from the world, to leave the planet purified and clean.

Despite Racine's preface, this longing for self-erasure is presented non-judgmentally, and therefore eerily, as just another pathological condition, similar to love, neither a virtue nor a vice. Racine underscores the passivity of passion by describing Phèdre's love for Hippolyte as the product of divine cruelty. Her crime itself, he says, is a punishment of the gods, not a product of her will.[72] But how can she be justly punished for an act of sadism committed against her? The God who incited Hippolyte's horses to run wild symbolizes perfectly the brutality of divine intervention. Dragged by the runaway animals, Hippolyte daubs the sharp rocks with bits of his torn flesh and gushing blood, his body being gruesomely macerated into one large meaty wound before he dies.[73] To be in love is to be a plaything of cruel gods. We are born combustible, we do not know why, but we are condemned for it anyway. There is no good reason why the gods treat human beings in this way, but they do. (In Christian theology, incidentally, the question is, Why does God give us a law, without the strength to obey it, and then condemn us for our inevitable disobedience? That Racine was conscious of this hint of cosmic sadism lying at the heart of Christian theology is beyond question.[74] In *Phèdre* he handles this problem discreetly, projecting inexplicable divine cruelty onto pagan gods whom Christians have no obligation to love.)

Phèdre, the eloquent surface of which I have barely scratched, reveals several vital assumptions of seventeenth-century French moral psychology, which help deepen and complete the Cartesian picture of human unreason. First, passionate love is a more dangerous motive than rational self-interest. Love can be more dangerous than interest because it involves mental fixation, and is therefore more difficult to influence strategically or guard against. Second, visceral self-hate is a common pathological condition, resulting from unmasterable conflict between unmasterable passions. Human beings neither love themselves nor act consistently for their own interest and preservation because their raw emotions vehemently collide. The conflict within Phèdre between love and shame reveals the most important theoretical implication of the play. The idea of suppressing the violent passion for glory by the mild passion for moneymaking, brilliantly examined by Hirschmann, must be located within a more general picture of multiple psychological antagonisms common in seventeenth-century works.[75] But countervailing passions do not necessarily lead to equipoise, balance, or moderation. This is a point first made philosophically by Descartes and later dramatized unforgettably by Racine. One motive set resolutely against another can lead to inner confusion and self-torture. The behavioral consequences of such irresolvable psychological strains are highly context dependent and therefore unpredictable. But inward warfare may well bring bloody aggression toward others, not merely suicidal self-hatred, in its train.

Conclusion

Neither Descartes nor Racine developed his subtle perspectives on human irrationality with political questions foremost in their minds. But their complementary analyses of mental fixation and irresolvable emotional conflicts are immensely persuasive and rich with implications. The implausible hypothesis that man is a rational maximizer of personal advantage, always strategically pursuing self-preservation and other subjectively valued goals, will naturally have problems gaining a purchase in cultures where works of this stripe are carefully studied and admired. It is no surprise, in any case, that those later liberals who wrote under the influence of French moral psychology incorporated these and similar insights into their more explicitly political theories. In fact, if liberal aspirations still survive in a turbulent world, it may well be because liberalism itself was originally crafted by theorists with a realistic appreciation, garnered from works like *Phèdre* and *The Passions of the Soul,* of the irrepressible follies and foibles of mankind.

Notes

1. That is, to "les dérèglements des passions." See René Descartes, *Les Passions de l'âme* (Paris, 1988), art. 156, p. 247; 161. All subsequent article and page citations are to this volume. Translations are mine.

2. Art. 28, p. 172; art. 52, p. 189.

3. Art. 202, p. 272.

4. Art. 76, p. 199.

5. Art. 143, p. 238.

6. Art. 202, p. 272.

7. Descartes, letter to Chanut, 6 June 1647, 1277; all letters are cited from Descartes, *Oeuvres et lettres,* ed. André Bridoux (Paris, 1953).

8. Art. 136, pp. 232–33.

9. Art. 47, p. 184.

10. Art. 13, p. 164.

11. Art. 52, p. 190; art. 137, pp. 233–34.

12. Art. 138, p. 234.

13. Art. 203, p. 273.

14. Letter of 6 Oct. 1645, to Princess Elizabeth, 1212.

15. There is no rational way to achieve one's goals when "l'âme se sent poussée presque en même temps et désirer et ne désirer pas une même chose" (art. 47, p. 184).

16. Often, "on se sent triste ou joyeux sans en pouvoir dire aucun sujet" (art. 51, p. 189).

17. Art. 147, p. 242.

18. Descartes's own term is *l'admiration*, or "wonderment" (art. 53, p. 190). According to Anthony Levi, *l'admiration* is "a stranger to the scholastic list" of the passions, and therefore seems to be a Cartesian innovation (Anthony Levi, *French Moralists: The Theory of the Passions 1585–1649* [Oxford, 1964], 275).

19. A parallel but contrary tendency is daydreaming or aimless mental drift: "notre pensée erre, nonchalament, sans s'appliquer à rien de soi-même" (art. 21, p. 168).

20. When the soul is stupefied, "tout le corps demeure immobile comme une statue" (art. 73, p. 198).

21. Art. 145, p. 239.

22. See for example the letter of 1 Feb. 1647, to Hector-Pierre Chanut, 1266.

23. Art. 138, p. 234. Cf.: "souvent la passion nous fait croire certaines choses beaucoup meilleures et plus désiderables qu'elles ne sont" (letter to Princess Elizabeth of 1 Sept. 1645, p. 1202); "toutes nos passions nous représentent les biens, à la recherche desquels elles nous incitent, beaucoup plus grands qu'ils ne sont véritablement" (letter of 15 Sept. 1645, to Princess Elizabeth, 1207).

24. Art. 167, p. 255.

25. Art. 90, p. 208.

26. Letter of 1 Feb. 1647, to Chanut, 1267.

27. Art. 175, p. 259.

28. Art. 174, pp. 258–59.

29. Art. 159, pp. 249–50; art. 205, p. 274.

30. The suggestion that discontent is almost inevitably psychotic (art. 198, pp. 269–70), that is, that people feel afflicted solely because they are irrational, is one of the most bizarre features of Descartes's retrieval of Stoic and Epicurean ethics.

31. Art. 177, p. 260.

32. Art. 191, pp. 266–67.

33. Filled with *dévotion,* it seems, "on ne craint pas de mourir" (art. 83, p. 204).

34. "De quoi on a vu souvent des exemples en ceux ceux qui se sont exposés à une mort certaine pour la défense de leur prince ou de leur ville, et même aussi quelquefois pour des personnes particulières auxquelles ils s'étaient dévoués" (art. 83, p. 204).

35. Art. 190, p. 266.

36. Nannerl O. Keohane, *Philosophy and the State in France: The Renaissance to the Enlightenment* (Princeton, N.J., 1980), 207.

37. Art. 182, p. 262.

38. Letter of Sept. 1646, to Princess Elizabeth, 1240.

39. Notice that "les princes n'ont pas coutume d'être enviés par le commun de leurs sujets" (ibid., 1240) because people will envy someone—that is, focus attention resentfully on his advantages—only if they believe themselves roughly comparable with him.

40. Art. 184, p. 263.

41. That is, "d'abaisser tous les autres hommes" (art. 158, p. 249).

42. Ibid.

43. Letter of 6 June 1647, 1276.

44. Art. 202, p. 272.

45. Art. 190, p. 270.

46. Letter to Princess Elizabeth of 1 Sept. 1645, 1203.

47. He recognizes that *la hardièsse* can be cultivated in soldiers only if they concentrate on the hope for "la gloire après leur mort" (art. 173, p. 258); this countervailing strategy is already lucidly described in *The Iliad*, bk. 11, lines 400–410.

48. Albert O. Hirschman, *The Passions and the Interests* (Princeton, N.J., 1977).

49. Art. 48, pp. 185–86.

50. Racine, *Phèdre*, in *Théâtre complète de Racine,* ed. Maurice Rat (Paris, 1947), 542. All subsequent page citations are to this volume. Translations are mine.

51. Phèdre's residual instinct for self-preservation seems to be externalized or projected onto her solicitous maidservant, Oenone, who eventually commits suicide herself. Note that Oenone, who is personally responsible for Hippolyte's tragic end, is herself motivated by selfless devotion—an extremely dangerous emotion, as Descartes, too, explained.

52. *Phèdre,* 546.

53. For example, "fureur" (566); "ardeurs insensées" (567); "mes transports / Les fureurs de mes feux" (581); and Hippolyte speaking about Thésée: "Quel funeste poison / L'amour a répandu sur toute sa maison!" (573).

54. Phèdre speaks of: "ma raison égarée" (552) and the "fol amour ceux qui trouble ma raison" (564).

55. *Phèdre,* 541.

56. Most strikingly, Phèdre describes her encounter with Hippolyte: "Je le vis, je rougis, je pâlis à sa vue; / Un trouble s'éleva dans mon âme éperdue; / Mes yeux ne voyaient plus, je ne pouvais parler; / Je sentis tout mon corps et transir et brûler; / Je reconnus Vénus et ses feux redoutables, / D'un sang qu'elle pursuit, tourments inévitables" (552).

57. Oenone says to Phèdre, "Vous nourrissez un feu qu'il vous faudrait éteindre" (566). Hippolyte is similarly fixated on Aricie, seeing her face wherever he looks (559).

58. In her words, "ma folle ardeur malgré moi se déclare" (562).

59. *Phèdre,* 580.

60. "C'est Vénus toute entière à sa proie attachée" (552).

61. In economic terms, Hippolyte is a positional good, a commodity made more valuable by the fact that other women have never been able to seduce him.

62. "Mais de faire fléchir un courage inflexible, / De porter la douleur dans une âme insensible, / D'enchaîner un captif de ses fers étonné, / Contre un joug ceux qui lui plaît vainement mutiné; / C'est là ce que je veux; c'est là ce ceux qui m'irrite" (557).

63. In praying that Hippolyte will fall in love with her, Phèdre begs Venus to avenge herself on him: "Déesse, venge-toi" (568).

64. To Hippolyte she says, "J'aime. Ne pense pas qu'au moment que je t'aime, / Innocente à mes yeux, je m'approuve moi-mème" (564).

65. After hearing of Hippolyte's love for Aricie, Phèdre says, "Il faut perdre Aricie" (581), but promptly realizes the injustice of killing an innocent person in a fit of passion. This particular seesaw between passion and reason contrasts sharply with the play's fundamental conflict between Phèdre's love and her shame. Her shame itself is feverish, nothing at all like a clear-eyed sense of the difference between justice and injustice.

66. She calls her passion incestuous, even though she has no blood relationship to Hippolyte: "Je respire à la fois l'inceste et l'imposture" (582).

67. In Oenone's words, "pour sauver votre honneur combattu, / Il faut immoler tout" (571).

68. This is Thésée's prayer: "étouffe dans son sang ses désirs effrontés" (576).

69. *Phèdre,* 578, 572.

70. "Je m'abhorre" (564), and "Je ne puis sans horreur me regarder moi-mème" (565).

71. "J'ai pris la vie en haine et ma flamme en horreur" (552).

72. He says in the preface, "son crime est plutôt une punition des dieux qu'un mouvement de sa volonté" (540).

73. *Phèdre,* 590.

74. Jocaste, in Racine's *La Thébaïde,* says: "Voilà de ces grands dieux la suprème justice! / Jusques au bord du crime ils conduisent nos pas; / Ils nous le font commettre, et ne l'excusent pas!" (act 3, scene 2).

75. These multiple overlapping conflicts appear even more complicated when we see that passions, interests, and norms may not only conflict, but may also reinforce one another. A particularly good example is Hippolyte's love for Aricie, which appears to have been at least partly provoked by the norm (promulgated by Hippolyte's father) of putting Aricie strictly off limits as a marriage partner. Since forbidden fruit is always sweeter, a prohibitory norm can awaken passions that otherwise would have remained dormant.

8

The Self Knowing the Self in the Work of Jean-Jacques Rousseau

Tracy B. Strong

Énigme	*Riddle*
Enfant de l'Art, Enfant de la Nature	Child of Art, Child of Nature,
Sans prolonger les jours j'empêche de mourir:	Without prolonging time, I keep death back;
Plus je suis vrai, plus je fais l'imposture,	The truer I am, the more an impostor.
et je deviens trop jeune à force de vieillir.	And my aging makes me too young.[1]

THE ANSWER TO ROUSSEAU'S RIDDLE is, of course, "My Portrait." Written at age thirty, in 1742, when Rousseau was first making his mark on Paris, the riddle and its answer reflect a lifelong concern. Any representation must by virtue of what it is betray the reality of that which it represents. This presented him, as a writer, with the problem of how to make available what he had to say to the world in such a manner that the world did not misread it. Nor was this a problem only in, as it were, art. What could be "true" knowledge of an other? The problem of the portrait is the problem of the knowledge of others.

Judith Shklar once declared to her somewhat stunned seminar on political thought from Locke to Kant that while she might be married to Bentham, she would have an affair with Rousseau. She meant, among other things, I think, that an encounter with Rousseau seem to forbid mediation, that his writings made a demand which was personal and not (just) institutional. The sense that Rousseau's books require a direct and unmediated response is not an invention of only latter-day readers, often desirous of placing blame for the political horrors of the twentieth century. Already in Rousseau's time, his readers wrote to him and spoke of him to others as if he were their personal friend.[2]

What is achieved by a writing that has such presence? Rousseau has often been criticized for a certain lack of philosophical rigor. He is compared unfavorably to, say, Hume or Kant, where, at least, one can find *arguments*. It is also quite true that one finds precious little of what might be called argument in Rousseau's texts. Instead, there are striking turns of phrase, novels, calculated and explicit ignorance of facts, dialogues, reveries, confessions. It is such a literary sensibility that if his work convinces at all, it convinces only in the way that art does. It is also the case that Rousseau sought quite consciously to write in such a manner that one could not avoid encountering him as a distinct individual. Kant, by counterexample, is only very rarely present to the readers in his texts. *The Critique of Pure Reason* appears to present itself to its readers more or less without its author. This is not the sense we have when reading Rousseau. There we feel the person.

The personal encounter demands a different quality of response than that which I might call intellectual, in that one cannot as easily hold a person at a distance in the way that one can hold a text, or even the author of a text. Indeed, one can probably not hold a person *as a person* at distance at all. Or, more accurately, one can only hold a person at distance by treating him or her not as a person but as an object. A person is not wrong or right in the way an argument is; indeed, one would not even raise such questions. It is precisely Rousseau's ability to achieve this kind of almost bodily presence to his readers that is at the root of his greatness. Rousseau wants to become part of our sensibility rather than convince us that he is right.

I want to explore in the words of Rousseau the relationship between the encounter with a person and the encounter with a text. It is clear that Rousseau thought the two had an intimate relation, one to the other. The text in which Rousseau broaches this question the most explicitly is the *Dialogues: Rousseau Judge of Jean-Jacques*. The immediate precipitant of the work is Rousseau's conviction that there existed a plot to defame him. The work consists of three dialogues between a Frenchman and "Rousseau." The topic of their exchange is "Jean-Jacques," whom the Frenchman dislikes and whom Rousseau is defending. The purpose of the *Dialogues* is for the Frenchman to see Jean-Jacques for what he is, to make available to others the "eye" with which Jean-Jacques (Rousseau) might actually be seen by others for what he is.

The dialogues themselves are preceded by a discussion of the "Nature and Form of this Writing," which explains that the dialogue form is appropriate to a discussion of whether or not there is a plot against

Rousseau, led by, among others Grimm, Diderot, and d'Alembert. They are followed by a "History of the Preceding Work." The architecture of the work closes it in on itself. In it Rousseau seeks to know himself and does so in the context of making himself known to another. It is thus an attempt to examine himself as the society for himself. In the *Confessions* he speaks of the "need for intimate society, as intimate as it could possibly be." Such a society would be so intimate that "the narrowest union of bodies would not have been adequate: one would have needed two souls in the same body. Without that I felt myself always in emptiness [*dans le vide*]."[3] The *Dialogues* are an effort to make his life available to himself and thus to others.

The task, then, as the beginning of the second dialogue makes clear, is to move from simply reading him to seeing him.[4] This has been difficult, for "Jean-Jacques" (the character in the dialogue, who is the subject of the portrait the author of the dialogue wants to paint) has by his behavior encouraged misrepresentation. "Rousseau" says:

> I have seen him in a unique and almost incredible position, more alone in Paris than Robinson [Crusoe] in his island, sequestered from interaction [*commerce*] with humans by the crowd pressing to surround him and keeping him from attaching himself to anyone. I have seen him voluntarily go along with his persecutors in order ceaselessly to render himself more isolated, and, while they worked without pause to keep him separate from others, he would distance himself more and more from others and from them.[5]

Feeling himself alone in the crowd, he cannot be seen. Rousseau (the author) even tries, in a paroxysm of hubristic despair, to deposit a copy of the manuscript of the dialogues on the high altar at Notre Dame, only to find his way barred by a grillwork which he claims has never to that day been there. The whole purpose of the *Dialogues* is bring the quality of the person, in this case both the author and the subject of the text, together with the text. At the end of the first dialogue "Rousseau" indicates that he is going off to see Jean-Jacques. The Frenchman indicates on the other hand that he is going to go and *read* "Jean-Jacques." The book is an attempt to bring the man and his words together so that he can be seen for what he actually is.

"Rousseau" has seen "Jean-Jacques," and throughout the second dialogue "Rousseau" attempts to depict "Jean-Jacques" as he "really" is, admitting even that the *Confessions* failed in its intent at making the real "person available to the world."[6] This time, the portrait works. The word picture drawn by "Rousseau" accords with the words of author as available in his books. But one could not see the reality of these words without having seen the author. Between the time of the second and third dialogues, the Frenchman reads "Jean-Jacques" while on a lengthy stay in the country and concludes that the author of these works is "the most hideous of all monsters and the horror of the human race." In demonstration of this, he has compiled a list of extracts from Rousseau's works that he now presents to "Rousseau." The Frenchman now can see in the works that Jean-Jacques is as he has been said to be by "Rousseau." What makes him a monster, however, is the "only thing" that astonished the Frenchman: that "an isolated stranger, without parents, without support, holding to nothing on earth, and wanting to say all these things, could have believed he might do so with impunity."[7] The citations the Frenchman has pulled out almost all emphasize the fact that Jean-Jacques's contemporaries are caught in institutions that do damage to them as human beings and which they are unable to change. Indeed, perhaps change is itself impossible. The reason that Jean-Jacques is misunderstood is that society is such that human beings no longer possess the categories to understand him.

> If you had not depicted your J. J. I would have believed that natural man no longer existed, but the striking relation of he whom you painted for me to the author whose books I have read leaves me no doubt that one was the other, although I have no other reason to believe it. . . . I may never love him, because that does not rest with me: but I will honor him because I want to be just, I believe him innocent, and I see him oppressed.[8]

Note that there is no reason to believe that the author of the books is the man described except that the image was so striking. This can only mean that the words that the Frenchman has read have the quality of being the words of Jean-Jacques—they are in his own voice, only the person described by "Rousseau" could speak them and have them be his own.[9] Thus, since the Frenchman now knows "Jean-Jacques" from "Rousseau's" portrait, that is, has found the speaker of those words, "his books have accomplished the work that you had begun."[10] Indeed, Rousseau was to note in his "Portrait" that "my book would rise up against me if I lie" about myself, as if his authorship was so reduced that he had no power over the content of his portrait.[11] The fear that one's portrait will betray the real person, that it will be given words which are not one's own, is a theme to which Rousseau returns again and again. Rousseau was one of the first true celebrity intellectuals. He received a vast amount of correspondence from what can only best described as fans, readers telling him how their lives had been changed by his books, women offering their souls and more (Rousseau informs us that he never took advantage of them).[12] In addition, like star-struck fans seeking studio photographs, many portraits were commissioned. In the *Dia-*

logues, the character Rousseau notes that in response to this demand, "Jean-Jacques" has had a quatrain placed under one of these portraits:

> Those knowing in the art of pretense
> Who give me such gentle features
> No matter how much you wish to portray me
> You will only have displayed yourselves.[13]

The attempt at representation, the depiction without the presence of the depicted, will not only fail but will be a projecting of the portrayer's wish fulfillments. Nietzsche, equally preoccupied by the need to be seen for what he was, will write in his autobiography, *Ecce Homo,* that

> ultimately, nobody can get more out of things, including books, then he already knows. . . . This is, in the end, my average experience and, if you will, the originality of my experience. Whoever had thought he had understood something of me, had made up something out of me after his own image.[14]

Without, as it were, the physical presence of the text, a text risks being only a kind of Rorschach inkblot for the reader. For both Rousseau and Nietzsche, the task will not and cannot be simply to find a way of writing which does not distort the representation. They seek instead a way of writing, of representing the world which does not allow the reader to distort him or herself. There is in Rousseau, as there will be in Nietzsche (and in Wittgenstein and even Heidegger) a transformation of the role of the text away from the impossible hope of an accurate representation of the world to an enforcement of honesty upon the reader/viewer. Note that the Frenchman does not come to like "Jean-Jacques" but merely no longer to create him in his own image. Rousseau wants the encounter with his text to be the encounter with another person.

This transformation of the idea of writing (and of representation in general) runs throughout Rousseau's work. In the drafts for the *Confessions,* for instance, we find: "For what I have to say one must invent a language that is as new as my project.[15] It is inherent in his well-known but little-understood hostility to representation in some spheres of politics; it is at the basis of his parallel hostility to representation in the theater.[16] The project of a new writing is central to the intention of the *Confessions* which is not so much to portray the person Rousseau as to portray ("for the first time," Rousseau claims somewhat grandiosely) a human being. The *Confessions* are, he claims "a first work for comparison." The problem that it is designed to remedy is the fact that "many think to know others, but they are wrong."[17] Men do not know anyone else as human beings, they do not know that they do not know, and most importantly they thereby do not grasp or acknowledge the human in themselves. Rousseau spells out the intent of the *Confessions:*

> To be able to know oneself well the rule for the proof is to know well another than oneself. Without this, one will never be sure not to be mistaken. . . . I want to make it possible that one may have at least one item for comparison, such that each person can know him or herself and another and that this other be me.[18]

The *Confessions* are not designed to portray Rousseau but to make it possible for others to know themselves. And to this effect he notes that every detail reveals the same thing but that to keep any detail back would be to lie about the whole. For the person to be present, every word must be the first word and the last word.[19]

Instead of further exploring how this is accomplished in the *Confessions*—which would require an in-depth study of the strategy of the text[20]—I should like to look more concretely at the theme of knowledge of self and others in relation to a text. That is, I should like to look at what happens when one person is confused about the difference between encountering another person and encountering a representation of a person, that is, an object, a work of art, some thing, not some one. The most available way to do this effectively is to use the device of the play within a play, that is, to look at how this problem is raised in dramatic form by Rousseau. The play within the play is a dramatic device whose role it is to precipitate a recognition of fact which leads to the unraveling of a situation previous thought other.[21] This is a theme which occupies many of the plays that Rousseau wrote, precisely because in a play one deals with characters, that is, persons acting as representations.

Looking at those plays of Rousseau which are about this question may give some clues as to what is involved in achieving the effect of this kind of writing. In 1740 or 1741, at age eighteen, Rousseau writes a play entitled *Narcissus, or The Lover of Himself.*[22] In the aftermath of the success of the *First Discourse* and with some retouching by Marivaux, it was first performed in 1752, on which occasion Rousseau wrote a preface for it. Attention has in recent years been paid to the preface, insofar as it seems to modify or soften the harshness of the claims apparently made against theater in the *Letter to D'Alembert.*[23] However, the play itself is in itself important. It has the structure of a modified Roman comedy. Two couples are to get married. The woman in one couple, Lucinde, has been receiving *billets doux* from an unknown admirer, who, unknown to her, is in fact her fiancé, Léandre. Intrigued, she finds excuses to delay her marriage. In the mean time, Lucinde surreptitiously places in her brother Valère's chambers a portrait of him. The portrait was commissioned by Léandre's sister, Angélique, to whom Valère is engaged. However, Lucinde has prevailed on Angélique to have the portrait represent Valère dressed as a woman. She notes that he is "a sort [*espèce*] of woman . . . and that this drag [*travesti*] portrait seems less to disguise him that to make apparent his natural state."[24]

We know from Valère's first words that he is almost solipsistically self-referential: "What pleasure it is going to give me to make Angélique happy!" Not surprisingly, he thus falls in love with his transvestite self. Not recognizing himself, he declares that he cannot marry until he has found the woman of the portrait. (His valet has no trouble recognizing the portrait as that of his master.)

With this, the stage is set. As noted, the play has the structure of a modified Roman comedy. In such plays, typically each of the pairs of lovers find, then lose, and then find each other again; the second finding establishes social and institutional bonds, usually marriage. Here the second finding and thus legitimated human society is threatened by a bond that cannot be: the solipsism of Valère's love of a self that he does not know to be himself. If one knew oneself, one would not know oneself. Only others can be loved. (As the valet notes, "This matter cannot be brought to accounts—*La chose est inpayable*.") Solipsism would not threaten if Valère could recognize himself for who he is. Note that it is not simply the reflection of himself that leads to solipsism: the mirror in front of which he preens does not satisfy him. It is not knowing himself.[25] Solipsism is to want oneself not as oneself. It is to desire a union with oneself as an object.

At first his fiancée, Angélique, finds this enchanting. She uses terms that reflect the passions of the state of nature: "He has seen himself by my eyes."[26] Much to his confusion, she even gives Valère permission to pursue the woman of the portrait for, as she says to him, "you will love her until your grave." But she is mistaken, she soon realizes, and as Valère persists, all relationships are threatened. As the valet remarks, Valère is not here for anyone else because he is looking for himself in order to marry himself. The father of Valère and Lucinde threatens to disinherit his son, send his daughter to a nunnery, and marry Angélique, his son's fiancée (Léandre is told that he will simply have to wait). All society will be reassumed under patriarchal domination. Just prior to this, in a key exchange, the particular quality of the social dynamic is expressed as follows:

VALÈRE. Go on. Remember that who loves nothing does not deserve to be loved.
ANGÉLIQUE. It is even better to love nothing than to love oneself.[27]

Angélique's line could be Rousseau's motto. Others are necessary, as others. But the simple existence of others is not in and of itself sufficient. Since the presence of others is not (logically) necessary—this was the point of the first part of the *Second Discourse*—there is nothing about their presence as presence that will provide the basis for a nonsolipsistic situation. The problem that the *Social Contract* will later resolve is how to combine self-love with the knowledge of similarity and the actuality of difference. Rousseau realizes that a human life with each other has to be learned, at least in this day and age.

In the *Second Discourse* no such solution to dehumanization is seen, or even attempted. Society as we presently experience it is in fact very much as if Valère had made the choice to pursue his distorted portrait. Here it is significant that the eventual marriages of the end of *Narcisse* are made possible by Valère's freely choosing Angélique over the portrait *before he knows that it is a portrait of himself.* The stage directions are explicit that he throw the portrait to the ground and that only then does he find out that it is a portrait of himself. Self-knowledge is consequent to and does not precede the recognition of others as other. Such recognition makes unnecessary the threatened semi-Hobbesian imposition of order for order's sake: hearing that the lovers have found each other, the father immediately withdraws his commands.

The portrait shows and it deludes. It is the doubleness of the work of art which must represent but cannot, which the purer it is, the more false it must be to itself, that fascinates Rousseau. Suppose, however, a work of art were alive, a representation were "real"—would that make a difference? In *Narcisse* Rousseau uses a representation both to threaten the world of humans and to make possible its restoration. The point of the preface he later appended to the play was to suggest that when society is as, well, narcissistic, as that of these players, art used and rejected might serve a function.[28] But suppose art took form and dwelt among us?

When Rousseau considers the natural condition of humans in the *Second Discourse,* he notes that, in nature, since humans are not wicked, they are "relieved of having to be good."[29] In nature, in fact, man is *nul.*[30] Individuals have no individual characteristics; even the word *individual* is misleading. With no qualities and few passions, men are "sufficient unto themselves."[31] Note Rousseau's language as he "concludes" (a conclusion that Voltaire annotated as that of "a very bad novel)":[32]

> Let us conclude that, wandering in the forests without industry, without
> speech, without settled abode, without war, and without ties, without any
> need of others of his kind and without any desire to harm them, perhaps
> even without ever recognizing any one of them individually, subject of

few passions and self-sufficient, centuries went by in the all crudeness of the first ages; the species had already grown old and man remained ever a child.[33]

Eight times *without:* absence is central. There is literally nothing to humans in the state of nature.[34] Thus the defining quality of the human is not to be defined or fixed. The definition that we might have is therefore acquired. And thus the acquisition of any substantive quality has the effect of differentiating one person from another and of keeping others from being available to me as I am to myself. The process of differentiation occurs as a consequence to the encountering of obstacles to human self-preservation. Different obstacles lead to different differences but the consequence of all of them is that humans tend increasingly to think of themselves *in relation* to others. First, the species distinguishes itself, but in doing so each "was from afar preparing an individual claim to pre-eminence."[35] While not necessary, this process is (almost) inevitable. Even in the *Nouvelle Héloïse,* Julie indicates that children depart "the state of nature almost from birth."[36] We are what we become; thus we must be careful about what we become.

For we certainly have become something. Our original state was negativity. If the quality of the human in nature is negativity, then the idea of human nature only makes positive sense in terms of the accomplishment of a complete denaturation and the translation of the negativities of the human into its actualized essence. The problem for Rousseau, one might say, is to retain the original nothingness as a interior quality of the human itself. Here I wish to turn to another play within Rousseau's play. How can denatured negativity make myself available to myself, others available to me, and myself to others? Why would it not become simply a form of solipsism? A stunning picture of the lure and possibility of this alternative is given at the end of Rousseau's playlet *Pygmalion.* Written in 1762 and set to music in 1770, it was performed at the Paris opera in 1772 without Rousseau's permission.

Pygmalion is in despair as to his ability only to find that it might possibly be rekindled by looking upon the statue of Galatea he has been sculpting. He lifts the sheet that veils his statue from him and then dreams of a relationship with Galatea like this: "I adore myself in what I have made."

He goes to chip away some of the clothing on the grounds that the statue is "not naked enough": the mistake here is to try and remove that which keeps him from seeing his creation. After one more blow of the chisel, he realizes that the attempt to remove barriers to transparency is futile and stops. In his effort to unveil her breasts, he feels the "pulsing flesh repulse the chisel."[37]

As he looks fully and completely on her, the statue comes alive, the talismanic "To be her, to see her" announces the melding of subject and object.

GALATEA [*She touches her self and her first word is*]. Me.

PYGMALION [*ecstatic*]. Me!

GALATEA [*touching her self again*]. It is me.

PYGMALION. Ravishing illusion which reaches unto my ears, ah! never leave my senses.

GALATEA [*takes some steps and touches a piece of marble*]. This is no longer me.
[*She touches him; he takes her hand and kisses it*] Ah! me again.

PYGMALION. Yes, dear and charming object: yes, master work fit for my hands, for my heart and for the gods. . . .It is you, you alone: I have given you all my being; I will only live through you.[38]

Whereas before Galatea came alive, Pygmalion had, like Valère, adored himself in what he made, now, with the actual presence of the other, he insists that he will live only through her, as he has given her "all his being." The story ends here. We are not meant, I think, to find the position in which Pygmalion finds himself at the end a disappointment. It seems to me in clear contrast with what he had hoped for prior to Galatea's coming alive. He proclaims: "Oh that Pygmalion might die to live in Galatea!"

Then he realizes the folly of this:

Heavens, what am I saying! If I were she, I would not see her, I would not be he who loved her! No, that my Galatea live and that I not be her. Ah! that I always be another, to want always to be her, to see her, to love her, to be loved by her.[39]

Here he wants to find himself in her, but not to be her. Retaining the sight of her means that he would not have given her all his being. I suspect that the reason the last lines of the story indicate that a complete transferal of self has happened precisely because Galatea is (as Pygmalion says in the same speech) a "dear and charming object." Not only can we not humanly love a creation, but we also cannot humanly love that which we create, even if that creation were to be alive.

Yet there is something very significant in the assertion here that at its best my encounter with others is an encounter with myself. From one reading it might appear sick—too great a narcissism. Indeed Rousseau's fascination with autoeroticism,[40] the constant youthful fear that pervades the *Confessions* of *being seen* when he had not shown himself, the insistence that no one can see him except himself: all this does not seem the material for a sound politics, not indeed for politics at all.

However attractive this possibility was to Rousseau (one thinks of his relations to Madame de Warens), this solipsistic view of commonalty is possible only in a play when an object a person has made comes to life. Rousseau may have longed on occasion for such an awful perfect community, but he knew enough to know that it was not one of human beings. That which was in common here had no commonalty at all. I cannot be human if the other for my being is a *thing*, even a living thing.

What this analysis suggests, however, is that in a society whose realities are legitimate and just, a human encounter with others will be to find in those others precisely that which constitutes me, like them, a human being. Being human, finding the human is in the realm of inequality, not something that comes easily. Consider:

> Why are kings without pity for their subjects? Because they expect never to be humans. Why are the rich so hard to the poor? Because they are not afraid of becoming such.[41]

Kings are *not human*, and they do not even feel this as a lack. The Turks, in fact, are "more human" than are the Europeans because their form of government is so arbitrary that anyone might one day find himself at the bottom of the heap. When is a person not a human being? When it seems that he is a king, or rich, or a noble—when he is *defined*. We all, for Rousseau, are in danger of being a Lear, of losing our humanity in the attractions and requirements of our role.

The elaboration of the achievement and retention of the human has two parallel courses in Rousseau, the one in *Émile* and the other in the *Social Contract*. Precisely because the element of the human is the same in human relations as it is in human society, I would argue that their courses are not only parallel but are indeed the same course, as, indeed, Rousseau himself makes clear by placing a summary of the *Social Contract* in the last book of *Émile*.[42] But it should be clear from this why Rousseau has a profound worry about the possibility that a written text might teach any one what justice might be. Unless a text forces the reader into his or her own presence, it will not bring the reader into the presence of the author. As Rousseau had hoped for his readers, so Judith Shklar achieved for her students. It was her greatness as a human being that her presence as a teacher allowed her students to find their presence to the texts she so loved. She neither required nor expected of us to find her, but only our own voices. Hers was a great spirit.

Notes

1. Jean-Jacques Rousseau, *Oeuvres complètes*, ed. Bernard Gagnebin and Marcel Raymond (Paris, 1959–), 2:1133. For a more complete account of the

matters in this essay see my *Jean-Jacques Rousseau: The Politics of the Ordinary* (Thousand Oaks, Calif., 1994).

2. See Robert Darnton, "Readers' Response to Rousseau," *The Great Cat Massacre and Other Episodes in French Cultural History* (New York, 1991), esp. 235ff. In addition, the claim of having had personal friendship with Rousseau was seen as a possible help to those in political trouble during the French revolution. The claim in 1790 by the Count d'Antraigues, then under indictment, to have received from Rousseau an outline of a sequel to the *Social Contract* on federations is almost certainly false. See R. A. Leigh's account in Jean-Jacques Rousseau, *Correspondance complète*, ed. R. A. Leigh (Geneva, 1965), 37:370.

3. *Confessions* 9, *OC* 1:414.

4. *Dialogues* 2, *OC* 1:773.

5. Ibid., 1:826.

6. Ibid., 1:903.

7. Ibid., 1:926.

8. *Dialogues* 3 *OC* 1:936.

9. On speaking in one's own voice, see Stanley Cavell, *A Pitch of Philosophy* (Cambridge, Mass., 1994).

10. *Dialogues* 3, *OC* 1:940.

11. "My Portrait," *OC* 1:1121.

12. See Darnton, "Readers' Response to Rousseau," *The Great Cat Massacre*, 235ff.

13. *Dialogues* 2, *OC* 1:778.

14. Friedrich Nietzsche, *Ecce Homo* (1908), in *On the Genealogy of Morals and Ecce Homo*, trans. and ed. Walter Kaufmann (New York, 1969), 261.

15. "Ébauches des Confessions" 1, *OC* 1:1153.

16. For a fuller discussion, see my *Jean-Jacques Rousseau: The Politics of the Ordinary*, 67ff., 91ff.

17. "Ébauches des Confessions" 3, *OC* 1:1153.

18. Ibid.

19. Ibid. For a revelatory discussion of this matter in relation to the case of Heidegger's silences on himself, see Babette Babich, "The Ethical Alpha and the Linguistic Omega: Heidegger's Anti-Semitism and the Inner Affinity of Germany and Greece, *Joyful Wisdom* 1 (1994): 3–25.

20. On the notion of strategy, see Helene Keyssar, "I Love You. Who Are You? The Strategy of Drama in Recognition Scenes," *PMLA*, Mar. 1977.

21. For a discussion, see my *The Idea of Political Theory: Reflections on the Self in Political Time and Space* (Notre Dame, Ind., 1990), chap. 2, esp. 64ff.

22. Few writers have seen how key this play is to Rousseauian themes. Among those who have, see Michael Brint, *Tragedy and Denial: The Politics of Difference in Western Political Thought* (Boulder, Colo., 1991), and Jean Starobinski, *The Living Eye* (Cambridge, Mass., 1989), 67–71.

23. See for example, Benjamin Barber, "Rousseau and Brecht," in *The Artist and Political Vision*, ed. Benjamin Barber and Michael McGrath (New Brunswick, N.J., 1981).

24. *Narcisse* 1, *OC* 2:977.

25. Starobinski makes a similar point in *The Living Eye*, 68.

26. *Narcisse* 6, *OC* 2:995.

27. Ibid., 2, 1002.

28. For a discussion of the dynamics of this, see my *The Idea of Political Theory*, chap. 2.

29. *Fragments politiques* 2 7, *OC* 3:476.

30. *Lettre à de Beaumont, OC* 4:936.

31. *Discourse on the Origins of Inequality.* 1, *OC* 3:151.

32. G. Havens, "Voltaire's Marginalia on the Pages of Rousseau," *Ohio State University Studies,* 6 (1933): 14; as usual, Voltaire was on to something, if off the mark, in his criticism of Rousseau.

33. *Discourse* 1, *OC* 3:160–61.

34. Pierre Burgelin notes that man was "une monade qui reflète un univers sans le distinguer de soi" (*La philosophie de l'existence chez Jean-Jacques Rousseau* [Paris, 1952], 251).

35. *Discourse* 2, *OC* 3:166.

36. *Julie, ou la Nouvelle Héloïse* V, 3, *OC* 2:571.

37. I resist to some degree the interpretation of Starobinski (in *Jean-Jacques Rousseau: Transparency and Obstruction,* 71ff.) in that it is important that the statue is not, as he claims, completely unveiled. Pygmalion allows Galatea the possibility of modesty and thus of life.

38. *Pygmalion, OC* 2:1230.

39. *Pygmalion, OC* 2:1228.

40. See Jacques Derrida, "Ce dangereux supplément," *De la grammatologie* (Paris, 1967).

41. *Émile, ou Traité de l'éducation* 4, *OC* 4:507.

42. See my *Jean-Jacques Rousseau: The Politics of the Ordinary* for an elaboration.

9

Shklar on Rousseau on Fénelon

Patrick Riley

JUDITH SHKLAR WAS USUALLY more concerned with Jean-Jacques Rousseau's striking originality—as a psychologist, as a pre-Freudian group psychologist, as the very prototype of the *homme revolté*—than with his intellectual debts. "His enduring originality and fascination," she urges in *Men and Citizens*, "are due entirely to the acute psychological insight with which he diagnosed the emotional diseases of modern civilization."[1] But she made two large exceptions in favor of John Locke and François Fénelon: she thought that Rousseau's debt to the psychological theory of Locke's *Essay Concerning Human Understanding* was huge and central, and that his debt to Fénelon's political and moral thought was equally massive. For Rousseau owed to Fénelon nothing less than the legitimation of his obsession with Greco-Roman antiquity: if an early Genevan reading of Plutarch set off this propensity, it was Fénelon's *Telemachus* (1699) and *Letter to the French Academy* (1714) which confirmed and dignified it; thus Fénelon's "Roman" *auctoritas* and *gravitas* were worth a great deal. In Shklar's view Rousseau owed to Fénelon (above all) the notion of seeing and using two ancient "Models" of social perfection—a prepolitical "age of innocence" and a fully political age of legislator-caused civic virtue—as foils to modern egoism and corruption.[2] Fénelon's familiar utopias of "Bétique" (celebrating pastoral innocence) and of "Salente" (depicting legislator-shaped *civisme*) in *Telemachus* were, for Shklar, echoed in Rousseau's "happy family" (in *La Nouvelle Héloïse* and *Lettre à d'Alembert*), and in his Spartan-Roman "fantasies" (in *Government of Poland* and the *Social Contract*). Small wonder, then, that Shklar should direct us toward "Rousseau's admiring remarks about Fénelon" in the *Confessions*, in *Rousseau, juge de Jean-Jacques*, in the *Rêveries du promeneur solitaire*, and in *Emile*.[3]

But none of this can become clear enough until Fénelon's social thought is exposed to the light of the present day. Rousseau may have known it by heart, as Shklar herself was later to do—but we no longer do. And therefore the first task is to recover those facets of Féneloni-anism that Rousseau found irresistible.

I

François de Salignac de La Mothe-Fénelon was born in Périgord in 1651, the son of an aristocratic provincial family which was distinguished but threadbare. Ordained a priest in 1675, he was within three years given an important ministry in the church—that of spiritual guide to the "New Catholics" (ex-Huguenots) in northern France. This ministry lasted for a decade (1678–99) and was crowned by the publication of the treatise *On the Education of Girls* (1687), which first revealed Fénelon's classicizing taste for the ancient pastoral simplicity depicted by Virgil in the *Aeneid* and the *Georgica*. By this time the Abbé Fénelon had caught the eye of Bossuet, the most powerful French ecclesiastic of the Grand Siècle. For the Bishop of Meaux Fénelon produced his *Réfutation de Malebranche* (1687–88), which attacked Malebranche's notion of a "Cartesian" *providence générale* operating through simple, constant, universal laws, and sustained Bossuet's notion (outlined in the *Histoire universelle*) of a *providence particulière* which had furnished David and Solomon to ancient Israel and Louis XIV to modern France. In 1689 he was named tutor to Louis's grandson, the Duc de Bourgogne (1682–1712), and it was for his royal pupil that he was soon to write *Telemachus, Son of Ulysses* (begun in 1693–95), and the *Dialogues of the Dead* (1690). Rhetorically, the high point of Fénelon's "court" period was his speech on being received into the Académie Française (1693), with its fulsome praise of the Sun King. The Archbishopric of Cambrai followed in 1695, carrying with it the titles of duke and prince of the Holy Roman Empire.[4]

But in the late 1680s, Fénelon had also become deeply interested in the quietistic notion of a "disinterested love of God" free of hope for personal happiness—a disinterested interest fanned by the mystical pieties of his friend Madame Guyon. His insistence that one must "go out of oneself," even "Hate oneself," finally eventuated in the *Maxims of the Saints on the Inner Life* (1697)—a work in which Fénelon argued for degrees of "purity" or "disinterestedness" in human love of God. At the lowest end of the scale one finds the love of God not for himself but for "the goods which depend on his power and which one hopes to obtain:" this Fénelon contemptuously calls "purely servile love." One small notch above this Fénelon places loving God not for "goods" which he can provide but as the "instrument" of our salvation; but even this "higher" love is still "at the level of self-love." At the third and fourth levels Fénelon finds a mixture of self-love and true love of God; but what really interests him is the fifth and highest degree, the "pure love" of God that one finds only in "saints." "One can love God," Fénelon urges, "from a love which is pure charity, and without the slightest mixture of self-interested motivation." In such a love, Fénelon adds, neither the "fear of punishment" nor the "hope of reward" plays any part at all.[5] As is well known, Bossuet and others—including Malebranche, in his *Traité de l'amour de Dieu* (1697)—argued that Fénelon's "disinterested" love excluded all hope of salvation, as well as all fear of justified punishment, and thus subverted Christianity: Fénelon's work was finally placed on the Index of forbidden books in March 1699. In this condemnation the prime mover was Bossuet, now Fénelon's greatest detractor: "To detach oneself from himself to the point of no longer desiring to be happy, is an error which neither nature, nor grace, nor reason, nor faith can suffer."[6]

A month later *Telemachus* was printed, without Fénelon's permission, through "the infidelity of a copyist." Louis XIV had already banished the "chimerical" Fénelon to his Cambrai diocese in 1697, and with the double disaster of 1699—condemnation at Rome followed within a few weeks by publication of the "Homeric" novel which Louis considered an attack on his faults—Fénelon was divested of his pension and of his tutorship to the Duc de Bourgogne. He never set foot in Versailles, or even Paris, again.

With the premature death in 1712 of the Duc de Bourgogne, whom Fénelon had carefully educated to be an enlightened successor to his grandfather, Fénelon's hopes for a renewed France collapsed like a house of cards. His *Demonstration de l'existence de Dieu* (1713) was a work of pure theology; and, indeed, had Fénelon not been a royal tutor for ten years, *Telemachus* and the *Dialogues of the Dead* would almost certainly never have come into existence. Conscientiously administering his half-Flemish diocese even as Louis XIV made perpetual war on its borders, and constantly engaging in a wide-ranging correspondence as spiritual counselor, Fénelon died, prematurely worn out, in January 1715. To this day many French Fénelonians view the Archbishop of Cambrai as a saint and martyr, the victim of the "interested" high politics of Louis XIV, Bossuet, and the Roman curia.

The year 1716 saw the posthumous publication of the magnificent *Letter on the Occupations of the French Academy* (written in 1714), in which

Fénelon contributed to the "quarrel between the ancients and the moderns" by offering glowing praise of Homer, Plato, Demosthenes, Virgil, and Cicero, and insisting that "it is our insane and cruel vanity, and not the noble simplicity of the ancients, which needs to be corrected." It was that "noble simplicity" which he had tried to illustrate in the demi-Platonic myths of "Bétique" and "Salente," in *Telemachus*:

> When the ancient poets wanted to charm the imagination of men, they conducted them far from the great cities; they made them forget the luxury of their time, and let them back to the age of gold; they represented shepherds dancing on the flowered grass in the shade of a grove, in a delightful season, rather that agitated hearts, and great men who are unhappy in virtue of their very greatness.[7]

Telemachus may have contributed to Fénelon's downfall, but the book was spectacularly successful: the most read literary work in eighteenth-century France (after the Bible). Cherished and praised by Rousseau, it was first translated into English in the very year of its publication, and was retranslated by no less a figure than the novelist Tobias Smollett, in the late 1760s. (In Rousseau's *Émile* the eponymous pupil is given *Robinson Crusoe* as his sole adolescent reading, then Fénelon's *Telemachus* on reaching adulthood—a striking concession from one who thought almost all literature to be morally suspect.)

II

Without doubt the two most important pieces of French political theory at the turn of the eighteenth century are Bossuet's *Politics Drawn from the Very Words of Holy Scripture* (completed in 1704) and Fénelon's *Telemachus*.[8] But while Bossuet offered the greatest of all defenses of divine-right monarchy—in which Louis XIV's rule is descended unbroken from Abraham's covenant with God in Genesis ("kings shall come out of you")—Fénelon by contrast theorized what might be called a republican monarchy in which the key notions are simplicity, labor, the virtues of agriculture, the absence of luxury and splendor, and the elevation of peace over war and aggrandizement. This proto-Rousseauian, demilitarized "Spartanism" led Louis XIV, of course, to read *Telemachus* as a satire on his luxuriousness and bellicosity, and Fénelon fell permanently from official favor. Fénelon combines monarchical rule with republican virtues in a unique way. After him Montesquieu was to draw a necessary connection between monarchy and "war and the enlargement of dominion," and to separate monarchy by a categorical gulf from republican simplicity and virtue. Rousseau was to restore a more nearly Fénelonian view of republican monarchy in his glowing Plutarchian encomium of Lycurgus—in a Sparta not just temporally and geographically but morally distant from Versailles.

It was no accident that Rousseau so greatly admired Fénelon's fable: for like *Émile*, *Telemachus* is the story of the moral and political education of a young man by a knowledgeable and virtuous tutor. While Émile, however, is in some sense Everyman, the tutor in *Telemachus*, Mentor, is preparing a young prince to succeed Ulysses at Ithaca. (As Rousseau says, "Émile is not a king, nor am I god, so that we are not distressed that we cannot imitate Telemachus and Mentor in the good they did.")[9] Fénelon himself, in a letter from 1710, indicates his objective in writing *Telemachus* for his royal pupil, the Duc de Bourgogne:

> As for *Telemachus*, it is a fabulous narration in the form of an heroic poem like those of Homer and of Virgil, into which I have put their main instructions which are suitable for a young prince whose birth destines him to rule. . . . In these adventures I have put all the truths necessary to government, and all the faults that one can find in sovereign power.[10]

Louis XIV, for his part saw nothing but the alleged "faults" of sovereign power in *Telemachus*—faults which Fénelon describes at length in his account of misrule by Idomeneus, former King of Crete. (Since Idomeneus kills his own son and is deposed and exiled, one can understand Louis's displeasure.) One of Mentor's long speeches to the slowly reforming Idomeneus (now King of Salente in book 10 of *Telemachus*) must have been read by Louis XIV as a veiled, mythologized version of what Fénelon would have wanted to say to, or rather against, Versailles:

> Have you sought after people who were the most disinterested, and the most likely to contradict you . . . to condemn your passions and your unjust feelings? No, no: let us see whether you will now have the courage to be humiliated by the truth which condemns you.
>
> You have exhausted your riches; you have never thought of augmenting your people, nor of cultivating fertile lands. Was it not necessary to view two things as the two essential foundations of your power—to have many good people, and well-cultivated lands to nourish them? I would require a long peace to favor the multiplication of your people. You should never think of anything but agriculture and the establishment of the wisest laws. A vain ambition has pushed you to the very edge of the precipice. By virtue of wanting to appear great, you let yourself ruin your true greatness. Hasten to repair these faults; suspend all your great works; renounce this display which would ruin your new city; let your people breathe in peace.[11]

That second paragraph, particularly, could be invisibly woven into Rousseau's *Social Contract,* book 2, chapter 11: "Devote your whole attention to agriculture, which causes man to multiply, and drive out the arts and crafts." (To be sure, both Fénelon and Rousseau have their roots in Cato's *De re rustica,* with its praise of Cincinnatus's virtues and its equation of moneylending with murder.)

Fénelon did not put such speeches only into the mouth of Mentor: at every turn, and in every chapter, the *inventions de la vanité et de la molesse* are denounced. In book 7, having escaped the seductions of Calypso, Mentor and Telemachus are told a story of the land of Bétique by Adoam—who reveals that the luxuries of Greece and Egypt are anathema in that simple prepolitical land:

> Among these people (Adoam says) we found gold and silver put to the same use as iron—for example, as plowshares . . . . They are almost all shepherds or laborers [who practice only] those arts necessary for their simple and frugal life . . . .
>
> When one speaks to them of peoples who have the art of making superb buildings, furniture of gold and silver, fabrics ornamented with embroideries and with precious stones, exquisite perfumes . . . they reply in these terms: "These people are very unfortunate to have used up so much labor and industry in order to corrupt themselves. This superfluity softens, enervates, torments those who possess it: it tempts those who are without it to want to acquire it through injustice and violence. Can one call good a superfluity which serves only to make men evil?" . . . It is thus, Adoam went on, that those wise men spoke, who learned their wisdom only by studying mere nature.[12]

(Rousseau must have remembered this Fénelonian inversion of the usual value of precious metals when, in *Government of Poland,* he suggested awarding gold medals to the lowest public benefactors, silver ones to those who contribute more, and plaques of steel to those who most advance the general good.)[13]

The unfortunate outgrowths of "vanity and flabbiness" are set in even higher relief by Fénelon's account of the austere and noble pleasures of "just kings" who live in the eternal daylight of the Elysian fields. In book 14 of *Telemachus,* Telemachus is ferried across the river Styx by Charon, where he sees rulers "who have governed men wisely" enjoying "a happiness infinitely greater than that of the rest of men who have loved virtue on earth":

> Neither blood-covered war nor cruel envy which bites with a venomous tooth, and which bears vipers wound around its middle and its arms, nor jealousy, nor mistrust, nor fear, nor vain desires, ever approach this happy abode of peace. . . . A pure and gentle light surrounds the bodies of these just men and covers them in its rays like a vestment.[14]

Here, of course, the Champs Elysées take on some of the coloration of a Christian Heaven—even if Fénelon's avowed models are Homer and Virgil.

But what is least "Homeric"—and also most Rousseauian—is the transformation of the notion of heroism in *Telemachus*. The nominal hero, of course, is Telemachus—the son of a greater hero, Ulysses. But the true hero of Fénelon's work is certainly Mentor, for it is he who educates and restrains a Telemachus who could easily degenerate into another Idomeneus. The true hero for Fénelon is not the wanderer on an Odyssey to Ithaca, nor a Louis le Grand who sacrificed real goods to apparent ones; the true hero is the moral-civic educator who "denatures" natural egoists—the man whom Rousseau later called "the true miracle" in the *Social Contract*. The proof comes at the very end of *Telemachus* when Mentor undergoes a metamorphosis and is revealed as Minerva (goddess of wisdom); the book ends abruptly before Telemachus is shown being reunited with Ulysses. The hero has already been resolved into pure wisdom: the nominal hero barely reaches Ithaca.

What that true hero teaches is a political version of Fénelon's quietistic "disinterested love of god;" just as one truly loves God only by renouncing self-interested *amour propre* (the hope for personal salvation), so too for Fénelon the "idea of pure disinterestedness dominates the political theories of all ancient legislators." In antiquity "it was not a matter of finding happiness in conforming to that order but, *au contraire,* of devouring oneself for love of that order, perishing, depriving the self of all resources." Fénelon completes this thought with a wonderful passage which Rousseau must have had in mind when he wrote his discourse on political economy for Diderot's *Encyclopédie* sixty years later: "All these [ancient] legislators and philosophers who reasoned about laws presupposed that the fundamental principle of political society was that of preferring the public to the self—not through hope of serving one's own interests, but through the simple, pure disinterested love of the political order, which is beauty, justice, and virtue itself." If one "brackets" God out of Fénelonian thought, the Rousseauian "civic" ideal is more than half in place. And what is displaced is virtually everything imagined or accomplished by Louis XIV. That is clearest, perhaps, in Fénelon's "On Pure Love":

> Nothing is so odious as this idea of a heart always occupied with itself: nothing delights us so much as certain generous actions which persuade the world (and us) that we have done the good for love of the good, without seeking ourselves therein. Self-love itself renders homage to this disinterested virtue, by the shrewdness with which it tries to take on the

appearance of it—so true is it that man, who does not bring himself about, is not made to seek after himself, but to exist solely for him who has made him. His glory and his perfection consist in going out of himself [*sortir de soi*], in forgetting himself, in losing himself, in being swallowed up in the simple love of infinite beauty.[15]

The central truth about Fénelon, then, is that the whole of his practical thought—religious, moral, political—is held together by the notion of disinterested love, of "going out of oneself" in order to lose oneself in a greater beyond (or, in the case of God, above). The disinterested love of God, without self-interest and hope for benefits, is pure "charity" (as in Pascal's *Pensées*, in which "the self is hateful" and charity is "of another order");[16] the disinterested love of one's neighbor is "friendship" (as in Cicero's *De amicitia*); the disinterested love of the *polis* is a proto-Rousseauian ancient civic virtue. On this view of the moral world, an austere Pascalian *charité* and a Platonic "sublimated" *eros* (that is, eros made sublime) meet. Small wonder that Fénelon, a brilliantly sympathetic classical scholar, loved the *Symposium* and the *Phaedrus* with non-concupiscent passion.[17]

IV

Since one cannot hope to point out every parallel between Fénelon and Rousseau, the best course is to bring out affinities between Fénelon's last work, the *Letter on the Occupations of the Académie Française,* and Rousseau's first—the *Discourse on the Arts and Sciences* (1750), the work which made Rousseau.

Fénelon's *Letter* was written soon before his death in January 1715, and was posthumously published in the following year. It is the *summa* of his thought, drawing together his favorite themes. But above all the *Letter* is celebrated as the most important turn-of-the-(eighteenth)century contribution to the "the quarrel between the ancients and the moderns"—the quarrel to which Rousseau was soon to contribute so much.

That quarrel itself, however, has a limited side, and a much broader significance. The limited quarrel was French, took place mainly from 1685 to 1715, and was fairly narrowly literary; the broader and more important quarrel was pan-European and political. The large quarrel goes back at least to Machiavelli's claim in *The Discourses* that the golden age of ancient Roman civic virtue remains a perfect model for intelligent imitation by modern men, whenever *fortuna* affords the opportunity,[18] and extends forward in time—after Rousseau's ardent "Spartanism"[19]—to Benjamin Constant's celebrated essay on ancient

versus modern liberty in the post-Napoleonic period. The quarrel between the ancients and the moderns then had a very long "run," and it
included phenomena as significant as Poussin's and Lorrain's paintings
of Greek and Roman pastoral felicity at the very moment of Louis XIV's
glittering Versailles ascendancy.

Fénelon was an important contributor to that large political-cultural
quarrel stretching from Machiavelli to Rousseau to Constant—though
his *Letter* was nominally concerned with a more parochial fight within
the Académie Française (between the classicist Boileau and the modernist Fontenelle, for example). Fénelon's *Letter*, to be sure, deals with
the local and narrow issues of the day—such as the question whether
French is less adequate and expressive than Greek and Latin, or
whether the rhyme schemes of Corneille are more forced and stilted
than those of Sophocles. But in subordinating the "insane and cruel
vanity" of the moderns to the "noble simplicity" of the ancients, in
praising Homer, Virgil, Plato, Demosthenes, and Cicero as nearly perfect models, Fénelon went well beyond Parisian academic quarrels
about rhetoric and diction to offer a general encomium of pre-
Christian civilization.

That is of course paradoxical, since Fénelon was not only a Christian
but an archbishop. But his view (in the *Maxims of the Saints*) was that
most modern Christians love God from a base and "interested" motive
(hope for personal salvation), while the ancients *disinterestedly* loved the
polis and sacrificed themselves for it. For Fénelon the Christians have
the right object (God) but the wrong motive (self-love); the ancients had
a lower if estimable object (the city) but a worthy motive (disinterested
affection). Here only Fénelon's own words in the *Letter* will do:

> Those who cultivate their reason and who love virtue—can they compare
> the vain and ruinous luxury which in our times is the plague of morality
> and the shame of the nation, with the happy and elegant simplicity which
> the ancients place before our eyes?
>
> Virgil, who saw all the magnificence of Rome from close up, turned
> the poverty of the King Evander into the grace and the ornament of his
> poem [the *Aeneid*]. . . . Virgil even goes to the point of comparing a free,
> peaceable and pastoral life with the voluptuous actions, mixed with trou-
> ble, which come into play with great fortunes. He imagined nothing
> happy except a wise mediocrity, in which men would be secure from the
> desire for prosperity, and [full of] compassion for the miseries of
> others.[20]

It is easy enough to see why Rousseau so cherished Fénelon, and
made Fénelon's *Telemachus* (with its quasi-Platonic utopias of pacific
and agricultural simplicity) the only book which Émile is encouraged to

read on reaching adulthood. (To be sure, one can understand the dismay of Archbishop Beaumont of Paris: Émile is not given Scripture, or even Bossuet's *Politics from Scripture;* he is given a "Greek" work bearing the subtitle "Continuation of the Fourth Book of the Odyssey." He is given Tertullian standing on his head: if we have Greece, what need of Jerusalem?) If, indeed, Rousseau had died in the early 1750s, before the writing of *Inequality* and the *Social Contract,* leaving the *Discourse on the Arts and Sciences* as his main legacy, he would now probably be thought of as a minor if eloquent embroiderer of familiar Fénelonian themes. For the *First Discourse* (1750) is Rousseau's first contribution to the quarrel between the ancients and the moderns; with its magnification of Spartan and Roman republican civic virtue and its denigration of Athenian aestheticism, it is an extension of the view that Fénelon had made famous in his 1714 *Letter.* It is almost as if Rousseau, on the road to Vincennes to visit Diderot in prison, were thinking of these Fénelonian lines:

> Nothing so much marks a declining nation as this disdainful luxuriousness which rejects the frugality of the ancients. It is this depravity which overturned Rome . . . . I love a hundred times better the poor Ithaca of Ulysses than a city [imperial Rome] shining through so odious a magnificence. Happy are the men who content themselves with pleasures which cost neither crime nor ruin; it is our insane and cruel vanity and not the noble simplicity of the ancients which needs to be corrected.[21]

Since Fénelon's *Letter* is so proto-Rousseauian, Jean-Jacques needed only to enlarge a long familiar subordination of modernity to antiquity in *Arts and Sciences;* mainly he needed to add Cato and Brutus to the Socrates whom Fénelon had already made a civic saint. And he did this, in effect, by collapsing Socrates into Cato and Brutus: Socrates is now the only acceptable Athenian, but that is because he willingly died for the sake of the laws. The Platonic Socrates who hears the harmony of the spheres and sees the *psyche* as a Pythagorean geometrizing echo of a consonant *kosmos* yields to Socrates the civic martyr in the *Crito.* Socrates displays "the general will one has as a citizen."[22]

But that last phrase reveals what is not yet present in the *First Discourse.* If what is ancient, à la Fénelon, is fully "there" in the *First Discourse,* what has not yet appeared is modern (indeed Lockean) "voluntary agreement" as the basis of legitimate government in the *Social Contract.*[23] There must be voluntariness as something morally crucial before "general will" can be a will of a particular kind; and that voluntariness is Augustinian/Christian—as is Rousseau's stress on "conscience" in the *Lettres morales,* and his insistence on the final arrival of adult moral autonomy at the end of Émile's denaturing, transformative education.[24] The civic *généralité* of Roman-Spartan antiquity has not yet been fused in the *First Discourse* with the autonomy and "will" of *Inequality* and the works that succeed it. Indeed, the key term *volonté générale* does not even appear until the *Discourse on Political Economy*.[25] In time Rousseau's thought became far richer and more complex, but the final worry is whether that thought is as coherent as it is complex— whether Fénelonian, Plutarchian, Lockean, Roman, Christian, Platonic, Machiavellian, Spartan, and Augustinian strands really cohere. Whether Rousseauian thought is truly a corpus, or just a basket of enthusiastic *disjecta membra,* is what is at issue. At the time of the *First Discourse* Rousseau was in his neo-Fénelonian vein: that is why he places Ovid on his title page ("here I am the barbarian because they do not understand me"); later he sought (and sometimes achieved) an equilibrium between ancient "generality" and modern voluntarism. And that is why the general will "expresses everything he most wanted to say."[26]

Fénelon's *Letter,* then, made a crucial contribution to one of the greatest ongoing modern disputes. If he was certainly no Machiavellian, he loved Rome as ardently as the celebrated Florentine, and he bequeathed that love to the most intense and eloquent of modern "romanists," Rousseau.

V

Having brought out what links Fénelon and Rousseau—the devotion to Greek and Roman antiquity, the subordination of self-love to a larger general good—it is important too to stress the things which separate them. And the main thing which distances them is the crucial difference between "generality" and true "universality." If the mature Rousseau consistently sought after a civic *general* will valid only for Sparta or Rome *en particulier*—so that "the general will one has as a citizen" is precisely particular with respect to the entire *genre humain*— Fénelon remained a believer in a Dantean universal *respublica christiana* held together by universal charity or "disinterested" love. (Unorthodox as Fénelon may have been, he was not about to deny Christian universalism; and indeed he and Leibniz were the last figures of the first rank to cling to the ideals of Dante's *De monarchia*).

To be sure, the young Rousseau had at one time clung to the venerable idea of a *morale universelle.* In an early, unpublished manuscript called *Chronologie universelle, ou Histoire Générale du temps* (1737) he had appealed to Fénelon's notion of a universal Christian republic:

> We are all brothers; our neighbors ought to be as dear to us as ourselves. "I love the human race more than my country," said the illustrious M. de

Fénelon, "my country more than my family and my family more than my-self." Sentiments so full of humanity ought to be shared by all men . . . . The universe is a great family of which we are all members . . . . However extensive may be the power of an individual, he is always in a position to make himself useful . . . to the great body of which he is a part. If he can [do this] he indispensably ought to.[27]

Later, of course—most notably in his attack on Diderot's notion of a reason-ordained "universal morality" in the first version of the *Social Contract*—Rousseau would abandon the *universelle* in favor of the *générale*, and exchange *respublica christiania* for more modest republics, such as Sparta, Rome, and Geneva. That is especially clear in the first of the *Lettres écrites de la montagne* (1764), in which Rousseau shows very clearly that his concern is to produce a civic general will that is peculiar to some particular nation, not a Fénelonian universal will for the good of the whole human race—even if this entails abandoning Christianity as a universal religion:

All the ancient religions, not excepting that of the Jews, were national in origin, appropriated to, and incorporated in, the state; forming the basis, or at least making a part of the legislative system.

Christianity, on the contrary, is in its principles a universal religion, having nothing exclusive, nothing local, nothing peculiar to one country any more than to another. Its divine author, embracing all mankind in his boundless charity, came to remove those barriers that separated the na-tions from each other, and to unite all mankind in a people of brethren . . . .

National religions are useful to a state . . . but they were hurtful to mankind in general. . . . Christianity, on the contrary, by making men just, moderate and peaceable is very advantageous to society in general, but it weakens the force of the political spring [and] . . . breaks the unity of the moral body.[28]

Rousseau ends this passage with a radical claim that proves how little he finally favored Christian universalism: "Christianity . . . inspires hu-manity rather than patriotism, and tends rather to the forming of men than citizens." In the end, for Rousseau, no *morale universelle*—whether given by Christ or reason—can help in the transformation of natural men into denatured citizens. The *générale* must be (somewhat) *partic-ulière*.

Admittedly in the *Political Economy*, a comparatively early transi-tional work, Rousseau seems to vacillate between *universalité* and *génér-alité*. There he first says that "any body politic" is "a moral being that has a will," and that "this general will which always tends to the preservation and welfare of the whole and of each part, and which is the source of the law, is . . . the rule of what is just and unjust." But this "rule of justice," Rousseau immediately adds, while "infallible" for citizens within a particular polity, "can be defective with [respect to] foreigners." This is simply because "the will of the state, though general in relation to its [own] members, is no longer [such] in relation to other states and their members." At this early point, however, Rousseau was not yet ready to say (as he does in the *Lettres écrites de la montagne*) that humanity must yield to patriotism, that men matter less than citizens; thus, having begun by making the general will the will of some particular body politic, Rousseau falls back on the more or less Fénelonian thought that "the large town of the world becomes the body politic, of which the law of nature is always the general will, and the various states and peoples are merely individual members."[29] In his mature, fully confident, and radically civic works, that last echo of the *Chronologie universelle,* of a Dantean-Fénelonian Christian *respublica* under Thomist natural law, finally vanishes altogether: after *Inequality* there is usually no natural law with which the general will can be equated, and after the *Lettres écrites de la montagne* and the *Government of Poland* the "various states" are no longer "members" of a world body politic. In the "Political Economy there is still some vacillation between the *polis* and the *cosmopolis,* the general and the universal; later that vacillation gave way to a radical constancy.

VI

If disinterested love of "Fénelonianism" will not explain everything in Rousseau, then, it nonetheless accounts for a great deal; at a minimum one must fold in Lockean "voluntarism" before one can begin to understand Rousseau's crucial insistence that "the general will is always right." Fénelonian antiquity and Lockean "will," subtly fused, do indeed provide the substructure of Rousseau's politics. And Rousseau captured his devotion to Fénelon's love of antiquity *and* to Locke's ardent modernism when he characterized himself, in a moment of brilliant insight, as one of those "moderns who has an ancient soul." No one ever saw this unorthodox and unexpected rapprochement within Rousseau between Fénelon and Locke as clearly as Judith Shklar. She was in the habit of seeing, not through a glass darkly, but face to face.

Notes

1. *Men and Citizens,* 1.
2. Ibid., 4–5.
3. Ibid., 4–6.

4. See Ely Carcassonne, *Fénelon: L'Homme et l'oeuvre* (Paris, 1946), chap. 1, and, above all, Jeanne-Lydie Goré, *L'itenéraire de Fénelon* (Paris, 1957).

5. Fénelon, *Explication des maximes des saints sur la vie intérieure* ed. A. Cherel (Paris, 1911), 118–30.

6. Bossuet, foreword to *Quatre écrits sur les maximes des saints,* cited in M. Terestchenko, "La doctrine de Fénelon du pur amour," *Les Études philosophiques* 2 (1992).

7. Fénelon, *Lettre sur les occupations de l'Academie Française,* in *Oeuvres de Fénelon* (Paris, 1835), 3:248–50.

8. Bossuet, *Politics Drawn from the Very Words of Holy Scripture,* trans. and ed. Patrick Riley (Cambridge, 1990); Fénelon, *Telemachus, Son of Ulysses,* trans. and ed. Riley (Cambridge, 1994).

9. Jean-Jacques Rousseau, *Émile,* trans. B. Foxley (London, 1910), 431.

10. Fénelon, letter to Letellier, *Oeuvres* 3:653–54.

11. Fénelon, *Telemachus,* 152–53.

12. Ibid., 109–10.

13. Rousseau, *Government of Poland,* in *Political Writings,* trans. F. Watkins (Edinburgh, 1953), 174.

14. Fénelon, *Telemachus,* 252.

15. Fénelon, "Sur le pur amour," *Oeuvres* 1:307–10.

16. See Blaise Pascal, *Pensées,* ed. L. Brunschvicg (Paris, 1914), nos. 473–83 and (above all) no. 792.

17. The notion that egoism is evil ties together figures as radically different as Plato, Augustine, Pascal, Fénelon, and Rousseau: in each of these there is a sublimated "ascent" from low to high. Here Kant is exceptional: for him all love is "pathological," and ethics needs "reason-ordained objective ends," not sublimated eros. See Imannuel Kant, *Critique of Practical Reason* (1788; Indianapolis, 1956), 126–36.

18. See Niccolò Machiavelli, *Discourses,* book 1, chap. 10; and book 2, introduction.

19. See Rousseau's claim that "I am a modern who has an ancient soul" in "Jugement sur la Polysynodie," in *Political Writings,* ed. C. Vaughan (Cambridge, 1915), 1:421.

20. Fénelon, *Lettre sur l'Académie Française,* 248ff.

21. Ibid.

22. Rousseau, *The Social Contract,* in *Political Writings,* 2:35–36.

23. Ibid., 105, 28.

24. Rousseau, *Émile,* 436.

25. See "General Will," 275ff.

26. *Men and Citizens,* 184.

27. Rousseau, "Chronologie universelle," cited in Riley, *The General Will before Rousseau* (Princeton, N.J., 1986), 206–7.

28. Rousseau, *Letters from the Mountain.* (Edinburgh, 1764), 34–37.

29. Rousseau, *Political Economy,* trans. R. Masters, in *On the Social Contract* (New York, 1968), 211–12.

10

Liberalism, Marxism, and the Enlightenment: The Case of Harold Laski

Isaac Kramnick

TOLERANT LIBERAL AND SUPERB TEACHER that she was, Judith Shklar would always urge students in her Enlightenment tutorials and classes to read Harold Laski's *The Rise of European Liberalism*, a book with which she passionately disagreed. It represented for her the quintessential Marxist misreading of the Enlightenment and the liberal tradition. Laski's spirited indictment of liberalism as serving bourgeois interests, with its tone of dogmatic certainty, violated Shklar's profound anti-ideological skepticism, and she hoped it would similarly offend her students, as it usually did. Occasionally, however, exposure to Laski served less to immunize students against a left ideological reading of liberalism than to infect them with it. If the student then moved on to C. B. Macpherson's even more virulent "misreading" of liberalism, there was little hope for recovery.

These two "misreadings" of liberalism were, of course, not unrelated, for much of Macpherson's understanding of political theory was, in fact, shaped by Laski. The teacher who most influenced Macpherson's undergraduate years at the University of Toronto between 1929 and 1932 was Otto B. Van der Sprenkel, a European émigré who had been a student of Laski's at the London School of Economics. Van der Sprenkel constantly cited Laski and his books as he introduced Macpherson to modern political thought. Macpherson then went to study with Laski himself in London from 1932 to 1935. (Van der Sprenkel went to Australia and a second career as a sinologist.) No reader of Macpherson's later *Theory of Possessive Individualism* can fail to see its roots in Laski's *Rise of European Liberalism*, which was published in 1936 from a set of lectures that Laski had developed at the London School of Economics in the previous two years and which Macpherson makes clear in his diary he had attended faithfully.

Just before he published the *Rise of European Liberalism,* Laski wrote to his dear friend Felix Frankfurter, then teaching at the Harvard Law School, hoping that he would not be too upset by the book's "crypto-Marxism."[1] And crypto-Marxist it was. Liberalism was a "new philosophy" which had evolved because "new material conditions . . . gave birth to new social relationships" and it provided "a rational justification for the new world which had come into being." What produced liberalism, according to Laski, "was the emergence of a new economic society at the end of the Middle Ages" and at its heart liberalism "was the idea by which the new middle class rose to a position of political dominance." It was, indeed, "a by-product of the effort of the middle class to win its place in the sun." To be sure, like Marx's praise of the bourgeoisie in *The Communist Manifesto* for playing its very revolutionary role, Laski concedes that "the triumph of liberalism" represented "real and profound progress" and that the "advent of the middle class to power was one of the most beneficent revolutions in history."[2]

Locke was "the prophet" of middle-class liberalism, "nothing so much as the successful missionary of a new faith." At the core of the new creed was the belief that the state exists to protect the right of the "industrious and rational" to accumulate and exploit property. Natural rights "proclaim a code of behavior the rational man will follow," which "protects the individual as he goes about his daily business; they are nothing so much as a specific for prosperity. They are what the business man needs if the hazards of his enterprise are to be minimal." While Lockean liberalism speaks in universal terms, its real message is intended only for "property owners," for "a fellowship of the successful man." It is meaningless to the man "with nothing but his labor to sell"; it unashamedly "invites to freedom those who are denied the means of reaching it."[3]

The Enlightenment's preoccupation with science, symbolized by the *Encyclopedia*'s dedication to Bacon and Newton as well as to Locke, principally served bourgeois economic interests, according to *The Rise of European Liberalism.* It is not, Laski wrote, "excessive to say that the new outlook codified in the *Principia* of Newton emerged from a nexus of problems presented to science by business men in the search for wealth." Science lent powerful assistance to "the rationalizing force of capitalism" by valorizing "the qualities and temper that the new business life demanded—precision, experiment, daring, the search for authority in the facts themselves."[4]

Luminaries of the Age of Reason like Voltaire and Diderot, with their assault on fanaticism, cruelty, and superstition and their commitment to religious toleration, were, in fact, motivated by class interests. "At bottom," Laski writes, "persecution is a threat to property. It endangers the conditions of sound business enterprise." Religious persecution was "incompatible with peace and order," a "hindrance to prosperity," and thus "toleration came because intolerance interfered with the access to wealth." Voltaire's outlook with its "healthy respect for property" was "the practical common sense philosophy of the successful man" and Voltaire's "value to the business man was effectively beyond measure." The tolerant social reformer par excellence, "Voltaire represents at its best the normal outlook of the good and humane bourgeois of his generation who recognizes the existence of profound wrong and is eager for improvement consistently with safety to his own well-being."[5]

Liberalism proclaims that if "the business man but free himself . . . thereby he frees mankind." But in reality "liberalism was a doctrine limited to the service of a narrow section of the community." A doctrine "that started as a method of emancipating the middle class" developed "into a method of disciplining the working class." All socialists, Laski concludes, should "reject the liberal idea" because they recognize it for what it is, "one more particular of history seeking to masquerade as universal."[6]

But Laski did not follow his own advice. His Marxism, crypto or real, never, in fact, required that all features of "the liberal idea" be rejected as mere bourgeois superstructure. Macpherson, in revisiting his London School of Economics teacher's lectures several decades later in his *Possessive Individualism,* perpetuated a distorted reading of Laski on liberalism and the Enlightenment, leaving out an entire dimension of Laski. Throughout his career, in his writings and his activism, Laski tempered his Marxist reading of the relativism and particularism of liberal rights with an abiding commitment to the universal and class free nature of liberal nonproperty-focused rights associated with the values of toleration, free inquiry, individuality, and nonconformity. Laski was, in short, a liberal Marxist.

He self-consciously announced this in his 1940 Hobhouse Memorial Lecture, the timing of which was by no means unimportant, since Britain was then at war with the fascist enemies of civil liberties. There were, he insisted, truly universal and eternal values in "the doctrines of liberalism." Free expression, tolerance, and free inquiry were differentiated from the sanctity of property and only the latter was seen as irredeemably linked to the historic and particularist use of the middle class, a middle class which when its own privileges were attacked was all too ready to abandon the civil liberties of its own liberal tradition. The non-possessive ideals of liberalism were, Laski urged in 1940, not simply "instruments of a system of vested interests."[7]

Laski, however, was not a late-in-the-day antifascist convert to the timeless and universal values of liberty. Throughout his life he consistently championed the civil liberties associated with liberalism and the Enlightenment, even as he wrote of their historically determined, class-based emergence. It was, for example, Laski's outspoken defense of the rights of the individual conscience and of the freedom of thought and expression against the state in his pluralist writings which was the source of his immense appeal to people like Oliver Wendell Holmes, Louis Brandeis, and Frankfurter. His writings and personal influence were among the sources of Justice Holmes's ringing defense of free speech in his dissent in the *Abrams* case in the fall of 1919, which rests on a philosophical defense of "free trade in ideas" with "fighting faiths" surviving the "best test of the truth," which was "the power of the thought to get itself accepted in the competition of the market," since "all life is an experiment" and no truth is accepted for ever.

At the very time that Holmes was sorting through his ambivalent feelings about unlimited free speech, he was being bombarded with a radical civil liberties perspective from his young pluralist friend Laski. Laski's crusade, he wrote to Holmes, "is to take away from the state the superior morality with which we have invested its activities and give them back to the individual conscience."[8] There was much in Laski's 1917 *Studies in the Problem of Sovereignty* to influence Holmes's views on free speech. The Darwinian vision of faiths fighting it out in a struggle was spelled out there in Laski's claim that evolution undermined dogma that claimed eternal truth. Laski railed against those who "make a fetish of obedience. To everyone there comes a point when to bow the knee is worse than death." The book was full of phrases that echo back in Holmes's dissent: "Progress is born from disagreement and discussion"; there is "no immutability of political form"; "the price of liberty is exactly divergence of opinion on fundamental questions."[9]

Even more directly influential on Holmes's *Abrams* dissent were the pleas for civil liberties found in Laski's *Authority in the Modern State*, dedicated to Holmes and read by him in the very months before he wrote his dissent. In his book Laski insisted that history's greatest truth was that the "only real security for social well-being is the free exercise of men's minds." There is a "realm within," the individual conscience, where "the state can have no rights and where it is well that it should have none." No mind was free, Laski wrote, "once a penalty is attached to thought as absolute . . . whether on the part of the individual or of a social group." For the state to claim it knows the one truth was to claim an obnoxious "centralized infallibility." Holmes's magisterial defence of free speech in his dissent was almost verbatim Laski's own amalgam of John Stuart Mill and Charles Darwin. Political ideas are adequate for the moment they were formulated, but since men are various and move in varied directions, no one single scheme of interpreting life ever lasts. "Political good refuses the swaddling clothes of finality. It is a shifting conception," Laski wrote. It is "in the clash of ideas that we shall find the means of truth. There is no other safeguard of progress."[10]

It was Laski's later criticism of communism in practice, just such a single scheme of finality, that evoked some of his most compelling arguments in defence of civil liberty. His little book *Communism*, so influential in directing intellectuals on the British left to the social democracy of the Labour Party and away from the Communist Party of Great Britain, describes as the most grievous fault of communism its assumption of dogmatic truth. Laski's tone is that of the skeptical *philosophes*. Communist Party discipline, requiring absolute and loyal obedience, "dispenses with the problems of conscience in much the same way as an *ex cathedra* pronouncement from Rome controls the attitude of its adherents." The dictatorship of the party "produces an artificial uniformity purchased at the expense of intellectual creativeness." Laski even conjures up the Enlightenment's archenemy to conclude his case against communist assumptions. "The Communist International resembles nothing so much," he writes, "as the Roman Catholic Church. There is the same authoritarian imposition of dogma and there is the same ruthless purging of dissident elements."[11]

In 1937, the year after his book on liberalism, Laski wrote that the Soviet Union, despite its socialist potential, "causes grief and disappointment to those who care for freedom all over the world." He publicly criticized the Webbs (Sidney James and Beatrice Potter), whose *Soviet Communism: A New Civilization* had paid no notice to the barbarism of the treason trials. "In the classic sense of liberalism," Laski wrote, "freedom does not exist in the Soviet Union." There is no liberty to criticize the regime, "to found a journal of opinion, to publish a book, or hold a meeting, to advocate views which . . . threaten the stability of the system." In the worlds of Soviet art, drama, music, and cinema there is, Laski laments, a tragic lack of freedom of expression. He even ridicules in 1937 Soviet efforts to demean rights of free thought as outdated "bourgeois notions."[12]

Laski practiced what he preached. Twice he was himself at the center of free speech crises. A speech to the wives of Boston's striking police in 1919 led to demands from the press and alumni that Harvard fire him, a move resisted by A. Lawrence Lowell, the president of the university, whose own illiberalism stopped at academic freedom. Fifteen years later some speeches Laski gave in Moscow led to calls for an investigation of both him and the London School of Economics, creating a furor that ended only after George Bernard Shaw and John Maynard Keynes weighed in on the side of free speech. Laski was a founding board member (along with Frankfurter) of Roger Baldwin's American Civil Liberties Union in his Harvard years and, more important, in 1934, even while writing the lectures that would culminate in *The Rise of European Liberalism*, Laski was a principal founder in Great Britain of its still existent National Council of Civil Liberties. Three years later, Laski warned that if Britain abandoned its "atmosphere of free discussion our fate will be no different from Russia's or Spain's."[13]

Laski's liberalism coexisted with his commitment to a Marxist reading of society throughout the 1930s and 1940s. He insisted that he was a Marxist socialist and not a Marxist communist, by which he meant a Leninist or a Stalinist. To be a Marxist was for Laski to be a real socialist as opposed to a social reformer, which is how he characterized the leadership of the British Labour Party. It meant that one believed class struggle dominated social life. It meant one sought a total collective transformation of society in which neither a mixed economy nor the profit motive survived. In Laski's tortuous balancing act, to be a Marxist socialist was not to advocate or belong to a party that wanted violent political change brought by a small group of conspirators, but to believe in parliamentary and electoral processes. To be a Marxist socialist was still to be a civil libertarian committed to the individual's right to think and speak freely, uncoerced by party line, unquestioned dogma, or proletarian dictatorship.

Laski was in many respects the very embodiment of the Enlightenment ideal, a *philosophe* in spite of his Marxism. There was, for example, his boundless faith in science. Laski had begun his intellectual life reading biology at Oxford, and he never lost the scientific optimism of his early Fabianism even when linking science to the bourgeois agenda. But it was more than simply that. To the scientific revolution goes the principal credit, according to Laski, for the liberation of knowledge from dependence on Christian dogma and authority. Science undermined "the idea of the heavenly city" by making clear that the reward for effort was not salvation in a life to come but happiness on earth itself.[14] Diderot, especially, and his *Encyclopedia* represent for Laski "the triumph of the scientific spirit over its religious rival." Science enshrines "the unlimited right of free inquiry, and insistence that reason not faith, intelligence, not dogma, are the tests by which truth is established."[15] Scientific progress subdues nature to human purpose and is the "key to that power which will unlock the hidden treasures of the universe."[16]

This wondrous potential of science is not realized under capitalism, however, where science and scientists are not free. Utterly dependent on politicians and businessmen, the "man of science waits cap in hand, as it were, upon the rulers of the society in which he lives."[17] Frustrated by service to the profit motive, science is unable to realize itself as "the servant of mankind." Only socialism will liberate science and enable it to produce abundance for all. Laski was convinced that in a socialist society, "the man of science will slowly, no doubt, but inescapably, come to have that place in society which, in the public imagination, the successful pioneer in business enterprise possessed, especially in the United States, in the period of capitalist expansion."[18]

Laski shared the Enlightenment's contempt for orthodoxy and its commitment to skepticism rooted in the rights of individual conscience and self-expression. Western civilization, Laski wrote, owes all its advances to its "habit of experimenting with taboos, . . . to men who have been deliberately skeptical about its orthodoxies." Yet in the 1930s "we are the slaves of custom," obedient "to certain expected canons of behaviour." The conventional has become infallible and "we do not experiment with ourselves." The political expression of a skeptical disposition was the questioning of authority. Following their consciences, citizens should challenge the state, even the socialist state, not approach it "in fear and trembling." They "owe no state or church a blind or unreasoning obedience," because in the realm of politics no faith is really possible "without a large margin of doubt. . . . There is not a simple certitude today which will not to the future appear meager and inadequate." While it was fascism which for Laski most heinously repudiated these ideals, Soviet communism, "which seeks to impress a particular creed upon every aspect of the life it controls," was equally condemned. The condition of freedom in any state, according to Laski, "is always a widespread and consistent skepticism of the canons upon which power insists."[19]

At the heart of Laski's skepticism and its urging of disobedience was a radical individualism that survived his socialism and his Marxism. His most popular lecture, which Laski gave annually at the London School of Economics, was on Martin Luther's "*Hier Stehe Ich: Ich Kann Nicht Anders.*" Laski's *Liberty in the Modern State,* which the *New York Times* described as the most brilliant defense of liberty "since John Stuart Mill's famous essay," is a veritable hymn to individuality.[20] "I am unique," it proclaims; "I am separate, I am myself; out of these qualities I must build my own principals of action." Laski remained convinced that liberty meant being faithful to oneself even as he acknowledged that it was inescapably "a doctrine of contingent anarchy." Leaders of democratic states, however, had much less reason to fear the anarchic potential of radical individualism than did the "enthusiasts of Moscow and of

Rome," who "differ only in the object of their worship." The latter-day *philosophe* Laski concludes that "enthusiasm has always been the enemy of freedom" and the only "dissolvement of enthusiasm is skepticism."[21]

A final expression of Laski's Enlightenment liberalism was his abhorrence of cruelty and persecution. Here, indeed, he comes the closest to Judith Shklar, who assigned him to her students, notwithstanding her profound disagreement with him. Laski's principal historical villain is not surprising. There was, he wrote, "no form of cruelty in human experience to which the religious spirit has not been able to accommodate itself."[22] Singled out was Roman Catholicism, "one of the permanent enemies of all that is decent in the human spirit."[23] Religious and political persecution must be opposed not because they disturb the peace and stability of a business culture, but for timeless reasons. Persecution assumes that "the persecutor has hold of truth and that he would betray its service by allowing it to be questioned." Criticizing Italy, Germany, and Soviet Russia in the 1930s, Laski wrote that "no man's love of justice is strong enough to survive the right to inflict punishment in the name of the creed he professes."[24] Laski suggests that it was, in fact, Diderot who best expressed his own bottom line political conviction: "the desire to end the needless infliction of pain."[25]

How alike in some respects, then, are the Marxist socialist Laski and the skeptical liberal Shklar. One can almost hear the passionate convictions of the latter in the words of the former as he ridiculed Soviet insistence after 1948 that Czech literature and music be systematically "rid of trash and reactionary rot and mildew." To be sure, Laski wrote, many bad books were published each year in the West for profit, and much was trash and escapism. "But this is surely a smaller danger than to give a Ministry the right to decide what shall be published in terms of a political directive that transforms both books and music into forms of pamphleteering which achieves success only by making its first canon of substance the orthodoxy which the officials of the Ministry will require."[26] One can also hear Shklar in Laski's bitter complaint that governments throughout history perpetually and inexcusably mistreat people, "sweat them in fetid dens, shoot, stab, hang, imprison, sink, burn, and destroy them in the name of law and order."[27]

Toward the end of his life, Laski turned his skepticism on his own Marxist faith in a new socialist Jerusalem built in England's green and pleasant land. Labour was in power, and Laski saw how difficult it was to achieve even a Keynesean managed economy and moderate welfare state, let alone true socialism. His seemingly unflappable belief in a socialist future was shaken. No Heavenly City would be produced by Clement Attlee and Ernest Bevin, but their lack of ideological socialist conviction was not the only reason why. In describing his doubt, Laski's

liberal skepticism was reinforced by an unlikely source, the conservative skepticism of Edmund Burke, the grave digger of the Enlightenment, whom Laski read often and wrote on extensively. "Man," Laski
wrote, "Is a conservative animal, whose ideas are imprisoned within a
framework he is not easily persuaded to abandon." It's a Burkean Laski
with a dash of Gramsci:

> We are trying to transform a profoundly bourgeois society, in which all
> the major criteria of social values have been imposed by a long indoctrina-
> tion for whose faith all the power of church and school, of press and cin-
> ema and radio, have been very skillfully mobilized; we have got to
> transform this bourgeois society into a socialist society with foundations
> not less secure than those it seeks to renovate. We have, moreover, to ac-
> complish this in a dramatically revolutionary period, in which quite liter-
> ally millions, afraid of the responsibilities of freedom, yearn to cling to
> whatever they have, however fragmentary, of a security with which they
> are familiar.[28]

How ironic that one way Laski dealt with his doubt was by turning to
religion, the very source of dreaded enthusiasm for the *philosophes*. After a career in which he had rarely made public mention of his Jewishness, Laski in his fifties became preoccupied with it. His Enlightenment
conviction that reason would inevitably triumph over darkness and evil
was devastated by the revelation of the Nazi atrocities. In the spring of
1943 Laski attended for the first time a meeting of the Poale Zion, the
Jewish Socialist Labour Party, an affiliated society within the Labour
Party. The members took it as a sign of Laski's return to his people as a
Jew, and, indeed, at the 1943 Labour Party conference, Laski spoke for
the National Executive Committee, on which he sat, in supporting the
resolution moved by the Poale Zion "expressing horror and indignation with which all civilized mankind witnesses Hitler's bestial campaign
of extermination of European Jewry," as well as reaffirming "the traditional policy of the Labour Party in favour of building Palestine as the
Jewish national home." From the platform Laski noted in his first sentence that it was "fitting that a member of the National Executive who is
also a Jew" should speak for the resolution. He proceeded to make a
public declaration of his Jewishness to the delegates: "I, as a Jew in the
fullest sense of the word, claim absolute equality of status in political,
social, and economic rights with any other people in the world." The
Jews, he went on, "are always selected as the first victims of reactionaries. For 2,000 years we have been the victims of persecution of this
kind. But we have stood at the grave of every one of our previous oppressors and we shall stand at the graves of our Nazi oppressors, too."[29]

In his last years the Zionist Laski spent as much time criticizing

Bevin's Palestine policy as he did the latter's overly obsequious partnership with America in the early years of the cold war. In the summer of 1948, in fact, Laski was taken to task about his identity as a Jew. He had written that with its failure to recognize Israel immediately, "the British government has done more damage to the honor and prestige of Britain than our enemies have been able to inflict on us since the evil days of Munich." The Tory *Spectator* asked to whom the word *our* referred; Were these the "words of a Jew or an Englishman?" Clearly, it went on, "Mr. Laski is a Jew first and an Englishman second." He had a perfect right to so order his loyalties, the *Spectator* conceded, "but if that is his choice, his right place would seem to be Palestine, not England."[30] In a talk to the Association of Jewish Ex-Servicemen about the revival of anti-Semitism in Britain, Laski answered the *Spectator:*

> Referring to Israel, Professor Laski said that the only ultimate enemies of Israel were the Jews who were ashamed of their Jewishness, afraid of their fellow-Jews, and who thought that their status as Englishmen or Americans or Frenchmen was compromised by the establishment of Israel . . . . Although by tradition and training he was in the intellectual climate of this country, and although his legal allegiance was as fully English as that of Mr. Bevin, he would feel safer if there was a Jewish government sitting in Tel Aviv with the right to interest itself in the Jews of England, just as the Vatican had the right to interest itself in the Roman Catholics.[31]

He had come full circle. From ridiculing the Vatican as the essence of intolerant dogmatism, Laski invoked it now as the exemplary model with which to resolve the dilemma of dual allegiance created by his new Zionist faith.

Shklar never discussed Laski's Zionism in class or tutorial; it was not that well known. But given her own skepticism and the interest she always had in the themes of exile and loyalty, how she would have relished exploring and exploiting the tensions and the paradoxes to which Laski, the Marxist *philosophe,* was led by his skepticism.

Notes

1. Felix Frankfurter Papers, Library of Congress, 28 Dec. 1935.
2. Harold Laski, *The Rise of European Liberalism* (London, 1936), 12, 17, 258, 18.
3. Ibid., 115, 116, 142, 155, 157.
4. Ibid., 75, 140.
5. Ibid., 61, 131, 170, 211–12.
6. Ibid., 182, 195, 208, 241.

7. Laski, "The Decline of Liberalism," Hobhouse Memorial Lecture, London School of Economics, 20 May 1940.

8. *The Holmes-Laski Letters*, ed. M. D. Howe (Cambridge, 1953), 1:113.

9. Laski, *Studies in the Problem of Sovereignty* (New Haven, Conn., 1917), 211, 236–37, 274.

10. Laski, *Authority in the Modern State* (New Haven, Conn., 1919), 55–56, 301, 166, 279.

11. Laski, *Communism* (London, 1927), 225, 229, 192.

12. Laski, *Liberty in the Modern State* (London, 1937), 18, 43, 210.

13. Laski, "Outlook for Civil Liberties," *Fabian Society* (London, 1937), 18.

14. Laski, *Faith, Reason and Civilization* (New York, 1944), 60.

15. Laski, "Diderot," in *Studies in Law and Politics* (New Haven, Conn., 1932), 54, 53.

16. Laski, *Faith*, 60.

17. Laski, *The Place of the Scientist in Post-war Administration* (London, 1945), 7.

18. Laski, *Reflections on the Revolution of Our Time* (New York, 1943), 50, 162.

19. Laski, *The Dangers of Obedience and Other Essays* (New York, 1930), 1, 3, 6, 23, 25, 26, 29.

20. Laski, *New York Times*, 30 Nov. 1930.

21. Laski, *Liberty*, 90, 92, 210–11.

22. Laski, *Reflections*, 4.

23. *Holmes-Laski Letters*, 2:1450.

24. Laski, *Reflections*, 202, 241.

25. Laski, "Diderot," 48.

26. Laski, *The Dilemma of Our Times* (London, 1952), 235–36, 238.

27. Laski, *Parliamentary Government in Britain* (New York, 1938), 154.

28. Laski, *The Road to Recovery* (London, 1948), 49–50.

29. Labour Party, *Report of the Annual Conference* (1943), 188.

30. *Spectator*, 11 June 1948.

31. Laski, in *Jewish Chronicle*, 24 Sept. 1948.

11

Thomas Hobbes's Antiliberal Theory of Liberty

Quentin Skinner

DITA SHKLAR WAS GREATLY INTERESTED in, and highly knowledgeable about, the early modern origins of our current beliefs about rights and liberty. Yet she never devoted any sustained attention to the philosophy of Thomas Hobbes, who arguably treated these issues with greater rigor and depth than any other early modern writer in the English language. While this neglect may at first sight seem surprising, it is perhaps not difficult to guess why Hobbes appears only fleetingly in Dita's pages, where he tends to be treated as a somewhat marginal although unquestionably impressive figure.[1] The clue is surely to be found in the fact that, from first to last, Dita always presented herself in her own political writings as a liberal: as someone whose historical interests centered on the origins of liberalism,[2] and whose main concern as a moralist was to vindicate what she eventually called, in a now-famous phrase, the liberalism of fear.[3]

To espouse this form of liberalism is to believe, on Dita's account, that cruelty is incomparably the worst of the vices, is indeed "the supreme evil"[4]. One of her own grounds for holding this belief was her sense that the infliction of cruelty, or even the threat of it, causes such anguish and fear as to enslave us, to undermine and take away our liberty.[5] She accordingly viewed despotism, as Montesquieu had done, as the politics of fear,[6] while defining liberal societies as those in which potential victims of cruelty and oppression are effectively protected in

This chapter draws on an article published as "Liberty and Legal Obligation in Hobbes's *Leviathan*," in *Jurisprudence: Cambridge Essays*, ed. Hyman Gross and Ross Harrison, 231–56, © Oxford University Press 1992. Reprinted by permission.

their freedom and security,[7] so that all citizens are liberated from terror and the cruelty engendering it.[8] One of her reasons, in short, for stigmatizing cruelty as the worst of the ordinary vices is that cruelty produces fear, and fear takes away liberty.

This is exactly what Hobbes denies. "Feare and Liberty are consistent," he declares in chapter 21 of *Leviathan*, so that although "a man sometimes pays his debts only for feare of Imprisonment," this is nevertheless "the action of a man at liberty." Freedom remains unaffected by coercion or fear of punishment, so that "generally all actions which men doe in Commonwealths, for feare of the law, are actions which the doers had liberty to omit."[9]

Hobbes's claim that free actions are compatible with coercion poses an obvious challenge to those who think of themselves—as Dita always did—as the heirs of classical liberalism. Within that tradition of thought, the absolute opposition between freedom and coercion always amounted to an article of faith. Henry Sidgwick, for example, expresses the point with complete confidence in analyzing the concept of freedom in his *Elements of Politics*, one of the most powerful summaries of the classical liberal creed:

> When employed without qualification, "freedom" signifies primarily the absence of physical coercion or confinement: . . . But in another part of its meaning—which from our present point of view is more important— "freedom" is opposed not to physical constraint, but to the moral restraint placed on inclination by the fear of painful consequences resulting from the action of other human beings.[10]

The incompatibility of freedom with coercion is here presented as a matter of definition: if we fail to recognize it we fail to grasp the meaning of freedom itself.

Owing to this commitment, liberal theorists have always felt it possible to offer a robust answer to Hobbes, an answer which has largely been endorsed and repeated in recent commentaries on his thought. Hobbes, we are told, was simply confused about the nature of liberty, and treats the concept incoherently.[11] Beginning with the dramatic but indefensible claim that liberty can be restricted only by physical force, he later admits that the liberty of subjects depends in virtually every instance on "the silence of the law." He thereby reverts, with obvious inconsistency, to the familiar claim that liberty can also be limited by the threat of force, and hence by the mechanism of fear.

These accusations of inconsistency are widespread, but I have come to feel that they fail to take account of the framework within which Hobbes's theory of liberty is situated, especially the framework provided by his fundamental distinction between the natural and artificial conditions of mankind. Once the force of that distinction is recognized, the apparent confusions in his analysis of the relations between coercion and liberty can, I think, be shown to dissolve. But this in turn means that Hobbes's challenge to liberal pieties remains to haunt us after all. It becomes clear that his underlying purpose is to defuse the allegedly radical implications of theories both about natural rights and government by consent, the two concepts central not merely to the revolutionary politics of his own age but to later liberal thought as well.

I

There are two striking features of Hobbes's most extended analysis of liberty, which he puts forward in chapter 21 of *Leviathan*, entitled "Of the Liberty of Subjects." One is the vehemence with which he insists that his own explication of the concept represents the only possible one. No comparable tone of urgency underlies his earlier discussions either in *The Elements of Law*, first circulated in 1640, or in *De cive*, first published in 1642.[12] By the time he came to issue *Leviathan* in 1651, however, Hobbes had clearly come to regard it as a matter of great importance to be able to declare that what he was offering was an account of "the proper signification" of liberty (91), what it "signifieth properly" (145), and how to understand it "in the proper sense" (147).

The other striking feature of Hobbes's analysis is its extreme simplicity. He first introduces the topic of human freedom in *Leviathan* in connection with his discussion of "the right of nature" in chapter 14. This he defines as "the liberty each man hath to use his power as he will himself for the preservation of his own nature" (91). (It should be noted that, in following the usage of time, Hobbes always equates human freedom with "the freedom of man." Regrettable though this is, I shall not be able wholly to avoid such turns of phrase myself in attempting to give an exegesis of his thought.) This freedom or liberty,[13] Hobbes at once stresses, must be defined in negative terms. The presence of liberty is always marked, that is, by the absence of something else. Specifically, it is marked by "the absence of externall Impediments" (91). And by *impediments* Hobbes simply means anything that can hinder a man from using his powers "according as his judgment and reason shall dictate to him" (91).

This analysis is subsequently taken up and elaborated at the start of chapter 21, at which point Hobbes presents his formal definition of what it means to be a free man. "A FREE-MAN is he that, in those things which by his strength and wit he is able to do, is not hindred to doe what he has a will to" (146). As this makes clear, Hobbes sees two essential elements in the concept of human freedom. One is the idea of possessing an underlying power or ability to act. As Hobbes had already observed in chapter 14, it is in relation to "a man's power to do what hee would" that we speak of his being or not being at liberty (91). The other is the idea of being unimpeded in the exercise of such powers. As Hobbes explains in chapter 21, the freedom of a man "consisteth in this, that he finds no stop in doing what he has the will, desire or inclination to doe" (146).

Hobbes's basic doctrine can thus be very straightforwardly summarized. He already hints as much at the start of chapter 14 of *Leviathan*,[14] but he says so most clearly at the end of *The Questions Concerning Liberty, Necessity and Chance*, his final reply to Bishop Bramhall on the problem of free will. A free man is he who, in respect of his powers or abilities, "can do if he will and forbear if he will."[15]

As Hobbes recognizes, however, this analysis is not yet a very illuminating one. We still lack an account of the kinds of limitations on human action that count as impediments. To put the point another way, we still lack a criterion for distinguishing between inherent limitations upon our powers themselves, and positive constraints upon our freedom to exercise or forbear from exercising those powers in accordance with our will and desires.

Turning to this further theme at the start of chapter 21, Hobbes distinguishes two ways in which freedom may be hindered or impeded. The first is common to human and inanimate bodies. It occurs when "the opposition of some externall body" intervenes in such a way that another body is tied—or, as Hobbes also says, is bound—so that "it cannot move but within a certain space."[16] Hobbes has just laid it down that to be free is to be unimpeded from doing or forbearing from doing something. But these are cases in which an agent is impeded from doing something. An action within the agent's powers is rendered physically impossible of performance. It follows that such agents "are not at Liberty to move in such manner as without those externall impediments they would" (146).

The other way we can be hindered from using our powers at will is considered in the same passage. This happens when we are physically bound or obliged to act in some particular way by the operation of an irresistible external force.[17] Hobbes assumes that, if we are to describe a man as free, we must not only be able to say that he is free to act; we must also be able to say that, when he acts, he performs his action freely, in that he "may refuse to doe it if he will" (146). If, by contrast, he cannot forbear from acting, then his action will not be that of "one that was free" (146). As Hobbes had already noted in his preliminary discussion in chapter 14, obligation and liberty "in one and the same matter are inconsistent" (91).

This second type of impediment might seem to be of merely residual significance, especially as Hobbes largely confines himself to illustrating it with such simple instances as that of someone who is "led to prison by force."[18] But in fact the category of actions we cannot forbear from performing is of considerable theoretical importance for Hobbes, since he takes it to be the means of defining two forms of human bondage.

One is that of slavery. According to Hobbes's analysis, both in *De cive* and *Leviathan*, the lack of liberty suffered by slaves is not simply that they are "kept in prison or bonds" (141). It is also that "their labour is appointed to them by another" in such a way that their bodies "are not in their own power" (447). A slave is thus defined as someone whose lack of freedom is in part that he is, literally, a bondsman: someone who is bound or forced to act and is not at liberty to forbear from acting.[19]

The other way human freedom is similarly forfeited is among those who admit God's providence. This too is stressed both in *De cive* and *Leviathan*, although in this case the earlier analysis is the fuller one. God's power, to those who recognize it, must appear as irresistible.[20] It follows that when God issues a command to those who believe in him—for example through the Scriptures, which many believe to be the word of God—then "they cannot forbear from obeying him."[21] They are tied or bound to obey in such a way "that their bodily liberty is forfeited."[22] As Hobbes summarizes in chapter 45 of *Leviathan*, all religious believers "are God's slaves" (447).

The whole of Hobbes's analysis thus depends on his initial distinction between power and liberty. We forfeit our liberty if an external force renders us powerless to act or powerless not to act in some particular way. The distinction is, I think, clear, but is nevertheless worth underlining. For as Hobbes himself stresses, it is all too easy for the two concepts to become confused.[23] The danger arises from the fact that, if we follow a Hobbesian analysis, we are bound to say of someone who is capable of exercising the power to act in some particular way that they are also at liberty to act in that way. Their power and liberty amount to the same thing. This being so, there is a temptation to add—as Hobbes notes in his reply to Bramhall[24]—that if someone analogously lacks the power to act, they must also lack the liberty.

This is certainly a temptation to which "negative" theories of liberty have regularly fallen prey in the twentieth no less than in the seventeenth century.[25] But as Hobbes rightly observes, it may or may not make sense to claim that an agent who lacks power also lacks liberty. It will not make sense where the impediment to motion lies in "the constitution of the thing it selfe" (146). To take Hobbes's own example, a man "fastned to his bed by sicknesse" lacks the power to move, but it makes no sense to say that he also lacks the liberty.[26] The reason why he cannot be said to be unfree is that nothing is impeding him from moving; he is simply incapable of movement. This contrasts with the predicament of a man "imprisoned or restrained with walls" (146). His plight is similar to that of the sick man in that he is unable to leave. But the sick man would still be unable even if the prison doors were to be opened, whereas the prisoner is only unable because the doors remain locked. He possesses an underlying power or ability to leave which has been "taken away" from him.[27] So while the sick man merely lacks ability, the prisoner lacks freedom.

If this interpretation is sound, it is worth adding that Hobbes's theory of human freedom seems to have been rather widely misunderstood. Hobbes is often singled out as the classic exponent of what is sometimes called the pure negative theory of liberty.[28] He is claimed, that is, to hold the view that an individual is unfree if and only if the doing of some particular action has been rendered impossible.[29] But this appears to be untrue to Hobbes's analysis in two distinct ways. Although Hobbes agrees that agents may be said to lack freedom if actions within their powers have been rendered impossible, he does not think that this is the only way in which unfreedom can be produced.[30] An agent will also lack freedom if tied or bound to act in such a way as to make it impossible to forebear from acting. The other misunderstanding is that, even if no one is rendering it impossible for an agent to act in a given way, it still does not necessarily follow for Hobbes that the agent is free to perform the action concerned.[31] This is because, as we have seen, the action in question may be beyond the agent's powers. It is true that, given the lines along which Hobbes analyzes the concept, he might be willing to admit that the agent is free to try to perform the given action—although he does not in fact pronounce upon that question at any point. But what is certain is that, for Hobbes, the question of whether the action is one that the agent is or is not free to perform simply does not arise.

Rather than being an instance of the pure negative theory of liberty, Hobbes's analysis serves to suggest that there may be something amiss with the theory itself. To state it in its positive and most widely accepted form, the theory holds that we are free unless an action within our powers has been subjected to "preventing conditions."[32] This formulation certainly avoids the awkwardness of claiming that we remain free to perform actions beyond our powers. But is still appears to confuse the general concept of social freedom with the more specific notion of being free to act.[33] It overlooks the possibility that our lack of freedom may derive not from being unfree to act, but rather from being unable to act freely.[34]

II

So far I have presented Hobbes's theory of human freedom as a simple and unambiguous one. But it must be admitted that this interpretation faces a difficulty. As I intimated at the outset, moreover, it is a difficulty which has caused many of Hobbes's commentators to conclude that his theory is not only more complicated than I have been implying but is seriously confused.

The main grounds for this accusation are furnished by the range of examples Hobbes uses to illustrate his theory at the start of chapter 21 of *Leviathan*. One of the cases he considers is that of a free gift. "When we say a Guift is Free," he maintains, "there is not meant any Liberty of the Guift, but of the Giver, that was not bound by any law or Covenant to give it" (146). Hobbes's point is that the agent is free in the sense of being able to act freely as opposed to being bound or forced to act. But his chosen instance seems to presuppose a view much broader than I have so far been suggesting of the range of ties that can properly be said to take away our liberty to forbear from acting. As well as the purely physical constraints of slavery, he now includes the bonds of covenants and law.

A further example Hobbes discusses in the same passage is that of freedom of speech. "When we speak Freely," the freedom we exercise "is not the Liberty of voice or pronunciation, but of the man, whom no law hath obliged to speak otherwise than he did" (146). Here Hobbes is making the contrasting point that the agent is free in the sense of being free to act as opposed to being prevented. But again he appears to expand his sense of the range of ties that are capable of stopping us from acting, and hence of taking away our liberty. As well as the purely physical bonds on which he initially concentrated, he again speaks of the bonds of law as another such potential impediment.

In the light of such examples, it is easy to see how the accusation of inconsistency arises. Hobbes first defines freedom as the absence of purely physical hindrances. But he then seems to allow that our liberty can also be limited by moral and especially legal ties. By passing, as one critic has put it, "from physical impediments to obligations" as his criterion of unfreedom, he leaves his analysis muddled and confused.[35]

As I began by suggesting, however, this criticism ignores the fact that Hobbes is interested in *Leviathan* in two separate "conditions of mankind."[36] One is our natural condition, in which we are free from legal constraints, and at the same time possess our natural liberty to the extent that we are capable of exercising our powers without being physically prevented or compelled.[37] But the other condition in which

Hobbes is interested is, in his own phrase, not natural but "artificial," a condition created by art in which we act as subjects of an "Artificiall Man" (9), the sovereign author of the "Artificiall Chains" of the law (147). It is in relation to this underlying duality—which runs throughout *Leviathan*—that we need to assess the coherence of Hobbes's views about coercion and liberty.

Hobbes is of course clear that the coercive powers of the law limit our liberty as subjects. To say that we are subjects is to say that we have covenanted to give up the condition in which we all naturally find ourselves, the condition of "meer Nature" in which, apart from our obligation to obey the laws of nature, we have no legal obligations at all.[38] There is therefore a sense in which, in agreeing to quit the state of nature, we must be deciding to give up a form of liberty. By covenanting to become subjects of a commonwealth, we agree to regulate our behavior according to the civil law. "But Civill Law is an Obligation, and takes from us the Liberty which the Law of Nature gave us. Nature gave a Right to every man to secure himselfe by his own strength, and to invade a suspected neighbour by way of prevention; but the Civill Law takes away that Liberty" (200).

It is the fulcrum of Hobbes's theory of the commonwealth to insist on the rationality of giving up this freedom from any obligation to obey human laws. Because everyone in the state of nature enjoys this freedom, and because "nature hath made men so equall" in power and strength (86–87), the state of nature can only be described as a condition of liberty in the most paradoxical sense. It can equally well be described as a condition in which we all enjoy an equal liberty to master and enslave our neighbors, while they enjoy the same liberty "to make themselves Masters" of our own "persons, wives, children and cattell" if they can manage it (88). The paradox is excellently summarized by Dita Shklar in the course of analyzing Hegel's theory of the state in her book *Freedom and Independence*. With Hegel, as she puts it, the "state of absolute liberty" is recognized as being "exactly what Hobbes said it was, a condition of universal fear of violent death."[39]

Nevertheless, there remains a sense in which liberty is forfeited when we take on the role of subjects.[40] Given that a subject is, by definition, someone subject to law, it follows that the liberty of a subject must basically depend upon "the Silence of the Law" (152). If there are "cases where the Soveraign has prescribed no rule, there the Subject hath the Liberty to do or forbeare according to his own discretion" (152). But where the law enjoins or forbids a certain course of action, there the subject is tied or bound to act or forbear from acting as the law and sovereign command.[41]

As Hobbes makes clear at the outset, however, these considerations apply to us only in relation to our "artificial" condition as subjects. It remains to ask whether he thinks that the coercive bonds of law serve at the same time to limit our natural liberty. For only in that case will it be justifiable to claim that his exposition is confused.

Before turning to that question, it is important to note that Hobbes allows one exception even to his doctrine that the liberty which characterizes our natural condition—liberty from human law—is canceled by the obligations we undertake when we covenant to become subjects. The exception is grounded on the fact that, when we covenant, "the motive and end for which this renouncing and transferring of Right is introduced is nothing else but the security of a mans person in his life and in the means of so preserving life as not to be weary of it" (93). It follows that, if "the end of Obedience is Protection" (153), there must be certain natural rights—and hence liberties of action—that "can by no Covenant be relinquished" (153). Specifically, I cannot consistently agree to relinquish my freedom to act in protection of my life and bodily liberty. For my sole aim in agreeing to the covenant was to assure a better protection for precisely those rights than I could ever have hoped to achieve by my own unaided efforts in the lawless condition of mere nature.[42]

Hobbes's main point, however, is a far more general and challenging one. It is that, even when our freedom from legal obligation in the state of nature is undoubtedly abridged by our duty as subjects to obey the civil law, this does nothing to limit our natural liberty to employ our powers in accordance with our will and desires.

Hobbes of course intends this conclusion to seem paradoxical. But the paradox can readily be resolved if we turn to the account he gives of the distinctive ways in which any system of law operates to ensure the obedience of those subject to it. There are two separate routes, according to Hobbes, by which a citizen can come to feel the force of a law and decide to obey it. First, all rational persons will, *ex hypothesi*, recognize that obedience is in their interests. For the basic aim of law is to seek peace by protecting life and liberty, and these are the goals that all rational persons seek above all. So the liberty of such agents to act as their will and desires dictate will not in the least be infringed by their obligation to obey the law. The dictates of their wills and the requirements of the law will prove to be one and the same.

This expresses a traditional view about the compatibility of liberty and legal obligation, one that John Locke was classically to restate a generation later in his *Two Treatises of Government:* "Law in its true notion is not so much the Limitation as the direction of a free and intelligent Agent to his proper interests." Locke draws the inference that, when we submit to the direction of such laws, this will constitute an expression rather than a restriction of our liberty. "That ill deserves the Name of Confinement that hedges us in only from Bogs and Precipices."[43] This is not merely a doctrine that Hobbes appears to endorse, but one that he enunciates in the form of a simile later echoed by Locke with remarkable closeness. "The use of Lawes," as Hobbes puts it in discussing the office of the sovereign in chapter 30 of *Leviathan*, "is not to bind the People from all Voluntary actions, but to direct and keep them in such a motion as not to hurt themselves by their own impetuous desires, rashnesse, or indiscretion, as Hedges are set, not to stop Travellers, but to keep them in the way" (239–40).

As Dita Shklar stresses in her book *Men and Citizens*, this view of the compatibility between law and liberty remained of great importance throughout the Enlightenment, and underlies Kant's moral thinking no less than that of Rousseau in the *Contrat social*. Both writers continue to assume that, so long as I am involved in the process of law making myself, then the laws I help to make must by definition be a product of my will, and hence an expression of my freedom rather than a limitation of it.[44]

To Hobbes, however, it is crucial to stress that this is not the reason why the generality of citizens obey the law, moved as they are by mere considerations of wealth, command, or sensual pleasure. The only mechanism by which they can be brought to obey is by making them more terrified of the consequences of disobedience.[45] There is admittedly no hope of employing this device outside the confines of the commonwealth. "Covenants without the Sword are but Words, and of no strength to secure a man at all" (117). But if a "visible Power" is erected "to keep them in awe, and tye them by feare of punishment," then there is every prospect of compelling them both to act in line with their obligations and at the same time to forbear from acting as partiality, pride, and revenge would otherwise dictate (117).

It is of course true that, where the mechanism of using fear to produce obedience works successfully, subjects will elect not to exercise their powers or abilities in various ways. The whole purpose of assigning the right of punishment to sovereigns is "to forme the wills" of their subjects in just this way (120). But the point on which Hobbes above all insists is that this does nothing to take away our continuing power or ability to act as our will and desires dictate. "The Consent of a Subject to Soveraign Power" is such that "there is no restriction at all of his own former naturall Liberty" (151).

To see how Hobbes can consistently defend this crucial conclusion, we need only recall his account of the means by which we are alone capable of forfeiting our liberty, in "the proper signification of the word" (91). An external impediment must intervene in such a way that we are

either stopped from acting or forced to act contrary to our will and desires. But neither fear nor any other passion of the soul can possibly
count as such an impediment. Rather, anyone who acts out of fear performs an action out of a desire to avoid various consequences which,
they fear, will otherwise befall them. Of such persons we may certainly
say that they act as they do because their wills have been "formed" or
"compelled."[46] But to compel someone's will is only to cause them to
have a will or desire to act other than the will or desire for the sake of
which they would otherwise have acted. When such persons act, it will
still be because they possess the will or desire to act in precisely the ways
in which they duly act. It follows that, even if the cause of their will is
fear, the actions they perform out of fear will be free actions. To illustrate his argument, Hobbes takes the familiar example originally considered by Aristotle at the start of book 3 of the *Nicomachean Ethics*, the
example of a man who "throweth his goods into the Sea for feare the
ship should sink."[47] The man certainly acts out of fear; so we may say if
we like that he felt compelled to act. But as Hobbes grimly adds—
challenging Aristotle's analysis[48]—"he doth it neverthelesse very willingly, and may refuse to doe it if he will: it is therefore the action of one
that was free" (146).

As we saw at the outset, Hobbes's basic contention is thus that "Feare
and Liberty are consistent." It follows that, if we speak of being tied or
bound by the laws, we cannot be speaking of natural ties, but only of
artificial or metaphorical ones. Hobbes is anxious to underline this
point, for he describes the artificial character of these bonds in a mem-
orably grotesque piece of imagery at odds with his usual expository
style:

> But as men for the atteyning of peace, and conservation of themselves
> thereby, have made an Artificiall Man, which we call a Common-wealth;
> so also have they made Artificiall Chains, called Civill Lawes, which they
> themselves, by mutuall covenants, have fastned at one end to the lips of
> that Man or Assembly to whom they have given the Soveraigne Power;
> and at the other end to their own Ears. (147)

Hobbes is alluding here to Lucian's version of the fable of Hercules. According to Lucian, the ancient Gauls thought of Hercules as a venerable
and exceptionally prudent orator, symbolizing his gifts of persuasion
by picturing him as drawing men along by fetters attached at one end to
his tongue and at the other end to his followers' ears.[49] Hobbes's original readers might perhaps have been surprised to come upon this sudden classical flourish, especially as Hobbes was to boast in his conclusion
that he had deliberately left *Leviathan* unencumbered with any such
conventional references to ancient authorities (490). But Hobbes would

undoubtedly have expected his original readers both to recognize the allusion and to grasp its relevance, especially as Lucian's claim that men can be "led by the ears" had already become a favourite humanist *topos* by the end of the sixteenth century.[50] The moral of the story, as Hobbes makes clear, is that while the chains of the law are of course sufficient to bind us in our artificial condition as subjects, these chains "in their own nature" have no binding force at all. They can only be made to hold "by the danger, though not by the difficulty of breaking them" (147). They may persuade, but they cannot force. As Hobbes puts it in a further classical allusion (this time to Plutarch's life of Solon),[51] all subjects retain at all times the natural liberty of "breaking through the Cob-web Lawes of their Country" if they will (204).

I cannot see, therefore, that there is any serious inconsistency in Hobbes's theory of human freedom. He does not contradict himself by first saying that liberty can only be constrained by external impediments and later that it can also be constrained by fear of the law. Rather his point is that the law and its penalties form part of an artificial world which supervenes upon, but does not of course abolish, the world of nature. The law binds us as subjects in such a way that, legally speaking, there are certain things we must and other things we cannot do. But these bonds are purely artificial; they leave entirely unimpaired our natural liberty to make use of our powers as we please.

III

I have now tried to lay out what I take to be Hobbes's view about "the proper signification" of liberty. But I am far from supposing that I have said enough to enable his theory to be fully understood. As I intimated at the outset, one of the most interesting questions raised by his analysis is why he should have insisted with so much vehemence that it constitutes the only possible way of thinking about the idea of human freedom. Having followed out his analysis, it now becomes possible to rephrase that question more pointedly. Why should Hobbes have been so anxious to insist on such a restricted account of the circumstances in which we can legitimately claim that our liberty has been infringed?

The answer, I shall argue, is that Hobbes's conclusions—as well as the special emphasis he places on them in *Leviathan*—follow in part from his anxiety to confront and overturn two prevailing theories about the nature and especially the limits of political obligation which he had come to regard as peculiarly dangerous. One was the claim that we all possess natural rights as part of our birthright; the other was the connected claim that, if governments are to possess any legitimacy, they must originate in an act of voluntary consent on the part of those who submit to them.

This is not to say that Hobbes repudiates the doctrines of natural rights and government by consent. On the contrary, he agrees that our natural condition is one of "full and absolute Libertie," and he treats our natural liberty and our natural rights of action as one and the same (91–92, 149–50). He also agrees that, because "all men equally are by Nature Free," there can be "no Obligation on any man which ariseth not from some Act of his own" (150). He agrees in consequence that conquest and victory can never in themselves yield any "right of dominion over the vanquished" nor any obligation on the part of the conquered (141–42). This is due to the fact that, where someone submits merely as a result of being "overcome," their obedience will be due to the fact that they have been "put into prison or chaines" and have found it impossible not to submit (485, 141). As we have seen, however, to be physically forced into submission in this way is, for Hobbes, to be in the condition not of a subject but a slave. If, by contrast, our obligation is to be that of a true subject, it is indispensable that our submission should take the form of an act of free consent.

What Hobbes opposes is not the doctrines of natural right and consent but the attempt to draw radical and even revolutionary conclusions from them. Among the groups he particularly denounces for attempting to draw such conclusions are the Levellers and sectaries who, as he puts it in *Leviathan*, are clamoring for liberty and calling it their birthright.[52] As Dita Shklar forcefully reminds us in her book *American Citizenship*, these groups and the demands they put forward in the course of the 1640s made a major contribution to the development of liberal thought.[53] This was the moment at which the demand was voiced for equal treatment to be accorded to citizens in virtue of their natural rather than their property rights, and hence in virtue of their birthright of freedom. Shklar goes so far as to add that "the future American citizen was born in the course of these exchanges."[54]

So much the worse, according to Hobbes, for the future American citizen. Hobbes insists that, once we have grasped the proper signification of liberty, we shall see that all such claims about liberty as a birthright are wholly and dangerously confused. Suppose we take it that what these agitators are demanding is "Liberty in the proper sense," that is, "freedome from chains and prisons." Then it is "very absurd for men to clamor as they doe' for this form of freedom, since they manifestly enjoy it (147). But suppose we instead take them to be calling for liberty in the sense of "exemption from Lawes"—what Hobbes has been describing as the liberty of subjects. To ask for complete freedom in this sense is no less absurd. For this is to demand a return to the state of nature. And as Hobbes has already shown, to call for this is to call in effect for slavery, since it is to ask for that form of liberty "by which all other men may be masters" of our lives (147).

Hobbes reserves his most detailed criticisms, however, for those who sought to derive radical conclusions from the doctrine of government by consent. One widely canvassed claim was that no legitimate government can ever originate in an act of submission to a victor in war—a claim repeated with great vehemence a generation later by Locke in his *Two Treatises*.[55] A second claim—also crucial to Locke—was that because all lawful government needs to originate in an act of free consent, those who submit to government must at the same time be able to declare the terms of their submission in such a way as to set limits to the powers of government over them.

Hobbes mainly focuses on these arguments in the Review and Conclusion of *Leviathan*, where he complains that "divers English Books lately printed" make it evident that no one has yet understood the relations between conquest, consent, and obedience (484). But it is in chapter 20 that he first takes up the question of "Dominion acquired by Conquest or Victory in war," and is thus led to examine the predicament of a man who, finding his sovereign vanquished, submits to his conqueror in order "to avoyd the present stroke of death" (141).

The first point Hobbes makes specifically about the liberty of a man in such a situation is that he is free to submit. If "his life and corporall Libertie" are given to him "on condition to be Subject to the Victor, he hath Libertie to accept the condition" (154). Here in turn Hobbes has two claims to make. The first, which he takes for granted, is that such a man is free in the fundamental sense that nothing is stopping him. Although Hobbes observes in his conclusion that such impediments can certainly arise, the only instance he mentions is that of someone prevented from submitting by the fact of being abroad at the time when his country is conquered (486). Hobbes's other and principal point is that such a man is also free as a subject. He is under no legal or moral obligation not to submit. The reason is that our obligations as subjects depend, as we have seen, upon our sovereign's capacity to protect us. If our sovereign is conquered, we lose any such protection and the commonwealth is dissolved. We thereupon cease to be subjects, and each of us is left "at liberty to protect himselfe by such courses as his own discretion shall suggest unto him" (230, 154).

The conclusion of *Leviathan* clarifies and expands this account of "when it is that a man hath the liberty to submit" (484). Hobbes reiterates that "for him that hath no obligation to his former Soveraign but that of an ordinary Subject," the moment comes "when the means of his life is within the Guards and Garrisons of the Enemy" (484). But he now adds the topical observation that, if the man is not merely a subject but a soldier in a civil war, the case becomes more complicated: "He hath not the liberty to submit to a new Power as long as the old one keeps the field and giveth him means of subsistence," for in that case "he cannot complain of want of Protection." As soon as that fails, however, he too is at liberty to "seek his Protection wheresoever he has most hope to have it, and may lawfully submit himself to his new Master" (485).

The other point Hobbes makes about the liberty of a man in this pre-dicament is also brought out in chapter 20, but is particularly under-lined in the conclusion. It is that such a man is not merely free to submit; if he submits, he will also be acting freely. Here again Hobbes has two claims to make. The first and obvious one is that such a man will be acting freely in the legal sense. He is clearly under no legal obligation to submit, since his predicament is such that he has no legal obligations at all. But Hobbes's central contention is that such a man will also be free according to the proper signification of the word. If he submits, his act will be that of a free man voluntarily consenting to a new sovereign power.

To see how Hobbes arrives at this crucial conclusion, we need only recall the conditions that would have to be met before it could properly be argued that such a man's freedom of action had been infringed. He would have to be physically tied or bound to submit in such a way that he could not forbear from submitting. As we have seen, this is of course a possible way of inducing submission. It describes the manner in which a slave, someone "not trusted with the libertie of his bodie," is forced to obey (154). It is Hobbes's principal aim, however, to establish that this is not the position of the man who submits to a conqueror in order to avoid imprisonment or death. The reason is that this describes the pre-dicament of a man who, unlike the slave, is offered a condition of sub-mission, and is thus at liberty to accept or refuse that condition "if hee will" (485). He is not forced to submit by being "beaten and taken"; on the contrary, "he commeth in and submitteth to the Victor" on condi-tion that "his life and the liberty of his body" are spared (141).

Hobbes's fundamental contention is thus that the man he is describ-ing is someone who, far from being forced to submit, freely consents to the terms of his own submission and thereby enters into a covenant with a new sovereign.[56] "Having liberty to submit to him, he consenteth ei-ther by express words or by other sufficient sign to be his Subject" (484). He may thus be said to "contract with the Victor, promising Obe-dience for Life and Liberty" (486). Hobbes's reason for treating it as an error to suppose that conquest ever gives rise in itself to lawful power is thus that "it is not therefore the Victory that giveth the right of Dominion over the Vanquished, but his own Covenant" (141). When a man submits to a conqueror to avoid the present stroke of death, his act of submission is the willing act of a free man. This in turn enables Hobbes to draw the polemical conclusion in which he is clearly most interested. Since the act of submitting to a conqueror is based on consent and expressed in a covenant, the man who submits in this way cannot possibly be described as a slave—as the Levellers and other radicals in the English Revolution had all sought to maintain. Rather he must be acknowledged to be a true subject with an absolute duty of obedience. The conclusion is first drawn at the end of the chapter on the liberty of subjects. If a man "hath his life and corporall Libertie given him, on condition to be Subject to the Victor, he hath Libertie to accept the condition; and having accepted it is the subject of him that took him" (154). The basic argument is then triumphantly reiterated in the closing pages of *Leviathan*. A man who finds himself conquered is at liberty to "submit himself to his new Master" and "may do it lawfully, if hee will. If therefore he doe it, he is undoubtedly bound to be a true Subject: for a Contract lawfully made, cannot lawfully be broken" (485).

Living as he did in revolutionary times, Hobbes knew all about what Dita Shklar describes as the liberalism of fear. But part of the abiding if disconcerting interest of Hobbes's political theory stems from the fact that he regarded the liberalism of fear as a self-deceiving ideology and treated it with unblinking contempt. When examining the predicament of those who submit to a conqueror to avoid the present stroke of death, he explicitly considers the possible objection that this cannot be regarded as a genuine act of consent on the grounds that the submission is merely extorted by fear. To this he retorts that, to anyone with a proper understanding of liberty, it will be obvious that such an objection amounts to nothing more than a "fraudulent pretence" (230). Although we may not agree with Hobbes, he stands as a powerful reminder that even liberals have no monopoly on the definition of liberty.

Notes

1. On the two main occasions when Dita Shklar specifically refers to Hobbes's doctrines, she treats them with much respect. The first is in her discussion of the metaphor of the body politic in her book on Rousseau, *Men and Citizens: A Study of Rousseau's Social Theory*, 198–200. The second is in her analysis of the state of nature in her book on Hegel, *Freedom and Independence: A Study of the Political Ideas of Hegel's Phenomenology of Mind*, 177–178. Hobbes also makes a brief appearance in the first of Dita's Tanner Lectures; see *American Citizenship: The Quest for Inclusion*, 32–33.

2. As she makes clear in *Ordinary Vices* (see 261), Dita Shklar completely rejected the suggestion put forward by such commentators as C. B. Macpherson and Ian Shapiro that Hobbes must in some sense be accounted a founding father of the liberal theory of the state. For Dita such founders mainly lived in the eighteenth century, the great names being those of Montesquieu, Madison, and Kant.

3. For the first occurrence of the phrase in Dita Shklar's writings see *Ordinary Vices*, 5. See also 237–38, where the phrase recurs and where the liberalism of fear is connected and contrasted with the liberalism of rights.

4. *Ordinary Vices*, 8.

5. On cruelty as a cause of fear, and fear as a constraint on freedom, see *Ordinary Vices*, esp. 4–5, 236–38, 241–44. It is worth adding that Dita usually preferred to speak not of liberty but of freedom, although she clearly regarded the terms as synonyms. The point is expressed most succinctly in one of her index entries, which reads: "liberty: see freedom." See *After Utopia*, 304.

6. See *Ordinary Vices*, esp. 242, and cf. the later and fuller discussion in *Montesquieu*, esp. 68–69, 84–85.

7. *Ordinary Vices*, esp. 214.

8. *Ordinary Vices*, 216, 237.

9. Thomas Hobbes, *Leviathan*, ed. Richard Tuck (Cambridge, 1991), 146. When quoting from *Leviathan* I have preserved original spelling and punctuation, except that I do not always follow Hobbes's copious italicizing and sometimes allow myself to thin out his commas. So far as possible I give references to *Leviathan* in the body of the text. All such numbers in the text refer to Tuck's edition, which is much the best available.

10. Henry Sidgwick, *The Elements of Politics*, rev. ed. (London, 1897), 45.

11. See for example J. Roland Pennock, "Hobbes's Confusing 'Clarity'—The Case of 'Liberty,'" in *Hobbes Studies*, ed. Keith C. Brown (Oxford, 1965), 102, 116; A. G. Wernham, "Liberty and Obligation in Hobbes," in *Hobbes Studies*, 120–21; David P. Gauthier, *The Logic of Leviathan* (Oxford, 1969), 62, 65–66; Ralph Ross, "Some Puzzles in Hobbes," in *Thomas Hobbes in His Time*, ed. Ralph Ross, Herbert W. Schneider, and Theodore Waldman (Minneapolis, 1974), esp. 55–56; D. D. Raphael, "Hobbes," in *Conceptions of Liberty in Political Philosophy*, ed. Z. Pelczynski and John Gray (London, 1984), esp. 30–34. But for two defenses of Hobbes's consistency see W. von Leyden, *Hobbes and Locke: The Politics of Freedom and Obligation* (London, 1982), 32–50, esp. 45–50, and M. M. Goldsmith, "Hobbes on Liberty," *Hobbes Studies* 2 (1989): 23–39.

12. Hobbes's discussion in *The Elements of Law* fails even to provide a formal definition of liberty. See Hobbes, *The Elements of Law*, ed. Ferdinand Tönnies (London, 1969), 134. The corresponding passage in *De cive* does offer a definition, but only alludes glancingly to the alleged dangers of failing to adopt it. See Hobbes, *De Cive: The Latin Version*, ed. Howard Warrender (Oxford, 1983), 167. As several scholars have recently argued, the English translation of *De cive* issued in March 1651 cannot possibly be by Hobbes, despite Warrender's assertions to the contrary. See Warrender, editor's introduction to Hobbes, *De Cive: The English Version* (Oxford, 1983), 4–8, and compare the skepticism voiced in Noel Malcolm, "Citizen Hobbes," *London Review of Books*, 18–31 Oct. 1984, 22,

and taken up in Tuck, "Warrender's *De Cive*," *Political Studies* 33 (1985): 310–
12. Since the 1651 translation has no standing—and indeed makes use of a political vocabulary partly at odds with the one Hobbes generally employs when
writing in English—I have preferred, when citing from *De cive*, to make my own
translations from Warrender's edition of the Latin text.

13. As Hobbes makes clear at the start of chapter 21 of *Leviathan* (145),
where he speaks of "liberty or freedom," he makes no distinction of meaning
between the two terms. I have followed him in using them interchangeably.

14. Hobbes, *Leviathan*, 189, where *right* is defined in terms of "liberty to do or
forbeare."

15. Hobbes, *The Questions Concerning Liberty, Necessity and Chance* (London,
1656), 301; see also Hobbes's opening formula, 28–29. For the complete bibliography of Hobbes's debate with Bramhall, see H. Macdonald and M. Har-
greaves, *Thomas Hobbes: A Bibliography* (London, 1952), 37–41.

16. Hobbes, *Leviathan*, 145; on being "tied," see also 91, 92–93.

17. Note that Hobbes distinguishes, with a fair degree of consistency, between being "forced" and being "compelled." I am compelled if my will is co-
erced. I am forced if it is rendered physically impossible for me to forbear from
acting in a certain way. For Hobbes, compulsion is compatible with liberty, although force is not. See especially the discussion in *Concerning Liberty*, 199–200,
208–9, 216–17. The point is well brought out in Wernham, "Liberty and Obligation in Hobbes," 123.

18. Hobbes, *Concerning Liberty*, 216–17. Hobbes earlier uses the same example in *The Elements of Law*, 63. The reason the category may appear residual,
even empty, is that Hobbes sometimes speaks as though an action we cannot
forbear from performing cannot be treated as an action: it is a case in which we
are acted upon, not a case in which we act. See for example the discussion in
Concerning Liberty, 209, 216–17. But the implication—that all actions are free
by definition—is one that Hobbes elsewhere rejects. See for example *Leviathan*,
146, where it is laid down that only actions which proceed from the will "proceed from liberty."

19. See Hobbes, *Leviathan*, 447, for the explicit distinction between "the service of Bondmen" and of "a voluntary servant."

20. Hobbes, *De Cive: The Latin Version*, 221; *Leviathan*, 246.

21. Hobbes, *De Cive: The Latin Version*, 223: "non-protest non obedire." For a
valuable discussion of this difficult passage, see Robert Orr, "Thomas Hobbes
on the Regulation of Voluntary Motion," in *Lives, Liberties and the Public Good*,
ed. George Feaver and Frederick Rosen (London, 1987), 58–59. There is certainly something unsatisfactory about Hobbes's argument at this point. He
holds that liberty can be taken away only by external impediments to motion. It
is clear that God's omnipotence will constitute such an impediment if it is a fact.
But it is not clear how it can be said to do so if it is merely believed to be a fact.
For further discussion of the passage from *De cive*, see M. M. Goldsmith,
Hobbes's Science of Politics (New York, 1966), 111–13, app. 4.

22. Hobbes, *De Cive: The Latin Version*, 223: "libertas . . . corporeis tollitur."

23. See Hobbes, *Leviathan*, 146, *Concerning Liberty*, 211.

24. Hobbes, *Concerning Liberty*, 209–11.

25. See for instance C. W. Cassinelli, *Free Activities and Interpersonal Relations* (The Hague, 1966), 28, for a contrasting discussion of an example very similar to the one Hobbes considers in *Leviathan*, 146. Felix Oppenheim, *Political Concepts: A Reconstruction* (Chicago, 1981), 87, gives a good criticism of Cassinelli's analysis.

26. Hobbes, *Leviathan*, 146, and *Concerning Liberty*, 211.

27. See the initial formulation in Hobbes, *Leviathan*, 91, and *Concerning Liberty*, 285.

28. See Michael Taylor, *Community, Anarchy and Liberty* (Cambridge, 1982), 142. As a paradigm of the pure negative theory, Taylor cites Hillel Steiner, "Individual Liberty," *Proceedings of the Aristotelian Society* 75 (1974–75): 33–50.

29. This is to allude to the definition given by Steiner, "Individual Liberty," 33. I formerly accepted this interpretation of Hobbes's theory myself. See Quentin Skinner, "Il concetto inglese di libertà," *Filosofia politica* 3 (1989): 83–85.

30. As appears to be assumed, for example, in J. P. Day, "Individual Liberty," in *Of Liberty*, ed. A. Phillips Griffith (Cambridge, 1983), 17–29, where Hobbes's analysis is treated as though he is concerned only with being free and unfree to act.

31. As appears to be assumed, for example, in Goldsmith, "Hobbes on Liberty," *Hobbes Studies*, 23–39, who claims that according to Hobbes, "to be unfree is to be restrained from acting as one wishes to act" (24). This implies that we remain free so long as no one restrains us from performing an action we may wish to perform. As we have seen, however, Hobbes's view is that, if the action in question is beyond our powers, the question of freedom does not arise.

32. See, for example, the classic essay by Gerald C. MacCallum, "Negative and Positive Freedom," *Philosophy, Politics and Society*, 4th series, ed. Peter Laslett, W. G. Runciman, and Quentin Skinner (Oxford, 1972), 176.

33. See the excellent discussion in Oppenheim, *Political Concepts*, 83–84.

34. This distinction is well drawn, however, in F. S. McNeilly, *The Anatomy of Leviathan* (London, 1968), 171. See also J. W. N. Watkins, *Hobbes's System of Ideas* (London, 1965), 120–22, and the valuable remarks on unfree action in Raphael, "Hobbes," 30.

35. McNeilly, *Anatomy of Leviathan*, 171. Similar criticisms are advanced by several of the commentators cited above in note 12. Note that, although *Leviathan* contains an extensive discussion of the concept of unfreedom, Hobbes at no point uses that word.

36. For an excellent analysis of Hobbes's distinction between the worlds of nature and artifice, see Gigliola Rossini, *Natura e artificio nel pensiero di Hobbes* (Bologna, 1988).

37. Hobbes, *Leviathan*, 86–90.

38. Hobbes, *Leviathan*, esp. 87, 91–92.

39. *Freedom and Independence*, 177–78.

40. As Hobbes puts it, "the Right of Nature, that is, the naturall Liberty of man, may by the Civill Law be abridged and restrained: nay, the end of making Lawes is no other but such Restraint" (*Leviathan*, 185). But this summary could perhaps be misleading. As Hobbes has already argued (145–46), to speak of

natural liberty is only to speak of the absence of external impediments. But this is not the form of liberty that defines the state of nature. What characterizes that state is freedom from the obligation to obey any human laws.

41. Hence Hobbes defines a crime as "the Committing (by Deed or Word) of that which the Law forbiddeth, or the Omission of what it hath commanded" (*Leviathan*, 201).

42. For this claim see Hobbes, *Leviathan*, esp. 98–99. For the list of the things that a subject, "though commanded by the Soveraign," may "neverthelesse without injustice refuse to do," see 150–52. Since these are taken (151) to include the right to refuse any dishonorable office, their range seems at once interminate and—especially in a society concerned with status and reputation—potentially very extensive. It is not clear how this can be reconciled with Hobbes's basic doctrine to the effect that the dictates of conscience can never be permitted take precedence over our obligation to obey the law.

43. John Locke, *Two Treatises of Government*, ed. Peter Laslett (1690; Cambridge, 1988), 305.

44. *Men and Citizens*, esp. 162–63.

45. Hobbes occasionally speaks of a still more direct mechanism: a citizen may be physically forced to act by an authorized agent of the commonwealth. For passages in which this seems to be envisaged, see Hobbes, *Leviathan*, 96, where the "common Power" of the state is said to be capable of compelling by force, and 151, where the sovereign is described as authorizing assault.

46. Because Hobbes distinguishes between bodily coercion, which takes away liberty, and coercion of the will, which does not, he has no objection to describing threats of punishment as coercing and compelling us to act, while insisting that the resulting actions will nevertheless be freely performed. For invocations of this vocabulary, see Hobbes, *Leviathan* 96, 100–101.

47. See Hobbes, *Leviathan*, 146, and Aristotle, *Nicomachean Ethics*, 1110a.

48. According to Aristotle, *Nicomachean Ethics*, 1110a, the action is "mixed": voluntary, although in a sense involuntary.

49. Lucian, "Heracles," in *Lucian*, trans. and ed. A. M. Harmon (London, 1913), 1:65.

50. See, for example, the reference to those who are "subjects a estre menez par les oreilles," in Michel de Montaigne, *Essais*, ed. Jean Plattard, 6 vols. (Paris, 1946), 2:55, and Montaigne's further reference to the same *topos* at 2:230 in the course of his discussion of oratory. See also the claim that "with his golden chaine/ | The Orator so farre mens harts doth bind,' in sonnet 58 of Philip Sidney, "Astrophel and Stella," in *The Complete Works*, ed. Albert Feuillerat (Cambridge, 1922), 2:265. Lucian's image of Hercules appears as emblem 181 in Andreae Alciati, *Emblemata* (Padua, 1621), 751.

51. Hobbes appears to be quoting from Thomas North's translation; see Plutarch, *The Lives of the Noble Grecians and Romanes, Compared Together*, trans. Thomas North (London, 1579), 89.

52. For these phrases see Hobbes, *Leviathan*, 147, 149. For evidence about the clamor for liberty, see Keith Lindley, "London and Popular Freedom in the 1640s," in *Freedom in the English Revolution*, ed. R. C. Richardson and G. M. Ridden (Manchester, 1986), 111–50.

53. *American Citizenship*, 43–46, esp. 45.

54. *American Citizenship*, 45.

55. Locke, *Two Treatises*, 2d treatise, chap. 16, 384–97.

56. Hobbes, *Leviathan*, 484–86. But if the man submits only on condition that his life and liberty are spared, this would appear to make the victor a party to the covenant. This would be contrary to Hobbes's basic contention that "he which is made Soveraigne maketh no Covenant with his Subjects beforehand" (122). This raises no problems in the case of what Hobbes calls a commonwealth by institution (121). The form taken by the covenant in such cases is simply that each prospective subject agrees with everyone else who shall be sovereign. Ever since Samuel Pufendorf stressed the point, however, in his *De ivre naturae et gentium* (1672), critics have complained that Hobbes contradicts himself when he comes to "a commonwealth by acquisition," and thus to the relationship of victor and vanquished (138). For in this case he explicitly states that the subjects covenant not with each other but with "him they are afraid of" (138). Hobbes's consistency can be rescued, however, if we interpret him as saying not that the conqueror covenants to allow life and liberty to those he has vanquished, but merely that he accepts their covenant by allowing them life and liberty, while remaining free from any obligation to respect these terms. This point is excellently brought out in Gauthier, *Logic of Leviathan*, 114–15.

Part Three

Liberal Theory and Practice

12

Hypocrisy and Democracy

Dennis F. Thompson

No criticism of politicians in liberal democracies is more common than the charge of hypocrisy. If true, the charge would seem to constitute a serious wrong. Hypocrisy, after all, is a species of deception, and no vice is more dangerous to democracy than deceit. As both politicians and philosophers have long emphasized, veracity is a precondition of liberal democracy. To hold their leaders accountable for any decision or policy, citizens must have truthful information about what leaders and their opponents have done and intend to do.

No theorist has insisted more consistently or eloquently on the need for accountability in moral and political life than has Judith Shklar. From her criticism of theorists of historical inevitability for their political evasions to her castigation of public officials for their indifference to passive injustice, she expresses nothing but contempt for people who exercise power without responsibility.[1] Nor did Shklar in her own writing or speaking, personally or professionally, hesitate to speak openly and candidly. "Facing up to" whatever problem was at issue (as in "Facing up to Intellectual Pluralism")[2] was her consistent counsel.

It is therefore surprising to find her in *Ordinary Vices* singing the praises of hypocrisy. In the most penetrating theoretical discussion of the subject since Hegel's critique of the "age of hypocrisy," Shklar vigorously defends hypocrites against their critics.[3] She argues that "hypocrisy is one of the few vices that bolsters liberal democracy."[4] Her "liberalism of fear" not only accommodates hypocrisy but welcomes it.

This benign view of hypocrisy is partly the consequence of the ordering of the vices that her liberalism prescribes: it puts cruelty (a form of violence) ahead of hypocrisy (a form of deceit). It is also partly the result of this liberalism's fear that "those who put hypocrisy first" will, like the Puritans or like Orgon in Molière's *Tartuffe*, promote oppression and tyranny (50–51). Shklar seems prepared to sacrifice democratic honesty to save liberal security. Her "liberalism without illusions," it appears, needs one grand illusion to sustain it: that its public officials are as moral as they say they are.

If we examine her arguments closely, however, we find that she generally does not make such broad claims, and when she occasionally does she cannot sustain them. Her strongest arguments call for tolerance of only a certain kind of hypocrisy—that which may be ascribed primarily to individuals. She does not try to justify, and indeed (along with most writers) mostly ignores another kind of hypocrisy—that which may also be imputed to institutions. By examining her arguments, and trying to sort out tolerable from intolerable kinds of hypocrisy, we can come to better understand the relationship between veracity and democracy. The connection between these values, she in effect suggests, is not so tight as it might first appear. There are reasons to believe that pushing veracity too far, calling for perfect candor, will actually harm democracy.

Shklar is surely right to urge us to pay less attention to individual hypocrisy, currently a dominant strain the discourse of our democratic politics. But in her charity toward the individual forms of hypocrisy, she disregards the dangers of its institutional forms. If this neglect is an objection to her analysis, it is an objection that can nevertheless proceed in the spirit of the method she recommends. Within the realm of hypocrisy, we should still try to put the worst forms first. We should still try to identify and protect the core of veracity that democracy presupposes. That core may be—like her barebones liberalism—only a barebones veracity, but it is no less essential for democracy.

Two Concepts of Hypocrisy

Among the varieties of individual hypocrisy that Shklar considers in political life, "moral hypocrisy" is the most clearly deceptive. This vice involves pretending that one's "motives and intentions and character are irreproachable when [one] knows that they are blameworthy"[5] (47). This fits precisely the standard conception of deception—causing or intending to cause someone to have a belief that one knows or should know is false. But it is a specific form of deception. The belief that one seeks to cause is about oneself, not about an impersonal state of affairs (and not even about one's own belief about an impersonal state of affairs). Nor is it a belief about the virtuousness of one's friends, political allies, or the parties and organizations to which one may belong. Moral hypocrites seek to make us believe that they themselves are better than they know they are.

This kind of hypocrisy is individual because it refers primarily to the motives and actions of individuals. But as Shklar makes clear, the individuals in question are thoroughly social creatures. Their hypocrisy is deeply embedded in the moral culture in which they live. With Hegel, she sees hypocrisy not as an isolated failing, but "a total environment."[6] It is "systematic, not occasional" (63). Hegel blamed the hypocritical character of our moral age on Kant, whose morality demanded such "inner purity and self-perfection" that only a hypocrite would claim to act morally.[7] That is hardly fair to Kant, who (as Shklar notes) abhorred hypocrisy no less than Hegel.[8] But Kant's followers, those who make personal conscience the sole basis of morality, do deserve much of the blame.

Shklar agrees with Hegel that this exaltation of conscience has contributed to a culture in which hypocrisy has become "a logical and psychological necessity of moral life."[9] But she declines to accept Hegel's prognosis—that conscience will so completely dominate moral discourse that charges of hypocrisy will cease to have any force. Other moralities persist, and they offer other perspectives—based in convention or tradition—from which the claims of conscience can be challenged. There is still plenty of room for antihypocrisy. Instead "what we have to live with is a morally pluralistic world in which hypocrisy and antihypocrisy are joined to form a discrete system" (62).

In this system, it is still the individual characters who attract Shklar's keenest interest. The most memorable and attractive of her hypocrites is Benjamin Franklin, who knew that in a democracy "a public man should try to make himself acceptable to his fellow citizens" (72). To this end, he deliberately concealed his superior intelligence, affected an air of uncertainty when his beliefs were really dogmatic, and cultivated an appearance of a humility quite beyond his natural character ("he would only be proud of it if he were to try it" [75]). Franklin saw "with perfect clarity what the demands of democratic assemblies were, even in their infancy" (74). His character could also take on whatever shape that his many public roles required in the various worlds in which he moved—whether in elegant society of Versailles, the provincial politics of Philadelphia or the intellectual milieu of the Royal Society.

Shklar's psychological portraits of historical and literary figures who, like Franklin, keep the "system" of hypocrisy humming are compelling. They are much more subtly drawn and richly analyzed than the brief sketch of her only example of hypocrisy that could be deemed institutional. The institution in question is "American representative democracy," and its hypocrisy lies in its failure to live up to its own ideals (68–

69). With a subject so general as a whole system of government, it is not surprising that Shklar does not pause to examine the specific ways in which this institution is hypocritical. She quickly moves on to the psychological traits of the individuals who must use hypocrisy to defend this democracy, and of those who criticize them. If we are prepared to consider institutions of lesser scope than whole systems, however, we may find that some of her own arguments about individual hypocrisy may apply to the institutional kind, though sometimes with opposite results.

Institutional hypocrisy involves a disparity between the publicly avowed purposes of an a institution and its actual performance or function. This disparity often develops over time as an institution comes to serve purposes other than those for which it was established. In some cases, no one is deceived and no harm is done to the democratic process. The electoral college may have once been supposed to provide an additional forum for democratic deliberation, but most citizens today would be more than surprised if the delegates decided to conduct a serious debate about the merits of the candidates and cast their votes according to their own best judgment.

But in other cases the divergence between the official purpose and the actual function is not so open and the consequences not so benign. In some—especially those involving almost any agency that can claim to be protecting national security—the institutional hypocrisy is often deeply deceptive. The National Security Council is supposed to provide the president with an independent source of advice and control over the conduct of foreign policy. When it becomes a tool for evading congressional oversight, as it did in the Iran-Contra affair, an appeal to its official purpose constitutes institutional hypocrisy that has serious consequences for the democratic process. Oliver North and John Poindexter tried to justify their congressionally unauthorized use of the NSC by arguing that the Boland Amendment banned only operational agencies from intervening in the conflict in Nicaragua. The NSC, they said, is merely a planning and advisory agency.[10] They thus exploited the official purpose of the institution while using it for other illegitimate purposes. The disparity was part of the cause as well as the consequence of the damage to the democratic process.

In all these cases it is individuals, most often public officials, who make the statements and carry out the actions that may be regarded as instances of institutional hypocrisy. To appreciate this kind of hypocrisy, it is not necessary to treat institutions as moral agents. Nor is it necessary to try to reduce all the actions of institutions to actions of individuals. But it is important to recognize that institutional hypocrisy and individual hypocrisy are not only distinct but often opposed. Institutional hypocrisy is sometimes made possible by the absence of individual hypocrisy.

Ollie North was not a hypocrite in any conventional sense.[11] He did not believe that his motives or intentions were reproachable. He could not be accused of acting out of self-interest in any of its usual disreputable forms. He believed in his cause, and believed that he was serving both his president and his nation in carrying out his scheme to trade hostages for arms to Iran and divert some of the proceeds to the Contras in Nicaragua. He was not even trying to make himself appear better than he thought he was, since he believed that if most citizens fully understood what he was doing they would consider him a hero. Had North been a conventional hypocrite, he would not have been so successful in enlisting others in support of his cause, and thereby in effecting the institutional hypocrisy that should count as his gravest wrong. His main moral fault was not that he failed to be true to himself, but that he failed to be true to those to whom he was accountable. In his individual sincerity, he created and sustained an institutional hypocrisy.

Four arguments in defense of hypocrisy emerge in the course of Shklar's reflections on the vice. All four assume that democracy requires that public officials be held accountable for their decisions and policies, and then seek to show either that hypocrisy directly encourages accountability or that it supports other values that are equally necessary to responsible democratic government. In all four it is individual hypocrisy that is shown to serve democracy. Applied to institutional hypocrisy, as we shall see, the arguments are more equivocal.

Deliberation

The best to be said for hypocrites, Shklar believes, is that they are better than their critics. Antihypocrisy does more damage to democratic deliberation than hypocrisy does. Since it is especially difficult in politics to prove that one's motives are pure, the best response to a charge of hypocrisy is often to hurl a countercharge of the same nature. "As each side tries to destroy the credibility of its rivals, politics becomes a treadmill of dissimulation and unmasking" (67). As citizens watch this spectacle, they confirm their impression that the motives of all politicians are suspect, but they will not learn much about the "actual misdeeds" of politicians, let alone their past and future policies (66).

What Shklar has in mind recalls Jeremy Bentham's objection on motive-based criticism. Although no more a utilitarian than Hegel or Kant, Shklar finds Bentham's no-nonsense conception of political argument attractive. With their obsession with motives, antihypocrites distract political attention from the decisions and policies that politicians make. In Bentham's inventory of political fallacies, "imputation of bad motive" is branded one of the weakest forms of argument.[12] The fallacy consists in inferring from the alleged bad motives of the person who proposes a policy that the policy is also bad. This is a mistake, Bentham notes, because "(1) motives are hidden in the human breast, and (2) if the measure is beneficial, it would be absurd to reject on account of the motives of its author."[13]

This fallacy, like its companion, "imputation of bad character," are expressions of a general "distrust": citizens are encouraged to oppose otherwise desirable policies on the grounds that "there lurk *more behind them* of a very different complexion."[14] Talk about motive and character in this way produces a political discourse that is accessible to only those who can see what is "hidden," what is "behind" policies, rather than in them. This is not a discourse that would support a common perspective from which democratic citizens could deliberate about policies and hold public officials accountable.

But we may ask, Does not Shklar herself encourage this general distrust by promoting a "liberalism of fear" that itself "institutionalizes suspicion"? "Only a distrustful population can be relied on to watch out for its rights" (238). The answer surely must be that everything depends on what the object of distrust is. A suspicious attitude directed toward the present and future policies of politicians is perfectly appropriate. Even some suspicions based on motives do not corrupt democratic discourse. Although Shklar does not make the distinction, we should acknowledge a difference with respect to the political effects of what may be called specific and general antihypocrisy.

Specific antihypocrisy is a criticism based on definite statements and actions attributable to an individual politician. The politician who opposes legalized abortion but helps his daughter obtain an abortion, the candidate who preaches family values but is guilty of marital infidelity, the mayor who gives antidrug lectures in the public schools while addicted to cocaine—all invite criticism pointing to the inconsistency between what they say and what they do. This may not be the most edifying form of political criticism, but it is relatively benign. The politician brings the criticism on himself. It is thus avoidable. More important, it is also answerable at least in principle. The charge and the evidence for it are sufficiently definite that citizens can determine whether the politician's explanation is satisfactory, and then move on to the policy issues.

Quite different are the effects of general antihypocrisy—the familiar charge that a politician is taking a position for "political" reasons. Although this charge could be made specific, it is usually based only on a general assumption that politicians act in their own political self-interest. The legislator may say she is voting for this bill because it is in the public interest, but we know better: her real motive is that it will benefit her district and improve her chances of reelection. The candidate may say he is in favor of capital punishment on moral grounds, but we suspect that it has more to do with the anticrime sentiments of voters. The trouble with such criticisms is that there is often nothing a politician can do to avoid or answer them. At best the criticism leads to a discursive draw; at worst, it becomes one more move in the "unending game of mutual unmasking" that Shklar dissects (67).

The general form of antihypocrisy is insidious because the assumption on which it rests is in an important sense valid. The charge of political motivation exploits a feature of democratic institutions that is both inevitable and desirable: representatives act on mixed motives. In any electorally based representative system, legislators are not only permitted but also required to take into account many different kinds of considerations in making decisions. They act for the benefit of particular constituents, for the good of the whole district or state, for the good of the nation, for their own interest in reelection or future political goals. Some of these motives may be more admirable than others, but none is illegitimate in itself, and all are in some measure necessary for accountability in our democratic system. So the assertion that a politician is politically motivated might as well be taken as a compliment as a criticism. It might even be better not made at all.

Under the circumstances of mixed motives, it is hard enough for any official, however conscientious, to separate proper from improper motives, and more generally to find the right balance of motives in making any particular decision. It is harder still for citizens, even well-informed and nonpartisan ones, to judge at a distance whether the official has actually found that balance. The charge that a politician is politically motivated therefore does not advance the political debate. Because it is inherently ambiguous, it leads to a deliberative dead end.

Recognizing the institutional dimensions of antihypocrisy in this way should help us see that some forms may be worse than others. But the critique is still directed against individual hypocrisy. What might institutional antihypocrisy look like? A case in point is the social security system—more specifically, the criticism that exposes the inconsistency between the rationale by which the system has often been defended and the way the system actually operates. The political popularity of social security is partly due to the widespread belief that the pensions that citizens receive when they retire come from the tax contributions they have made in the past. Public officials who want to expand or protect the program find it convenient to encourage this mistaken view of the rationale for the system. But this same view makes it difficult to reduce benefits for wealthy citizens or otherwise to bring under control a system that in fact depends largely on current tax revenues. Pointing out the discrepancy between what has often been taken as the official purpose of the system and how it actually operates may enhance democratic debate. In this respect, the charge of institutional hypocrisy can constitute a necessary step toward making officials more accountable for social security policy as it actually operates.

No doubt the greatest institutional hypocrisy in our history was the disjunction between the principles of liberty and equality so grandly proclaimed in our constitution and the practice of slavery also legitimized in the same document. Although Shklar does not regard it as a form of hypocrisy, it is precisely the historical contradiction that animates her study of American citizenship: "From the first, the most radical claims for freedom and political equality were played out in counterpoint to chattel slavery . . . the consequences of which still haunt us . . . . The equality of political rights . . . was proclaimed in the accepted presence of its absolute denial."[15] It would be hard to deny that pointing out this discrepancy, even today, is a contribution to democratic accountability. It should also be clear that this kind of criticism is more constructive than the parallel charge of individual hypocrisy— such as those traditionally leveled against Thomas Jefferson and Patrick Henry, only the most celebrated of our predecessors who defended liberty while owning slaves.

Legitimacy

To sustain the consent of the governed on which any democracy depends, the "rhetoric of legitimation" in democratic discourse sets high standards and raises great expectations (78). Political leaders in a democracy not only have to devise good public policies, but also have to convince citizens that these policies fulfill the legitimating ideals of the society (69). The "disparity between what is said and what is done" is bound to be great, and is likely to be greater the higher the political leader aims. This is why presidents like Abraham Lincoln and Franklin Delano Roosevelt who (admirably, in Shklar's view) raise the moral expectations of citizens are especially vulnerable to charges of hypocrisy. It is also why politicians inevitability disappoint us if we insist, with Nathaniel Hawthorne, that we should take the "private and domestic view of public men" (74). Shklar prefers Franklin's view, which measures true character by the "manner of acting one's roles," instead of the conformity of one's actions to some singular "private self" (74). In these and other ways, the needs of democratic legitimation are bound to produce much disappointment, and therefore to breed much hypocrisy. To prevent the disappointments from undermining the system, and thereby tempting citizens to seek remedies like regimes of tyranny that would be worse, we should tolerate the pretense that leaders are better than they are.

Shklar is surely right that we should learn to tolerate some inconsistency between the promises and performances of politicians, and perhaps even more between their private and public lives. No representative democracy, not even one that institutionalizes distrust, can endure unless citizens maintain some degree of confidence in the government and its leaders. One of the most striking trends in democratic politics of the past several decades is the massive decline in trust in government.[16] Whether part of the cause or only an effect, "professional antihypocrites" (46) further erode public trust and encourage a public cynicism that impedes efforts to restore that trust.

No doubt politicians have done too little to earn our trust. But in a healthy democracy our criticism would focus more on the public deeds of leaders and less on their political promises or private lives. The value of this more specific, more accessible criticism lies not only in the improvement in accountability already noted, but also in the cultivation of legitimacy invariably needed. It is difficult for politicians to regain public confidence, even if they promise less and perform better, as long as they are judged mainly by how far they fall short of their expressed ideals, whether in public or private life. In the climate of pervasive cynicism promoted by the "unending game of mutual unmasking," legitimacy is bound to lose. Politicians (and governments more generally) stand a better chance of winning the kind of trust that democracy needs if they are judged by how well they do their job relative to how well their rivals are likely to do it.

Dwelling on the discrepancies between institutional promise and performance may also damage democratic legitimacy in some of these same ways. But in at least one important respect institutional hypocrisy is less tolerable than individual hypocrisy, and its critics therefore are more useful. When an institution systematically fails to fulfill its purposes, it cannot be so readily replaced as can an individual who habitually falls short. To preserve the legitimacy of such an institution, the only alternatives are usually to ignore its failures or to correct them. The first is usually not sustainable, since the effects of the failures become obvious to those whom the institution is supposed to serve, even if critics do not point them out.

The second, more constructive alternative calls for institutional reform, a task to which the critics of institutional hypocrisy can make worthwhile contributions. It was Montesquieu (one of the theorists most appreciated by Shklar) who saw most clearly the need to criticize an institution for betraying its "principle" and its distinctive "end."[17]

The legislator, whether founding or reforming institutions, needs the insight that such criticism can provide. In our time on a less grand scale, criticisms of governmental agencies help set the agenda for institutional reform. The critics who charge a federal regulatory agency with serving the interests of the industries it is supposed to regulate more than the interests of the citizens it is supposed to serve not only identify the need for reform but can indicate the form it should take. The long-term legitimacy of these and other such institutions depends on establishing more coherence between their official purposes and their actual practices.

Compromise

The "politics of persuasion," Shklar emphasizes, is inherent in "any openly competitive political system" (75). The "back-and-forth of charges and counter-charges" that make up the rituals we call elections provides an ample "fund of hypocrisy" (70). To win political support in a pluralist society, candidates have to appeal to many different audiences, whose interests and ideals conflict with those of the candidates and with each other. This means first that politicians have to appear better than they are, or (like Franklin) worse than they are. They "pretend to a common touch, youthful poverty and inordinate virtue" (72). But the demands of persuasion go further. They also require politicians to adapt their public statements to the prejudices and opinions of their audience; they may have to compromise with what they regard as their true beliefs. Some earlier liberals like John Morley may have hoped that free discussion would gradually eliminate the need for compromise and the hypocrisy that inevitably accompanies it; they assumed that the pursuit of truth would gradually shrink the realm of politics (67–68). But contemporary liberals, Shklar suggests, should know better. Compromise is a desirable part of the art of democratic politics, and therefore so is whatever hypocrisy is necessary to sustain its artists.

Shklar would not accept on this point the claim of the modern followers of Plato, like Hannah Arendt, who argue that the "political realm" is "at war with truth in all its forms."[18] It is not that Shklar denies the possibility of objective truth; it is rather that she thinks the kind of truth appropriate for political theory and democratic politics is quite different from that which most of those who condemn compromise and hypocrisy have in mind. Political theory as a form of persuasion is "closer to what Aristotle called rhetoric, than the sort of discourse which is clearly scientific or purely formal."[19] If "all political theorists must be . . . competent rhetoricians,," then *a fortiori* so must all politicians.

So we should perhaps not be so hard on the politician who alters his campaign speech to cater to the opinions or prejudices of the audience to whom he is speaking. On the campaign trail in Florida in 1976 where his chief rival in the Democratic primary was George Wallace (the darling of reactionary southern whites), Jimmy Carter conveniently dropped Martin Luther King from the standard list of "great Americans" he had used in his speeches in northern states[20]—John F. Kennedy and Eleanor Roosevelt were quite enough. Although we may wish that Carter had shown more courage, we surely must acknowledge Shklar's point that in our electoral system such hypocrisies are inevitable, perhaps even desirable. If we accept that point, though, it is partly because we know that the inconsistency can be readily discovered, and that citizens can then make up their own minds about its significance. It is quite another matter when a candidate is elected on a promise to end a war (as Lyndon Johnson was), even while he is planning to escalate it.

Institutions not only have to make compromises to accomplish their goals, but the goals themselves may constitute a compromise. When they promote the competing purposes of different groups, they may have to present themselves to one audience as serving one purpose, and another as serving a quite different purpose. Bentham made this point more explicit than most theorists or legislators would think sensible. Recognizing that in a representative democracy legislators must represent both the general interest and particular interests of their constituents, Bentham asks how these contradictory demands can be resolved. His answer, characteristically mechanical in form, is an institutional procedure that assigns each demand a specific role. He designs a legislature in which representatives speak for their own views of the public interest but then vote according to the views of their constituents.[21] To their constituents, the representatives can say that I voted for you. To those who care about the public interest, the representative can say that at least he spoke for it, even if he could not act on it.

Bentham's procedure is not entirely pointless, since the speeches might change the minds of constituents, as Bentham in fact hoped, and thus enable representatives in the future to bring their votes into line with their words. But in the absence of further social and political reforms to encourage public-spirited citizenship, this institutional hypocrisy could scarcely be thought to serve any useful democratic purpose. Some of Bentham's other proposals go even further. To avoid the disutility of capital punishment while preserving its deterrent effect, he would have the government simulate public executions.[22] The convicted criminal would be given what appeared to be a deadly poison, and then later in secret an official would administer an antidote. Even if the ruse could be kept secret (the criminals could be told that the next time the antidote might not be available), secrecy about such a fundamental policy could hardly be acceptable in a democracy.

There is, of course, no danger that either of Bentham's proposals will be adopted, but there is some point in identifying the sources of their mischief, since they represent, in only a slightly more extreme form, features of some existing institutions in contemporary democracies. One source is the tendency of one of the avowed purposes of an institution simply to be ignored. The problem is not merely that the institution presents a different face to different audiences, but rather that it pays only symbolic attention to one of them. The public interest gets the glory while the particular interests get the gains.

This institutional lip service is common in all branches of democratic government, but because of the conflicting roles of its members, legislatures may be even more prone to its temptations than other institutions. In the United States Congress, members running for reelection must solicit contributions from wealthy groups and individuals, many of whom expect favors in return. The norms of the institution frown on favoritism: members publicly proclaim that contributions do not influence their legislative judgment, and most members also insist that they consider the claims of all constituents equally on the merits. Although money may not buy votes, it often still buys access.[23] Further, some members privately remind contributors, in subtle and not so subtle ways, that it does.

Some of these practices were dramatically exposed in the early 1990s during the hearings of the "Keating Five." The case involved a group of United States senators charged with assisting savings and loan financier Charles Keating in his dealing with the government while accepting large contributions that he had raised for their campaigns. One of the five made the connection between the contributions and the favors explicit in a now famous episode when he "came up and patted Mr. Keating on the back and said, 'Ah, the mutual aid society.'"[24] In this way, members tell some constituents that money does not matter and tell other constituents that it does. The institution does not force members to practice this hypocrisy, but it creates the conditions that encourage it. To the extent that the contradictory demands are built into the institution, the resulting hypocrisy is more institutional than individual.[25]

Our criminal justice system provides ample illustration of the source of the problems of institutions like Bentham's other two-faced device, the scheme for simulated executions. Any attempt in a democracy to send differential messages to different publics about general policies as fundamental as criminal justice is likely to miscarry. The audience with the most to lose (or the most to gain) usually gets the real message first, and the general public is the last to know. The American criminal justice system sends a different message to the public than it does to criminals—but with just the opposite effect from what Bentham or anyone else presumed. To convince the public that they are vigorously fighting crime, politicians enact popular get-tough measures on crime—longer prison terms, mandatory sentences, and capital punishment for more crimes. But without adequate institutional support for these measure (such as police and prosecutors to enforce the laws, judges and juries prepared to impose the sentences, and prisons to house adequately the convicted criminals), the measures are not likely to reduce crime and may even merely result in more plea bargains, more parole, and fewer convictions. The system tells the criminal on the street that, despite the public rhetoric, the actual risk of getting caught, let alone serving a long term, is not high. Institutional hypocrisy of this variety not only fails to further political compromise, but also defeats its own policy aims.

Civility

Liberal democracy "cannot afford public sincerity," Shklar argues. "Honesties that humiliate . . . would ruin democratic civility in a political society in which people have many serious differences of belief and interest" (78). In modern democracies, citizens "heartily dislike one another's religious, sexual, intellectual and political commitments." They also privately disdain the ethnic, racial and class character of many of their fellows. If their public conduct really mirrored their "private, inner selves," racist and anti-Semitic remarks would be expressed freely and frequently. We may not be convinced that all our fellow citizens are entitled to a certain minimum of social respect, but most of us always act as if we believe that they are, and "that is what counts."

Shklar's sharp separation of "public manners" and "private laxities" should not be taken as implying (or requiring) any deep view about the comparative moral status of human nature and society. She does not intend to reverse the Rousseauian story of the social corruption of the goodness of natural man.[26] Nor is she committed to any part of the Kantian anthropology that finds "man is evil by nature."[27] Insofar as she is presupposing any moral psychology, it is more in the spirit of Aristotle. She hopes that as citizens practice good civic habits in public, they will eventually bring their private attitudes into line with their public postures. But she does not count on this process of internalization to eliminate the need for a separation of private views and public positions. Her main concern is political—the health of democratic politics in pluralist society—and she does not expect, or wish, that the differences that divide citizens disappear. She hopes that by behaving "better as citizens and public officials than as actors in the private sphere," we can make democracy safe for disagreement.

That is why those theorists are so seriously mistaken who believe, as Michael Walzer does, that the antihypocrisy reveals moral agreement. Walzer writes that "the exposure of hypocrisy . . . may be the most important form of moral criticism" because it appeals to a shared commitment that goes "deeper than partisan allegiance and the emergencies of the battle."[28] It is the tribute that vice pays to virtue.[29] Shklar has no patience with this defense. Rather than being a sign of shared moral knowledge, the discourse of antihypocrisy manifests "moral confusion and ideological conflict" (79). In the absence of shared commitments, political rivals can criticize each other only for failing to live up to their own commitments; they cannot attack the commitments directly. The moral argument has no substance, and democratic civility suffers.

Shklar's advice on democratic manners may not present the most edifying portrait of democratic citizens, but it provides a fitting framework for democratic politics in the conditions of conflict that are likely to persist in a pluralist society. Although her advice applies primarily to individuals in their social relations with each other, it also has implications for political institutions. In particular, it suggests a view about what kinds of arguments or justifications are appropriate in public forums. In the contemporary debate about the nature of public reason in liberal theory, a chief point of contention is the extent to which private or personal views (such as moral and religious convictions) should be brought into the public forum.

It might seem that the institutional analogue of Shklar's advice implies that the public forum remain neutral: the terms of public justification should not presuppose any conception of the good, whether moral or religious. We should seek "political neutrality" based on "a universal normal of rational dialogue."[30] Shklar's counsel to keep some of our deepest commitments to ourselves may seem to fit well with this idea of a neutral public forum.

Such strict liberal neutrality is not sustainable in theory or practice. It cannot be coherently justified because any attempt to defend the restrictions it would place on other moral views exposes its own substantive moral assumptions. It cannot be consistently practiced because so many important issues of public policy are inseparable from their moral implications. Indeed, Shklar herself could accept these objections. Despite the drift of some of her comments on hypocrisy, her own liberalism makes no claims to this kind of neutrality at all. On the contrary, she is committed to the principle that "a diversity of opinions and habits is not only to be endured but to be cherished and encouraged," and that this principle itself is as much an ideology as any other.[31] Years before the debate on public reason assumed its current shape, Shklar argued forcefully against the neutralist idea that political language and institutions could ever make good any claim to stand independent of ideology.[32] Even (perhaps especially) legal institutions cannot escape the ideological conflicts that characterize a healthy democratic politics.

The institutional implications of her defense of hypocrisy fit somewhat better with the recent work of John Rawls. When discussing and voting on the most fundamental political questions, citizens, Rawls argues, should not appeal to "the whole truth as they see it."[33] They should limit themselves to public conceptions of justice, principles that could not be reasonably rejected by any citizen, rather than those based on distinct religions or comprehensive moralities held only by some citizens. Rawls explicitly denies that public reason and his own theory more generally are morally neutral in the sense that they "ensure all citizens equal opportunity to advance any conception of the good they freely affirm."[34] His theory depends on a fundamental moral conception of citizens as free and equal persons, and it gives priority to the right over the good.

Shklar's objection to philosophical theories of justice such as Rawls's is not so much against what they assert as what they neglect. She complains that philosophers refuse to think about injustice as deeply or subtly as they do about justice.[35] Instead of constructing only "accounts of what we ought to be and do," we should look more closely at "our many injustices." In this spirit, the debates in Shklar's public forum would range more widely and welcome more diversity than theorists of justice may imagine. Imitating (palely) her own writings, they would include literary stories, historical chronicles, and cultural myths, along with weighty philosophical claims and ordinary political rhetoric. It may not be politically realistic to expect citizens to check their moral and religious convictions at the door of the public forum, but it is morally reasonable, she would insist, to require citizens to don a mantle of civility as they join the democratic debate. That is the least that should be demanded by a liberalism that makes tolerance a "primary virtue."[36] Civility may still depend on the lesser vice of hypocrisy, but it should enjoin citizens to aspire to the higher virtues of democratic citizenship.

•   •   •

In Dante's *Inferno*, the circle in hell reserved for the deceitful is closer to the center than the circle for the violent.[37] Deceit is worse than violence, presumably because its victims have no way to defend themselves. Dante did not have government in mind, but his insight is just as relevant to liberal democracy as to personal morality. Deception is the worst democratic vice because it makes possible all the others. To put it more positively, veracity is the political precondition for democratic virtue. We might suppose this ordering to be no less applicable to hypocrisy, which after all is a species of deception.

Yet Shklar, always alert to the ironies of political life, is not so sure. She suspects that in our age, moral vice serves political virtue more often than we like to admit. Like it or not, some kinds of hypocrisy facilitate democracy. Some hypocrites therefore may not deserve to burn in hell, and certainly not as much as those who criticize them. In this ordering of the vices, she may also be true to Dante, who assigned the "'sowers of dissension" an even hotter circle than the hypocrites.[38] Yet both Dante and Shklar are less sensitive to institutional hypocrisy, and as we have seen, its machinations do democracy no good and often much harm. It is its perpetrators who may be entitled to a special place in hell.

Notes

1. See, for example, *After Utopia*, 263–64, and *The Faces of Injustice*, 6–7, 63–64, 125–126.

2. See "Facing up to Intellectual Pluralism," 275–95.

3. The relevant sections of Hegel's *Phenomenology* and *Philosophy of Right* are discussed by Shklar in *Freedom and Independence*.

4. *Ordinary Vices*, 248; subsequent page references in the text are to this book unless otherwise indicated.

5. The other varieties are "religious hypocrisy," which is less relevant to politics, and states of mind such as "complacency and self-satisfaction," and "insincerity and inauthenticity," which are not intended to deceive other people, and may not count as deception at all in the usual sense.

6. *Freedom and Independence*, 192.

7. Ibid., 186.

8. See Immanuel Kant, *Religion within the Limits of Reason* (1793), trans. Theodore M. Greene and Hoyt H. Hudson, 2d ed. (La Salle, Ill., 1960), 37–38, 168, 176–77. Nevertheless, in fairness to Hegel we should also notice that the hypocrisy that Kant most severely criticized was that which involved acting on the moral law from any motive other than pure duty: "All homage paid to the moral law is an act of hypocrisy, if, in one's maxim, ascendancy is not at the same time granted to the law as an incentive sufficient in itself and higher than all other determining grounds of the will" (37n).

9. *Freedom and Independence*, 193; and *Ordinary Vices*, 57, 61.

10. Theodore Draper, *A Very Thin Line: The Iran-Contra Affairs* (New York; 1991), 25–26, 33–37, 344.

11. It may thought that North fits the profile of the Hegelian hypocrite whose life is "wicked" but whose heart is "pure" and who can justify "any sort of crime as long as it can be said to promote some noble personal ideal" (*Freedom and Independence*, 192–93). But this self-deception or inauthenticity is quite different from the moral hypocrisy that leads officials to conceal their base motives. It does not in itself require, or lead to, deception of other people. Furthermore, as Shklar points out, no one could escape being a hypocrite if states of mind such as self-deception, inauthenticity, and insincerity, rather than acts intended to deceive others, were grounds for charging hypocrisy (*Ordinary Vices*, 47).

12. Jeremy Bentham, *Handbook of Political Fallacies* (New York, 1962), 86–87.

13. Ibid.

14. Ibid., 100.

15. *American Citizenship*, 1.

16. See Arthur H. Miller and Stephen A. Borelli, "Confidence in Government During the 1980s," *American Politics Quarterly* 19 (April 1991): 149–50.

17. *Montesquieu*, 75, 78–79.

18. Hannah Arendt, "Truth and Politics," in *Philosophy, Politics and Society*, 3d ser., ed. Peter Laslett and W. G. Runciman (Oxford, 1967), 113. This is not of course to imply that Arendt's thought in general is Platonic.

19. *Men and Citizens*, 225–26.

20. So as not to single out Jimmy Carter, one may wish to take note of a bipartisan list of similar hypocrisies: Michael Oreskes, "Thrust of TV Campaign Ads Can Vary with the Territory," *New York Times*, (1 Nov., 1988), A1, 28.

21. Bentham, *Constitutional Code*, ed. Frederick Rosen and J. H. Burns (Oxford, 1983), 1:44 (6.1.A11).

22. See Shirley Letwin, *The Pursuit of Certainty* (Cambridge, 1965), 173; Letwin refers to portfolio 96, f.10, p. 190 in the Bentham manuscript collection of University College.

23. In a careful study of three House committees, two political scientists found that although political action committee money did not purchase members' votes, it "did buy marginal time, energy, and legislative resources" during formal markups and committee action behind the scenes. See Richard L. Hall and Frank W. Wayman, "Buying Time: Moneyed Interests and the Mobilization of Bias in Congressional Committees," *American Political Science Review*, 84 (Sept. 1990): 797–820. This study also shows that the distribution of mobilization favors financially better-off groups.

24. U. S. Senate, Select Committee on Ethics, *Preliminary Inquiry into Allegations Regarding Senators Cranston, DeConcini, Glenn, McCain, and Riegle, and Lincoln Savings and Loan*, Open Session Hearings, 101st Cong. 2d sess., 15 Nov. 1990–16 Jan. 1991 (Washington, D.C., 1991), part 4, 14 Dec. 1990, 178.

25. The conflicting demands also produce other anomalies, which members themselves see as forms of hypocrisy. During a debate on gift reform, Senator John Glenn remarked, "It is a little *hypocritical* for members to say they could be bought for a $21 lunch, yet turn around and pick up a phone to a PAC and ask

for a contribution over 200 times that amount" (*Congressional Record*, daily edition, 5 May 1994, S5229 [emphasis added]).

26. *Men and Citizens*, chaps. 1–2.

27. Kant, *Religion within the Limits of Reason*, 27.

28. Michael Walzer, *Just and Unjust Wars* (New York, 1977), xv, 19–20.

29 "L'hypocrise est un hommage que le vice rend à la vertue" (Duc de La Rochefoucauld, *Maximes*, 218).

30. Charles Larmore, *Patterns of Moral Complexity* (Cambridge, 1987), 53–59; see also Bruce Ackerman, *Social Justice in the Liberal State* (New Haven, Conn., 1980), 11, 61.

31. *Legalism*, 5.

32. Ibid., 5–28.

33. John Rawls, *Political Liberalism* (New York, 1993), 216.

34. Ibid., 192–93.

35. *The Faces of Injustice*, 16.

36. *Legalism*, 5.

37. Dante Alighieri, *The Divine Comedy* (1321), trans. Carlyle-Wicksteed (New York, 1950), 3–5, 123–27.

38. Ibid., 5.

13

Active and Passive Justice

Bernard Yack

JUSTICE, JUDITH SHKLAR NOTED, is a rather cold virtue.[1] It is, after all, hard to get excited about the innumerable just actions we experience everyday—the return of correct change at the supermarket, waiting patiently in a queue, impartial acceptance of any paying customer into a store or restaurant. We expect, or demand, that just actions be the norm and we are, accordingly, disinclined to take special note of them. But even a single act of injustice, as when someone fails to perform one of the actions described above, usually grabs our attention and inflames our passions. The just acts of fellow citizens provide conditions under which we can continue to pursue whatever it is that occupies our hearts and minds. They thus do not attract much attention or passion. Unjust actions, in contrast, directly prevent us from achieving our goals. No wonder then that we expend so much energy each day passionately describing and denouncing them.

Nevertheless, there is a kind of justice, admittedly far rarer than that of the ordinary law-abiding citizen, that inspires the kind of warmth and passion ordinarily associated with injustice. Think of the way in which we laud the wisest "Solomonic" judges, the most far-seeing legislators, or the most admired of public officials. We can get very enthusiastic indeed about the justice we associate with such figures. Like the Greek poet cited in the *Nicomachean Ethics*, we treat this sort of justice as "more admirable than morning and evening star."[2]

How can we reconcile these two familiar reactions to justice? One might argue it is not really justice at all that excites our admiration in great judges and legislators, but rather some other virtue such as wisdom, beneficence, or magnanimity. I want to suggest, instead, that

191

these contrasting reactions to justice point to two different forms of justice and reflect important elements of our everyday social and political experience. I shall call these two forms of justice *active* and *passive* justice, in imitation of Shklar's distinction between active and passive injustice in *The Faces of Injustice*.[3]

Shklar notes that most theories focus their attention almost exclusively on "active injustice," the injustice of those who violate laws and other recognized general standards of justice. By doing so, Shklar complains, they ignore the large part of our claims about injustice that center on "passive injustice," the injustice of those who allow harm to come to others despite having the power to prevent it. As citizens, we are passively unjust when "we fail to report crimes, . . . when we let the wife beater next door go to it rather than interfere, or when we close our eyes to a colleague who routinely grades randomly and arbitrarily out of sheer laziness."[4] As public officials, we are guilty of passive injustice when we evade responsibility for the disasters we could have foreseen and prevented or when we fail to make full use of our powers and abilities to prevent cruelty to those caught in the system of justice. Shklar argues that ignoring passive injustice encourages the false and arrogant belief that some systematic body of rules and principles can capture the full range of actions that inspire reasonable complaints about injustice.[5]

Shklar's distinction between active and passive injustice suggests a parallel distinction between forms of justice. Active justice, the form of justice that excites such enthusiasm among us, is the virtue of those who make the most of their powers and abilities to prevent harm to others, in other words, the virtue of those who do the most to avoid what Shklar calls passive injustice. Passive justice, the colder and more familiar form of justice, is, in contrast, the virtue of those who faithfully and impartially follow laws and other recognized standards of justice, in other words, the virtue of those who avoid active injustice.

Since actively just individuals are those who make the best use of their power to prevent harm to others, it is not surprising that we associate active justice especially with those who have the most authority to determine our fate. Expectations of actively just behavior rise in proportion to the power that individuals have to affect our lives, which explains why active justice surfaces in political rhetoric most often when one speaks of great founders, legislators, and judges. Nevertheless, I do not think that we should treat what I am calling active justice as a superogatory virtue, a form of behavior to be associated only with moral saints and political virtuosi. We look for active justice in our everyday encounters with individuals who have some power over us, even if we do not expect them to live up to our standards for moral and political greatness. When someone has even a small degree of power over us, we hope not only that they will impartially apply recognized standards of justice, but also that they will make the most intelligent and conscientious use of that power.

Active justice depends upon the ability to exercise whatever other virtues a particular situation demands. Just as the lazy immigration clerk or the cowardly judge is likely to commit a whole range of passive injustices, so only the individual who can call on the requisite energy, courage, and prudence is likely to make the best use of their power to prevent harm and improve the lot of other individuals. Active justice, like the concept of general justice that Aristotle opposes to distributive and corrective justice,[6] potentially involves the exercise of all of the other moral virtues. Although it is a very demanding virtue, we are, I suggest, constantly complaining about its absence.

Passive justice, in contrast, is clearly a much narrower and more familiar virtue. It is far easier to determine and meet its standards. Passive justice only requires that we follow some recognized standard—such as a law, a custom, a moral principle or divine command. It is the operative concept of justice in most theories of distributive and corrective justice. Individuals are just, according to these theories, when they follow and impartially apply the particular standards advanced by these theories. Whether these standards are conventional, as in positivist theories, or are rooted in higher standards of divine or natural reason, the justice they define is passive in that it demands that we follow standards of distribution and rectitude rather than actively make the best use of our power to affect the lives of others.

Following rules and other general standards is not, however, the merely formal or mechanical process often portrayed in critiques of legalism. One must possess powerful virtues of character in order to resist the innumerable invitations to depart from general rules and standards of justice, most importantly, the virtues of fidelity and impartiality. Passively just individuals faithfully cling to their standards of justice and impartially apply them to all other groups and individuals, no matter their personal loyalties and friendships. It is this combination of fidelity and impartiality that makes passive justice such a cold virtue.[7] Personal fidelity touches our emotions quite deeply. Clinging faithfully to one's commitments to other human beings, despite the pains and adversity that life throws in our way, usually warms our hearts. But clinging faithfully to an impersonal standard of distribution or correct behavior and applying it impartially, despite competing claims of personal and group loyalty, is much harder to love. We may admire the steely will that it takes to suppress the warmth of personal relations in making one's judgments. But it is still a cold and rather unattractive virtue that requires looking away from human connectedness in making our moral judgments.

Passive justice's reliance on fidelity also focuses our attention on acts of injustice, rather than acts of justice, as the noteworthy events in our lives. Passive justice requires *continued* faithfulness to a set of standards of justice. Violating the standards of justice, even if only once in many opportunities to do so, eliminates one's claim to the virtue of passive justice; we are, after all, quite reluctant to call someone just who only rarely steals or takes a bribe. Active justice, in contrast, focuses attention on the acts of justice achieved, rather than the innumerable possibilities of passive injustice that surround every such act. It is measured by an accumulation of actions making good use of political power, rather than an uninterrupted display of fidelity. Thus someone who occasionally fails to act or makes a misjudgment may still be described as actively just in light of the great predominance of actions he or she has taken over the years.

Because most theories of justice develop an exemplary set of general rules and principles for us to follow—what Shklar accurately describes as "the normal model of justice"[8]—they have focused primarily on passive justice and its characteristic virtues, fidelity and impartiality. But these virtues are too narrow to support the ways in which we ordinarily talk about justice. For we use justice to characterize not only the actions of those who faithfully and impartially apply recognized standards, but also the actions of those who *choose* the right kinds of standards to apply. A much broader range of virtues than fidelity and impartiality is needed to make such choices well: the combination of energy, intelligence, sensitivity, and courage that we expect from actively just individuals.

There have, of course, been attempts to use the narrower virtues of passive justice to justify a choice among competing standards of justice. The most of influential of these attempts has been John Rawls's theory of justice as fairness. By arguing that justice is the choice of principles made by people who are constrained, by ignorance of their own personal identity and characteristics, to reason fairly, Rawls, in effect, uses the virtues of impartiality and fidelity to generate his principles of justice.[9] In his theory of justice the same virtues that we employ in the application of these principles justifies their original selection.

But why should we accept this way of determining principles of justice? Answering that we must do so because it is the only *fair* way of choosing our standards begs the question, since it assumes that fairness, which is grounded in the virtues of fidelity and impartiality, must take precedence in generating our principles of justice. Even if we value these virtues as highly as Rawls suggests that we do, that does not mean that we all believe that justice is nothing but the principles constructed by fair reasoners. Indeed, I would suggest that Rawls mistakes our strong appreciation of fairness in our everyday social interactions as evidence of our "considered judgment" that justice itself must reflect the outcome of a fair process of reasoning.

Rawls's later arguments about how restricting justice to fairness represents a political choice concerning how to deal with the "fact of diversity" in a pluralistic society offers a plausible answer to the question about why we should use the virtues associated with fairness to generate our principles of justice. In a pluralistic society one must, he argues, apply the principle of toleration to reasoning about justice itself. We must use the kind of impartiality toward different ways of life that we expect of public officials to generate our choice of principles in order to create a stable liberal democracy.[10]

But these arguments extend the range of virtues that we associate with justice well beyond fairness and impartiality. They reflect a judgment about the best way of ordering things in a liberal society, the kind of judgment that we look for in actively just individuals. Rawls is arguing, in effect, that a just person is someone who recognizes that the best way of promoting social peace and moral decency in a liberal democracy is by restricting our understanding of justice to principles selected by fair or genuinely impartial reasoners. But why do just individuals come to that conclusion, according to Rawls? Not because they are fair but because they come to certain conclusions about the best way of promoting the common good in conditions of diversity. It is this judgment about how to make the best use of their power, not their impartiality or fidelity to principle, that makes them just. In the end, even Rawls invokes the virtues of active justice in order to justify choices among competing standards of justice.

Passive Justice and Law

I have argued that the distinction between active and passive justice helps make sense of a significant part of our social experience and also plays an important, if unacknowledged role in major theories of justice. If so, why does this distinction receive no attention in these theories?[11]

Moral and political philosophers have, it seems to me, shied away from the distinction between active and passive justice for two reasons. First of all, there is the tremendous influence of law and legal judgment on the way in which philosophers have conceptualized justice. Law clearly emphasizes passive justice's virtues of fidelity and impartiality. To the extent that models of legal judgment influence philosophical theories of justice, they push these theories toward the purely passive conception of justice. Second, there is the tendency of moral and political philosophers to abstract from power relationships when conceptualizing justice, a tendency that turns our attention away from the conditions that promote expectations of active justice. I shall deal with law's influence on models of justice in this section and the abstraction from power relationships in the following section.

Law is, among other things, an extraordinarily useful instrument of justice. Its hallmark, I suggest, is it celebration of passive justice, its insistence that power be exercised as the faithful and impartial application to particular cases of rules and other general norms. Of course, judges must often act creatively, especially in appellate courts, to meet new situations, iron out inconsistencies, and apply relative open-ended statutes. But the emphasis in legal judgment is clearly on following norms rather than on the virtues that allow us to choose them. Straying into the territory of active justice, which judges must inevitably do at times, threatens the coherence and political legitimacy of legal judgment, which is one reason why legal theorists exercise so much desperate ingenuity to portray judicial lawmaking as if it were really nothing but fidelity to the higher preexisting norms that judges discover in the fabric of law and society.

The success of legal justice in creating relatively decent forms of social order has greatly influenced the way in which moral and political philosophers conceptualize justice. Shklar's normal model of justice, with its emphasis on discovering a bounded set of determinate rules and principles for ordering a community, is in effect a legalist or adjudicatory model of justice.[12] For it assumes, as does legal judgment, that the task of a theory of justice is to discover and apply the means of adjudicating competing claims. Legal judgment seeks to discover and apply norms to situations of social disagreement and conflict. Similarly, the most influential theories of justice seek to discover and apply the norms that will allow us to adjudicate competing claims about the best standards of justice to choose. The success of law in adjudicating social disagreement, I am suggesting, has led moral and political philosophers to see themselves as the articulators of the "common point of view from which their claims [about the basic norms of justice] may be adjudicated."[13] The adjudicatory efforts of judges help make it possible to exercise the passive virtues of justice, since they give us a determinate set of legal standards that we can faithfully and impartially follow. The adjudicatory efforts of moral and political philosophers aim at a parallel goal. By providing us with a determinate set of norms against which to measure competing views of justice, they make it possible to exercise the passive virtues of justice when choosing basic standards of justice. We need only faithfully and impartiality apply that set of norms in order to come up with the right standards. This adjudicatory model of justice, like most models of legal judgment, leaves little or no room for what I have called active justice.

The problem that bedevils all such models is, of course, the justification of the higher set of determinate norms used to adjudicate our disagreements about justice. It is hard enough to justify claims about the determinate content of statutory and constitutional norms. It is far more difficult to justify claims about the determinate content of extralegal norms of justice, which is probably why so much philosophic ingenuity is devoted to the task.

Philosophers have tried to identify the determinate standards of extralegal justice dictated by nature, God, human reason, custom, our shared experience, our implicit consensus, or any combination thereof. Even though most contemporary moral and political philosophers disdain any appeal to natural or divine standards of justice, they usually try to eliminate the characteristic indeterminacy of extralegal standards of justice. Rawls identifies determinate standards against which to measure the justice of our social and political institutions by asking which principles of justice rational individuals would choose if they were constrained to reason fairly by a "veil of ignorance" that concealed from them their personal identity and characteristics. Ronald Dworkin offers a path to "right answers" about questions of justice when he insists that our legal and political institutions, when viewed as a coherent whole, contain implicit principles of justice that allow us to resolve even the most difficult of hard legal cases.[14] Even Michael Walzer, who firmly rejects the kind of appeal to transhistorical standards of justice that he finds lurking in Rawls's and Dworkin's arguments,[15] still insists that we can identify a determinate standard against which to measure the justice of our various social institutions. He bases such a standard on the "shared understandings" of the goods that we distribute in different spheres of social interaction. These understandings may change from one historical period to another, but, Walzer assumes, they are sufficiently clear and distinct at any particular time to yield citizens determinate standards against which to measure their judgments about justice.[16]

All three of these philosophers deny that justice is waiting to be discovered "out there" in the nature of the world or of human reason. Nevertheless, they all still insist that we can discover determinate extralegal standards of justice if we reason properly—whether, as with Rawls, by a process of hypothetical reasoning based on assumptions about fairness, or, as with Dworkin and Walzer, by empirical reasoning about the determinate standards implicit in "our" cultural, legal, and political systems. Proper reasoning, they argue, well lead us to discover the standards that we must faithfully and impartially apply when measuring the justice of practices and institutions.

Since the relative indeterminacy of extralegal standards of justice introduces considerable instability and tension into our lives, it is hardly surprising that moral and political philosophers seek to discover more determinate standards for us to follow. But they can only provide us with such standards by making highly controversial and unrealistic assumptions about our moral reasoning.

Rawls, for example, can generate his two principles of justice only by making highly controversial assumptions about the "primary goods" of citizens and the rational strategy—maximizing one's minimum return—for attaining them. In order to maintain the claim that his principles of justice can adjudicate competing claims about the common advantage of a community, Rawls has to treat these assumptions as if they follow from relatively uncontroversial understandings of individual rationality. But these understandings of primary goods and rational strategies are themselves highly controversial. We can only choose among such understandings with reference to the kind of life and goods we want to use our power to promote. Similarly, Michael Walzer tries to represent inherently controversial judgments about the best standards to promote the common good as if they necessarily follow from the shared "historical meanings" of goods. His highly implausible claim that economic democracy, the shared control of factories and other large-scale operations, necessarily follows from the "shared understandings" of property and power in modern America shows just how far he is willing to go in using this argument to support inherently controversial claims about the common good.[17]

The quest to give all norms of justice the degree of determinacy found in legal standards has led philosophers to defend highly unrealistic assumptions about moral reasoning and social consensus. By recognizing the role of active justice in choosing from competing standards of justice, we might escape the need for such assumptions. The price of that escape, however, would be the acceptance of a rather high degree of indeterminacy in our standards of justice. Fidelity to some norm is far easier to measure and agree upon than the best use of one's power, which is what we expect from actively just individuals. Whether we find reasonable ground for complaints about failure to meet such expectations of justice will depend, to a great extent, on our subjective preferences and expectations. Clearly, one person's Solomon can be another's Savonarola.

Nevertheless, I think it better to face up to the relative indeterminacy of the standards of justice that we employ rather than continue on a fruitless quest for an uncontroversial set of determinate norms to guide our choice of standards of justice. Arguments about justice ordinarily refer to two kinds of standards: the relatively determinate standards embodied in the fund of norms familiar to the members of a community and the much vaguer and more indeterminate standards by which the justice of these norms is measured. Where these relatively determinate standards are available, passive justice's virtues of fidelity and impartiality can guide our behavior. But it is a mistake, a mistake encouraged by legalist models of justice, to think that such standards are available for the whole of our demands about justice.

Active Justice and Power

Why insist on describing the virtue of those who make the best use of their power as a form of justice rather than as some other virtue, such as prudence, beneficence, or public-spiritedness? One reason for doing so is, as we have seen, in order to capture best the sense of justice associated with choosing as opposed to applying principles of justice. Another, equally important reason is to conceptualize a part of the social experience of justice and injustice that is missing in theories that focus exclusively on passive justice, namely, being in someone else's power.

Justice, it is often said, is the preeminently social virtue. Unlike the other cardinal virtues of wisdom, moderation, and courage, justice is exercised only as part of a relationship with others. It concerns, in particular, the claims that we make upon each other's rights and resources. But claims of justice and injustice most often involve a particular kind of social relationship: one in which someone has power over the lives of others. When we complain about injustice, we complain about the use that has been made of this power to affect our lives. When we demand justice be done, we demand a particular exercise of power to correct or prevent suffering injury from others.

This aspect of the circumstances of justice strikes us most strongly when we lay our fates in the hands of a judge or jury or public official. But it is present even in the most ordinary circumstances of justice, quite apart from the occasions when we defer to the judgments of individuals empowered to render justice in the name of the community. When, for example, we put a large bill in the hands of a shopkeeper or sign any sort of contract, we are to a greater or lesser extent, putting ourselves under the power of another. It is the use others make of such power that leads us to complain about injustice.

Theories of distributive justice, especially those that derive their principles from bargaining games or constrained reasoning of identically situated individuals, tend to obscure the unequal power relations that constitute part of the ordinary circumstances of justice. In order to construct morally preferable principles of distribution, these theories abstract from the social relationship to a powerful distributor that looms so large in the experience of distributive justice and injustice. In these theories distribution is something that "society" as a whole does with its rights and resources. In our actual social experience of justice, however, distribution is done by a range of individuals and groups that have power over us in particular situations. Typically, an individual or group of individuals has the power to distribute some good, such as grades, admission, promotion, or raises, to another group of individuals. The experience of being dependent on the power of other individuals to make such decisions is one of things that lead us to demand justice in the first place.

Proponents of many liberal theories of justice argue that they abstract from these power relations precisely in order to correct the distortions that unequal power relations introduce into principles of justice. Abstracting from the subordination characteristics of our actual experience of justice is for them the best way of regulating the behavior of participants in social hierarchies. But however effective and important these efforts to regulate social hierarchies, conceptualizing justice in this way hides from view that large part of our social expectations associated with active justice and passive injustice. Sharing an authoritative conception of passive justice gives us a means of holding others accountable; it does not eliminate their power over our fates. Even in the most egalitarian society, injustice would still involve an exercise of power. A more egalitarian society would simply offer a far more equal distribution of the opportunities to exercise such power over each other. It could not eliminate these opportunities altogether.

Theories that focus solely on what I have called passive justice deflect our attention away from this important aspect of the circumstances of justice. These theories encourage us to view justice primarily as a relation between individuals and general norms against which they should measure their behavior rather than as a social relationship among individuals who have different kinds of power over each other's fate. Viewing justice in this way may be harmless in the many everyday situations of contract and exchange where all we expect others to do with their power is follow norms stipulating particular levels of return. But it will impede our view of the more complex situations in which others have power to affect our lives.

As Shklar strikingly demonstrates in *The Faces of Injustice*, we still complain about the injustice of the behavior of people who have power over us even when they conscientiously follow all of the recognized general standards of justice. Laziness, stupidity, cowardice, or a whole range of lesser vices may keep them from making the best use of their power to serve their fellow citizens. When we are harmed by their failure to use their power to protect us, we complain about the injustice we have suffered at their hands. We have little patience with their exculpatory claims that our suffering was a misfortune "that couldn't be helped."[18] In doing so, we are measuring the justice of their behavior against our expectations, however subjective and indeterminate they may be, that public officials will make the best use of their power to prevent harm to us. In other words, we include expectations of active justice in our judgments about whether public officials have acted justly. How far we go in demanding that public officials live up to these expectations will depend on the nature of our public goals and political institutions, as we shall see in the following section.

Active Justice in Liberal Democratic Regimes

Different political regimes tend to rely on different balances between the virtues of active and passive justice. Aristocratic regimes are likely, given the great political inequalities that constitute them, to place a far greater emphasis on active justice than liberal democratic regimes—which may explain why Aristotle, who celebrates an aristocratic understanding of the moral virtues, seems so much more familiar with the concept of active justice than contemporary liberal theorists. Although Aristotle insists on the importance of fairness and its passive virtues, he characterizes them as a mere part of the larger whole of "general justice," the range of actions taken by completely virtuous individuals to promote the common good.[19] In Aristotle's aristocratic best regime, the majority of the population depends almost completely on the virtues of the small group of rulers for whatever justice they receive. In his less utopian model, the mixed regime, Aristotle balances such dependence with greater respect for law and, accordingly, greater reliance on the virtues I associate with passive justice.

Liberal democratic regimes, in contrast, usually seek to deemphasize the significance of active justice. They do so, first of all, because they seek to diminish the depth and extent of our dependence on individuals exercising power by promoting equal civil and political rights. Liberal democracies should simply present far fewer and less important opportunities for the exercise of active justice than aristocracies and monarchies. Second, many liberal practices and institutions reflect doubts that the active virtues of Aristotelian and Christian aristocrats can provide a stable and reliable foundation for social justice. Liberals have often expressed these doubts by arguing that universal vices or emotions, such as self-interest or fear, provide a far more reliable foundation for social justice than moral virtue. I would modify these familiar arguments somewhat by adding that liberal practices also rest upon replacing extremely demanding and rare virtues, such as active justice, with less demanding and more generally achievable virtues, such as passive justice. Many familiar liberal institutions, such as the rule of law and the constitutional separation of powers, are usually portrayed as resting solely on a set of mechanical checks and balances whereby the vices of one public official constrain the vices of another. I suggest that these institutions depend just as much on the development in citizens and rulers of a disposition to apply a regime's written and unwritten general standards faithfully and impartially, in other words, on the spread of the virtue of passive justice.

One might, accordingly, wonder whether active justice has any role at all in liberal democratic politics. It certainly seems to have disappeared from contemporary liberal theory. Perhaps it should have no place in liberal politics either.

Clearly, I disagree. While much less important than in aristocracies and monarchies, the claims inspired by expectations of active justice still arise in liberal democratic regimes for the simple reason that individuals still exercise power over others within them. Liberal democratic politics may offer less opportunity for the exercise of active justice and liberal democrats may expend great efforts to hedge the exercise of power with general rules and procedures, but they cannot eliminate the innumerable situations in which our fate depends on the choices made by those who have power over us. When the rude and sadistic immigration officer scares away petitioners, when a lazy and doddering judge decides cases without listening closely to arguments, when the selfish and insensitive politician harms exposed minorities by exploiting inflammatory rhetoric, we complain about the injustice—Shklar's passive injustice—that we have suffered at their hands. Even if they never break faith with the general standards of passive justice that we recognize, we still frequently complain about the injustice of their actions. In doing so we are measuring their actions against the more subjective and indeterminate standards of active justice. We are answering negatively the question, did these public officials make the best use of their power to avoid harm?

Liberals may have very good reasons for reserving coercion for those who fail in certain duties of passive justice. But they delude themselves if they think they can capture all of justice within the framework of passive justice's set of general standards. Politicians, judges, lawyers, and even private citizens will make worse use of their power, I suggest, if they believe that their actions can never cause complaints about injustice as long as they faithfully and impartially apply the general rules and principles recognized by their society. Such an exclusive focus on passive justice obscures the special concerns about justice and injustice inspired by power over others.

Finally, there may be a specifically liberal understanding of the goals of active justice. Our understanding of the "best use" of political power will depend to a great extent on the way in which we perceive the purposes of political power. Aristotle's very broad understanding of the goals of active justice, namely, promotion of the common advantage,[20] reflects his very broad understanding of the purpose of political power: helping individuals gain the security and character virtues that ground a flourishing human life. Liberals, who tend to favor far narrower understandings of the purpose of political power, are likely to favor much more limited understandings of active justice.

In this regard I find it quite revealing that Shklar speaks about the failure to use power "to *prevent harm*,"[21] rather than a broader and more positive formulation, such as failure to promote the good life, as the source of our complaints about passive injustice. Preventing harm, especially the kind of fear of cruelty that is, according to Shklar, the major enemy of liberal politics,[22] is a characteristically liberal way of understanding our expectations of public officials. Like most liberal theories, it views liberal politics as a means of securing the conditions within which to pursue our various understandings of the good life rather than as a means of promoting any particular view of human happiness and goodness. Those who expect their public officials to promote private virtue or religious truth will have considerably broader expectations of their public officials and, accordingly, broader conceptions of passive injustice.

Shklar's relatively narrow conception of passive injustice suggests, in turn, a specifically liberal understanding of active justice. What we expect of people with unequal political power, according to this liberal understanding of active justice, is that they make the best use of their power to prevent the most serious harm that may come to those whom their actions affect. Indeed, most liberal regimes erect public standards of passive justice to keep public officials from going beyond this relatively narrow conception of active justice.

Liberal politics thus not only places a greater emphasis on passive justice in its practices and institutions, it curtails the rather broad goals associated with active justice in more aristocratic societies. Nevertheless, we will misunderstand and misrepresent a large part of liberal democratic politics if we pay heed only to the claims of passive justice. As long as some individuals hold power over the fate of others, expectations of active justice, along with complaints about passive injustice, will be common features of liberal democratic politics.

Notes

1. *The Faces of Injustice*, 103–6. See also J. R. Lucas, *On Justice* (Oxford, 1980), 4.

2. Aristotle, *Nicomachean Ethics*, 1129b28.

3. *The Faces of Injustice*, 5–14, 40–50.

4. Ibid., 6, 43.

5. I provide a fuller discussion of Shklar's distinction between passive and active injustice in "Injustice and the Victim's Voice," *Michigan Law Review* 89 (1991): 1334–49.

6. Aristotle, *Nicomachean Ethics*, 1129–30.

7. Of course one can develop a passion for impartiality and fidelity, and many people do. But that passion is, in effect, a passion for a certain coldness in manner and behavior.

8. *The Faces of Injustice*, 17.

9. See John Rawls, *A Theory of Justice* (Cambridge, Mass., 1971).

10. See Rawls, *Political Liberalism* (New York, 1993), 89–211.

11. In chapter 5 of *The Problems of a Political Animal* (Berkeley, Calif., 1993), I argue that Aristotle recognizes the distinction between active and passive justice and conceptualizes it in his undervalued distinction between general and particular justice. But this is a relatively unusual interpretation of Aristotle's theory of justice. Aristotle's theory is much more often treated—including by Shklar (see *The Faces of Injustice*, 17)—as a straightforward theory of what I have described as passive justice.

12. For this understanding of legalism, see *Legalism*. I discuss the legalism of Shklar's normal model of justice in "Injustice and the Victim's Voice."

13. Rawls, *A Theory of Justice*, 5.

14. Ronald Dworkin, *Taking Rights Seriously* (Cambridge, Mass., 1977), 47, 100.

15. See Michael Walzer, Philosophy and Democracy," *Political Theory* 9 (1981): 379–99.

16. Michael Walzer, *Spheres of Justice* (New York, 1983), xiv, 6–10.

17. Ibid., 291–303.

18. *The Faces of Injustice*, 3.

19. Aristotle, *Nicomachean Ethics*, 1130b15. I develop this interpretation of Aristotle's understanding of justice in *The Problems of a Political Animal*, 157–66.

20. See Yack, *The Problems of a Political Animal*, 163.

21. *The Faces of Injustice*, 40–50.

22. See *Ordinary Vices*, 7–9, 237–49, and "The Liberalism of Fear."

14

The Political Case for Constitutional Courts

Bruce Ackerman

Escape from Politics?

UNTIL THE SECOND WORLD WAR it was plausible to view the constitutional role of courts in America as a historical curiosity—just another example of the New World going crazy in its Enlightenment enthusiasms. After the war it was plausible to view the success of judicial review in Germany, Italy, (and Japan?) as a product of American imperialism—just another example of a military hegemon mistaking its historical peculiarities for universal laws of reason.

But it is now time for European theory to take the constitutional role of courts seriously. However differently the revolutions of 1989 are playing themselves out in Eastern Europe, they are alike in this—all the new regimes are embracing judicial review in their emerging constitutional systems. Europe's domestication of an alien institution[1] is suggested by the fact that it is German, more than American, models of judicial review that are having the greatest impact in the current round of constitutional discussions in the former Communist zone.[2] At the same time, the courts have been playing an increasingly aggressive role in organizing the emerging legal order of the European community.[3] What *is* going on?

An easy answer: an escape from politics and, even more ominously, an escape from "the political."[4] This flight proceeds, it appears, on two levels. On the level of ideas: in the effort by liberal political philosophers (like the present writer) to reassert the possibility of a form of constitutive rationality that might serve as a putatively neutral foundation for judicial supremacy.[5] On the level of institutional reality: in the effort by judges and bureaucrats to oust politicians and voters from the central role in policy formulation.

This easy answer serves, of course, as prelude for not-too-agonized condemnation: the time to liberate ourselves from abstract philosophy and juridicobureaucratic management is *now*, before the iron cage closes irrevocably upon beleaguered *zoon politikon*, and Weber's nightmare becomes Europe's reality.

But there is another view: judicial review arrives on the scene to redeem the promise of the political, not to kill it. The real enemy of genuine politics is not the judges, but Europe's imperfect liberation from its monarchical past. It is this monarchocentralist tradition which has distorted the dominant European understanding of democratic politics in ways that make judicial review seem alien.

Let me explain.

Where Does Politics Occur?

In the nation's capital, says the courtier. That's where the king is. That's where the important people meet and greet and cheat one another in their effort to influence the highest and mightiest.

Now this simple thought, I submit, endures—especially in London, Paris, and Rome.[6] The king is dead, but the political life of the nation remains concentrated in a single square mile at the center. "Democracy" comes into the picture in a single way: the unwashed get a chance, once in a while, to vote the courtiers in or out. That's enough of the political life for them; we in the center, however, get to taste it on a day-to-day basis.

It is this simple picture that gives intuitive appeal to the easy answer with which we began. The intervention of judges into the foreground of courtesan politics threatens to take the joy out of life—as least for the (democratized) courtesans. These judicial eminences dressed in black, spouting Kantian maxims as if they were revealed truths, even look like the humorless Prussian party-killers that they are.

But the scene changes its aspect if we question its background premise: should we continue to think of genuine politics as the monopoly of the center? If not, how does this change the relationship of judicial review to the (reconstructed) domain of the "political"?

My argument proceeds in four steps. The first three constrain the political freedom of the center by elaborating upon the political freedom of the periphery—in different ways. The final step returns to the more traditional "liberal" understanding of judicial review, and inquires into the relevance of the preceding "political" stages in the argument. I conclude with a passing glance at the present European scene, and the potential relevance of my remarks for the constitutional future.

Step One: A Reconstructed Centralism

In the centralist picture, there is only one moment when the masses get into the act, namely, the point at which they elect one set of courtiers, rather than another, to represent them before the (dead) king. While I mean to question this setup, let us first examine it more closely. Isn't there room within the centralist framework for a more robust notion of the political presence of the periphery? If so, how can it lead to a new appreciation of constitutional review by courts?

Answers to these questions have been at the forefront of constitutional theory in both the United States and Germany in the last generation.[7] The simple two-step logic goes like this: first, politicians at the center cannot *credibly* claim to speak for the people if, for example, they run an election in the totalitarian manner of old-style Communist states. Instead, representation must be the result of a robust electoral process through which the people at the periphery have a free and fair choice among alternatives.

But if this is so, an institutional point comes into view. There is an obvious danger involved in giving politicians in the center full freedom to control the terms under which they will be challenged electorally. What will prevent them from manipulating this power in ways that unfairly disadvantage their challengers, perhaps to the point where the electoral process becomes a sham?

Here is where the judges enter.They offer an institutional mechanism though which the manipulative ambitions of the reigning politicians may be controlled. Since judges have long tenure that is not dependent on electoral victories, they can look upon the incumbent representatives' efforts to stack the electoral system with a plausible claim to impartiality. By declaring offensive legislation unconstitutional, the judges are undoubtedly constraining the political freedoms of the center—but in the name of enhancing the political will of the periphery.

This argument can lead to some very powerful conclusions—depending on meaning of the "free and fair" electoral process which the judges are constitutionally committed to safeguard. At a minimum it will require the judicial protection of the right to vote, to speak on political matters, and to run for office, as well as protection against criminal (and other) punishment for political activities.

But this is only the minimum, and most contemporary partisans of this first rationale for judicial intervention have been remarkably timid in exploring the further reaches of their organizing thought.[8] *Can* an election be fair and free if a large group in the electorate lack the schooling required to comprehend the leading lines of political debate? Or if they are starving or working under oppressive conditions for most of their waking hours?

My answer is no. If you agree, this first rationale allows you to prepare a conceptual path to consider how far judges should be constitutionally empowered to intervene on these social matters as well. Of course, granting such a power might be limited by all sorts of prudential considerations. But my concern here is with basic principle: in empowering judges to insist upon a "democratic floor" in the evaluation of welfare and educational measures proposed by the reigning politicians, I am not advocating the "death of the political," but its reorganization and extension—from a concern with the center to the protection of the political life experienced in the periphery.

Step Two: Dualist Democracy

Thus far, I have been operating within a *monistic* model of democracy, which allows the mass of citizens to enter into the picture at only one point: the moment they cast a ballot to select their rulers for the next period. During the days and years between elections, the centralist constitution—even when subjected to the preceding reorganization—is firmly fixed upon the national capital. In John Ely's pregnant phrase, the model of reconstructed centralism aims to purify the electoral process so that it can "reinforce" the claim of elected representatives to rule in the name of the rest of us. In allowing the judges to police the electoral process for fundamental fairness, it aims to eliminate, once and for all, the need for asking all troubling questions about the extent to which a few hundred politicians in the nation's capital can ever adequately represent the people.

In contrast, the *dualist* model seeks to problematize normal political representation—without delegitimating it. On this view, there are certain great occasions in political life in which the people intervene more directly and authoritatively than they do when they go to the polls in normal times to choose between competing politicians. During these episodes, a mass citizenry insists on doing something more than merely selecting their rulers, something that is better interpreted as giving their rulers marching orders. I have called these episodes constitutional moments—the people speak with a different accent than they maintain during normal politics. They exercise their "popular sovereignty," "*pouvoir constituant*," "*verfassunggebende Gewalt*"—in contrast to the "delegated power," "*pouvoir constituée*," or what have you, normally exercised by elected politicians in the capital.

This dualism is well entrenched in the modern language of constitutionalism, as well as its obscurities and dangers. The crucial problem is the people with a capital *P*. We all know what it is for an individual to decide something, but what is it for a collectivity so grand as the People to enter constitutional politics in a meaningful way?

Perhaps the modern writer to beg this question most outrageously was Carl Schmitt. His *Verfassungslehre* is a piece of "negative theology," with the crucial exception that Schmitt's god-term is the *Volk*: he tells us a lot about how the will of the *Volk* should not be confused with normal acts of political representation, but he is very weak in developing affirmative criteria for identifying the magical event. Indeed, his efforts along this line sound like the "thirteenth chime of the clock—not only absurd in itself, but calling into doubt all that has come before." Consider, for example, his remark that "the natural way in which the People expresses its immediate Will is through a shout of Yes or No by an assembled multitude, the Acclamation."[9] Once Schmitt "solves" the problem of identification in this brutalized way, his Nazism follows immediately: the rallies at Nuremberg are just the kind of remedy for the disease of modernity that Schmitt is prescribing in his *Verfassungslehre*.[10]

And yet I do not think we should allow Nazis like Schmitt to discredit the entire idea that modern citizens can, on occasion, organize their political will in a way that deserves special constitutional respect from their elected politicians. This point has, at least, served as one of my principal preoccupations over the last decade—serving as an organizing theme of my two last two books, *We the People* and *The Future of Liberal Revolution*.[11] Building on the American experience with dualist democracy, I propose a number of criteria for identifying an appropriate act of constitutional will. The first has to do with time: it should not be enough to elicit majority or supermajority support for a constitutional principle at one single moment. A very substantial period—measured in years, not months—should be provided in which a constitutional initiative can be debated in a multitude of decision-making forums before its fate is determined.

But the mere passage of time should not be enough. Before an initiative deserves passage it should gain support that is qualitatively different from normal legislation in at least three respects—depth, breadth, and decisiveness.

Breadth and decisiveness speak, in largely quantitative terms, about the degree of majority support that is required before a constitutional initiative is enacted. Breadth specifies the minimum percentage—should it be 50 percent or higher? Decisiveness, in turn, addresses the problems of social choice theory raised first by the Marquis de Condorcet and given its modern formulation by Kenneth Arrow.[12] As Condorcet and Arrow teach us, it is quite possible for an initiative to gain (super-)majority support through artful manipulation of the agenda even though it could be defeated if it were paired against alternatives suppressed by agenda manipulators. Given this analytic point, it is necessary to elaborate a concept of a *decisive* majority in a rather technical way—which it is not the task of this chapter to address.[13]

More important for present purposes is the last criterion, depth. This involves the extent to which citizens have invested time and energy in deliberating upon the constitutional initiative. Here I want to position myself at the opposite pole from Schmitt. He believes that the only *verffassunggebende Gewalt* worthy of the name is a shout that expresses the "natural and necessary life-assertion of a particular People."[14] I am looking for a different kind of political will, one that is expressed by a decisive majority only after an extraordinary amount of time and energy has been invested in collective deliberation.

At the same time, I want to disavow the potentially Kantian overtones that others may attribute to my view. I do *not* suppose that the collective process of deliberation either could or should lead to a politics of pure reason, divorced entirely from passion or self-interest. The aim of a dualist constitution is to provide a realistic structure for the serious collective exercise of democratic deliberation in which passion and interest are subjected to *serious* moral testing in a common search for the public good—on those relatively rare occasions upon which modern citizens want to take on this burden. The dualist constitution, however, remains a tool for citizens, not philosophers—though one that calls them, in a realistic way, to take their citizenship responsibilities seriously.

A pious hope? I refer the skeptical reader to my recent work where, among other things, I explore the extent to which the American constitutional practice, over the past two centuries, approximates the dualist conception of democratic life. For now, I will help myself to my conclusion so as to elaborate a second fundamental dimension in the political case for judicial review.

That is, I want you to assume the existence of a functioning dualist constitution, containing two lawmaking tracks. One is a normal lawmaking system in which democratically elected politicians are empowered to enact laws they think serve the public interest. The other is a higher lawmaking system in which, through a series of plebiscites and other, more deliberative, devices, a movement for constitutional politics finally wins the deep, broad, and decisive consent of the People. Assume finally that some constitutional program has indeed survived this demanding test of public deliberation and decision: the People have spoken.

What next? Here is where the judges enter, once again, to provide an institutional mechanism to assure that the People's words will be taken seriously by the normal politicians who continue to govern in the nation's capital. These members of parliament and the executive may have all sorts of reasons to ignore the People's will, ranging from personal vendettas to party strategies to moral convictions. And there are a host of reasons the simple process of regular electoral competition will not serve as a reliable constraint upon their evasions, ranging from conceptual matters elaborated by social choice theorists like Kenneth Arrow to matters of party organization more compelling to political hacks.

To fix ideas, suppose that after much political mobilization and debate, the People have decided to embrace the principle of freedom of intimate association, thus barring the state from restricting the kinds and number of sexual relationships into which individuals may enter in their private lives. Despite this solemn decision, five years later the dominant parliamentary coalition strikes a deal with the Catholic Church to proscribe birth control devices, thinking this tactic will maximize its opportunities for victory in the next election. When our hypothetical constitutional court intervenes and strikes down the statute, it is wrong to look upon this act as an assault on "the political."

Instead, it is simply telling the political elite in the nation's capital that they have a lot more work to do before they can earn the right to overturn a considered judgment of the People. Rather than contenting themselves with the daily triumphs of the normal lawmaking system, they will have to take on the more onerous task of higher lawmaking: mobilizing a sustained constitutional movement that will succeed, over time, in convincing the majority of the citizenry to give their broad, decisive, and deep evidence that the People have changed their mind.

In empowering the judges to act in this way, the dualist constitution is, once again, reorganizing the political rather than abolishing it. To make my point, let me adapt a useful metaphor floated by Michael Walzer a few years ago when he invited us to speak of "spheres" of justice—each sphere marking off a different realm that is appropriate to different principles of justice.[15] Walzer thinks that liberal theorists like myself are incapable of recognizing the importance of differentiating between different spheres of life, taking each sphere's distinctive character into account.

Although he was wrong about this complaint even when he published it,[16] the present occasion provides me with a chance to join him publicly in praise of his idea. Like Walzer, I want to insist on the need for boundaries between different areas of life. But in the present case I want to insist on the need for boundaries within the sphere of the political, as well as between the political and other spheres, like education or the marketplace. In the dualist conception, the judges operate to police one of these crucial intrapolitical boundaries. When they invalidate an ordinary parliamentary enactment as inconsistent with previously considered judgments of the People, they force the politicians of the capital to mobilize the broad and deep consent needed to support the proposition that the People have changed their mind. In enforcing the Constitution in this way, the judges do not kill "the political" but give it new life and structure, thus forcing the politicians in the capital to share the exercise of public deliberation with the country at large.

Step Three: Federalism

The dualist cuts a boundary through time: he emphasizes that modern citizens are only rarely prepared to make a sustained and considered judgment on matters of fundamental principle. He therefore proposes to structure and register these rare popular judgments with the constitutional seriousness they deserve.

But there is another boundary worth establishing within the political. This one cuts over space rather than time. When placed within the present framework, the minimal federalist thought is this: rather than allow one elite to enjoy an intense political life in a single capital, why not allow elites in a variety of regional centers also to engage in a rich political life?

This minimal thought can, in turn, be maximalized in either or both of the two preceding ways: the Constitution can take energetic steps to provide the bases of democratic citizenship to all so that they may participate in the regional electoral process with a sense of self-awareness, and it can embrace a dualistic structure, enabling the citizens of a region to give marching orders to their regional rulers through an appropriate form of constitutional politics. But it is enough here to remark upon the way in which the federalist idea—whether minimal or maximal—opens up a third path for the judges.

Consider that politicians operating at the center and in the regions will predictably enact statutes that are at cross purposes with one another. The center will assert X, some region will assert Y, which is completely or partially incompatible with X. Who wins?

Since this will be an endemic problem, it will not be enough for the Constitution to elaborate the basic principles for allocating legislative authority between the center and the regions. A forum will be required for resolving the ongoing tensions in a regularized and relatively impartial way. Enter, once again, the judges. No better institution has yet been devised for generating case by case moderately thoughtful decisions that attempt to mediate the competing claims of national and regional legislation.

In making these determinations, the judges will regularly declare that the politicians at the center or the region (or both) have overstepped their constitutional bounds. Once again, these determinations are part and parcel of the process of carving up political space into more manageable dimensions, and by no means signify the death of the political.

Step Four: Liberal Rights?

I am a liberal. I am a republican. I am a democrat. There are tensions between these three commitments. But there are also complementarities: *liberal democratic republicanism* is not an oxymoron, but provides the soundest way of dealing with the perplexities of political life in the modern world.

This chapter has done no more than glimpse this possibility through a single prism, the problem of judicial review. Nonetheless, we can try to elaborate a bit on the ideal of liberal democratic republicanism by considering how far the "political" case for judicial review extends to the protection of fundamental liberal rights. Let us reconsider our three-point program with this end in view.

Reconstructed Centralism

The position I ascribed to the reconstructed centralist is too narrow for all liberals and may also be too broad for some.

Begin on the narrow side. All liberals will appreciate that the reorganized centralist insists on the constitutional protection of such basic liberties as free speech and freedom from arbitrary criminal prosecution. But they will bridle at the narrowly political way these freedoms are conceived. Men and women not only have a fundamental right to talk about politics, they have a right to talk about anything that interests them. Nor should they be guaranteed merely against arbitrary arrest provoked by their political opposition to the powers that be; they have a right to force the police to respect their privacy on all occasions, except when there is probable cause to believe they have committed a clearly specified crime.

Of course, the reconstructed centralist might try to accommodate these points by broadening his notion of "politically relevant" speech and conduct—to the point, perhaps, where any speech or conduct will be encompassed within his argument for judicial intervention. While I applaud the liberal spirit that lurks behind such expansions, I think that, beyond a certain point, they misrepresent the character of the political in modern life. In contrast to Sparta or Stalinist Russia, everything we moderns do or say *isn't political* in any meaningful sense of the term, and the reconstructed centralist should not lose sight of this point in a good-hearted effort to expand his constitutional rights to reassure his liberal comrades. Far better to recognize that there is a limit to this first political rationale for judicial review which liberals will find unsatisfactory.

Now turn the coin and consider the possibility of overbreadth. Here the problem is raised by the fact that the reconstructed centralist may well find himself advocating a host of "welfarist" measures to establish a relatively high floor of educational and material preconditions for effective political participation. Some laissez-faire extremists—Hayek? Nozick? Gauthier?—may find this offensive.

However this may be, it is a mistake to allow these reactionaries to dominate our vision of contemporary liberalism. While I am hardly an unbiased observer, I believe that modern liberalism has something better to offer than warmed-over versions of nineteenth-century capitalism. This activist liberal vision—of the kinds developed by Rawls, Dworkin, as well as the present writer[17]—contemplates a far more robust place for both the state and democratic political life in liberal society. Within this evolving structure of liberal thought there seems no reason to worry about the overbreadth of the reconstructed centralist's guarantees of a material and educational foundation for political life.

To the contrary, the activist liberal's concern with social justice will converge with the reorganized centralist's concern with the social preconditions for a genuinely democratic electoral competition.

Dualist Democracy

The dualist, no less than the reconstructed centralist, places a special value on political freedoms, though his emphasis is slightly different and a bit broader. Dualism continues to emphasize the crucial role of the ballot box—in determining both the ongoing struggle for political office and the fate of the more plebiscitary initiatives debated before the People in the higher lawmaking system. But it also casts a very protective eye upon phenomena characteristically associated with high levels of political involvement, namely, the protest march and the mass demonstration. While the reconstructed centralist is also alive to their importance, the dualist judiciary will be even more protective since they will see these kinds of demonstrations as manifesting the kind of engaged politics that may (or may not) yield the mobilized consensus that is central to the exercise of the People's constituent power.

Turning to the protection of the broader range of rights prized by liberals, dualist democracy is not as narrow as reorganized centralism. Its problem, instead, is that it is entirely open ended. The status of fundamental rights like the free exercise of religion, personal privacy, private property, and freedom of contract depends on the will of the People, as expressed through successful exercises of constitutional politics. If the People have affirmed these fundamental freedoms, dualist courts will intervene to protect them—challenging incumbents to take to the higher lawmaking track if they wish to establish that the People have changed their mind in illiberal ways. If not, not.

We cannot, in short, determine the relationship between dualism and liberalism in the abstract; it all depends upon the content of the People's will, as revealed in the historical development of a particular constitutional system.

This point leads me to emphasize the importance of a worldwide trend. Since the Second World War there has been an accelerating effort to *positivize* the fundamental rights developed by the liberal tradition, to translate the conclusions of liberal political philosophy into law through acts of political will. While the United Nations declaration was important in inaugurating this process, no less important has been a series of regional political initiatives that have made the protection of fundamental rights a fundamental part of operating legal systems.

This process has been especially advanced in Europe, where, in addition to increasingly active human rights interventions by courts at the European level,[18] constitutional courts (especially in Germany, Italy, France, and Spain) have been aggressively implementing the political judgment made on behalf of liberal freedoms in the aftermath of the Second World War. The recent revolutions in Eastern Europe may push this process of dualistic postivization even further.[19] As my conclusion suggests, the next great test will come in the construction of a constitutional order for a federal Europe: Will the Europeans use the resources of dualist democracy to proclaim a broad and deep commitment to a bill of rights that expresses the deepest aspirations of contemporary liberal philosophy?

If so, the open-ended character of dualist democracy will be resolved in a way that will greatly reinforce the viability of democratic liberal republicanism in the coming historical period.

Federalism

With the aid of the federalist principle, one may carve two additional paths to the judicial protection of a broad array of liberal rights—one conceptual, another causal. Concepts first. The very idea of a federal system implies the protection of certain basic liberal rights. Most obviously, no federation worthy of the name can deny the right of citizens to trade and move between federal units without undue impediment. But this, in turn, yields a predictable causal dynamic that expands the domain of liberal freedoms yet further.

Suppose, for example, we looked into the crystal ball and found that the Europe of the 2020 and found that the basic situation with regard to the European Union had not changed fundamentally from today: on the one hand, all citizens of the union still have the right to move and work and trade wherever they like within the union's (expanded) borders; on the other hand, the political structure of Europe remained centered on the nation-state—if an Italian moved to Germany, he couldn't vote in German national elections or run for office. Despite this loss of political rights, market incentives have induced millions of people speaking French, Spanish, Portuguese, Greek, Italian into the German-speaking zone. (Of course, if the union is expanded further, there would be even more Turks, Poles, and Hungarians than there are today.) Within this emerging polyglot society, I do not think it would be politically feasible for Germans to restrict linguistic or cultural freedoms of minority groups on the regional level, except at the cost of breaking the union apart.[20] While some xenophobes will find this attractive, it will be increasingly difficult for them to convince their fellow German-speakers to accept the enormous economic costs generated by a breakup of the increasingly tight economic web generated over decades of market interdependence. Indeed, given this causal dynamic, I predict that the Germans would over time authorize their regional parliament in Berlin to grant an increasing number of fundamental liberal rights to *Ausländer*.[21] And as Germany goes, so will the other members of the union?

As with all causal arguments, I am talking about tendencies, not certainties. Nonetheless, it is wrong to overlook entirely the economics of xenophobia. Federalism not only commits the federation to the protection of some fundamental liberal rights; over time it increases the chances that the regions will also extend liberal rights to their burgeoning minorities.[22]

Europe: Yesterday, Today, and Tomorrow

Before 1989, on the national level, especially in Italy and Germany but also in France, courts were aggressively implementing the fundamentally liberal decisions made in their postwar constitutions. On the European level, the most important development was the success of the

Court of the European Community in gaining the cooperation of national courts in a vigorous use of the federalism rationale to protect liberally oriented market rights.[23]

Today the situation has changed radically. The Soviet Union is gone and America is retreating, its military presence will be reduced to such a degree that it will function as a very ambiguous symbol of trans-Atlantic concern. For the first time since the war, Europeans are free to determine their fate, though it will take some time for them to believe this, even more to act upon this new awareness.

A crucial forum will be the European Union. At present it is a child of the previous period, a creature of business and political elites anxious to construct a credible alternative to the "red menace." As the shaky popular reception to Maastricht reveals, the democratic foundations of a federal Europe remain to be built. Unless and until there is a deep and broad mobilization of support for a federal Europe, the process of integration can easily disintegrate. Even if the status quo is maintained, the federalist kind of judicial intervention by the community court will be continue to be perceived as part of a distant bureaucratic structure unrelated to democratic political aspirations.

The future status of judicial review, and much else besides, depends then on the future of European politics. Will the next generation respond to its new freedom of action by recurring to the nationalistic madness of the twentieth century? Or will it have the political strength, and wisdom, to mobilize itself for a federal Europe?[24]

This essay is dedicated to the memory of my great teacher Judith Shklar, who would, I am sure, be the last liberal on earth to answer these questions with a confident affirmative. Uprooted from her native soil by Hitler's legions, her entire life and work was marked by a pervasive skepticism about the power of modern men and women to use law creatively to establish an enduring liberal republic.[25] Hers was a liberalism of fear;[26] mine is a liberalism of hope.

In part, the difference is merely tactical. She wrote in the aftermath of the Holocaust. I write after the fall of the Berlin Wall. Different worlds, different fears. She feared the repetition of the cruel barbarism that emerged so stunningly from the very center of Western civilization. I hardly wish to trivialize this fear, but I believe that the liberalism of hope provides the best response to it in the present European context. For the moment at least, liberalism is politically ascendant on the Continent. The question is whether liberals will use this moment to maximum advantage, by grasping the power of constitutional law to give enduring structure to a liberal and republican politics.

Much more than this will be required to sustain the liberal project against Hitlerian regression. Indeed, it would be hopelessly naïve to suppose that constitutional law could ever propose a definitive solution to the demonic complexities that Shklar unearthed in her philosophical psychology of Western man.[27] At best all we can hope for is one legalistic expedient after another, each adapted to the balance of power at the moment, each trying to tip that balance to the advantage of liberal republican politics.

Before us lies the prospect of unending struggle without final reward or resting place. However skeptically she might greet the rest of my vision, I suspect that Judith Shklar would respond to this last prospect with a grim amen.

Notes

1. Perhaps *alien* is too strong a word. There are prewar examples of something that looked like constitutional review by courts—in Austria, Italy, Germany, and even in the Holy Roman Empire. Nonetheless, a careful study of these examples reveals that they are quite exceptional and provide a weak foundation for emerging judicial practices.

2. This was also true in Spain when it emerged from its fascist legacy.

3. See Joseph Weiler, "The Transformation of Europe," 100 *Yale Law Journal* 2403 (1991).

4. For an incisive appraisal of this perennial complaint by liberalism's critics, see Stephen Holmes, *The Anatomy of Antiliberalism* (Cambridge, Mass., 1993).

5. See my *Social Justice in the Liberal State* (New Haven, Conn., 1980), 310–11.

6. I build here on an old thought of Tocqueville's. See his *The Old Regime and the French Revolution* (1856; New York, 1993). While the English under Margaret Thatcher and John Major have reinforced the royalist-centralist impulse, the French under Mitterrand have made serious steps to deconstruct the ancien régime by building up federalist structures. Not coincidentally, this exercise in decentralization has been accompanied by fundamental changes in French judicial practice. See Alec Stone, *The Rise of Judicial Politics in France* (New York, 1992).

7. Compare John Ely, *Democracy and Distrust* (Cambridge, Mass., 1980), with Hans Klein, *Die Grundrechte im demokratischen Staat* (1974).

8. This timidity is especially marked in the work of John Ely, the leading modern theorist of this school; see his *Democracy and Distrust.*

9. Carl Schmitt, *Verfassungslehre* (Berlin, 1928) 83; (my translation).

10. As this paragraph suggests, I am very skeptical about the now fashionable effort to rehabilitate Schmitt by splitting him into the "good German" who wrote the *Verfassungslehre* and the "bad German" who emerged as the great Nazi jurist only a few years later. But I leave this particular bit of trendiness for serious consideration at another time.

11. Bruce Ackerman, *We the People: Foundations* (Cambridge, Mass., 1991); *The Future of Liberal Revolution* (New Haven, Conn., 1992).

12. See Kenneth Arrow, *Social Choice and Individual Values* (New Haven, Conn., 1963).

13. See *We the People*, 275–77, for an introduction to these complexities.

14. Schmitt, *Verfassungslehre*, 83–84.

15. Michael Walzer, *Spheres of Justice* (New York, 1983).

16. See Brian Barry, review of *Spheres of Justice*, *Columbia Law Review* 84 (1984): 806. In my own book *Social Justice in the Liberal State* I distinguish between a large number of different spheres, each to be regulated by its own distinctive principles. Thus the liberal education system is run by very different principles from those that govern the distribution of property or the regulation of the market economy, let alone the distribution and structure of liberal political power.

For more (but not enough) on this matter, see my "Neutralities," in *Liberalism and the Good*, ed. R. Bruce Douglass, Gerald Mara, and Henry Richardson (New York, 1990), 29–43. While I have my disagreements with Walzer's *Spheres of Justice*, they lie elsewhere, namely, in the concrete way he define his spheres and the substantive principles he proposes for their regulation.

17. See John Rawls, *A Theory of Justice* (Cambridge, Mass., 1970); Ronald Dworkin, *Law's Empire* (Cambridge, Mass., 1986); and Ackerman, *Social Justice in the Liberal State*.

18. Not only the specialized court in Strasbourg, but—even more significantly—the European Community Court has been increasingly active in this area over the course of the 1980s. See Weiler, "The Transformation of Europe."

19. The Hungarian Constitutional Court has been especially active here, probably hyperactive. I discuss recent developments in *The Future of Liberal Revolution*, chap. 6.

20. To make my point, I am assuming here that these German residents will still vote in elections in their "native" regions. Of course, if they gain political freedoms in Germany as well, my point is only stronger.

21. In fact, the German *Grundgesetz* already grants foreigners many of these rights.

22. I am building here on some thoughts expressed by Albert Hirschmann, *The Passions and the Interests* (Princeton, N.J., 1977).

23. See Weiler, "The Transformation of Europe."

24. For more on this theme, see my *Future of Liberal Revolution*, chap. 3.

25. See, for example, her early book *Legalism*.

26. See "Liberalism of Fear."

27. See *Men and Citizens*, *Freedom and Independence*, and *Ordinary Vices*.

15

The Freedom of Worthless and Harmful Speech

George Kateb

IN THE LATE SUMMER of 1992, not long before she died, Dita Shklar and I had a long conversation on the phone. She said that she was going to Israel at the end of the year for a conference and that she planned to present a paper on toleration. I told her that I too had been thinking about this subject; in particular, speech codes at universities and the effort to limit toleration of ugly speech. I indicated my views. She seemed quite sympathetic to the drift. What she would have thought of the final essay I would not presume to say. I can only hope that she would have remained sympathetic.

In this chapter I say ungenerous things I wish I did not feel I have to say. But the First Amendment is worth any amount of gracelessness when it is in trouble—as it always is.

• • •

In recent times, we have witnessed sharp spasms of hostility to expression, whether artistic or literary, or some mode less exalted. These incidents have occurred in countries supposedly committed to freedom of expression as well as in places that scorn it. Where freedom of expression does exist, it seems to be hated, resented, and violated more than any other right. It seems the most menacing. Therefore, perhaps, it is now and always has been the most vulnerable. Of course, all rights are vulnerable. It is as if people resent any right they see being used until

I am indebted for criticisms to Michelle Browers, Julia Driver, Amy Gutmann, and Andrew Koppelman.

they discover they are using it; and they make the discovery because they engender resentment in other people.

If the right of free expression has always been vulnerable in constitutional societies, I think the reason is that people live by words and images, by their intended and unintended meanings, by their understood and misunderstood suggestions. Everything important in human life is or depends on words and images. They constitute our life; they are its currency, its medium, its substance, and most of its pleasures and pains. It is inevitable, consequently, that people will be sensitive to what is expressed, and become passionate about it, and may try to control it.

Free expression grows yet more vulnerable because of the incredible abundance and profusion of words and images in the age of publicity and the mass media. Everyone's world is now porous to an unprecedented degree: words and images, and hence meanings and suggestions, never leave us alone. We are bathed in them. There is no convenient escape from their public and commercial sources. One feels constantly exposed, imposed on, invaded. This abundance and profusion make us all the more sensitive to what is expressed. There is more to frighten us, or to disgust or outrage us. We grow acutely concerned with the effects on others, or we resent what we see and hear for what it is in itself. We tire of expression and wish to limit it. We imagine a world rid of much of what is now expressed, and filled, instead, with expression we admire or that comforts or flatters us. Suppression, which used to be mostly the policy of political and religious elites, is now also the policy of practically everybody.

Such inevitable feelings in oneself or others must be resisted. We must not give in to our sense of grievance toward the right of free expression. Now, I know from myself how deep that sense of grievance goes. I fantasize about, among other things, censoring commercial advertising, abolishing political advertising, and commanding news coverage. Other people have other grievances and other compensatory fantasies. I have all the instincts of suppression. But I know that, as a matter of right, the instincts to suppress are out of place. It makes no difference how strong or upright or self-persuaded they may be. If you put all our grievances together, very little allowable expression would be left that was not conventional or passionless or indifferent.

I want to defend almost unrestricted freedom of expression. My background assumption is that the arguments I put forth are relevant to a free society, a society of rights. I do not intend what I say to persuade rulers or members of unfree societies (say, traditional ones or stable despotisms), or even to sound plausible to them. The theory of freedom of expression is only part of the overall theory of a free society, although there is no part more important. Of course, I also know that my arguments may prove unacceptable to those who believe in rights but would prefer to defend the rights of expression on grounds other than those I give.

I prefer to say "freedom of expression" rather than "freedom of speech" (despite my title) because it is commonly thought proper to expand the range of protection to various nonverbal artistic media. But another more conceptual reason for choosing this phrase is to make the point that the defense of almost unrestricted freedom is not the defense of literally every utterance, but rather *expression*. If we were to mean literally every utterance, we would include all sorts of messages and verbal acts that have their place and owe their occurrence to defined institutional settings, or to regulated practices, where many utterances are guided by or specified by determinate rules so that the work of these institutions and practices can be done. The question of freedom would not ordinarily arise; as, for example, it does not arise in prosecutions for perjury. When we speak of freedom of speech or expression, we do not and cannot mean literally every utterance. On the other hand, we have *expression* when persons are to some real extent not playing a role or performing a prescribed duty in an institution or a practice, but are as it were independently engaged, even when institutionally situated, in making some essentially mental act of creation or in apprehending one; or in making an unprompted communicative contribution or receiving one. (I know that the distinction I am trying to make is made imprecisely; but made more precisely, it would still be open to dispute.)

Naturally the defense of free expression as a right is in the first instance a defense against governmental abridgment (whether as prior restraint or after-the-fact punishment). But we move easily to speaking of the right of free expression as a claim against abridgment in any institution where independent or spontaneous expression is a prominent part of the institution's life—for example, colleges and universities. Another obvious but noteworthy point is that when they abridge expression, government or institutional authorities sometimes act on their own initiative, but they often also act under pressure put on them by private and social groups and individuals. These days show evidence of both initiative by public or private authorities and initial pressure on them. But on two matters currently salient—speech codes at universities and attempted suppression of pornography—most of the initiating pressure has come from social groups. Thus, on the matter of freedom of expression, though public or private authorities are the direct and official sources of the effort to impose or try to impose an abridgment of expression, and though resistance to them is in the name of a right against government or a private authority, we know that the source of the will to abridge—in regard to speech codes and pornography—is often not a power interest held by authorities but a passion that comes from one social group or another. Yet even when they act under pressure, authorities bear the principal responsibility and hence the burden of blame. They either offer little resistance when they could offer more or they supply the administrative procedures that transform inchoate or coercive feelings into legitimized deeds. The standing interest that officials have in finding new work to do or new power to wield is fed. Whether the results are beneficial or harmful, democracy is a process of mutual legitimation between the passions and interests of people and those of government.

A rough generalization concerning the motives to abridge expression—or to put it more starkly, to suppress it—is as follows. The most important source of attempted suppression is the desire of many groups in society not to have certain things expressed. They want the world purged of what outrages or disgusts them, what shocks them or hurts their feelings. This is the main and undying passion behind suppression. The fear of the contagious effects on crude and easily seducible minds is often present, whether stated or not. But I think this motive is, for most suppressors, a good deal less important. What powerfully moves people to intolerance is often the mere fact that someone has dared to express certain thoughts or feelings in any of the modes of expression. Among these thoughts and feelings are those that are radical or irreligious or wrongly religious or obscene or pornographic or insulting or painful or divergent or simply new and unconventional. How dare they be expressed? These expressed thoughts and feelings, it is claimed, do not deserve protection against public or private authorities.

To say it again, I too often find myself fantasizing about suppression. My own motives—and they matter only if they are representative of the motives of some other people—are not exactly those I have just attributed to social groups now active in the cause of suppression. I would put the matter this way: first, I find much publicly disseminated expression worthless and harmful. Thus I use the word *worthless*—a word not always used by those who want to suppress. The phrase used about obscenity, "utterly without redeeming social importance,"[1] is not equivalent to *worthless* as I use it. I will shortly say what I mean by this word. And second, I do worry a lot about the contagious effects of much worthless expression, not because the minds of the many are crude and easily seduced, but because all minds are necessarily subject to unsolicited influence. Some main part of the harm of harmful expression is attributable to such influence. But I also think that we can try to resist being influenced, as I shall indicate at the end.

I am willing, then, to grant, indeed to insist, that much publicly disseminated expression is worthless; of that, much in turn is harmful. Yet

I still want to defend and as a matter of right almost unrestricted freedom of expression.

The complication of course is that what I find worthless and harmful, many other people do not—perhaps most other people do not; also, that what I value, others may not. And I will try to build that complication into the defense of almost unrestricted freedom of expression. But let me disregard it for the moment.

Before turning to the defense, I want to say why I think much (a fair amount, at least) of actual expression (which others think is excellent or good or at least unproblematic) is and has been worthless; and then why, in turn, much worthless expression is and has been harmful. What, first, do I mean by *worthless*?

I have five categories of the worthless:

1. expression that is ignorant, while presuming to know, especially on matters that are of great importance, or are thought to be
2. expression that is mendacious, while pretending (in a self-aware or self-unaware manner) to be truthful, especially on matters that are of great importance, or are thought to be
3. publicly disseminated expression in bad taste or that is trashy
4. publicly disseminated expression that is stupid or base
5. publicly disseminated expression that is mediocre or that panders to a low average

Here are some examples in each of these five categories:

1. expression that is ignorant while presuming to know: religion, often
2. expression that is mendacious while pretending (in a self-aware or self-unaware manner) to be truthful
   a. religion, often
   b. much political speech of citizens and candidates for office, including political campaigning, advertising, and debate; the speech of officials is not at issue for they do not typically have to appeal to the First Amendment
   c. almost all commercial advertising

Examples (3), (4), and (5) cover a lot of popular or mass entertainment. An academic audience may tend to agree that what I put into categories 3, 4, and 5 deserves to be there, and I will not spend time on its alleged worthlessness. Many of us would tend to put commercial advertisement in category 2, some may agree that much political speech is worthless. I suppose that putting religion in both categories 1 and 2 would be strenuously challenged. (I subsume freedom of religion under freedom of expression.) Notice that I do not (yet) mention hate speech, which I also consider worthless, or pornography, which many consider worthless.

I must therefore elaborate a little on my contention that much of religion is worthless. The criticism of religion is the premise of all criticism. These are the words of Marx, of course;[2] but the analysis I have in mind is not Marx's but Nietzsche's in *The Anti-Christ*. In that book, harsh as it is, Nietzsche provides a subtle account of the theological and the religious predispositions. He sees the convergence and mutual reinforcement of self-confident ignorance, self-deception, and mendacity. Indeed, it is hard to distinguish these properties; each easily turns into each:

> faith: closing one's eyes with respect to oneself for good and all so as not to suffer from the sight of incurable falsity. Out of this erroneous perspective on all things one makes . . . a holiness for oneself, one unites the good conscience with seeing falsely . . . what a theologian feels to be true *must* be false: this provides almost a criterion of truth. . . . "Faith" means not *wanting* to know what is true . . . . I call a lie: wanting *not* to see something one does see, wanting not to see something as one sees it. . . . The most common lie is the lie one tells to oneself; lying to others is relatively the exception.[3]

As he proceeds, Nietzsche extends his analysis of faith to include all convictions, and to the party spirit that results from convictions. But the theological and religious mentalities supply him with the models for all self-deceptions. Deliberate deception—manipulative or paternalist lying—is not central, certainly not in *The Anti-Christ* (as distinct from *On the Genealogy of Morals*). Yet self-deception has the force of a lie when received by others; or if not quite a lie, then an untruth that is avoidable with greater effort.

No matter how thoughtful, complex, and seemingly attuned to human needs, religion is—or, say, religions are—usually based on unwarrantable assumptions, which are always traceable to faith. Why should anyone have faith? Where is the starting place? A choice to accept is made but not always recognized as a choice; the line that separates faith from (Sartrean) bad faith is regularly crossed. Is it not the case that only urgent or needy motives are at work: the will to believe, or an indeliberate aestheticism, or an attempt to populate emptiness, or a demand for consolation, or some hidden secular motive?

My point, however, is that there should be freedom to disseminate religion even though much of it is, in the judgment of more than a few, worthless expression, when taken on its own terms. I do not deny that religion in the form of theology is often fascinating and intricately intellectual though built on indefensible foundations. I do not deny the capacity of religion to inspire extraordinary human achievements. But judged by the test of truth, which figures provisionally in John Stuart Mill's defense of liberty of thought and discussion, and decisively in Supreme Court First Amendment jurisprudence, theology, like religion, can be said to fail the test. Many religious utterances are demonstrably false. And most religious people say their religion is truthful, not that it is suggestive or allegorical or metaphorical or poetical (as it often is). They are religious, if not for the sake of the truth, then at least not for the sake of stimulating their imagination. The literalness of their belief, however, often vitiates the content of their belief. If theology were put forth only as speculation, it would cease to be theology, and it would not do its work. Similarly, if religion were put forth only as fiction or myth, it could not inspire or energize, console or frighten or discipline. We would be truly in a sorry state if we had to conclude that mendacity and belief in systematic error were indispensable for great effects, good and bad. Is the worthless the foundation of the worthwhile, not only of the harmful?

In regard to political speech, is it wrong to call most of it mendacious? Think of the constant stream of outright political lies, distortions, evasions, hypocrisies; they are the *primary* stuff of free political expression as we receive it in the media, because of the political class or because of the very nature of the media. The primary stuff is sickening. Yet I still want to defend its freedom, and to do so with a whole heart. I do not just want to say that without free political expression there could be no democracy. That is true, but it is not the whole truth. The truth of this position turns false if it is used to contend that free expression exists primarily for the sake of maintaining democratic politics. We could just as rightly say that democracy exists for the sake of maintaining free expression.

As for commercial advertising, it used to be thought too close to fraud to be entitled to protection under the Constitution. Yet I sympathize with the effort to extend constitutional protection to it, even though I am aware that it is not spontaneous expression but commissioned utterance, just as a lot of mass or popular entertainment is. My sympathy here has almost exclusively to do with fear of governmental regulation, which I take up later.

I now want to suggest that much of this worthless expression is also harmful. I go on the assumption that publicly disseminated expression is, in normal circumstances, other-regarding activity, not self-regarding. That is, such expression *affects* those who hear or see it, and does so often without "their free, voluntary, and undeceived consent"; whether we "like it" or not, we are affected (to borrow from Mill).[4] I cannot therefore base my defense of free expression on the grounds that expression is self-regarding activity, affecting solely the expresser or affecting others only with their consent. (No defense can be so based.) Just because it is so influential, disseminated expression *is* other-regarding activity. It is therefore capable of being harmful. And the extent and depth of its effects are often imagined to be so great that the only possible source of regulation and penalty could be government, directly or ultimately. It does not matter that attempted suppression often starts locally and in particular institutions. Incidents are invested with a sense of their typicality.

The closest parallel to the influence of expression is the influence exerted by examples of self-regarding conduct engaged in either by an individual or by a more or less enclosed voluntary association. (I believe that the distinction between self-regarding and other-regarding or social activity continues to have its uses.) But the concentrated social influence of publicly disseminated expression is, of course, much greater than that of instances of unconventional or self-injuring or exemplary self-regarding conduct, at least for the production of harm. Nevertheless, one's contemplation of people's self-regarding conduct may provide a model for one's reception of their expression. Which is to say, one could hope to live in a society where, to an ever larger extent, expression became self-regarding—that is, we would be influenced only with our consent by what we heard, read, and saw. Our approval would be more thoughtful and our antagonism would unbalance us less. We would also expect our own expression to be received with more reserve. Again, let me hold off on this point.

Why, then, do I call so much expression not only worthless but harmful? The very qualities that make expression worthless may also make it harmful. The worthlessness of self-confident ignorance is intrinsic: it exhibits the vice of presumptuousness. It becomes harmful when it spreads errors that are used to instigate or legitimize harmful deeds and policies. The worthlessness of mendacity is intrinsic: mendacity is a vice; it expresses disrespect for its recipients. But it often engenders harmful effects. Expression that is trashy or base or pandering is aesthetically condemnable, but what is aesthetically condemnable can have harmful effects. A sense of beauty permeates the production and reception of the aesthetically inferior, and, as we know, a lot of harm flows from the vicissitudes of aesthetic urges. To be sure, some publicly disseminated worthless expression can be innocuous in its effects. When it is harmful, it is gratuitously or avoidably or unnecessarily harmful. Not all harmful speech is worthless: it may sometimes be the source of necessary harm.

By *harmful expression* I mean expression that leads clearly and directly to the invasion of human individual rights by government or to fundamentally immoral conduct on a significant scale by groups or strategically placed individuals in society. This is the core meaning of *harm*. Second, expression is harmful when its long-term tendency or indirect but appreciable result is the invasion of rights or fundamentally immoral conduct on a significant scale. Relatedly, expression is harmful when its steady or intermittent cultural effect is to weaken or contaminate democratic citizenship and to discourage the aspiration to democratic individuality. This last kind of harm is the most tenuous, and to worry too much about it is likely to be productive of harm in the first two senses. Let me add that I reject the view that the notion of harm includes giving or feeling offense or outrage.

My main point is that the harm done by expression that scarcely anyone would think of abridging far exceeds the harm (if any) done by expression that is already abridged. Specifically, freedom of conventional religious expression and everyday political expression does far more harm than hate speech or pornography or the political speech and writing of radical sects and movements. If I am right, then all the standing abridgments of expression need reconsideration, just as all suggested new ones carry a burden of presumptive invalidity. The only exception I make to this skepticism is expression that exploits children, of which the principal example is child pornography. Children cannot take care of themselves.

Consider religious utterance first. I meant to paint with a broad brush.

I am not claiming to be able to enter an overall judgment on the comparative weight of the good and the harm that any particular religion does, or that all religions, believed in and practiced, do in any society. But I would offer the suggestion that a frequent harmful effect of religion is the discouragement of morality. And when such an effect is politically influential, it leads to the denial of one or another right. Is that not the worst harm possible? If I am correct, this result is all the more glaring because people often say that religion is the custodian and indispensable guarantor of morality; that indeed without religion people would be even more immoral than they already are; and that "if God is dead, everything is permitted." To the contrary, I find that historically, religion has often fomented war because it has inculcated bigotry, exclusiveness, fanaticism, narrow-mindedness and single-mindedness; it has often sanctified unjust social systems; and it has habituated people to a mental childishness that then lets itself be enlisted in atrocious causes that may have no tie to religion.

It is good to recall the spirit of the Enlightenment in this discussion. Kant, for one, gave differences of religion as one of the two main obstacles to human intermingling and hence a main source of war, the worst evil. (The other main obstacle is differences in language.)[5] Think also of Tom Paine's deconstruction of Scripture in *The Age of Reason* (1794–95), written from the perspective of freedom and rational morality. I grant, of course, that sometimes religion—say, Quakerism—has inspired protest in the name of justice. But I doubt that this is the preponderant direction of religion's influence—at least of organized religion's influence. Of course the contribution of religions to investing life with meaning and purpose is incontestable. But in defending freedom of religion as part of freedom of expression one should be aware of the whole range of effects of religion, some of which are as harmful as anything can be. Religious people, in the forefront of suppression of free expression on grounds of harm, never think to apply their argument to themselves. We should do so for them. They harm us not only in wanting to abridge our expression but also in sponsoring denial of various substantive rights and legitimate claims. Further, when spokespersons for some religions say they are guarding the morals of society, what they often really mean is sexual practice, thus implying that the most morally important sector of one's conduct is sexual conduct. This is a very harmful assumption. The main concern has often seemed to be to discipline female sexuality. All attempts to achieve women's sexual equality have had to overcome religious opposition. I suppose a case can be made for the religious regimen; but not a case, in many of its leading parts, that many of us find persuasive. On the matter of sexuality, then, it is arguable that some religions have had profoundly harmful influence. But, to say it again, religious bigotry is equally important and equally harmful. It has been a constant source of inflamed religious group identity that seeks either to convert others or to punish them for religious difference or for their supposedly disgusting or unclean nature, or to shun them or shut them out as inferior. And all this, on no credible basis. It is for sufficient reason that Nietzsche thought religions to be systems of cruelty, even apart from his indictment of Christianity in particular as "the metaphysics of the hangman."[6]

On political expression, whether that of citizens or candidates, or the various mass media on their own, think of the often degraded condition of free public opinion—the hysteria, the obsessions, the gross disproportions of attention, emphasis, and sympathy; the bigotry and jingoism; the indifference to suffering; the irrationality; the steady incitement to do or allow or ignore wrong. The free press and media comprise a reliable war-making machine. The reiterated patriotism, insistent, unwearying, is a continuous source of moral corruption. All these tendencies and attitudes feed actual decision making, and if sometimes they are manipulated by officials or cultivated by the media, we can say that to a considerable extent these attitudes are as it were spontaneous—that is, instilled from an early age, and at all ages acquired from a thousand sources—because of human susceptibility and impressionability. Think of the harm done to human rights and other basic interests by the decisions occasioned by such political expression. Of course, not only harm has occurred. But if you start with the precept that we should first of all avoid harm, then the record of this society, like that of any, including all free ones, contains an appalling amount of harm done at home and abroad—especially abroad—thanks to the free expression of political opinion. Freedom of expression may be used to protest harm, or prevent it, but freedom is the source, also, of a tremendous amount of harm. But would we be silent? I am so far from urging regulation of citizenly political speech, much of which I deem harmful, that I am wholeheartedly for as much freedom as possible.

Concerning commercial advertising, much has been powerfully and sensibly said on the harmful nature of its effects: on the mindless, insatiable, irrational consumerism that advertising promotes; the general lesson of normalized discipline it is always promoting by its messages; and the corrupting effects of its programmed exaggerations and distortions. The harm is to citizenship and the aspiration to individuality. The corrupting effects are in fact admitted on all sides, whether or not the protests are made in behalf of individuality or citizenship.

Let us continue to leave aside the harm of popular and mass entertainment. I cannot help saying, however, that I do agree that the prevalence of violence in the movies and on television is, most likely, a corrupting influence on the whole society; perhaps especially on children and adolescents, but not only on them. The worst impulses are constantly confirmed and hence legitimized and hence strengthened, just by being represented as the stuff of entertainment. I see less catharsis than encouragement.

Now, if many people agree that much commercial advertising and much popular and mass entertainment are both worthless and harmful, it is clear that many would contest my characterization of religion, and maybe quite a few would object to my characterization of political speech. My proposal, nevertheless, is that two recent objects of attempted suppression—namely, hate speech and pornography—are no more worthless and much, much less harmful than a lot of religious expression and a lot of political expression; and to fill out the thought I would say that hate speech and pornography are of a piece with a lot of popular and mass entertainment in that they are no more worthless; also, they are much less harmful. Actually, religious speech is often hate speech, and so is some political speech, just as a lot of advertisement (and mass and popular entertainment) are semipornographic.

If I am right, then any case made to regulate pornography, or hate speech as such (as distinct from its failed or successful incitement to "imminent lawless action"),[7] could also be made to abridge much religious and political expression, and much of the content of the culture around us. My judgment is that the moral advantage is on the side of hate speech and pornography because the harm they do is, at most, minor. On the other hand, the content advantage may not be with them, but it is not against them: there is rough parity of worthlessness. If I am mistaken, what follows? Where there is disagreement, no side should act intolerantly on its judgments. There is good sense in the dictum "One man's vulgarity is another's lyric."[8]

I condemn as I do, and I still want almost unrestricted freedom of expression, and as a matter of fundamental right. I sustain myself in that view because I think that it is only common sense to admit that no society—whether or not it recognized almost unrestricted freedom of expression as a right—could ever contain a preponderance of truth, truthfulness, moral sense, and good taste in its publicly disseminated expression. The human condition is a condition of failure. But perhaps what success there is, is necessarily embedded in failure: only if rare and desperately wanted could the highest qualities emerge, be visible, and be recognized for what they are.

I can therefore grant a measure of assent to some powerful elements in the politically radical critique of the consequences of toleration made by, say, Herbert Marcuse,[9] and to some also powerful elements in the normally conservative critique made by, say, Walter Berns,[10] and still reject the suppressions they urge. If ascendant, a systemically censorious regime, whatever its ideological nature, would only replace old harms with new ones, and most probably would do greater harm domestically than what critics or I complain of. I do not wish to deny—I wish to insist on—the gross harms that often issue from governmental action influenced or legitimized by free religious and political expression. But political harms, political evils, will always come into existence, whether the offending society allows or rejects the right of free expression. I also do not wish to deny that when we take into account foreign policy it is impossible to say whether free or unfree societies on balance do more harm. Nevertheless, given the inescapable fatality of wrongdoing and the uncertainty of the overall moral reckoning, let us grant the benefit of the doubt to free societies and almost unrestricted freedom of expression. If not always self-correcting, free societies are at least regularly apologetic.

• • •

The defense of worthless and harmful expression must be at the center of the defense of freedom of expression as a fundamental right. This formulation is, I grant, mournful. It is especially mournful when, adopting the ultimacy of the moral perspective, we grant decisive importance to the category of the harmful and relegate that of the worthless to the margins. Expression is thus a kind of harmful other-regarding activity that should not be regulated or even deemed, without grave compunction, suitable for regulation. Mill, from whom I borrow so much, refuses to put the point in this manner, but rather contents himself with saying that though publication is an other-regarding activity, "conduct . . . which concerns other people," it must remain unregulated because its freedom is "almost of as much importance" as freedom of thought ("the inward domain of consciousness") and is "practically inseparable from it."[11] I suppose that Mill, as a utilitarian, was not able to say that public expression could ever be broadly harmful, if he was to defend a libertarian thesis. On the other hand, I am defending an almost unrestricted right, but one that I concede is often harmfully exercised. I do not think that any other basic right need be conceptualized in this way, not even the right of property.

Mill does defend so-called error, but it turns out that he does not think there is such a thing as mere error in metaphysical, political, legal, and moral doctrines.[12] Though he was infuriated by a lot of what he read and heard, I think he felt that most of it had to be said and served some legitimate purpose or other, or was appropriate for its time. In any case, he may have thought that expression as such was good, or at least better than prescribed pieties or conformist silence. The practice of free expression was rare, comparatively new, and rather fragile—why feed skepticism to it so early in its uncertain career? For strategic reasons, and doubtless others, he would therefore not have lent himself to the formulation I propose.

Well, why defend almost unrestricted freedom of expression, as a fundamental right, despite the harsh judgments one is disposed to make? (I will omit use of the point that is indispensable in American practice; namely, that freedom of expression is guaranteed by the Constitution.) Here I go over mostly familiar ground. Let me leave aside the appeal to peace as the reason to tolerate, though it is an important consideration, and refer instead to more positive reasons (which I will only sketch.) I believe that all of them can be used no less by those who want to engage in hate speech or to receive pornography than by those who want to express themselves religiously or politically.

One reason is suggested by Mill's third defense of liberty of thought and discussion, in chapter 2 of *On Liberty*. What some people claim is worthless or harmful is actually not. The categories of worthless and harmful are contestable at any time, and historically changeable. People profoundly disagree in their estimations. Full toleration keeps every expression available and even encourages expression, to begin with. Who knows what merit may one day be found, for example, in pornography? In regard to hate speech, only the epithets, not its doctrinal exposition, are almost always devoid of all claim to the attention of an audience. The same considerations apply with no less strength, of course, to religion or political speech or advertising or entertainment that we may now find worthless and harmful, but also with no more strength.

A second reason to allow almost unrestricted freedom of expression is respect for the sincerity of those who engage in or wish to receive worthless and harmful expression. They often are persuaded that what they express or want to receive is excellent or good. We can be absolutely certain that they are wrong and still respect their sincerity, and find in that sincerity a reason—perhaps a sufficient reason—to want to tolerate them almost absolutely.

A third and related reason is that much expression comes out of the character of the expressers. Their expression is not only theirs, it is them. To tolerate their expression is to tolerate their being. Or to put it less statically, to tolerate expression we find worthless or harmful is to tolerate what people need not so much to *be* themselves as to find or change themselves—to engage in a process, the process of growth and self-development, or what some want to call autonomy, or what I have called democratic individuality in its positive aspect. Any sort of communicative ingredient, though condemned by others, may contribute to that process.

We could add a fourth reason: to be refused freedom of expression is painful; to be allowed expression is pleasurable. (The same goes for receiving the expression of others that one wants or hopes to receive.) Once we decide to grant prominence to the simple facts of pleasure and pain, we have to say more to defend our tolerance, but our starting point has some credibility.

To say it again, everyone—no matter what we think of their expression—can appeal to any or all of these reasons to defend their right to free expression. They therefore can be used to defend toleration of hate speech and pornography. All in all, these reasons have weight.

Notice that I have so far only briefly referred to the commonly held view, found in Mill and in the Supreme Court's First Amendment jurisprudence, that the right of almost unrestricted freedom of expression is instrumentally necessary to the attainment of truth or to morally good conduct or (we can add) to beauty. If such various human excellence were, in fact, the best reason for the right of freedom of expression, the whole question of freedom of expression would have be re cast. We would, however, have to possess uncontestable standards of excellence, and be able to show, beyond challenge, that excellence is society's reason for being. But whatever the Supreme Court may find it convenient to say when it is either protecting, or allowing the abridgment of, expression in the name of the First Amendment, the promotion of excellence cannot possibly be given as the best reason for this freedom. There is no society-wide agreement on excellence, or its place. It is not a constitutional idea, so to speak. But leaving these problems aside, we would still have to face a further problem.

Those achievements of the past, whether in the pursuit of truth or beauty, that are thought by some people to be really excellent, rarely appeared in free societies. More often they appeared in coercive and disciplined ones. There were almost no free societies in which they could have appeared. Athens was only a magnificent exception. But even if a whole society could agree on what excellence is—and it may be much easier to do so than it is to agree on what is worthless and harmful or on what is intermediate and acceptable and useful—we could nevertheless conclude that excellence needs freedom of expression less than any other grade of expression. Genius or near genius or high talent will out, if suppression is not utterly ruthless and if, at the same time, enticements exist to call forth creativity, as they often have in unfree or partly free societies. Mill said that "genius can only breathe freely in an atmosphere of freedom."[13] I doubt he is right, if he is suggesting that the only effect of an unfree society on genius and talent is inhibition. Restraint, too, and even fear, can incite and help to shape the endeavors of those who are truly gifted.

I am not saying that excellence in the pursuit or achievement of truth and beauty does not benefit from freedom. Freedom for intellectuals and scholars clearly favors honesty, and honesty can favor excellence in the utterance of truth. Freedom for artists favors experiment, and experiment can favor beauty (or something equivalent) in the creation of artworks. However, those in a position to contribute directly to excellence are few in number, even though those few are endlessly dependent, in turn, on countless obscure and anonymous indirect contributions. Can we justify the principle of almost unrestricted freedom of expression on grounds of excellence when only a few put such freedom to admirable use? And when the truth and beauty achieved are often of little or only attenuated importance to any but a few? And when, to begin with, many fields of endeavor have historically flourished in excellence without much freedom of expression—indeed often without any vivid sense of the very idea of freedom of expression as a right or even as a privilege?

Concerning morally good conduct, we can say freedom of expression may undeniably favor it. I have in mind processes of deliberation that take place amid circumstances of frank and uninhibited public speech—what the Greeks called *parrhesia*. But openness hardly guarantees justice, especially in the treatment of those beyond national borders. It often favors injustice, or worse.

If, on balance, we can say plausibly, though not dogmatically, that the best reason for almost unrestricted freedom of expression is not its contribution to the attainment of excellence; and if at the same time we believe that almost unrestricted freedom of expression does lead to a tremendous amount of worthless and harmful publicly disseminated expression (which is perhaps the majority of expression), while the positive reasons I gave earlier are weighty, but perhaps not as weighty as we would wish, not even in compatible combination—what then? Is there a better reason for almost unrestricted freedom of expression? I can think of only one, and it is a rather negative reason; it is not very inspiring when stated outright, but I believe that, in the form of a powerful sentiment, it has in fact inspired some of the energies of political action that led to the emergence and spread of toleration, and beyond that, to the development of the theory and practice of almost unrestricted freedom of expression. I mean the idea that unless there is almost unrestricted freedom of expression the people develop, in the face of government and of all authorities in all spheres of life, the mentality of dependence, while thinking themselves free. This can happen in supposedly free societies. They come to learn to speak and perhaps to think and feel by permission. I am not talking about the sway of public opinion which caused deep anxiety to Tocqueville and Mill. What society could ever be free of that? I refer to concerted efforts to police thought and expression.

The Athenians held that democracy meant living as you like.[14] But expressing yourself as you like and taking in what expression you like is an inextricable part of living as you like. The reason for one is the reason for the other. I do not posit autonomy as the value at stake here—autonomy in the now common non-Kantian sense of attaining one's distinctive individuality. (In a democracy we could call it positive democratic individuality.) That word is too grand to be the antithesis of dependence. I settle for modest free agency as definitive of being human, of living a life, of living one's own life—that is, the right of people to move freely through life without feeling the need to be answerable or accountable to authority, provided they do not invade others. That they do not attain a distinctive individuality or that they have no settled or deliberate plan of life does not matter to the defense of free expression, any more than it matters that the expression they make and receive is often worthless and harmful. Free agency is much less problematic than autonomy or democratic individuality, much easier to recognize, and far more usual; and respect for free agency is a large part of respect for human dignity, which is the source of all individual rights. I do not denigrate autonomy but see it as a possibility which in its democratic form grows out of a society in which rights are guaranteed and defended on simple grounds.

I am aware that I am defending the human dignity of those who live acceptingly in a world largely made up of what I think is worthless and harmful expression, the human dignity of those who vest their identities in such a world or derive their identities from it. Am I inconsistent? Am I attributing dignity to those I really think are undignified because they have forfeited their dignity?

In answer, I say two things. First, I am sufficiently uncertain about how to apply my categories of the worthless and harmful to leave open the possibility that I misapply them, and by doing that I leave open the possibility that I grossly exaggerate the quantity of the worthless and harmful.

Second, I believe there is scarcely anything—except for outright despotism or tyranny—that is worse than the condition in which people are imprisoned by the mentality of dependence and live by permission, as they must so live, if they express and receive expression by permission. The wrong done them is beyond repair, no matter how wise the censors and tutors are. But censors and tutors are not usually wise. Abridgments of expression introduce not merely a despotic or tyrannical element into supposedly free societies, but the very essence of despotism or tyranny. The injury inflicted on unearned human dignity by authority when it surveys all expression with the intent of locating areas of possible regulation outweighs the injury to our earned dignity (in the sense of being respectable or admirable) that is done by and to us by worthless and harmful expression, or by the more narrowly self-inflicted injury to dignity (in the latter, lesser sense) of certain kinds of self-indulgence, like expressing hatred or enjoying pornography—that is, if pornography is at all questionable to begin with. Of course I am not saying that the harm of being dependent (as sponsored by government), which degrades people whether they are "aware of it or not,"[15] outweighs all the substantive harms that free expression helps to cause government to produce, and thus forgives them. Rather, the harm of dependency is tremendous; and on the other hand, to say it again, it must be that harms will come, free expression or no.

A reasonably close analogy I find for my argument in behalf of tolerating worthless and harmful expression is with a possible attitude toward abortion (which in fact I hold). One may think abortion wrong because it prevents the actualization of a potential human life, but also think that prohibiting abortion is a worse wrong because prohibition instrumentalizes or conscripts or degrades pregnant women (and perhaps all women as such). Prohibition of abortion is a harm done to the human dignity of women: it is a harm to their status as human beings. It is a denial, that is to say, of a significant right that reaches to the very personhood of a human being. Such harm done by government to an individual is qualitatively worse than the substantive harm done by an individual's questionable use of freedom when a fetus is aborted.

I find that in order to shore up these sentiments of toleration for worthless and harmful expression in myself I try to develop a kind of *civil* courage. This is the story I tell myself. It goes most against our human dignity if we need courage to face government (or other authority). *Political* courage should not be needed to live a life. Our constant accompaniment would be fear—fear of penalty. Most of us would cower and become subdued. On the other hand, looking to authority to assuage our hurt from expression is also pernicious. Both fearing and relying on government (or other authority) spreads to all persons the mentality of dependence. Expressing and receiving expression by permission becomes the norm.

This degrading condition is self-inflicted when the seemingly beneficent government (or authority) is constantly invited to intervene. It thus accumulates precedents for intervention and will inevitably use the precedents in ways that its beneficiaries will eventually deplore. To look constantly to authority for relief against expression that offends us is to think that society consists of persons who must be perpetually supplied the very rudiments of civilization. Such an outlook could never have originated the idea of free expression and cannot now be counted on to transmit that idea to future generations.

Justice Holmes said in *U.S. v. Schwimmer* (1929) that freedom is "freedom for the thought we hate."[16] The meaning is that freedom of expression is genuinely respected only when extreme expression is protected—expression at the margins. The margins must be safe if the center is to be safe. Even more, freedom has the most meaning when the temptation is strongest to abridge it and the temptation is resisted.

As Judith Shklar said in *Legalism*, "Now it is hard to see whom the First Amendment protects if not the obnoxious."[17] The thought we hate must include hate thought; freedom is freedom for hate thought.

For related reasons I am also reluctant to see the spread of governmental subsidies to scholarship and the arts. The official patron easily turns into the authoritative regulator. Further, the view that government is needed, by subsidy and regulation, to establish or enable the expression of the disadvantaged or the unequal, signifies a disturbing reliance on government. Rights undergo a self-inconsistent transformation when they are conceptualized as what governmental policy must positively provide or promote. I know that it is too late to undo this transformation completely; this would not be desirable anyway. But more skepticism is in order.

To avoid needing political courage in the face of government (or other authority), when expressing and receiving expression, citizens instead should develop civil courage, which is courage in regard to one another's expression. Civil courage means two things. First, it means the willingness to use expression in order to counter expression we find worthless or harmful. That means to speak up and risk defeat or censure or embarrassment, but perhaps, after a while, to reach the point of finding our own expression more regularly pleasurable, apart from the provocation we may have felt when first we engaged in it. This aspect of civil courage, this love of speaking up and speaking out, supplements our explicitly political or dutiful involvement in discussion of public policy.

Second, civil courage means the willingness to manage one's impressions, to use an old stoic concept from Epictetus. (I mean to confine the application of Epictetus's concept to receiving expression, and not extend it, as he did, to accepting every direct invasion of one's life, liberty, or property.) To manage one's impressions is to try to reduce the shock or outrage or disgust or hatred one feels in encountering certain kinds of expression. It also means that we try to stop seeing such expression as harm, whether to us or others. One tries to handle the expression of others so that it ceases to be other-regarding activity, activity that the expresser hopes will affect others unfreely and almost helplessly. I mean that one tries to reduce one's impressionability, one's tendency to be overcome or seduced or taken in. Rather, one tries to receive expression more nearly on one's own terms. It may help, in this process, to receive the expression of others through a filter or screen made up of some mixture of the positive reasons we gave earlier for defending almost unrestricted freedom of expression. I do not say that one should try to receive expression in a spirit of indifference or impermeability to its content, but rather that one should, if one feels distressed by it, try to receive it in an attitude that makes room for these sentiments: what strikes us as worthless and harmful now may strike us differently later, or may now strike others as valuable and beneficial; and those who express themselves worthlessly or harmfully are sincere, and their expression may come from their very being or is needed by them to find or change themselves. (A concern for the pleasure of the expresser strikes me as not especially relevant to building up civil courage.) One also cultivates a capacity for second thoughts, for retrospection. And one remains on guard against regulatory authority, no matter how seemingly well-intentioned. This stoicism of response is hard work, but it may be part of the character of the good democratic individual, and part, also, of the character of the good democratic citizen.

Some people may think this effort of mine worthless or harmful. But I have written it, not needing political courage, but only a very mild form of civil courage; and in regard to those who do think it worthless or harmful, their civil courage may steady them and increase their patience. Fear of and reliance on authority can be kept at bay.

Notes

1. *Roth v. United States*, 352 U.S. 476, 484 (1957). See also the formulation in *Miller v. California*, 413 U.S. 15, 24 (1973): worthless expression "lacks serious literary, artistic, political or scientific value."

2. Karl Marx, *Contribution to the Critique of Hegel's Philosophy Right: Introduction*, in *The Marx-Engels Reader*, ed. Robert C. Tucker, 2d ed. (New York, 1978), 53.

3. Friedrich Nietzsche, *The Anti-Christ* (1895), trans. R. J. Hollingdale (New York, 1968), 9: 120; 52: 169; 55: 173.

4. I borrow from John Stuart Mill's extended definitions of self-regarding activity in *On Liberty* (1859), in *Collected Works of John Stuart Mill*, ed. J. M. Robson (Toronto, 1977), 18:225, 276.

5. Immanuel Kant, *Perpetual Peace: A Philosophical Sketch* (1795), in *Kant's Political Writings*, trans. H. B. Nisbet, ed. Hans Reiss (Cambridge, 1970), 113–14.

6. Friedrich Nietzsche, *Twilight of the Idols* (1889), trans. Walter Kaufmann, in *The Portable Nietzsche* (New York, 1954), 500.

7. *Brandenburg v. Ohio*, 395 U.S. 444, 447 (1969).

8. *Cohen v. California*, 403 U.S. 15, 25 (1971).

9. Herbert Marcuse, "Repressive Tolerance," in *Critique of Pure Tolerance*, ed. Robert Paul Wolff (Boston, 1965).

10. Walter Berns, *Freedom, Virtue and the First Amendment* (Baton Rouge, La., 1957), and *The First Amendment and the Future of American Democracy* (New York, 1976).

11. Mill, *On Liberty*, 18:225–26.

12. Compare the dictum concerning the First Amendment in *Gertz v. Robert Welch, Inc.*, 418 U.S. 323, 339 (1974): "there is no such thing as a false idea."

13. Mill, *On Liberty*, 18:267.

14. See Aristotle, *Politics*, bk. 6, chap. 2, 1317b.

15. John Stuart Mill, *Considerations on Representative Government, Collected Works* of John Stuart Mill, 19:470.

16. *United States v. Schwimmer*, 279 U.S. 644, 655 (1929).

17. *Legalism*, 214.

16

The Unfinished Tasks of Liberalism

Rogers M. Smith

Assessing Liberalism

WHAT IS THE STATE OF LIBERALISM TODAY? What are its prospects for the future? Recent years have produced wildly different assessments. They range from Francis Fukuyama's celebrated claim that no significant ideological opposition to liberal democracy remains today to John Gray's equally assured contention that our age is "distinguished by the collapse of the Enlightenment project on a world-historical scale."[1] The most plausible answer is less discussed. If we presume to scan the grand vista of "world history," liberalism seems a movement with many extraordinary successes, but with much left to do if the world is to be remade along liberal lines. It is too early to say that liberalism has either triumphed or failed. We can, however, assess where it is succeeding and failing, what it might mean for it to succeed further, and what obstacles stand in its way.

Here I essay some such assessments. I conclude that liberalism, understood as a historical set of movements, has much left to do, and that much of this work is not being done adequately, to the discredit of writers advocating liberalism, as Judith Shklar argued forcefully in her later years. But liberalism's work is made difficult by features in it that may not be remediable. Above all, liberalism suffers from a profound inability to provide unassailable assurances of people's worth, even as it prescribes disturbing transformations in their lives. These points suggest the proper tack for liberals now is not to worry about the Enlightenment's triumph or failure. It is to try to see if, and how, the liberal project of enhancing human freedom and dignity can be strengthened and extended—and then to do so.

Liberalism's Record: The American Case

Liberalism originated historically with partly interlinked seventeenth- and eighteenth-century movements of resistance to absolutist and hierarchical systems in economics, government, religion, philosophy, education, culture, and social and familial relations.[2] Although a full evaluation of the success of these movements would need to be truly world historical, it seems legitimate in a brief essay to focus on the polity most identified with liberalism, the United States of America. If the Enlightenment project has triumphed worldwide, its triumph should be pervasive in the United States. If it has failed, its defeat should be most wrenching where it has been thought to be most firmly entrenched.

Liberal Economics

Start with what critics often take as the root feature of liberalism: its advocacy of property rights that spur industrious activity via the creation of markets for goods, services, and capital that stimulate production, trade, investment, and consumption. In 1994 this part of liberalism was so globally ascendant that prophets of liberal doom had to insist, correctly, that markets can be severed from other aspects of liberalism, as in the authoritarian systems of Singapore and China.[3] Many former communist societies still exhibit great resistance to rapid privatization. But in the years ahead, few expect anything other than the further incorporation of all the world's peoples into the international market economy, though they will be incorporated in very different ways.

Few would deny, either, that the spread of market systems has fostered spectacular growth in the world's material wealth over the last several centuries. In 1989, for example, the United States gross national product was $5 trillion, having grown by over a trillion (constant) dollars since 1980.[4] Those figures would have been inconceivable at most earlier stages in United States history. They reflect, no doubt, American advantages beyond liberal market systems, such as great natural resources. But few would contend they could have been obtained without market institutions; and today few here or abroad can conceive of doing other than pursuing rapid economic growth via capitalist markets. The Enlightenment's old economic foes are so long vanquished they seem storybook fantasies. Since its revolution, the United States has never had any real support for aristocratically dominated, static agrarian systems. Elsewhere today hereditary aristocrats like the oil-rich Arab sheikhs are eager participants in world markets. With these long-lasting and still-increasing levels of growth and popularity, how can the "Enlightenment project" be said to have failed in the economic sphere?

The short answer is that it has not; but it is sometimes said to have failed in enough other regards to be judged a failure overall. That claim is plausible but debatable. A more damaging response is that despite tremendous successes, even in economic terms, Enlightenment institutions have failed to live up to crucial parts of their promise. Initially, liberals like John Locke promised that the rising tide of growth generated by market systems of economic liberties would indeed lift all boats. Even humble day laborers in England would be fed, lodged, and clad better than the wealthiest Indian chiefs in America. All inequalities would be justified in terms of differences in the productive contributions of each, without large concentrations of idle wealth.[5] Many nineteenth- and early twentieth-century liberals modified or abandoned those claims. In America today no one pretends that they have been realized.

The late nineteenth-century economic Darwinists who championed laissez-faire admitted that many ended up impoverished in competitive labor markets and defended this condition as a natural process of weeding out the unfit. Many twentieth-century proponents of the minimal state acknowledge that market systems often reward blind luck and inherited wealth rather than the sort of rational, productive activity espoused by Locke.[6] And the disparities and suffering visible even in the incredibly productive United States economy are massive. Using the draconian definition of poverty employed by United States policymakers, nearly 36 million Americans were poor in 1991.[7] Few analysts believe people can survive for long in America with income at the official poverty level; only slightly more realistic poverty estimates put the number at 47.5 million, or almost one of every five Americans. It is nonetheless probably true that most of today's working-class Americans, like Locke's English day laborer, are better off materially than American Indian "kings" of the early seventeenth century. But material goods like cars, radios, and phones are needed to participate in modern economic, political, and kinship systems as much as the arrows and smoke signals of yesteryear. And it is not likely that many Indian *kings* died of malnutrition in precolonial America. Every year several thousand Americans do. Many more live undernourished.

American wealth is also staggeringly, and increasingly, concentrated. In 1988, the wealthiest 20 percent of the American people received 44 percent of the nation's pretax income, while the poorest 20 percent received only 4.6 percent. Those disparities had been growing. From 1977 to 1988, average family income declined for 80 percent

of the American population but increased 16.5 percent for the most affluent 10 percent, with the top 5 percent increasing 23.4 percent, and
the top 1 percent expanding their income by 49.8 percent. The differences do not simply reflect different levels of industrious, rational labor. The vast majority of Americans increased their working hours
during that period, while the wealthiest profited from favorable governmental tax policies and gains from mergers, takeovers, junk bonds,
and other paper deals that did not always enhance productivity.[8]

Tocqueville predicted that if hereditary aristocracy should arise
again in America, it would be an aristocracy of wealth. These statistics
suggest Americans may indeed have just such a monied aristocracy—or
oligarchy.[9]

The Enlightenment economic project has faltered in another much
noted regard. Productivity impelled by market systems has often been
catastrophically shortsighted, blind to the costs of too rapid and massive
exploitation of natural resources. Even if we set aside aesthetic and scientific concerns with the loss of rare forms of flora and fauna and diverse ecosystems, the economic burdens and the threats to human lives
posed by environmental degradation are enormous. They raise the
specter of a world which runs out of fuel, overheats because of a damaged ozone layer, is poisoned by toxic wastes, or suffers from some
other environmental catastrophe. There is, to be sure, nothing in Enlightenment goals that explicitly urges these outcomes. Wasteful, destructive exploitation of natural resources is hostile, not instrumental,
to the goals of peace, prosperity, cultural progress, and personal liberty
that Enlightenment traditions espouse. The real issue, however, is
whether Enlightenment economic and governmental institutions can
control the pressures for vicious environmental abuse that are generated by the pursuit of rapid growth in fiercely competitive markets.

Liberal Politics

As in regard to market institutions, so in regard to the Enlightenment's espousal of representative political institutions the case for success is impressive. In the United States, the Revolution abolished
monarchical and aristocratic political privileges even more emphatically than their accompanying economic doctrines and legal institutions. Despite important transformations, the national Constitution,
which Henry May termed "perhaps the greatest monument of the
Moderate Enlightenment," has endured in its basic features longer
than any extant government.[10] It has maintained selection of legislative
and executive officials via regular competitive elections, checks on officials via separated powers, and procedural and substantive limits on
governmental authority to invade personal liberties. No nation has

precisely duplicated these particulars. But first with the decline of European colonial empires, then with the collapse of the Soviet Union, newly independent nations have generally adopted some form of competitive elections, limited term legislative and executive officers, a separate judiciary, and legal guarantees of basic freedoms, in place of traditional hereditary familial governance or one-man or one-party rule. Again, it is hard to deny Enlightenment political innovations real triumphs.

This success can, however, be exaggerated. The endurance of American institutions may be primarily due to the country's natural advantages and cultural features besides its liberal elements. Elsewhere, before the Soviet Union's demise, only about one-third of the world's nominally independent countries had institutions sufficiently liberal and democratic to be termed "polyarchies" by Robert Dahl. That ratio had not much increased in a half-century.[11] Furthermore, the experience of the end of colonialism suggests that new nations with ostensibly democratic arrangements may quickly succumb to forms of illiberal dictatorship. That prospect is already a reality in parts of the former Soviet bloc. As during the rise of totalitarian regimes in the 1920s and 1930s, so today analysts can reasonably argue that truly democratic governments are not the wave of the future, even if capitalist economies are. Perhaps authoritarian capitalist societies like Singapore will prove unstable. But it is optimistic to assert that representative democracy will be the pattern across the globe anytime soon.

Yet those facts merely show that liberal democratic values and arrangements have not won the war, not that they have failed. No alternative arrangements are more prestigious, more emulated, more successful. Again, the more serious criticism comes from recognizing the realities of political life today in advanced liberal nations like the United States. The basic blueprint of liberal democratic constitutionalism remains, but its lived reality calls into question its meaningfully liberal or democratic character. The scale of American government has grown vast; a fantastically complex array of regulatory and administrative bureaucracies has been overlaid on and around traditional governmental units. The functions of government have reached a complexity that no scholar or politician can master, much less busy private citizens. As a result, Americans can still vote to throw the rascals out, write their representatives, and sometimes get a hearing before a judge or bureaucrat. But few feel they have any true power to control the choice of candidates, to influence the legislative agenda, to shape effective legal arguments, or to do much more than satisfy the demands of the bureaucracies they regularly encounter. Success in these endeavors requires wealth, knowledge, and social status that few approach. Indeed, understanding and managing the system frustrates virtually all involved, whatever their position or possessions.[12]

There are many further, arguably deeper pathologies in American governance that could be discussed as failures of American liberalism. But no problem seems more basic than the impossibility of even conceiving how citizens might engage in competent collective self-governance to any significant extent while retaining the scale and complexity that so incline modern democracies to become near oligarchies, weakly and clumsily constrained by mechanisms of popular accountability. Thoughtful observers are driven to palliatives, such as exemplary deliberations by randomly selected "citizen assemblies," that simultaneously seem utopian and inadequate.[13]

Religious Liberty

Nowhere are assessments of liberal success more clashing than in regard to religious liberty. On the one hand, liberal celebrants adduce as proof of the wisdom of liberal religious toleration that the United States, the first nation founded on separation of church and state, is one of the most religious in the world and one devoid of truly destabilizing religious conflicts. Polls confirm that over 90 percent of Americans express belief in a supreme being, with 89 percent having a specific religious preference. Some 63 percent belong to one of almost 360,000 churches. And though over 90 percent of those church members are Christians—63 percent Protestant, 28 percent Catholic—they belong to over 140 substantial denominations, with countless tinier groups.[14] The evidence is clear that religious faith and diversity are flourishing in the land said to be most shaped by the Enlightenment.

It can rightly be claimed as well that, alongside this vigorous religiousness, the United States is devoted to Enlightenment science and rationalistic education. Nearly 14 percent of its public expenditures go to education, over $377 billion in 1990. The federal government also spent $78.9 billion for "scientific" or "research and development" programs. Almost 80 percent of America's citizens over age twenty-five have completed high school; 35 percent have had some form of higher education; over 21 percent are college graduates, most educated in secular public schools. The 23 percent of Americans attending universities exceeds any other nation. Japan has only 13 percent; Britain 9 percent.[15] Enlightenment hopes to promote scientific inquiry and education thus seem to be abundantly realized in the United States.

Now the buts. Although cross-national comparisons are extremely unreliable, many argue that American students perform worse than those in many other nations, especially in the sciences and math. Some contend, too, that contemporary American intellectual life displays a loss of confidence in Enlightenment rationalism in favor of skeptical postmodernist outlooks.[16] And the statistics on American religion can be adduced as further proof of the failure, not the success, of liberalism. Enlightenment theorists like Locke, Paine, Kant, and Jefferson repeatedly tried to reformulate Christianity to make it compatible with reason.[17] But the forms of religion that are most prevalent and rapidly growing in the United States are evangelical, often fundamentalist forms of Protestantism (and kindred forms of Catholicism). Though measures are controversial, it is likely that at least one-fourth of all Americans subscribe to some version of Christian fundamentalism.[18] These believers reject forms of rationalism that deny what they see as the literal meaning of biblical revelation. Their rise since the mid-1960s, along with the increased power of antirationalist strains in Islam and other faiths around the world, and the linked phenomenon of resurgent ethnically and religiously defined nationalisms, form the main evidence for claims that Enlightenment rationalism is now being decisively repudiated.[19] At a minimum, we must concede that the forms of rationalistic religion urged by Locke, Kant, and Jefferson have largely failed to gain and hold adherents anywhere in the world, including the "enlightened" United States.

Racial and Ethnic Parochialism

Enlightenment thinkers rarely doubted the superiority of their cultures to non-Western societies, and some created "scientific" classifications of humanity into hierarchically arrayed races. Nonetheless, it has mattered that writers like Locke not only denied differences in the salient natural endowments of various peoples but also argued for universal human rights, grounded in divine law and the possession of reason. Those doctrines, embodied in the Declaration of Independence, the French Declaration of the Rights of Man, and other Enlightenment documents, have served as prime vehicles for assaulting the legitimacy of ascriptive hierarchies based on race, ethnicity, and gender. Hence, though it is correct to say that Enlightenment liberalism long failed to launch any major assaults on Western racism and ethnocentrism and provided many arguments to legitimate them, it is still plausible to contend that the logic of Enlightenment liberalism is hostile to those forms of inequality.[20]

How, then, is the Enlightenment project faring in this regard? Again there are striking successes. The United States abolished slavery 130 year ago and banned legal systems of racial apartheid 40 years ago. At roughly the same time, it eliminated ethnic restrictions on naturalization. It abandoned the ethnic basis of its system of immigration about 30 years ago, at a time when new national laws prohibited racial discrimination in commerce, housing, education, and many other spheres of life. Worldwide, liberalism has come to be understood as standing for principles of racial and ethnic equality more firmly than ever. These principles are embodied in numerous international legal documents, such as the United Nations Charter of Human Rights.

But nowhere, perhaps, are the failures of American and global liberalism more striking than in matters of racial and ethnic equality. In 1992, black families in America still earned only 67 percent of what white families earned. Hispanics were only a bit better off, at 69 percent. The black unemployment rate was almost twice that of whites, with Hispanics again only a percentage point less than blacks. Blacks were much more likely than whites to be employed in low-level service and production jobs, instead of managerial, professional, or highly technical work. Although blacks were slightly *more* likely than either whites or Hispanics to be enrolled in elementary and secondary schools, only about 67 percent of blacks over twenty-five, and only 53 percent of Hispanics over twenty-five, had completed high school in 1992, as opposed to 81 percent of whites. The percentage of whites holding college degrees was similarly higher than that of blacks, 22.1 percent to 11.9 percent. And these figures actually understate the inequalities because they describe the noninstitutional population; blacks were vastly more likely to be incarcerated. In 1991 blacks made up 47.5 percent of all prison inmates, almost four times their share of the population as a whole. Grimly, they were also almost seven times more likely than whites to be victims of homicides.[21]

The inferior, indeed life-threatening material conditions experienced by many African Americans is still not the whole story of American liberalism's failure in regard to race. I have argued elsewhere that, because liberal democratic reforms are disruptive of traditional structures of economic, political, and social life and meaning, we should always expect efforts to find new ways to justify traditional hierarchies to appear after constellations of forces favorable to reform alter.[22] After the Civil War, enthusiasm for racial inclusiveness waned among whites, and new intellectual ideologies of racial inferiority arose to justify Jim Crow and race-based immigration restrictions. Similarly, as cold war tensions waned after the Vietnam era, American whites began to display less support for the reforms of the modern civil rights movement, and arguments assigning racial minorities chief responsibility for their disadvantaged conditions have multiplied. Many analysts now contend the nation has an "ethno-underclass" characterized by "welfare dependency, drug use, and violent crime," that has "values, attitudes, and life-styles" that seem "almost foreign" to other Americans.[23]

Some whites see this "ethno-underclass" as confirming old racial stereo-
types and conclude that the problems of minorities are due to their own
deficiencies. Other analysts are reviving laissez-faire arguments to urge
repeal of the 1960s civil rights laws.[24] And a growing chorus of scholars
now argues explicitly that blacks tend to be intellectually inferior to
whites, so that efforts to boost blacks up the socioeconomic ladder are
misguided and unproductive.[25] Polls show support for immigration restriction is the highest since the 1940s; and patriotism verging on jingoism is in no danger of giving way to rootless cosmopolitanism in
American political culture. It is, in sum, far from clear that American
liberalism has laid to rest the longstanding defenses of racial, ethnic,
and nativistic hierarchies that should be recognized as incompatible
with the Enlightenment's aim of ending ascriptive inequalities.

Gender Equality

A more optimistic story can be told in regard to gender in America,
but claims of full success remain vastly premature. Political theorists
continue to debate whether the philosophies of early liberals like Locke
were *essentially* committed to a "sexual contract" relegating women to
inferior status in a private sphere, and to gendered notions of human
rights, or whether their views had liberating potential for women. But
even if the endorsements of sexual hierarchy in writers like Locke were
not contingent or corrigible, American women have still used the liberal language of individual rights as a key weapon in their struggles for
greater equality.[26] Influenced by these among other arguments, the
United States extended the vote to women in 1920 and included
women in major civil rights laws of the 1960s and 1970s. Today, overt
legal discrimination against women is no longer the norm. Women
have made strides in entering prestigious educational institutions and
professions, including law and government; in reducing pay inequities;
and in gaining legal recourse against abusive husbands, sexually ha-
rassing employers, and regulators who would deny women reproduc-
tive freedoms. In 1975, for example, fewer female high school
graduates went on to college than male graduates; in 1991, more did.
By 1993, women held 72 statewide elective offices in the United States
and 1,417 seats in state legislatures.[27] And liberals now uniformly endorse gender equality, though what that means remains controversial.

Again, however, the story has another side. The Equal Rights
Amendment failed in the 1970s, defeated in part by women who
wanted to preserve major aspects of traditional gender roles and protections.[28] Though more women have joined the labor force—from
35.5 percent in 1960 to 53.8 percent in 1992—many did so out of need,

not choice. Although more women than men were in college after 1980, by 1992 it remained true that more men than women had completed college, and the gap had not much altered from 1965. Women had also not reached equal representation in managerial and professional occupations, and women's median weekly earnings were still only 75 percent of men's. And as one indication of ongoing problems of female safety, the rate of forcible rape rose by 62 percent from 1975 to 1991.[29]

Courts generally stood firm against overt forms of sexual discrimination, harassment, and violence. But after 1976, the judicial standard for gender discrimination settled at "intermediate scrutiny," a level that provides less protection than the "strict scrutiny" the Supreme Court imposes on racial classifications (though some contend lesser scrutiny facilitates judicial support for governmental aid to women, such as affirmative action). In 1992 the Supreme Court also relaxed, though it did not abandon, constitutional restraints on laws discouraging women from abortions, a step many saw as limiting women's control over their lives.[30]

The increased receptivity to abortion restrictions was part of a rising trend of concern over gender-related developments that many traced to feminism and saw as detrimental to families and children. Marriage in particular appeared to be in trouble by the 1980s, as divorce rates rose 34 percent from 1970 to 1988 and children involved in divorces increased by almost 20 percent. Meanwhile marriage rates went down and children born out of wedlock went up, to over 25 percent in 1989, and above 60 percent for blacks. Partly as a result, families maintained by women rose from 14 percent to 17 percent between 1980 and 1992. The median weekly earnings of those families were a meager 49 percent of those headed by married couples (and just 74 percent of families led by single men). Women maintained 40 percent of black families, and those families' median earnings were 47 percent of the national average. Hence almost three-fourths of the children who live in single-parent families experience poverty during their first ten years.[31]

These statistics have led many policy analysts to fear the decline of two-parent families, a decline some connect with the liberating legacies of the civil rights and women's movements.[32] Combined with perceptions of feminism as increasingly repressive, due in part to free-speech controversies, these concerns about the corrosive consequences of female emancipation for marriage, children, and "family values" helped make *feminist* a pejorative term to many by the 1990s. Despite real successes, then, the cause of gender equality also is far from triumphant today.

Liberties of Expression

For many liberals, the core of a free society is its system of free expression for political, scientific, and artistic communication. During the cold war, Westerners regularly invoked the liberties of speech and press as evidence of the superiority of liberal democracy to communism. In comparison with most societies elsewhere in the world and throughout history, it still is plausible to cite these freedoms as achievements of liberalism, though perhaps not liberalism alone.

But here, too, there is room for doubt about the extent and the desirability of these liberal triumphs. Even though its record pales against the repressions of totalitarian societies, the United States has a long, ugly history of jailing dissidents, of concealing information on public affairs, of banning artistic works as obscene, and of imposing sanctions like unemployment and deportation on advocates of unconventional views. From the Alien and Sedition Acts to antebellum laws banning abolitionist tracts to the many convictions under the World War I Espionage Act to the arrests of proselytizing Jehovah's Witnesses in the 1930s to the McCarthyite prosecutions of Communists under the Smith Act and other laws in the 1950s, political and religious repression have rarely been absent. Local governments have used obscenity laws against classic works like James Joyce's *Ulysses* and acclaimed films like *Carnal Knowledge*. In recent years the federal government has sought and sometimes succeeded in preventing press access to politically charged trials, to government documents like the Pentagon Papers and military operations like the Grenada invasion, and to the finger-pointing memoirs of public employees. Some scholars have therefore argued that the United States has never had more than freedom for the speech that few wanted to repress anyway.[33] If that conclusion is overstated, the notion that expression has flourished uninhibitedly in America is at least equally exaggerated.

But here, too, the greatest disappointments of Enlightenment hopes come not so much from their explicit repudiation as from the ways they are undercut in practice by other features of modern liberal societies. Even as science has generated extraordinary communications technologies on vast scales, the costs of gaining access to the most pervasive of those technologies have become exceedingly high, even in regulated market systems. The economic inequalities that characterize American life are thus central structural features of American systems of expression. Air time on broadcast and cable channels is heavily weighted toward wealthy corporate interests and to those political and intellectual elites financed by them. The communications industry itself—in all its forms, including book publishing, newspapers, film, telephone, computer networks, radio and television broadcasting and cable systems—displays increasingly concentrated ownership. It is terribly difficult for individual citizens with ordinary financial resources to gain access to truly influential media. The Supreme Court, moreover, has regularly upheld the highly unequal access to influential media that flows from disparities in resources as forms of inequality that are sheltered by the First Amendment.[34]

And the challenges posed by technology to expressive freedoms are mounting. As advanced nations construct the "information superhighway" in which virtually all forms of data will be electronically available through interconnected computer, telephone, and television networks, personal capacities to control expression about oneself, to keep information private, are profoundly jeopardized. The Clinton administration's "Clipper" proposal, to include in new technology devices that would permit continuing governmental access to many kinds of communication, is but one example of the threats to personal choices over what to communicate that arise in the emerging brave new electronic world. Again, nothing in Enlightenment ideals licenses unlimited corporate and governmental access to information persons wish to keep private, and much militates against such access. But the technologies spawned by Enlightenment scientific aspirations and the economic and governmental systems in which they are enmeshed may produce that result all the same.

More dramatic are the renewed controversies over governmental censorship that have burgeoned in the 1980s and 1990s. The courts have vigilantly struck down new restraints on speech proposed by feminists and minority activists in the form of antipornography statutes and "hate speech" codes.[35] But those movements show that commitments to free expression are now sharply contested even among intellectuals, who have long defended them. The battles are fueled by undeniable insights. In a social reality that is constituted in significant measure by the understandings language provides, the permissibility of racist and sexist discourse, and its glamorization in erotically charged media, may well play a role in maintaining systems of ascriptive domination that a liberal democratic society should try to eradicate. Yet systems of censorship risk imposing stifling repressions of their own, while delegitimating the causes they mean to serve. The new alliances between feminists and religious conservatives to repress offensive sexual depictions, in particular, has reinforced a pattern of court decisions upholding restrictions in the name of "traditional" moral values while dismissing more feminist concerns.[36] The result thus may be restraints that bolster the old hierarchies many proponents of new restrictions wish to oppose.

So far, these controversies have not greatly transformed the extent of expression allowed in the United States. It would be wrong to take them as proof that the Enlightenment project has failed in this area. But they are signs that here, too, it is in important respects not well.

Two Categories of Liberal Failings

Overall, then, evidence from the United States, seen in light of broader global developments, points strongly in support of the thesis that the liberal "Enlightenment project" has been successful in many respects but can hardly be viewed as triumphant. What can be said about the reasons for liberalism's shortcomings?

The sources of liberal failings fall into two main categories. Contemporary liberal theorists can be faulted for failing to address either of these two sorts of problems adequately, though I will argue that the picture is not altogether bleak. The first category includes failings that arise because there are deep tensions among richly valued liberal goals and liberals lack any means of resolving those tensions without sacrifice. A reassuringly large number of the failings of Enlightenment liberalism belong under this less troubling head. For example, liberal goals of prosperity and scientific progress, spurred by market systems, often result in grossly unequal wealth and environmental havoc. Pursuing economic growth and diverse individual opportunities creates an affinity between liberalism and large-scale, heterogeneous polities, but such societies make accessible and competent self-government hard. The modern media can violate privacy and drown out minority voices more than they facilitate expression and understanding. And so on.

These problems are chronic and important; they must always be addressed; they can be ameliorated to some degree, but they probably cannot be eliminated. Yet they are, I think, capable of being alleviated sufficiently so that their persistence should not lead to the conclusion that Enlightenment liberalism has failed. They merely indicate that with liberalism, as with life, the Rolling Stones are right. We can't always get what we want, but if we try, we can get what we need.

Problems in the second category are more serious and I shall focus upon them here. They are problems stemming from human desires and aspirations that, even at its best, liberalism is not likely to meet to most people's satisfaction. Longings for certainty that one's particular community is specially marked as worthy by nature and God, that one's life has an intrinsic meaning grounded in some transcendental order, that one is assured of salvation from the woes of this world and the painful prospect of oblivion at its end, all such yearnings for support from some higher powers as we navigate this vale of tears cannot be satisfied by liberalism alone. It is this philosophic failing, at bottom, that leads many to argue that the Enlightenment project cannot succeed. The charge is serious, for in truth liberals cannot honestly provide these sorts of assurances. They must insist defensively that no one else has the key to any such overflowing moral vaults. To be sure, liberals can and should say more than this; but as long as this is part of their answer, it will remain doubtful how far most people can be persuaded to be wholehearted partisans of the Enlightenment project.

The difficulties that center on the demands that liberalism cannot meet include, perhaps most famously, problems of justification for liberal principles. Early liberals like Locke blended appeals to divine will, rationalistic natural law, and human consent in politically palatable but philosophically unstable combinations, leaving the true intellectual and moral foundations of liberalism unclear. Theological and natural law defenses lost much credibility through the nineteenth and early twentieth centuries, however, and modern liberals have generally tried to eschew them, although recently religious and secular forms of natural law have made modest comebacks.[37] Following John Rawls, many liberals have tried to reduce their justificatory burdens by not trying to offer any robust theory of the human good. Instead they defend only what they describe as minimal conceptions of the good that are sufficient to justify allegiance to liberal theories of justice or right. That move has rightly prompted a thundering chorus of criticism that liberal "neutrality" is misleading. Liberalism narrows the range of permissible conceptions of the good in ways that must be defended not merely as just but also as good.[38]

But the deeper justificatory posture adopted by modern liberal theorists is much less contested. Virtually all rely on a pragmatic model of justification derived from Dewey and Quine. These views hold that in moral reasoning we must recurrently compare some of our inherited beliefs against others and against our perceived experiences of the world. We continue with such comparisons successively, amending or discarding notions that appear implausible, until we finally reach a "reflective equilibrium." This equilibrium is a point at which our moral notions and understandings of the ways the world works all cohere reasonably well. They also give us an account of how we should live that we find satisfactory, at least for now.

I do not think liberal reasoning, or any reasoning, can ultimately rest on any foundation other than such "reflective equilibrium."[39] It describes what reasonable moral reflection must involve, given the capacities and limitations of our minds. It is, however, a method of justifying liberalism that is unsatisfying for two reasons. First, its tasks are huge, open ended, and always ongoing. We are always having new experiences, and there are always moral views, new and old, that shape our lives but that we have not yet had time to ponder fully. It may well be when these experiences and perspectives are considered, they will alter the results of our reflective moral equilibrium.

Hence, second, our moral conclusions must always be viewed as preliminary, tentative, and uncertain, the best we can do now, when we must decide, but not unshakable eternal verities. Thus the Enlightenment's commitment to moral understanding within the limits of reason alone has today issued in an acknowledgment that liberal values, however specified, rest on probabilistic judgments, not self-evident truths. For many people, this probabilistic pragmatism seems too shaky a foundation for standards that guide their lives. They are therefore willing to follow those who purport, falsely, in my view, to be able to offer them something more.

This problem of the uncertainty at the bottom of modern liberal justifications is probably liberalism's greatest philosophic weakness, but not its only one. Even if we accept reflective equilibrium as a method of justification, we still need substantive arguments as to why the equilibrium we should reach is some version of liberalism. These arguments must be only sketches of what full process of reaching reflective equilibrium would entail, but they must nonetheless make a case for preferring some of the conflicting values we perceive in our minds and hearts over others. It is not enough to imply, as pragmatic theorists like Richard Rorty and Michael Walzer do, that we should simply give weight to the values we discern as "dominant" in our societies.[40] Approaching reflective equilibrium means finding reasons of logical coherence and compatibility with perceived experiences to judge some values more reasonable than others, and those judgments may involve rejection of dominant values.

If liberal writers have been correct since the early 1980s to insist increasingly that liberalism represents a choice in favor of a broad family of conceptions of the human good and a rejection of others, then liberals need arguments as to what defines that family of conceptions and why we should prefer it. To justify those conceptions as widely applicable across time and across many human contexts, I believe liberal arguments must emphasize features of human experience that seem generally if not universally shared, enduring, and of fundamental importance to us. But all choices of what experiences to feature and all arguments based upon them will be controversial, compounding the perceived fragility of the case for liberal values. Perhaps because these sorts of arguments are so difficult to make compelling, even most writers who contend liberalism must have a theory of the good have not gone far toward justifying one. Hence today, although the philosophic credibility of "neutral" liberalism has been undermined, visions of a more "purposeful" liberalism remain theoretically less developed.[41] This failing compounds the difficulties of liberals in winning allegiance to their precepts, reinforcing their more basic inability to claim that liberalism rests on eternal truths. Though few attend to the details of philosophic debates, most people today seem to have some sense that modern rationalism fails to provide the moral assurances they seek. That awareness is one reason why so many adhere to fundamentalist faiths in the teeth of even the best supported findings of the Enlightenment sciences.

But profound as that problem is, it is likely that many more people could live with uncertainty if the pursuit of liberal purposes proved otherwise fulfilling for them. It is surely liberalism's success in providing greater peace, prosperity, enlightenment, and personal freedom to many that accounts for its triumphs, much more than the appeal of any foundational argument. And liberal purposes remain satisfying, indeed inspiring, to many. Peace and prosperity is still the best platform on which to run for president. Millions still thrill to the visions of the progress of civilization inspired by scientific discoveries and by the futurist fiction and films that are perhaps the Enlightenment's distinctive contribution to popular culture. And hopes for greater personal liberty and democratic self-governance still stir great political efforts throughout the world.

Yet there is also ample evidence that the pursuit of liberal purposes, as defined in ways almost all modern liberals would accept, also generate massive dissatisfactions. Insofar as liberal economic and political systems are actually in place, they impose great demands on individuals. Insofar as they are not in place, and many forms of communal life even in advanced industrial societies are *not* ordered on liberal democratic principles, the Enlightenment project still threatens transformations many find alarming, even immoral. The forms at risk include ones so basic as family structures, racial and ethnic group identities and hierarchies, the existing boundaries of political communities, and most if not all conventional religions.

Here I can only list, not document, these disturbing aspects of liberal purposes. First, liberal market systems place virtually all individuals under pressure to work mightily in order to flourish in a competition that inevitably produces winners and losers, one that even many winners experience as draining and demoralizing. Redistributive programs generally lack the scale, effectiveness, and moral legitimacy to keep these competitive pressures, inequalities, and economic failures from generating great unhappiness with life in liberal societies. On the other hand, liberal calls to pursue more genuine opportunities for all create moral pressures for redistribution that the affluent often fear and resent.

Second, systems of democratic self-governance in practice seem either to place wildly unrealistic demands on citizens or to be largely shams, forms through which well-equipped elites prevail. Few wish to sacrifice social standing by giving up the right to vote, but few find much meaning in exercising it, as Judith Shklar argued.[42] Yet many experience more strenuous efforts to participate politically as so stressful and disappointing that they settle for being "bad," apathetic citizens, at some cost to their self-esteem.

Third, we have already seen that traditional forms of male dominance over women and white dominance over blacks have only been partially eroded in most American institutions. Similar gender, racial, and ethnic inequalities abound in other modern societies. Their elimination would involve staggering changes. Work would have to be reorganized extensively if men and women were to share child rearing and domestic labor on anything like a fully egalitarian basis. Housing, school, and employment patterns would have to be drastically altered if racial and ethnic minorities and women were to be integrated throughout the geographic, educational, and economic structures in existing liberal societies. Those alterations would be so bitterly attacked that they are left off most mainstream political agendas.

And even if a truly integrative public agenda is not adopted, liberalism's advocacy of expansive individual freedoms, exercised with the aid of ever increasing material and technological resources, still poses both intellectual and practical challenges to many existing forms of communal life. Enlightenment traditions suggest that humanity's division into national, religious, racial, and ethnic groups reflects neither biology nor divine ordinances but rather humanly constructed cultural and political inheritances.

People may, to be sure, find on reflection that their cultural and political identities are so vitally important to them that they decide to sustain them. But in liberal eyes, none of those identities are natural and none should be imposed on individuals who find them barriers to their self-realization. Many members of national, religious, racial, and ethnic groups wish instead to give those communal identities firmer "essentialist" groundings, viewing them as so constitutive of persons that they cannot morally be renounced. Because liberalism rejects such essentialism philosophically, it is an intellectual enemy of such communities. And insofar as liberal political, legal, educational, and economic institutions both expose members of particular communities to alternative ways of life and insist they be given the freedom to pursue those alternatives if they wish, then the Enlightenment project often proves corrosive to these communal identities not just in theory but in practice.

It is particularly important to stress that these Enlightenment challenges go to membership in any political communities that do not rest on actual consent. Locke insisted early on that "a Child is born a Subject of no Country or Government."[43] That position is too radical for any political regime ever to have accepted, including the United States. Most governments have instead claimed inherent authority over all "native-born" citizens, justifying their power through arguments that their members have natural affinities, if not natural allegiances, that make them one political community. Most people have responded with a measure of genuine loyalty to their governments, probably because they *wished* to feel they were a part of a polity whose members "belonged" together in some profound way.

Liberal democratic theorists have not addressed very fully the issue of how the character and bounds of membership in political communities should be defined.[44] That failing is of major practical importance in today's world, where political lines are being redrawn on a large scale. Yet here, too, the deepest problem is not liberalism's failure to provide answers, but the unpopularity of the answers it gives. If political communities are not natural, if they are human creations, at best forged by consent, more often by force, then their worth to human lives must be viewed as instrumental, not intrinsic. If human beings can best realize lives of freedom for all by maintaining the sorts of organization into particular groups that they have always had, then nothing in liberalism stands in their way. But if inherited boundaries and memberships are sources of unjust inequality, economic inefficiency, unreasonable nationalistic conflicts, and international domination, then liberalism implies that different structures ought to be sought. This insistence on the tentativeness of any particular set of political communities, identities, and boundaries makes liberalism unpopular with those exercising power under existing arrangements. It is also deeply unsettling to many who dwell within current borders and want to believe they are good and right.

Finally, the Enlightenment project suggests that most if not all the prevalent forms of religious doctrine, and hence the church organizations built in their name, rest on shaky if not false intellectual foundations. But in place of these systems of value and meaning, so profoundly important to millions, such a basic source of guidance and consolation in dealing with life's burdens and especially the threat of death to ourselves and those we love, liberalism offers only an uncertain and mundane vision of enhanced comfort, freedom, and understanding in this life. That vision is hardly without appeal, but it is no surprise that many find it less than adequate in the face of the enormous risks, pains, and disappointments human life presents. Many also doubt they can count on the behavior of others should religious justifications for moral conduct give way to the less potent teachings of Enlightenment rationalism, a consideration that gave even Locke and Jefferson pause. And many more are daunted by the fact that, after it discredits many cherished religious guides, modern liberalism provides only rather general standards on the forms of meaning they may then embrace. Instead it bestows upon them the dubious blessing of having great freedom to decide on the meanings they will pursue. That liberty has always been experienced as emancipating by some, but as a crushing burden by others. So for many, if Enlightenment liberalism suggests that much in the world's religions is ill founded, the response is to say that liberalism must to that degree be disregarded.

The Prospects for Liberal Progress

If the Enlightenment project today is in important respects unfulfilled, if it displays chronic tensions that cannot be eliminated, and if its message is unsatisfying to many on both high philosophic and concretely political levels, what are its prospects? Is it true after all that aspects of liberal institutions may continue, but the Enlightenment project at its heart is dead? I do not think so; but liberals have much work to do if they are to shore up liberalism against resurgent illiberal forces and carry it further. Although none of its enduring problems can be "solved," even the deepest difficulties of liberalism can be sufficiently alleviated, I believe, if liberals find better ways to include all in fuller realizations of liberal goals.

There remain important theoretical challenges to address. On the level of justification I have indicated that liberals need clearer and stronger defenses for liberalism's basic purposes, even though they will probably never be able to ground them to the satisfaction of those who must have nature and God on their side. I also think such defenses can be found as liberal theorists pursue their recent turn to purposeful pragmatism.

But overall, liberal thinkers need to focus less on high theory and more on how to alleviate the chronic tensions of liberalism, exploring more responsive and accountable yet competent and deliberative forms of political representation and administrative regulation; more productive and yet equitable and environmentally protective systems of economic organization; new family structures and new ways of structuring work that can diminish involuntary, unjust distributions of the work of child rearing, home keeping, and market production; means of expanding political, educational, economic, and social opportunities for racial and ethnic minorities without valorizing such identities as natural or ineradicably primary; ways of building productive transnational political arrangements—the list should go on for some time.

Many of these issues are being creatively addressed by thinkers from a whole range of traditions—feminism, socialism and other forms of communitarianism, modern versions of Aristotelian, religious, and postmodernist perspectives, and others. Many in these traditions are understandably wary of calling themselves liberals because that label is identified with the status quo they are seeking to improve. But insofar as their ideas fit with liberalism, liberals should learn from them; insofar as they do not, liberals should not leave such vital work to others.

Ultimately, only successful work of this sort can confront liberalism's greatest weakness, the fact that many are not satisfied with the answers it provides them concerning the meanings they can find and create in their lives. If people genuinely felt that, as individuals and as societies, they were increasing their material well-being, their abilities to shape their personal and collective lives harmoniously and successfully, and their capacities to understand and enhance themselves, their loved ones, and their social and natural worlds, my guess is that they would regard their lives as not only worthwhile but profoundly fulfilling. To be sure, we are not likely to make such enhancement so constant an experience for so many people that dissatisfactions with liberalism vanish. Whether we will ever be able to eliminate the rival appeal of powerfully affirming faiths in races, ethnicities, nations, or revelatory gods can well be doubted. But the Enlightenment project certainly cannot succeed if those who profess commitment to its goals fail to be dedicated to the unfinished work which those who fought for liberalism in the past have thus far so nobly advanced.

Notes

1. Francis Fukuyama, *The End of History and the Last Man* (New York, 1992); John Gray, "Against the New Liberalism: Rawls, Dworkin, and the Emptying of Political Life," *Times Literary Supplement*, 3 July 1992, 13.

2. See Stephen Holmes, *The Anatomy of Antiliberalism* (Cambridge, Mass., 1993); Brian Barry, "How Not to Defend Liberal Institutions," *British Journal of Political Science* (20 Jan. 1990): 1–4.

3. See Gray, "Agonistic Liberalism," paper presented to the Yale Political Theory Workshop, 11 Jan. 1994: 27.

4. U.S. Department of Commerce, Bureau of the Census, *Statistical Abstract of the United States*, 113th ed. (Washington, D.C., 1993), 852.

5. See John Locke, *Two Treatises of Government* (New York, 1965), 333, 338–40.

6. See William Graham Sumner, *What Social Classes Owe to Each Other* (Caldwell, Idaho, 1982), 114–15; Friedrich A. von Hayek, *Economic Freedom* (Oxford, 1991), 325, 334–40.

7. United States policymakers define poverty as less than the income needed to spend one-third of a household's budget on food supplying minimal nutritional requirements (Daniel H. Weinberg and Enrique J. Lamas, "Measurement of Need: The U.S. Poverty Line," *1993 Proceedings of the Social Statistics Section, American Statistical Association*).

8. Kevin Phillips, *The Politics of Rich and Poor: Wealth and the American Electorate in the Reagan Aftermath* (New York, 1991), 13, 17, 52, 115.

9. Alexis de Tocqueville, *Democracy in America* (12th ed., 1850; Garden City, N.Y., 1969), 555–58.

10. Henry F. May, *The Enlightenment in America* (Oxford, 1976), 100.

11. Robert A. Dahl, *Democracy and Its Critics* (New Haven, Conn., 1989), 239.

12. Dahl, "The Problem of Civic Competence," *Journal of Democracy* 3 (Oct. 1992): 47–51. Perhaps for these reasons, participation by voters in national elections has not risen above 60 percent since 1968 (Bureau of the Census, 284).

13. See James Fishkin, *Democracy and Deliberation* (New Haven, Conn., 1991); and Dahl, "The Problem of Civic Competence," 54–57.

14. Bureau of the Census, 67–69; Kenneth D. Wald, *Religion and Politics in the United States* (New York, 1987), 6–12.

15. Bureau of the Census, 150, 154, 332–34, 850.

16. For example, see John E. Chubb and Terry M. Moe, *Politics, Markets, and America's Schools* (Washington, D.C., 1990), 8; Allan Bloom, *The Closing of the American Mind* (New York, 1987).

17. John Locke, *The Reasonableness of Christianity* (Stanford, Calif., 1958); Thomas Paine, *The Age of Reason* (Cutchique, N.Y., 1976); Immanuel Kant, *Religion within the Limits of Reason Alone* (New York, 1960); Thomas Jefferson, *The Jefferson Bible* (Greenwich, Conn., 1961).

18. Bureau of the Census, 67–68.

19. Gray, "Agonistic Liberalism," 13.

20. Rogers M. Smith, "Beyond Tocqueville, Myrdal, and Hartz: The Multiple Traditions in America," *American Political Science Review* 87 (Sept. 1993): 549–66.

21. Bureau of the Census, 151, 153, 154, 195, 211, 395, 398, 409, 427.

22. Smith, "Beyond Tocqueville."

23. Lawrence H. Fuchs, *The American Kaleidoscope: Race, Ethnicity, and the Civic Culture* (Hanover, N.H., 1990), 489.

24. See Richard A. Epstein, *Forbidden Grounds: The Case against Employment Discrimination Laws* (Cambridge, Mass., 1992).

25. See Richard J. Herrnstein and Charles Murray, *The Bell Curve: Intelligence and Class Structure in American Life* (New York, 1994); and J. Philippe Rushton, *Race, Evolution, and Behavior: A Life History Perspective* (New Brunswick, N.J., 1995).

26. See Carole Pateman, *The Sexual Contract* (Stanford, Calif., 1988), 38, 41, 54, 94; and Smith, "'One United People': Second-Class Female Citizenship and

the American Quest for Community," *Yale Journal of Law and the Humanities* 1 (May 1989): 234–35.

27. Bureau of the Census, 169, 281.

28. See Jane J. Mansbridge, *Why We Lost the ERA* (Chicago, 1986).

29. Bureau of the Census, 153, 195, 395, 409, 426.

30. See *Craig v. Boren*, 429 U.S. 190 (1976); and *Planned Parenthood of Southeastern Pennsylvania v. Casey*, 505 U.S. 112, S. Ct. 2791 (1992).

31. Bureau of the Census, 100–101, 427; see William A. Galston, *Liberal Purposes: Goods, Virtues, and Diversity in the Liberal State* (Cambridge, 1991), 268.

32. See Galston, *Liberal Purposes*, 268, 283–88.

33. See Robert Justin Goldstein, *Political Repression in Modern America, 1870 to the Present* (Cambridge, Mass., 1978); and Mark A. Graber, *Transforming Free Speech: The Ambiguous Legacy of Civil Libertarianism* (Berkeley, Calif., 1991).

34. See Jeffrey B. Abramson, F. Christopher Arterton, and Gary R. Orren, *The Electronic Commonwealth: The Impact of the New Media Technologies on Democratic Politics* (New York, 1988); Ben H. Bagdikian, *The Media Monopoly* (Boston, 1990); and *Buckley v. Valeo*, 424 U.S. 1 (1976).

35. See *American Booksellers Association v. Hudnut*, 771 F. 2d (7th Cir.) 323 (1985); and *Doe v. University of Michigan* 721 F. Supp. (Eastern District Mich.) 852 (1989).

36. Cf. *Hudnut* to *Paris Adult Theatre v. Slaton*, 413 U.S. 49 (1973).

37. See for example, John Finnis, *Natural Law and Natural Rights* (Oxford, 1980); Robert George, *Making Men Moral: Civil Liberties and Public Morality* (Oxford, 1993); and Sotirios A. Barber, *The Constitution of Judicial Power* (Baltimore, 1993).

38. Cf. Rawls, *A Theory of Justice*, (Cambridge, 1971) 395–98; Galston, *Liberal Purposes*; Smith, *Liberalism and American Constitutional Law* (Cambridge, Mass., 1985); and Joseph Raz, *The Morality of Freedom* (Oxford, 1986).

39. Devices like an imaginary "original position," "ideal speech situation," or other "thought experiments" work only insofar as their elements are justifiable in reflective equilibrium. They clarify our notions but provide no independent grounds for them.

40. Michael Walzer, *Spheres of Justice: A Defense of Pluralism and Equality* (New York, 1983), 313–15; Richard Rorty, *Contingency, Irony, and Solidarity* (Cambridge, 1989), 48–50.

41. Leading accounts include Raz and Galston, but each focuses more than one would wish on the problems of neutrality and less on what justifies liberal conceptions of the good. In *Liberalism and American Constitutional Law* I argued, following Locke, that the experiences of human consciousness are what we should build upon.

42. *American Citizenship*, 15–19.

43. Locke, *Two Treatises*, 391–92.

44. Dahl, *Democracy and Its Critics*, 139, 146–47.

Appendix

A Life of Learning

Judith N. Shklar

I AM A BOOKWORM. Since the age of eleven I have read and read, and enjoyed almost every moment of it. Yet I was very slow to learn how to read at all, and I hated school, avoiding it as long and as often as I could, without being an actual dropout. It was certainly not in the various schools that I attended so unwillingly that I learned to read or to write. In fact, my exasperated parents had to hire a tutor to get me started. Nor were my first encounters with literature always happy, though they certainly made a deep impression upon me. The first book I ever read through by myself was a German translation of *David Copperfield*. I read it over and over again and I still love it. The second book was a children's novel about two boys in the Thirty Years War, which led me to look it up in a wonderful illustrated world history in many volumes in my parents' library. I was hooked for life on fiction and history. It was not, however, all pleasure. One day I picked up the first volume of Shakespeare in the Schlegel-Tieck translation. The first play was *Titus Adronicus*, and I read it all. To this day I can still feel the fear and horror it inspired. I was so afraid and confused that I could not even bring myself to tell anyone what was bothering me. Finally I managed to spill it out to my oldest sister. As soon as I told her, I, of course, felt infinitely relieved, especially as she assured me that these things did not really happen. The trouble was that both she and I knew that far worse was going on all around us. By 1939 I already understood that books, even scary ones,

Originally delivered as the Charles Homer Haskins Lecture, American Council of Learned Societies, Washington, D.C., 6 April 1989, and published as ACLS Occasional Paper no. 9. Reprinted by permission.

263

would be my best refuge from a world that was far more terrible than anything they might reveal. And that is how I became a bookworm. It was also the end of my childhood.

Biography, novels, and plays are the delight of young readers, and they certainly were mine. But I also very early on began to read about current events and political history. The reason for this precocious taste was obvious enough, just as there was nothing random about my later professional interests. Politics completely dominated our lives. My parents had a hard time getting out of Russia, where the First World War had stranded them, after the Revolution, but they did manage to return home, to Riga, which was now a Latvian city. At first they prospered, but soon it too became a very hostile place. We were essentially German Jews, which meant that almost everyone around us wanted us to be somewhere else at best, or to kill us at worst.

My parents were well-educated, well-to-do, and liberal people, and in a wholly unobtrusive way they were completely unconventional. They had an absolute confidence in the moral and intellectual abilities of their children and treated us accordingly, which made the extreme contrast between a family with high personal standards and an utterly depraved external world inescapable. And this induced a certain wariness, if not outright cynicism, in all of us. My father had wanted to leave Europe for many years, but we had many family ties binding us to Riga, and my mother, who was a pediatrician, ran a slum clinic which she could not easily abandon. In the event, just before the Russians arrived, my uncle put us on a plane to Sweden, where we remained far too long, until well after the German invasion of Norway. By then there was only one route out of Europe, the Trans-Siberian railroad, which slowly took us to Japan. It was not an easy trip, but miraculously we escaped. In Japan we were able to buy, in effect, a visa to Canada, which had, as is now common knowledge, a less than generous immigration policy. Not long before Pearl Harbor we took a boat to Seattle where we were locked up for several surrealistic weeks in a detention jail for illegal Oriental immigrants. If I were asked what effect all these adventures had on my character, I would say that they left me with an abiding taste for black humor.

When my father was at last able to settle his financial affairs, we finally went to Montreal. It was not a city one could easily like. It was politically held together by an equilibrium of ethnic and religious resentments and distrust. And in retrospect, it is not surprising that this political edifice eventually collapsed with extraordinary speed. The girls school that I attended there for some three years was dreadful. In all that time I was taught as much Latin as one can pick up in less than a term at college. I also learned some geometry, and one English teacher taught us how to compose précis, which is a very useful skill. The rest of the teachers just stood in front of us and read the textbook out loud. What I really learned was the meaning of boredom, and I learned that so well that I have never been bored since then. I report without comment that this was thought to be an excellent school. I dare say that there were better ones around, but I remain unconvinced by those who respond with vast nostalgia to the manifest inadequacies of high school education today.

I do not look back fondly to my college days at McGill University, either. That may have something to do with the then prevailing entrance rules: 750 points for Jews and 600 for everyone else. Nor was it an intellectually exciting institution, but at least when I arrived there, just before my seventeenth birthday, I was lucky to be in the same class as many ex-servicemen, whose presence made for an unusually mature and serious student body. And compared to school, it was heaven. Moreover, it all worked out surprisingly well for me. I met my future husband and was married at the end of my junior year, by far the smartest thing I ever did. And I found my vocation.

Originally I planned to major in a mixture of philosophy and economics, the rigor of which attracted me instantly. But when I was required to take a course in money and banking it became absolutely obvious to me that I was not going to be a professional economist. Philosophy was, moreover, mainly taught by a dim gentleman who took to it because he had lost his religious faith. I have known many confused people since I encountered this poor man, but nobody quite as utterly unfit to teach Plato or Descartes. Fortunately for me I was also obliged to take a course in the history of political theory taught by an American, Frederick Watkins. After two weeks of listening to this truly gifted teacher I knew what I wanted to do for the rest of my life. If there was any way of making sense of my experiences and that of my particular world, this was it.

Watkins was a remarkable man, as the many students whom he was to teach at Yale can testify. He was an exceptionally versatile and cultivated man and a more than talented teacher. He not only made the history of ideas fascinating in his lectures, but he also somehow conveyed the sense that nothing could be more important. I also found him very reassuring. For in many ways, direct and indirect, he let me know that the things I had been brought up to care for—classical music, pictures, literature—were indeed worthwhile, and not my personal eccentricities. His example, more than anything overtly said, gave me a great deal of self-confidence, and I would have remembered him gratefully, even if he had not encouraged me to go on to graduate school, to apply to Harvard, and then to continue to take a friendly interest in my education and career. It is great stroke of luck to discover one's calling in one's late teens, and not everyone has the good fortune to meet the right teacher at the right time in her life, but I did, and I have continued to be thankful for the education that he offered me so many years ago.

From the day that I arrived at Harvard I loved the place, and I still do. By that I do not mean that it was perfect. Far from it. In fact, I think it is a far better university now than it was when I got there. But whatever its flaws, I found the education there I had always longed for. The government department was then as now very eclectic, which suited me well, and I learned a lot of political science, mostly from the junior faculty. My mentor was a famous academic figure, Carl Joachim Friedrich. And he taught me how to behave, how to be professional, how to give and prepare lectures, how to deal with colleagues and how to act in public, as well as a general idea of what I would have to know. And though he was not given to praise, he did not seem to doubt that I would manage to get ahead somehow. In fact, I can recall only one nice comment he ever made to me. After my final thesis exam he said, "Well, this isn't the usual thesis, but then I did not expect it to be." Eventually I realized that he hoped that I would become his successor, as I indeed did, after many ups and downs. In retrospect it seems to me that the best thing he did for me was to let me go my own way as a student and then as a young teacher. Like many ambitious young people, I was inordinately concerned about what other people thought of me, but having seen a good many graduate students since then, I realize that I was relatively self-assured, and I have Carl Friedrich to thank for it.

There are always many very bright graduate students at Harvard and I really liked many of my contemporaries there, several of whom have remained my close friends. Seminars were lively and there was fair amount of good talk over coffee. There were also some brilliant lecturers, whom I found it thrilling to hear. And most of all I loved and still love Widener Library.

In many respects the Harvard that I entered in 1951 was a far less open scholarly society than it now is. The effects of McCarthyism were less crude and immediate than subtle and latent. The general red-bashing was, of course, a colossal waste of energy and time, but I cannot say that it deeply affected day-to-day life at the university. What it did was to enhance a whole range of attitudes that were there all along. Young scholars boasted of not being intellectuals. Among many, no conversation was tolerated except sports and snobbish gossip. A kind of unappetizing dirty-socks and locker-room humor and false and ostentatious masculinity were vaunted. With it came an odd gentility: no one used four-letter words and being appropriately dressed, in an inconspicuous oxford gray Brooks Brothers suit, was supremely important.

More damaging was that so many people who should have known better, scorned the poor, the bookish, the unconventional, the brainy, the people who did not resemble the crass and outlandish model of a real American upper-crust he-man whom they had conjured up in their imagination. For any woman of any degree of refinement or intellectuality, this was unappealing company.

To this affected boorishness was added a slavish admiration for the least intelligent, but good-looking, rich, and well-connected undergraduates. Their culture was in many respects one of protected juvenile delinquency. Harvard undergraduates were easily forgiven the misery they inflicted on the rest of Cambridge. High jinks included breaking streetlights and unrailing trolley cars. Conspicuous drunkenness on the streets was normal on weekends. One of the nastiest riots I ever saw, long before the radical sit-ins, was an undergraduate rampage set off by the decision to have English rather than Latin diplomas. Several tutors were physically assaulted and injured. All this was seen as high spirits, and secretly admired. Nor were these private school products particularly well prepared. Few could put a grammatical English sentence together, and if they knew a foreign language, they hid it well.

The real ideal of many teachers at Harvard in the fifties was the gentleman C-er. He would, we were told, govern us and feed us, and we ought to cherish him, rather than the studious youth who would never amount to anything socially significant. There was, of course, a great deal of self-hatred in all this, which I was far too immature to understand at the time. For these demands for overt conformity were quite repressive. Harvard in the fifties was full of people who were ashamed of their parents' social standing, as well as of their own condition. The place had too many closet Jews and closet gays and provincials who were obsessed with their inferiority to the "real thing," which was some mystical Harvard aristocracy, invented to no good purpose whatever. What was so appalling was that all of this was so unnecessary, so out of keeping with America's public philosophy. It was also a bizarre refusal to think through the real meaning of the Second World War.

In some ways I found Harvard conversations unreal. I knew what had happened in Europe between 1940 and 1945, and I assumed that most people at Harvard also were aware of the physical, political, and moral calamity that had occurred, but it was never to be discussed. Any American could have known all there was to know about the war years in Europe by then. Everything had been reported in the *New York Times* and in newsreels, but if these matters came up in class, it was only a part of the study of totalitarianism, and then it was pretty sanitized and integrated into the cold war context. It was very isolating and had a lot to do with my later writings. Yet in an intellectually subdued way there was a shift in the local consciousness. A look at the famous "Redbook," which was the plan for the general education program at Harvard, is very revealing. Its authors were determined to immunize the young against fascism and its temptations so that "it" would never happen again. There was to be a reinforcement of *The Western Tradition*, and it was to be presented in such a way as to show up fascism as an aberration, never to be repeated. I would guess that in the prewar Depression years some of the young men who devised this pedagogic ideology may have been tempted by attitudes that eventually coalesced into fascism, and now recoiled at what they knew it had wrought. They wanted a different past, a "good" West, a "real" West, not the actual one that had marched into the First World War and onward. They wanted a past fit for a better denouement. I found most of this unconvincing.

Harvard in the fifties was in appearance in a conservative moment, but it was, in fact, steadily changing, becoming perceptibly more liberal and interesting. The 1960s as a period and phenomenon did nothing, however, to hasten this progress, quite on the contrary. I do not remember the sixties kindly. What went on was brutish and silly and the spectacle of middle-aged men simpering about how much they learned from the young, and flattering the most uncouth of their students as models of intellectual and moral purity, would have been revolting had it not been so ridiculous. The only lasting legacy of that time is a general flight from the classroom. Many teachers simply quit and withdrew to their studies when confronted with all that abuse. Moreover, a whole new generation has grown up unprepared and unwilling to teach. If you do not trust anyone over thirty in your teens, you will not like young people once you reach forty. Instead we now have a constant round of conferences and institutes which do not inspire scholarly work good enough to justify the time and effort spent on them. Still, all in all, I don't lament. As I look at my younger colleagues, I am heartened by their intelligence, competence, openness, and lack of false prejudices. And Harvard's student body is certainly more alert, versatile, self-disciplined, and above all, more diverse and fun to teach, than it ever was before. What was it like to be woman at Harvard at the time I came there? It would be naïve of me to pretend that I was not asked to give this lecture because I am a woman. There is a considerable interest just now in the careers of women such as I, and it would be almost a breach of contract for me to say nothing about the subject. But before I begin that part of my story, I must say that at the time when I began my professional life, I did not think of my prospects or my circumstances primarily in terms of gender. There were many other things about me that seemed to me far more significant, and being a woman simply did not cause me much academic grief. From the first there were teachers and later publishers who went out of their way to help me, not condescendingly, but as a matter of fairness. These were often the sons of the old suffragettes and the remnants of the Progressive Era. I liked them and admired them, though they were a pretty battered and beaten lot, on the whole, by then. Still, they gave me a glimpse of American liberalism at its best. Moreover, I was not all alone. There were a few other young women in my classes, and those who persevered have all had remarkable careers.

Nevertheless, all was not well. I had hardly arrived when the wife of one of my teachers asked me bluntly why I wanted to go to graduate school when I should be promoting my husband's career and having babies. And with one or two exceptions that was the line most of the departmental wives followed. They took the view that I should attend their sewing circle, itself a ghastly scene in which the wives of the tenured bullied the younger women, who trembled lest they jeopardize their husbands' future. I disliked these women, all of them, and simply ignored them. In retrospect I am horrified at my inability to understand their real situation. I saw only their hostility, not their self-sacrifices.

The culture created by these dependent women has largely disappeared, but some of its less agreeable habits still survive. Any hierarchical and competitive society, such as Harvard, is likely to generate a lot of gossip about who is up and who is down. It puts the lower layers in touch with those above them, and it is an avenue for malice and envy to travel up and down the scale. When I became sufficiently successful to be noticed, I inevitably became the subject of gossip, and oddly I find it extremely objectionable. I detest being verbally served for dinner by academic hostesses, so to speak, and I particularly resent it when my husband and children are made into objects of invasive curiosity and entertainment by them.

These nuisances are surely trivial, and I mention them in order not to sound too loyal to Harvard. Though perhaps I am, because my experiences have not made me very critical. Certainly in class and in examinations I was not treated differently than my male fellow students. When it came to teaching Harvard undergraduates in sections there was a minor crisis. It was thought wonderful to have me do Radcliffe sections, but men? It had never been done! I said nothing, being far too proud to complain. After a year of dithering my elders decided that this was absurd and I began to teach at Harvard without anyone noticing it at all.

When I graduated I was, much to my own surprise, offered an instructorship in the Government Department. When I asked, how come? I was told that I deserved it and that was that. I did not, however, know whether I wanted it. I had just had our first child and I wanted to stay with him for his first year. That proved acceptable. I rocked the cradle and wrote my first book.

To the extent that I had made any plans for my professional future at all, I saw it in high-class literary journalism. I would have liked to be a literary editor of the *Atlantic* or some such publication. This was a perfectly realistic ambition and had obvious attractions for a young woman who wanted to raise a family. I was, moreover, sure that I would go on studying and writing about political theory, which was my real calling. My husband, however, thought that I ought to give the Harvard job a chance. I could quit if I didn't like it, and I might regret not trying it out at all. So I more or less drifted into a university career, and as I went along there were always male friends telling me what to do and promoting my interests. I did not mind then and I wouldn't mind now, especially as thinking ahead is not something I do well or often.

For a number of years everything went smoothly enough. I was almost always exhausted, but like both my parents I have a lot of energy. The crunch came predictably when the matter of tenure finally came up. My department could not bring itself to say either yes or no. It had done this to several male aspirants, who hung around for years while this cat and mouse game was being played. That was more humiliation than I could bear, so I went to the dean and asked him if I could have a half-time appointment with effective tenure and lecturer's title. It was not exactly what I wanted, but it was what I decided to arrange for myself rather than wait for others to tell me what I was worth. My colleagues accepted this deal with utter relief, and it certainly made life a lot easier for them, as well as for me. I had three children by then and a lot of writing to do. So it was by no means a disaster and it saved my self-respect, no doubt a matter of excessive importance to me. It also relieved me for years from a lot of committee and other nuisance work, though half-time never turned out to be exactly that. Do I think my colleagues behaved well? It is, of course, unreasonable to be a judge in one's own case, so I will answer the question indirectly. There are very many scholars whom I regard as my superiors in every way and whom I admire without reserve, but I have never thought of myself, then or now, as less competent than the other members of my department.

What did this experience do for or to me? Not much. In time, things straightened themselves out. Do I think that matters have improved since then? In some ways I am sure that they have. We treat our junior colleagues with far more respect and fairness now. They have more responsibility and also a more dignified and independent position. Their anxiety about tenure remains, of course, but at least we do not go out of our way to demean them any longer. The atmosphere for women is, however, far from ideal. There is certainly far less open discrimination in admissions, hiring, and promotions, and that is a very genuine improvement. However, there is a lot of cynical feminism about that is very damaging, especially to young women scholars. The chairman who calls for hiring more women, *any* women, for, after all, any skirt will do to make his numbers look good, and to reinforce his own liberal credentials. The self-styled male feminist who wildly overpraises every newly appointed young woman as "just brilliant and superb," when she is in fact no better or worse than her male contemporaries, is not doing her a favor, just expressing his own inability to accept the fact that a reasonably capable woman is not a miracle. The male colleague who cannot argue with a female colleague without losing his temper like an adolescent boy screaming at his mother, and the many men who cannot really carry on a serious professional conversation with a woman, are just as tiresome as those who bad-mouth us overtly. And they are more likely to be around for a long, long time proclaiming their good intentions without changing what really has to change most of all, they themselves.

For me, personally, the new era for women has been a mixed blessing. It is not particularly flattering to be constantly exhibited as the "first" woman to have done this or that, just like a prize pig at a county fair. The pressure, which is inevitably internalized, to do better than anyone else becomes debilitating and it erodes any self-confidence one might have built up with the years. Nothing now ever seems good enough, however hard I try. Nevertheless, in spite of these side-effects, I have much to be pleased about. Harvard has become a much less mean-spirited place than it used to be. In any case, the idea of making an ideological issue of my own career difficulties never occurred to me at all. Which is one of the reasons why I am not a real feminist. But it is not the only one. The idea of joining a movement and submitting to a collective belief system strikes me as a betrayal of intellectual values. And this conviction is an integral part of what I have tried to do as a political theorist, which is to disentangle philosophy from ideology. I am obliged to acknowledge that this is a characteristically liberal enterprise, which is a paradox, but classical liberalism can at least claim that it has tried to rise above its partisan roots rather than to rationalize or conceal them.

•   •   •

As I said at the outset, I took up political theory as a way of making sense of the experiences of the twentieth century. What had brought us to such a pass? In one way or another that question has lurked behind everything I have written, especially my first book, *After Utopia*, which I began when I was twenty-two. At the time the very idea of such an undertaking was dubious. There was some doubt whether political theory itself could or should survive at all. For over a hundred and fifty years political thinking had been dominated by those great "-isms," and the outcome was plain to see. No one wanted to relive the thirties. We had suffered enough intellectual disgrace. Ideologies were the engines of fanaticism and delusion, and we should never talk like that again. Instead we should limit ourselves to clarifying the meaning of political language, sort out intellectual muddles, and analyze the dominant concepts. In this way we could help political planners to recognize the alternatives available to them and to make reasonable choices. We would clean up the ideological mess and acquire an austere and rational style of exposition. It was not an ignoble intellectual ideal. Indeed, that passionate effort to free ourselves of affect can be recognized not only in philosophy, but in the aesthetics of that time as well. I was deeply under the spell of these intellectual aspirations, which were so obviously tied to hopes for a humane and efficient welfare state. The trouble with this way of thinking was that it did not help me much with the questions that I wanted to answer. So I turned to history.

What puzzled me when I wrote *After Utopia* was that none of the explanations for Europe's recent history made sense. And as I investigated them it seemed clear to me that most were really updated version of nineteenth-century ideologies, whether romantic, religious, or conservative-liberal, and not one of them was adequate to cope with the realities they tried to account for. Unhappily, I was so absorbed in the history of these ideas that I never quite got to my main topic, but I did get at least one point across: that the grand ideologically based political theories were dead and that political thinking might not recover from its obvious decadence. In this I was wrong, as were a great many other people. When Leo Strauss in a celebrated essay wrote that political theory was "a pitiable rump" left over by the specialized social sciences, he was being comparatively optimistic; at least he thought something remained.

What was gone was the "great tradition" that had begun with Plato and expired with Marx, Mill, or possibly Nietzsche, a canon of commanding quality, encompassing scope, and philosophical rigor. No one was writing anything comparable to *Leviathan*, and no one ever would. Only Isaiah Berlin, ever hopeful, claimed that as long as people would argue about fundamental political values, political theory was alive and well. Nonsense, I said, only political chatter and the vestiges of ideology were around. No *Social Contract*, no Rousseau, no political theory! Most of us believed that in the age of the two world wars both the utopian and the social-theoretical imagination had dried up in disenchantment and confusion. Only criticism remained as a vapid gesture of no substance, and as testimony to a general inability to understand the disasters that had overcome us, or to rise above them. What I thought was needed was a realistic adaptation to an intellectually pluralistic and skeptical eclecticism, but that could hardly get the old juices flowing.

There were other explanations for the apparent paralysis, of course. It was suggested that theory was stifled in a bureaucratic political order, where only functional thinking was encouraged, as in Byzantium, for example, where there also was no speculative thought, but just guarded little bailiwicks of ideas appropriated by an unoriginal master and his troop. I was not persuaded by this line of thought because I knew some Byzantine history and could see no resemblance to us at all. More persuasive was the medieval analogy. There had been plenty of philosophical talent and imagination, but it had all been concentrated on theology and not politics. With us it was the natural sciences. A rather different claim was that it was just as well that speculative theorizing had stopped. To be sure, there once had been a wonderfully rich and diverse variety of ideas and forms of public argument, but it was no longer possible to go on in that manner. We could and should work at improving the quality of intellectual history. That appealed to both certain democratic as well as aristocratic impulses, rather hard to recapture now. For the aristocrat the great canon was a cultural treasure to be preserved by and for the very few who could appreciate it. But for others, myself among them, it was the hope that by making these ideas and texts accessible to as many people as possible there would be a general deepening of the self-understanding that comes from confronting the remote and alien. The idea was to make the past relevant to all now.

What is now called the linguistic turn had very similar aspirations. Its hope was to be of use to all citizens by clarifying the entire vocabulary of politics and also to illuminate the alternatives available to those who had to make political choices. In addition, it might also serve the social sciences by giving them a stable, unemotive, and reliable language. I was certainly inclined to believe that the prospects of the social sciences as predictive and practical knowledge were good, and that theory could do much to sustain them. Theorists would analyze the prevailing terms of political discourse and see how it functioned in different contexts. This would help the public to free itself from ideological distortions and inconsistent impulses, and would provide the social sciences with an aseptic vocabulary. I think it fair to say that I was not atypical in caring more about being honest than about finding the truth, which only agitated traditional and radical critics at the margins of the intellectual map.

Those of you who have grown up in the midst of the vigorous debates around John Rawls's *A Theory of Justice* and the literature that it has inspired can no longer even imagine this state of mind. In retrospect it seems to me that there were stirrings of creativity under the surface all along, and that the inhibitions and hesitations of the postideological age were neither futile nor mindless. They were a pause, and not a worthless one, either. It got us over the disgrace of the immediate past.

To return to my younger self. The attention that *After Utopia* received had one funny result. My editors rather than I had hit upon the title, and many people thought that I had written a book about utopias. It was a fashionable topic, and I was soon asked to participate in scholarly conferences. I was in no position to refuse at that stage of my young career, and so I boned up on utopias. No subject could have been less suited to my temperament or interests, but I plowed on and even got to be quite fond of the utopian literature and eventually became a minor expert.

Utopian fantasies did not, however, liberate me from history or its burdens. I found, in spite of my dispiriting view of the discipline in general, that historical interpretation was not yet out of style, nor as irrelevant as I had originally feared. One could do more with it than just discuss who said what when. And so I soon returned to the events of the Second World War. I had been teaching a course on the history of modern legal theory for a number of years and had been reading up on the subject. Although it had nothing to do with the course itself, I thought that it might be interesting to take a good look at political trials generally and at the International Tribunals at Nuremberg and Tokyo specifically. In order to do that systematically I realized that I would have to think through for myself the very traditional problem of the relations between law, politics, and morals. As I did so, I was struck very forcefully by the difference between legal and political thinking and by the professional constrictions of jurisprudential thought, especially when it was extended beyond the limits of normal court business. Nothing could have been more remote from my mind, however, than to attack legal scholarship, lawyers, or the integrity of our legal system, but the majority of law journals were really upset at the very notion that politics structured the law very significantly. Nor were they exactly thrilled to read that one could justify the Nuremberg trials only on political grounds and the Tokyo ones not at all. I was told in no uncertain terms that only lawyers could really understand the perfection of legal reasoning. I look back with some amusement at this episode because my skeptical inquiry into the traditional orthodoxies of legal thought was so mild and so qualified, compared to the assaults that Critical Legal Studies have mounted against the basic assumptions of the legal establishment since then. And it is with some dismay that I now find myself treated as the purveyor of standard ideas, known to and accepted by all, even by the most conservative academic lawyers. To recognize that professions have their self-sustaining ideologies is hardly news today, but it was in 1964. And so *Legalism,* which is my favorite of the books that I have written, went quickly from being a radical outrage to being a conventional commonplace.

Going through all the published and unpublished documents relating to the war trials in the Treasure Room of the Harvard law library had a very liberating effect upon me. It was as if I had done all I could do to answer the question, How are we to think about the Nazi era? I knew that there was much that I would never understand, but perhaps I knew enough about the essentials. At any rate, I was ready to do other things.

Since my undergraduate days I had been absolutely mesmerized by Rousseau. Watkins had given some absolutely first-rate lectures and had urged me to write short and long papers about Rousseau. I was not the first reader to discover that Rousseau was addictive. It is not just that debates about him always seemed to touch upon the most vital and enduring questions of politics, but that when I read him, I knew that I was in the presence of an unequaled intelligence, so penetrating that nothing seemed to escape it. To read Rousseau is to acquire a political imagination and a second education. For someone as naturally and painlessly skeptical as I have always been, it is, moreover, a continuing revelation to follow the struggles of a mind that found skepticism both inevitable and unbearable. Above all, Rousseau has fascinated me because his writings are so perfect and lucid, and yet so totally alien to a liberal mentality. He is the complete and inevitable "other," and yet entirely integral to the modern world that he excoriated, more so than those who have accepted it on its own terms. It is difficult to like the author of the *Confessions,* but it is a riveting work, and even if one disagrees with the *Social Contract,* who can deny the brilliance of its arguments, or not be compelled to rethink political consent? I read Rousseau as a psychologist—as he said of himself, he was "the historian of the human heart"—and a rather pessimistic thinker, which makes him unique among the defenders of democracy and equality. It is, I believe his greatest strength. As a critical thinker he just has no rival, apart from Plato.

I am not, however, so besotted with Rousseau that I do not admire the great writers of the Enlightenment upon whom he cast his scorn. Quite on the contrary, in reaction to him, I was especially drawn to them, and am convinced that just those intellectual bonds that identify that diverse group—skepticism, autonomy and legal security for the individual, freedom and the discipline of scientific inquiry—are our best hope for a less brutal and irrational world. My favorite is Montesquieu, the most authentic voice of the French Enlightenment, its bridge to America, and an acute political scientist.

Anyone who does intellectual history recognizes more or less clearly that she owes a debt to Hegel, who laid down its philosophical principles: that history, endured as the conflict between incomplete epistemologies, is resolved when we recognize this process as the totality of our collective spiritual development. The study of that experience becomes the master science. No more powerful defense of the enterprise can be imagined, and in some more modest version, intellectual historians cling to it. The grounds of Hegel's argument were to be found in his *Phenomenology* and so I spent some five years unraveling its endless allusions and tying its political theory together. I was not altogether successful, but I would still defend my reading of Hegel as the last of the great Enlightenment thinkers. I should also, for the sake of honesty, confess that I do not understand Hegel's *Logic* and that the commentaries that I have read have not helped me. And while I am at it, I must also admit that there are a vast number of paragraphs by Heidegger that mean absolutely nothing to me. I quite simply do not understand what he is saying. I am not proud of these lapses, and I have no one to blame but myself, but it is better to own up than to hide them, especially from one's students.

Although I sometimes have students in mind when I write, I tend to keep writing and teaching apart. I have many friends who write their books as they lecture, but I somehow cannot do that, though I wish that I could. I think of the two as complementary, but different. In class I have to think of what the students must be taught; when I write I have only myself to please. I do not even find that the two compete for my time, and rather that mysteriously and semiconsciously, they interact. I have had the good luck to have taught some absolutely wonderful young people. Some of the Harvard seniors whose undergraduate theses I have directed are the most intelligent, stimulating, and delightful people I have known, and preparing for their tutorials has certainly done a lot for my own education as well.

Graduate students are not as easy to get on with at first, because they are in such a difficult position, having just fallen from the top of their undergraduate class to the very bottom of a very greasy pole. I certainly prefer frank and independent students to ingratiating and flattering ones, and trust those who take charge of their own education most of all. Ultimately they can be the most gratifying people for a teacher. The graduate students who become professional quickly and develop a real passion for their studies may soon be one's friends—their success is in some way one's own—and they are often the best partners for discussion, whether we agree or not.

The reason why I teach political theory is not that I just like the company of young people, but that I love the subject unconditionally and am wholly convinced of its importance and want others to recognize it as such. It has therefore been quite easy for me to avoid becoming a guru or substitute parent. I really only want to be a mother to our three children, and do not like disciples. And I fear that the students who so readily attach themselves to idols lose their education along with their independence.

Much as I have enjoyed teaching, I am inclined to think that I would have written more or less the same kinds of books if I had not accepted that unexpected Harvard job. The one subject that I might not have taken up is American political theory. I originally started reading American intellectual history entirely in order to prepare an undergraduate lecture course, but it soon became an avocation and I have thought and written about it with much pleasure and interest. I do not treat it as a peculiarly local phenomenon, "a poor thing but our own," but as intrinsically significant. Apart from the early establishment of representative democracy and the persistence of slavery, which do give it a special character, American political thought is just an integral part of modern history as a whole.

The study of American history has certainly done nothing to lessen my awareness of the oppression and violence which have marked all our past and present. And it also has sharpened my skepticism as I consider the illusions, myths, and ideologies that are generated to hide and justify them. With these thoughts in mind I quite naturally turned to Montaigne's essays. He increasingly has become my model as the true essayist, the master of the experimental style that weaves in and out of the subject rather than hitting the reader over the head. As I read Montaigne I came to see that he did not preach the virtues but reflected on our vices, mostly cruelty and betrayal. What, I asked myself, would a carefully thought-through political theory that "puts cruelty first" be like? I took it as my starting point that the willful infliction of pain is an unconditional evil and tried to develop a liberal theory of politics from that ground up. That exploration led me to consider a number of other vices, especially betrayal, in their tendency to enhance cruelty. The book I built around these notions, *Ordinary Vices*, is very tentative, an exploration rather than a statement, an effort to worry rather than to soothe.

From betrayal to injustice is a short step. I am now revising a short book on injustice, and I mean to be unsettling. I want to examine the subjective claims of the aggrieved and I try to look at injustice from the vantage point of those who have experienced it, not on the model of a court of law, but in a far less rule-bound way. It is a perspective that does not make it any easier to tell misfortune from injustice, and it decidedly is not the way those who govern tend to draw the line between the two. I hope to shift the accepted paradigms a bit.

What makes a scholar choose the subjects of inquiry, and change her interests over time? Because I am too busy to be very self-reflective, I find that question hard to answer, and perhaps I had better begin by looking at others who are like me. My guess is that there is a mixture of external and internal pressures that direct scholars working within a discipline such as political theory. I think that the years of postwar passivity did not exhaust the possibilities of textual commentary, though the methods of interpretation are now all up for intense rethinking in response to too many repetitive readings. The practical limits of the linguistic turn duly emerged as well, and though we will certainly have to continue to refine and clarify our terms of discourse, few if any of us still believe that this will improve the world or even the social sciences. To be sure, muddled, emotive, and intuitive thinking would only make matters worse. So the two main postwar endeavors did not lead us to a dead end after all. In fact, they opened the door to new prospects. Practical ethics is now deeply engaged with the political choices imposed by new technologies and administrative institutions. Analytical thought, originally so finely honed for its own sake, now has a new function here. These theoretical ventures are, I think, inspired both by events in the social world and by the fatigue induced by the remoteness of pure analysis. The stimulus of political radicalism has, in contrast, been brief and less distinguished, leaving behind it a desiccated and abstract Marxism. The career of social criticism has also floundered. As its rituals lost their charm, hermeneutics replaced prophecy, and a return to the cave in order to interpret rather than to judge politics suggested itself. Scholars now try to read their cultures as once they read their texts. I do not find these researches particularly impressive, and often they amount to little but an unspoken conservatism. What are the search for "shared meanings" and the articulation of deep intimations but celebrations of tradition? I much prefer an open and direct defense of the habitual and customary. Far more exciting, to my mind, is the enlarged scope of political theory today, as literature and the fine arts are integrated into reflections about the nature of government and its ends. It preserves the canon by expanding it.

Evidently I have some notion of how scholarly changes occur in general, but each one of us is, of course, different and has personal motives for making specific intellectual decisions. As I look at myself I see that I have often been moved to oppose theories that did not only seem wrong to me, but also excessively fashionable. I do not simply reject out of hand the prevailing notions and doctrines, but complacency, metaphysical comforts, and the protection of either sheltered despair or of cozy optimism drive me into intellectual action. I do not want to settle down into one of the available conventions. Perhaps this reflects the peculiarity of the kind of refugee I was. We had never known poverty or ignorance. My sister and I both spoke elegant English when we arrived. It made it very easy for us to adapt quickly, but we did not have to alter fundamentally to do so. And I have participated happily enough in what goes on around me, but with no wish to be deeply involved. It is a very satisfactory situation for a scholar and a bookworm.

Works by Judith N. Shklar

Books

1957 *After Utopia: The Decline in Political Faith*. Princeton, N.J.: Princeton University Press.

1964 *Legalism: An Essay on Law, Morals, and Politics*. Cambridge, Mass.: Harvard University Press. 2d edition, with new preface, 1986.

1966 *Political Theory and Ideology* (ed.). New York: Macmillan.

1969 *Men and Citizens: A Study of Rousseau's Social Theory*. Cambridge: Cambridge University Press. 2d edition, with new preface, 1985.

1976 *Freedom and Independence: A Study of the Political Ideas of Hegel's Phenomenology of Mind*. Cambridge: Cambridge University Press.

1984 *Ordinary Vices*. Cambridge, Mass.: Harvard University Press. In Italian, *Vizi Communi* (Bologna: Il Mulino, 1986). In Spanish, *Vicies Ordinaires* (Mexico City: Fondo de Cultura Economiaz, 1990).

1987 *Montesquieu*. Oxford: Oxford University Press.

1990 *The Faces of Injustice*. New Haven: Yale University Press. In German, *Über Ungerechtigkeit* (Berlin: Rotbuch Verlag, 1992).

1991 *American Citizenship: The Quest for Inclusion*. Cambridge, Mass.: Harvard University Press. In French, *Citoyenneté américaine* (Paris: Calmann-Levy, 1991).

1996 *Essays on American Political Thought*. Edited by Stanley Hoffmann. Forthcoming.

1997 Collected Essays. Edited by Stanley Hoffmann. Forthcoming.

Articles and Essays

1958 "Bergson and the Politics of Intuition." *Review of Politics* 20:634–56.

1959 "Ideology-Hunting—The Case of James Harrington." *American Political Science Review* 53:662–92.

1964 "Decisionism." In *Nomos 7. Rational Decision*, ed. Carl Friedrich, 3–17. New York: Atherton.

"Rousseau's Images of Authority." *American Political Science Review* 58:919–32.

1965 "Political Theory of Utopia: From Melancholy to Nostalgia." *Daedalus* 94:367–81. Reprinted in *Utopias and Utopian Thought*, ed. Frank E. Manuel (Boston: Houghton Mifflin, 1967).

1966 "In Defense of Legalism." *Journal of Legal Education* 19:51–58.

"Rousseau's Two Models: Sparta and the Age of Gold." *Political Science Quarterly* 81:25–51.

1968 "Facing up to Intellectual Pluralism." In *Political Theory and Social Change*. Ed. David Spitz, 275–95. New York: Atherton.

1971 "Hegel's *Phenomenology*: An Elegy for Hellas." In *Hegel's Political Philosophy*, ed. Z. A. Pelczynski, 73–89. Cambridge: Cambridge University Press.

"Hegel's *Phenomenology*: Paths to Revolution." In *Theory and Politics: Festschrift zum 70. Geburtstag für C. J. Friedrich*, ed. K. von Beymel, 162–81. The Hague: Martinus Nijhoff.

1972 "Subversive Genealogies." *Daedalus* 101:129–54. Reprinted in *Myth, Symbol, and Culture*, ed. C. Geertz (New York: Norton, 1971).

1973 "Comment on Avineri." *Political Theory* 1:399–404.

"General Will." In *Dictionary of the History of Ideas*, ed. P. P. Wiener. 5 vols., 2:275–81. New York: Scribners.

"Hegel's *Phenomenology*: The Moral Failures of Asocial Man." *Political Theory* 1:259–86.

1974 "The Education of Henry Adams." *Daedalus* 103:59–66.

"Phenomenology: Beyond Mortality." *Western Political Quarterly* 27:597–623.

1975 "Hannah Arendt's Triumph." *New Republic* 173, 27 Dec., 8–10.

1977 "Publius and the Science of the Past." *Yale Law Journal* 86:1286–96.

"Rethinking the Past." *Social Research* 44:80–90.

1978 "Jean-Jacques Rousseau and Equality." *Daedalus* 107:13–25.

"Politics and the Intellect." *Studies in Eighteenth Century Culture* 7:139–51.

1979 "Let Us Not Be Hypocritical." *Daedalus* 108:1–25.

"Reading the Social Contract." In *Powers, Possession and Freedom*, ed. Alkis Kontos, 77–88. Toronto: University of Toronto Press.

"Virtue in a Bad Climate: Good Men and Good Citizens in Montesquieu's *l'Esprit des Lois*." In *Enlightenment Studies in Honor of Lester G. Crocker*, 315–28. Oxford: Voltaire Foundation.

1980 "Learning without Knowing." *Daedalus* 109:53–72.

1981 "Jean d'Alembert and the Rehabilitation of History." *Journal of the History of Ideas* 42:643–64.

1982 "Putting Cruelty First." *Daedalus* 11:71–27.
1983 "Hannah Arendt as Pariah." *Partisan Review* 50:64–77.
   "Rousseau and the Republican Project." *French Politics and Society* 7:42–49.
1985 "Nineteen Eighty-four: Should Political Theory Care?" *Political Theory* 13:5–18.
1986 "Injustice, Injury and Inequality: An Introduction." In *Justice and Equality Here and Now*, ed. Frank Lucash, 13–33. Ithaca, N.Y.: Cornell University Press.
   "Squaring the Hermeneutic Circle." *Social Research* 53:449–73.
1987 "Alexander Hamilton and the Language of Political Science." In *The Languages of Political Theory in Early-Modern Europe*, ed. Anthony Pagden, 339–55. Cambridge: Cambridge University Press.
   "Political Theory and the Rule of Law." In *The Rule of Law: Ideal or Illusion*, ed. A. Hutchinson and P. Monahan, 1–16. Toronto: Carswell.
1988 "Why Teach Political Theory?" *Teaching Literature: What Is Needed Now?* ed. J. Engell and D. Perkins, 151–60. Cambridge, Mass.: Harvard University Press.
1989 "Giving Injustice Its Due." *Yale Law Journal* 98:1135–51.
   "The Liberalism of Fear." In *Liberalism and the Moral Life*, ed. Nancy Rosenblum, 21–38. Cambridge, Mass.: Harvard University Press.
   "A Life of Learning." Autobiographical essay. Washington, D.C., American Council of Learned Societies Publications no. 9. Reprinted in this volume.
   "Montesquieu en Amérique." *Lettre internationale* 22:10–12.
1990 "American Citizenship: The Quest for Inclusion." In *Tanner Lectures*, 11:385–439.
   "Emerson and the Inhibitions of Democracy." *Political Theory* 18:601–14.
   "Montesquieu and the New Republicanism." In *Machiavelli and Republicanism*, ed. Gisela Bock, Quentin Skinner, and Maurizio Viroli, 266–79. Cambridge: Cambridge University Press.
1991 "Hawthorne in Utopia." In *In the Presence of the Past*, ed. R. J. Bienvenue and M. Feingold, 215–31. Kluwer Academic Publishers.
   "Redeeming American Political Theory." Presidential address to American Political Science Association. *American Political Science Review* 85:3–15.
1992 *The Bill of Rights and the Liberal Tradition*. Colorado Springs: Colorado College.
   Foreword to Wolf Lepennies, *Melancholy and Society*. Cambridge, Mass.: Harvard University Press.
   "Justice without Virtue." In *Nomos 34. Virtue*, ed. John Chapman

and William Galston, chap. 13. New York: New York University
Press.
1993 "Obligation, Loyalty, Exile." *Political Theory* 21:181–97.
"Pictures of America." *Yale Journal of Law and the Humanities*
5:191–200.
"Politics and Friendship." *Proceedings of the American Philosophical
Society* 137: 207–12.

Reviews

1961 *An Immortal Commonwealth: The Political Thought of James
Harrington*, by C. Blitzer. *American Political Science Review* 55:606–
7.
The Future of Mankind, by Karl Jaspers. *Political Science Quarterly*
76:437–39.
1963 *Between Past and Future*, by Hannah Arendt. *History and Theory*
2:286–91.
1967 *The Enlightenment*, by Peter Gay. *Political Science Quarterly* 82:477–
79.
Rousseau and the French Revolution, by Jean Macdonald. *Journal of
Modern History* 89:458.
1968 *The Early Rousseau*, by Mario Einaudi. *Political Science Quarterly*
83:477–78.
The Political Philosophy of Rousseau, by Roger Masters, and *Rousseau
and the Spirit of Revolt*, by W. H. Blanchard. *Political Science
Quarterly* 83:612–13.
1969 *Warrant for Genocide*, by Norman Cohn. *Mosaic* 10:50–59.
1971 *Rousseau's Social Contract*, by Lester G. Crocker. *Political Science
Quarterly* 86:315–16.
1972 *Montesquieu's System of Natural Government*, by H. J. Merry. *American
Historical Review* 77:1131–32.
1973 *La politique de la solitude*, by Raymond Polin. *Political Science
Quarterly* 86:315–16.
Political Justice, by William Godwin. *Political Theory* 1:486–88.
1974 *Hegel*, by Raymond Plant. *American Political Science Review*
68:1744–46.
Natural Law in Political Thought, by Paul Sigmund. *American
Political Science Review* 68:266–67.
1975 *Condorcet*, by Keith Baker. *Political Theory* 3:469–74.
Jean Bodin and the Rise of Absolutist Theory, by Julian Franklin, and
Richelieu and Reason of State, by W. F. Church. *Journal of Modern
History* 47:134–41.
On Human Conduct, by Michael Oakeshott. *Times Literary
Supplement*, 12 Sept., 1018–19.
1976 *The Social Problem in the Political Philosophy of Rousseau*, by John
Charvet. *American Political Science Review* 70:606–7.

National Consciousness, History and Political Culture in Early-Modern Europe, by O. Ranum. *Review of European History* 2:507–14.

Rousseau—Stoic and Romantic, by K. F. Roche. *American Historical Review* 81:156–57.

1978 *Human Nature in Politics*, ed. J. R. Pennock and J. Chapman. *American Political Science Review* 72:1384–85.

The Political Works of James Harrington, ed. J. G. A. Pocock. *Political Theory* 6:558–61.

Inventing America, by Gary Wills. *New Republic* 179 (26 Aug.): 32–34.

1979 *Foundations of Modern Political Theory*, by Quentin Skinner. *Political Theory* 7:549–52.

1980 *Against the Current*, by Isaiah Berlin. *New Republic* 182 (5 Apr.): 32–35.

1981 *Utopian Theory in the Western World*, by Frank and Fritzie Manuel. *Political Theory* 9:278–93.

Explaining America, by Gary Wills. *Yale Law Journal* 90:942–53.

1982 *Models and Means of Political Reflection in the 18th Century*. *Journal of Modern History* 54:576–80.

1983 *Jean-Jacques: The Early Life and Works of Rousseau*, by Maurice Cranston, and *Will and Circumstance: Montesquieu, Rousseau and the French Revolution*, by Norman Hampson. *London Review of Books* 5 (29 Oct.): 10–11.

Rousseau's Social Contract, by J. B. Noone. *Ethics* 93:405–6.

1984 *Writings*, by Thomas Jefferson. *New Republic* 191 (5 Nov.):29–35.

Jefferson's Extracts from the Gospels, ed. Dickinson Adams, and *The Pursuit of Happiness*, by Jan Lewis. *London Review of Books* 5 (17 May): 6–7.

1985 *Dominance and Affection: The Making of Pets*, by Yi-fu Tuan. *London Review of Books* 4 (18 Apr.): 12–13.

1986 *Society, Government, and the Enlightenment*, by C. B. A. Behrens. *New Republic* 194 (30 June): 38–39.

1987 *Voltaire*, by A. J. Ayer, and *Rousseau and the Republic of Virtue*, by Carol Blum. *New Republic* 196 (2 Mar.): 36–40.

Law's Empire, by Ronald Dworkin. *American Political Science Review* 81:261–62.

The Needs of Strangers, by Michael Ignatieff. *Political Theory* 15:141–45.

Sources of Social Power, by Michael Mann. *Journal of Interdisciplinary History* 18:331–32.

Novus Ordo Seclorum, by Forest McDonald. *Times Literary Supplement*, 11 Sept., 996.

The Cycles of American History, by Arthur Schlesinger. *Times Literary Supplement*, 13 Mar., 267–68.

Montaigne in Motion, by Jean Starobinski. *Political Theory* 15:653–57.

1988 *Rousseau: Confessions*, by Peter France. *History of European Ideas* 9:750–51.
  The Great Triumvirate: Webster, Calhoun and Clay, by M. D. Peterson. *New Republic* 198 (22 March): 39–41.
  Jean-Jacques Rousseau: Transparency and Obstruction, by Jean Starobinski. *New Republic* 198 (27 June): 38–40.
1990 *Morality, Politics and Law: A Bicentennial Essay*, by Michael J. Perry. *Ethics* 100:427–28.
1991 *Sources of the Self: The Making of the Modern Identity*, by Charles Taylor. *Political Theory* 19:105–9.
1992 *We, The People*, vol. 1, *Foundations*, by Bruce Ackerman. *American Political Science Review* 86:775–76.

Contributors

Bruce Ackerman, professor of law and political science at Yale University, is the author of many books, including *Social Justice in the Liberal State* and *We the People*.

Seyla Benhabib, professor of government at Harvard University, is the author of *Critique, Norm and Utopia* and *Situating the Self*.

John Dunn, Fellow of King's College and the professor of political theory at Cambridge University, is the author of numerous books, including *Western Political Theory in the Face of the Future* and *The Political Thought of John Locke*.

Amy Gutmann, the Laurance S. Rockefeller Professor of Politics and dean of faculty at Princeton University, is the author, most recently, of *Democratic Education* and coauthor of *Democracy and Disagreement*.

Stanley Hoffmann is the Douglas Dillon Professor of French Civilization and chairman of the Center for European Studies, Harvard University. He is the author of numerous books in international relations and French politics.

Stephen Holmes, professor of law and political science at the University of Chicago, is the author of *Benjamin Constant and the Making of Modern Liberalism* and *Passions and Constraint: On the Theory of Liberal Democracy*.

George Kateb, professor of politics at Princeton University, is the author, most recently, of *The Inner Ocean* and *Emerson and Self-Reliance*.

Isaac Kramnick, professor of government at Cornell University, is the author, most recently, of *Republicanism and Bourgeois Radicalism* and *Harold Laski: A Life on the Left*.

Patrick Riley, professor of political science at the University of Wisconsin, Madison, is the author of, among other works, *The General Will before Rousseau* and *Will and Political Legitimacy*.

Nancy L. Rosenblum, professor of political science at Brown University, is the author of *Bentham's Theory of the Modern State* and *Another Liberalism*.

Quentin Skinner, the professor of political science at Cambridge University, is the author, most recently, of *Reason and Rhetoric in the Philosophy of Hobbes*.

Rogers M. Smith, professor of political science at Yale University, is the author of *Liberalism and American Constitutional Law* and numerous articles on American citizenship.

Tracy B. Strong, professor of political science at the University of California, San Diego, and editor of the journal *Political Theory*, is the author of *Nietzsche and the Politics of Transfiguration* and *Jean-Jacques Rousseau and the Politics of the Ordinary*.

Dennis F. Thompson, the Alfred North Whitehead Professor of Political Philosophy at Harvard University, is the author of, among other books, *J. S. Mill and Representative Government* and *Political Ethics and Public Office*.

Michael Walzer, the UPS Foundation Professor of Social Science at the Institute for Advanced Study, Princeton, is the author of numerous books, including *Just and Unjust Wars* and *Spheres of Justice*.

Bernard Yack, professor of political science at the University of Wisconsin, Madison, is the author of *The Longing for Total Revolution* and *The Problems of a Political Animal*.

Index